# Real and Financial Economic Dynamics in Russia and Eastern Europe

Springer
*Berlin*
*Heidelberg*
*New York*
*Hong Kong*
*London*
*Milan*
*Paris*
*Tokyo*

Timothy Lane · Nina Oding
Paul J. J. Welfens (Editors)

# Real and Financial Economic Dynamics in Russia and Eastern Europe

With 50 Figures and 63 Tables

Springer

Dr. Timothy Lane
International Monetary Fund
700 19th Street, N.W.
Washington, D.C. 20431
USA
tlane@imf.org

Dr. Nina Oding
Leontief Centre
Pereulok Antonenko 6
190000 St. Petersburg
Russia
oding@leontief.spb.su

Professor Dr. Paul J. J. Welfens
Jean-Monnet-Professor for
European Economic Integration
President of EIIW;
University of Wuppertal
Gauss-Straße 21
42097 Wuppertal
Germany
welfens@uni-wuppertal.de
http://www.euroeiiw.de
and
http://www.progressinfo.net

ISBN 3-540-00910-8 Springer-Verlag Berlin Heidelberg New York

Cataloging-in-Publication Data applied for
A catalog record for this book is available from the Library of Congress.
Bibliographic information published by Die Deutsche Bibliothek
Die Deutsche Bibliothek lists this publication in the Deutsche Nationalbibliografie; detailed bibliographic data is available in the Internet at <http://dnb.ddb.de>.



Springer-Verlag Berlin Heidelberg New York
a member of BertelsmannSpringer Science+Business Media GmbH

http://www.springer.de


Printed in Germany



Hardcover-Design: Erich Kirchner, Heidelberg

SPIN 10922279 43/3130-5 4 3 2 1 0 – Printed on acid-free paper

# Contents

## E. Structure and Growth of Private Consumption in Russia and East Germany

*Cathleen Faber and Hans Gerhard Strohe*



## F. Labor Market Transformation and Hidden Unemployment in Russia

*Nina Oding*

## G. Principles of Market-Oriented Labor Market Policies

*John T. Addison*



## H. Rent-Seeking and Rent-Setting: Government Versus Competition (The Case of St. Petersburg)

*Andrei Zaostrovtsev*

## I. Powerful Groups and Corruption

*Frank Bohn*



## J. Regional Dimension of the Market Transformation in Russia

*Ruslan Grinberg and Leonid Vardomsky*

## K. Foreign Trade Policies in Transformational Russian and Ukrainian Economies

*Olga Nosova*



## L. The Role of Foreign Direct Investment in Transformation

*Roland Doehrn and Natalja v. Westernhagen*

# Introduction

The early years of Russia's economic transition were marked by a substantial and persistent decline in economic activity as many obstacles to the functioning of a market economy remained to be overcome. Russia's cumulative decline of output in the 1990s was about 40 %, much larger than the decline that occurred in the United States during the Great Depression. Only in 1997 was a modest positive rate of growth achieved, but this was interrupted by crisis of 1998, which reflected an inconsistent configuration of domestic policies combined with significant external shocks. By the year 1999, growth had revived as the effects of the crisis had worked themselves out and as fundamental uncertainties about the course of economic policies were attenuated under President Putin. In the years 1999–2002, Russia's GDP growth averaged close to 6 %, obviously benefiting from high oil and gas prices in world markets and a renewed confidence on the part of domestic and foreign investors.

Russia is a relatively special country among the transition economies. It is larger than and as resource-rich as Canada, with a population half that of the US, but per capita income is roughly one-fifth of that in North America. Given Russia's short history of a market economy prior to Lenin's revolution of 1917, one might expect that the country could return to its historical track of a large industrialized country, which in 1913 ranked fifth in the world. In this optimistic scenario, the new Russia—having embraced effective transformation later than the east European Visegrad countries—would follow the more successful transition cases in central and eastern Europe in achieving high sustained growth: attracting high capital inflows, modernizing both the industry and services sector and increasing trade with OECD countries and other countries. The removal of distortions in factor markets, with enhanced competition, would be expected to further expand Russia's production possibilities.

In the face of these advantages, Russia's failure to achieve high and sustained growth reflect, to a large extent, the many inherited institutional shortcomings and distortions: a very short tradition of the rule of law, a lack of newly created firms, a massive shadow economy, and capital flight that reduces the savings available to finance capital accumulation and growth. Moreover, some questionable decisions in the early stage of transformation set the stage for difficulties later on—notably the disastrous banking crisis of 1998 that destroyed public confidence in the banking sector. Moreover, Russia's abundance of natural resources may in some respects turn out to be a curse—the so-called "Dutch disease", under which the rapid growth of the natural resources sector can be a barrier to growth of other sectors.

Russia's economic transformation and growth clearly face important challenges. In facing these challenges, Russia has much to learn from the rich experience of transition and economic opening of almost 30 transition countries. Applying these lessons wisely should help Russia avoid policy pitfalls and achieve sustained growth in line with its vast potential.

The papers collected in this volume examine a variety of aspects of economic transition in Russia and other Eastern European countries. The paper by *Timothy*

*Lane, Leslie Lipschitz,* and *Alex Mourmouras* examines the forces leading to capital inflows in many European transition economies. The authors first note that the large real currency appreciations experienced by many transition economies, to the extent that they reflect rising productivity associated with the economic transformation, create a strong incentive for cross-border lending at any positive nominal interest rate. Another metric for gauging the potential volume of capital inflows is the real differential in the marginal productivity of capital associated with wide discrepancies in capital stocks in transition economies compared with their Western neighbors. From either of these perspectives, one would predict capital inflows that are much larger than actually observed. The authors then examine the reasons actual capital flows are smaller than those implied by their analysis, suggesting in particular that institutional factors may play an important role in limiting capital flows to many countries. Finally, they note that the capital inflows to these countries, even though they are smaller than those implied by the real forces of capital scarcity and productivity growth alone, pose a dilemma for policymakers, as they expose the recipient countries to turbulence in global financial markets. Key policy recommendations are exchange rate flexibility and steps to enhance the financial system's resilience in the face of capital market volatility, but in some cases market-friendly controls over capital inflows may need to be considered.

*Evgeny Gavrilenkov* analyzes structural change and productivity growth in Russia. His starting point is that in 1999/2000 the growth rates of industrial output and investment have increased very strongly; private consumption, which contracted sharply in the 1998 crisis, rebounded in 1999. Gavrilenkov then asks whether Russia's higher growth can be sustained, as is widely believed: he points out that growth potential will be limited by the long-term dynamics of population and working-age population, which will decline after 2008. He then presents a broader macroeconomic analysis which shows that the high savings rate, which increased again in 1999/2000, goes along with ongoing high capital flight, reaching almost 10% of GDP at the beginning of the 21st century. With respect to Russia's economic growth strategy, Gavrilenkov points to the need to internationalize Russia's economy. This would require a strong government that is able to support Russian economic interests in the world economic system. But a strong government in turn would require a strong domestic economy, whereas the Russian economy has only a few strong and dynamic sectors while other sectors lag behind in modernization. More generally, he emphasizes that opening up the Russian economy will mean not only economic internationalization but also cultural globalization, with a convergence of the attitudes and the aspirations of Russian citizens towards West European patterns. In this regard, Gavrilenkov stresses the need to mobilize the entrepreneurial spirit of Russians, long suppressed by the collectivist values which he argues were artificially implanted by the Communist regime. Such a shift in values could be quite important in driving the modernization of an economy that suffers from an aged capital stock and a variety of ineffciencies, plus a potentially serious foreign debt problem.

The contribution by *Jungmittag* and *Welfens* examines the links between innovation, growth and wages in transforming countries. As the starting point of their analysis, the authors contrast the economic dynamics in newly industrializing countries in Asia and the sustained structural backwardness of some countries in Africa. In order to highlight the relevance of industrial exports and technology intensive production, Jungmittag and Welfens focus on the relative technological capability share and the R&D intensity of transition countries. There is a clear positive correlation between R&D intensity and growth of industrial output in transition countries, pointing to the importance of national innovation systems. But by the late 1990s, most transition countries were still lagging in this area—both with regard to the numbers of R&D personnel and (with the exeptions of Slovenia and Hungary) international patent applications per capita. Another key factor, as highlighted by a broad analysis of Asian NICs, is the positive link between industrial modernization and export position. Here, transforming countries had a negative revealed comparative advantage in high-tech exports (with the exceptions of Hungary and Kyrgyzstan). Another thorny issue examined is the link between economic opening and wage structures. Jungmittag and Welfens point out the enormous income differentials in Russia as compared to other transforming countries, noting that struggles over income distribution could undermine prospects for industrial modernization, innovation and exports, aimed at economic growth.

*Ralf Wiegert* explores the role of the financial sector and human capital development as factors underpinning economic growth in Russia. Russia's transition process is considered to be at critical stage: the pickup in growth following the 1998 crisis to large extent reflects a rise in oil prices and the depreciation of the Rouble, leaving the question of how to harness Russia's considerable growth potential. The author discusses the poor state of Russia's financial sector, which diminishes growth prospects. Reforming the financial sector, especially with regard to the functioning of banks and other financial institutions as intermediaries, should have a high marginal pay-off in efficiency gains and enhance growth. From a longer term perspective, the failure of Russian policymakers to implement needed education reform—in view of the importance of human capital as a core factor for economic growth—undermines Russia's effort to catch up with developed market economies.

*Cathleen Faber* and *Hans Gerhard Strohe* focus on the structure and growth of private consumption in Russia and East Germany. The measurement of private consumption poses some particular challenges in Russia due to the importance of barter trade and problems of price index measurement. The authors present new data on the developments in Russia, but also new data on the former GDR (East Germany) that show considerable changes over time. There is no doubt that consumption patterns in both Russia and the former GDR have been influenced by western patterns, including advertising. The authors note that East Germany's core consumption patterns have converged rather quickly to those of West Germany although, a decade after German unification, some important differences remain.

*Nina Oding's* paper examines labor market transition and hidden unemployment in Russia. The author looks at national and regional unemployment rates in Russia, noting the important differences between national measures of unemployment and ILO standards. She also discusses some key problems of the informal sector, which clearly plays an important role in Russia. Hidden unemployment is shown to be a crucial element of Russia's economy. Oding illustrates that enterprise behavior is crucial for understanding major problems in Russia's labor market. Some key aspects of regional employment patterns are also discussed, using St. Petersburg as a case study.

*John T. Addison* examines the development of employment policy in western nations, providing insight for transformation economies. The author focuses mainly on the experience in the United States—which displays considerable diversity in manpower programs and long-standing attempts to evaluate their impact—although European policies are also discussed. The author presents the case for active labor market policies, followed by a review of mainstream U.S. training measures and their evaluation. He notes that while many of these standard policies are controversial, while there is wider agreement on the benefits of other measures such as early childhood interventions and certain reforms of the unemployment insurance system. The wider issues raised by the U.S. experience are then summarized, prior to a review of the European experience. The concluding section discusses the lessons for transition economies.

*Andrei Zaostrovtsev* looks into a neglected topic of transformation in Russia: the rent-seeking problem within the context of regional authorities, specifically in the case of St. Petersburg. Regions compete for mobile capital and investors, respectively, at the same time employees and civil servants working for regional government or local authorities enjoy discretionary decision options; having only low wages and incomes, respectively, those working for government can exploit opportunities to obtain part of the rent accruing to investors under alternative decisions. Regional investment incentives, special rules for economic development zones and licensing procedures plus customs rules all create opportunities for rent-seeking. Under external pressure, the city of St. Petersburg has streamlined some regulations and created a more transparent institutional setup which should reduce rent-seeking incentives. However, there still is the fact that unclear and inconsistent rules create uncertainty and raise transaction costs, in turn impairing investment and employment growth.

*Frank Bohn's* contribution is a theoretical examination of the link between corruption and the power structure of society. He analyzes a non-cooperative Nash game involving bureaucrats, corrupt capitalists, and honest entrepreneurs. In his model, the corrupt capitalists decide on the degree of corruption and the government can redistribute income by using taxation and paying salaries to the bureaucrats. Policies that affect the power structure are shown to have implications for the degree of corruption and the level of output. While the model is simplified, it can be extended to cover a richer range of possibilities.

*Ruslan Grinberg* and *Leonid Vardomsky* provide insight into the regional dimensions of the transition in Russia, describing some of the key heterogeneities within the Russian Federation. They note the wide regional disparities in income, with some sparsely populated regions as well as the centres of Moscow and St. Petersburg having the highest per capita incomes. They note that these disparities create special problems in fiscal federalism and also stimulate potential migration. New federalism has encouraged regional economic development. Across regions, the degree of internationalization of economic activity differs considerably. Moreover, regional policy approaches also show different strategies. Relations between centre and periphery changed during the 1990s, as the metropolitan regions gained in terms of relative economic weight: for instance, the share of Moscow and its regions in total GDP increased from 14 % in 1995 to almost roughly 20 % by the end of the decade. The authors also characterize regional patterns of FDI. They illustrate some medium term dynamics that might aid in overcoming Russia's territorial fragmentation, noting the absence of consensus in discussions within Russia. The authors also suggest some constitutional amendments that should support efficient Russian federalism.

*Olga Nosova's* contribution pertains to the foreign trade patterns and policies of Russia and Ukraine. She notes the links between trade and capital flows, especially foreign direct investment. She contrasts the ratio of FDI inflows to private investment in Russia and Ukraine during the 1990s to those observed in the the Asian and Latin American NICs. She notes the volatility of Russia's trade flows during the 1990s, reflecting the importance of oil and gas exports as well as fluctuations in imports. She also examines the composition of trade, noting that the share of machinery and equipment in total imports is well below levels that would be associated with successful economic modernization. With regard to the trade patterns of Ukraine, she notes that Russia and other former Soviet Union countries respectively are still the leading trading partners. Finally, the paper discusses the problems and policy options for trade policy, including the constraints posed by the budgetary importance of tariff revenues.

Once industry in former socialist countries had to face international market conditions, its low level of productivity, the narrow range of products, and often low quality, became evident. Modernizing and restructuring existing enterprises and building new industries are essential, but given the low savings rates and distorted financial system, there is insufficient domestic financing for the structural changes and high rates of capital accumulation that are needed. Among external financial sources, Foreign Direct Investment (FDI) is expected to play an important role in the modernization process not only as a source of additional capital, but also as a means of transferring technology and knowledge to the economy as a whole. The paper by *Döhrn* and *von Westernhagen* examines these issues. It takes a broader look at FDI issues in transforming economies and compares the two countries which were rather successful in attracting FDI—Hungary and Poland—to the three largest CIS countries: Russia, Belarus and Ukraine, where FDI has hitherto played a comparatively more minor role. They first review theoretical approaches to the role of FDI in transformation and then discuss some statistical aspects of FDI in the countries investigated. They analyze the dynamics of FDI in these countries and present some projections, as the basis for further discussion of the role of FDI in fixed capital formation.

We hope that this book will stimulate national and international discussion about Russia's economic situation and help in formulating a response to major policy challenges, reflecting both Russia's history of transition from central planning and the current economic environment characterized by globalization and rapid advances in information technology. The European Institute for International Economic Relations will continue to monitor and analyze the Russian transformation process with these issues in mind.

We are grateful to the *Leontief Institute, St. Petersburg*, which hosted the international workshop at which most of the papers contained in this volume were presented; also included are papers from the Transatlantic Transformation and

Economic Development Research Group (Trans@lantic-Transfo.Net). We also thank the *Alfried Krupp von Bohlen und Halbach Foundation* for their support for the underlying research project project and for the website www.progressinfo.net, dedicated to promoting growth and stability in Russia and prosperity in Europe as a whole. Finally, we greatly appreciate the editorial assistance provided by Karl Hummel, Albrecht Kauffmann, Ralf Wiegert, and Tim Yarling.

Washington DC, St. Petersburg and Potsdam, April 2003

*Timothy Lane, Nina Oding and Paul J.J. Welfens*

# A. Capital Flows to Transition Economies: Reasons, Risks, and Policy Responses

Timothy Lane, Leslie Lipschitz, and Alex Mourmouras

## 1 Introduction

Substantial private capital inflows have been a fact of life for many of Europe's transition economies over the past decade (Figure A1).[1] Capital flows to economies undergoing far-reaching structural change are to be expected, as they reflect investment opportunities in excess of those that can be financed by domestic savings.

But recent emerging market financial crises – in Mexico, Asia, Brazil, Russia, and most recently Argentina and Turkey – serve as a reminder that capital flows are a good servant but a bad master. In most of the countries affected by the Asian crisis, for example, the capital inflows that preceded the crisis were widely regarded as benign, particularly as they corresponded to high levels of domestic investment in economies that were growing rapidly and had strong fiscal positions and high domestic savings rates. Only in hindsight did it become evident that the capital inflows, together with rapid domestic credit expansion, were contributing to a highly vulnerable financial and corporate structure.[2] This experience has underscored the need for countries receiving substantial capital inflows to consider carefully the reasons for these flows and the appropriate policy response.

This paper discusses the factors driving capital flows the resulting policy issues in transition countries of central and eastern Europe (CEE), the resulting risks, and the possible policy responses.[3] The remainder of the paper is structured as follows. Section II discusses the capital flows, the motivations for these flows, and their consequences. Section III discusses possible policy responses to capital inflows in light of international experience, and especially the recent global financial crises. In considering these issues, the note draws on the lessons from experience elsewhere in the world – especially the Asian crisis countries, Brazil, and Mexico. Section IV presents some concluding observations.

---

[1] For a general discussion of the determinants and systematic consequences of capital flows, see for instance Goldstein, Mathieson, and Lane, 1989.

[2] See for instance Lane and others, 1999; Boorman and others, 2001.

[3] The other CIS countries are not included in this comparison, as they face a quite different set of issues: a greater role of government rather than private sector borrowing, greater reliance on official rather than private sector lending (except in some oil-producing countries); and a different stage of transition. See for instance McGettigan 2000 and EBRD 1997.

## 2 Capital Flows and their Motivation

Capital inflows to the CEE countries with market access have financed current account imbalances (Figure A2) associated, to varying degrees, with relatively high levels of investment spending and with consumption smoothing (as well as, in some cases, fiscal imbalances). Such deficits have been particularly large in the three Baltic countries as well as Hungary and Poland.[4]

Foreign direct investment (FDI) has been a major component of capital inflows (Figure A3). While its macroeconomic consequences are similar to those of other forms of capital inflow, FDI plays a role different from other flows at the microeconomic level, for instance by facilitating the transfer of technology and management techniques. Moreover, compared with other kinds of capital inflows, FDI is less likely to be unwound quickly in response to changes in market sentiment and some of the impact of such a change on the country's external position is absorbed by changes in market valuation – although experience shows that net FDI flows can nonetheless be quite volatile (Dooley, Fernandez-Arias, and Kletzer, 1994), as also illustrated by the marked decline in FDI in Russia in the aftermath of its 1998 crisis.

At the same time, several countries in the region have experienced substantial short-term capital inflows, including portfolio investment and bank claims (Figure A4). In the Czech Republic and Estonia, for instance, portfolio investment and other inflows amounted to around 5 percentage points of GDP in 1999. Such short-term inflows have in some cases been quite volatile; they played an important role in the buildup of vulnerabilities leading to the Russian crisis of 1998.

These capital flows have, to a large extent been driven by strong real forces. These forces can be seen from two different perspectives, either of which suggests a compelling motivation for large capital inflows and some real dilemmas for policy. [5]

### 2.1 Real Appreciations and Interest Rate Differentials

Capital inflows are linked to the real appreciations of exchange rates that many transition countries in the region have undergone (Figure A5) – and which are likely to continue, although one cannot predict to what extent. Inflows may, in part, be motivated by the anticipation of real appreciation. Inflows may also support the real appreciation: huge starting disparities in capital/labor ratios and real rates of return lead to both large capital flows and large productivity gains which may differ as between tradable and non-tradable goods sectors, resulting in equilibrium real appreciations associated with the Balassa-Samuelson effect.

---

[4] Keller et al. 2000 analyzes various indicators of external vulnerability in the Baltic countries, arguing in particular that current account deficits may overstate the degree of external vulnerability.

[5] These are discussed in greater analytical detail in Lipschitz, Lane, and Mourmouras, 2001.

The motivation for capital flows can be illustrated with reference to the basic uncovered interest parity relationship, linking nominal interest rates to the expected nominal depreciation of the transition country's currency:

$$i^C = i^G + (\Delta e/e) \tag{1}$$

where superscripts refer to a transition country C and the industrial country G, i is the nominal interest rate, and e is the exchange rate expressed in units of currency C per unit of currency G. This implies the following relationship between real interest rates and the rate of real appreciation of the transition country currency:[6]

$$r^C = r^G - (\pi^C - \pi^G - \Delta e/e) \tag{2}$$

where the expression in parentheses on the right-hand side represents the rate of real appreciation of the currency of the transition country, expressed in terms of consumer price indices, and $\pi^i$ is the rate of consumer price inflation in country i.

This relationship can be considered in light of the substantial real appreciations experienced by a number of transition economies. Table A1 presents illustrative calculations for the real interest rates for selected European transition economies implied by the right-hand side of (2), on the assumption of uncovered interest parity vis - à - vis Germany, and assuming that the average rates of real appreciation experienced since 1995 are expected to continue.[7]

These results indicate that, under the assumptions made, unfettered capital mobility would drive real interest rates well into negative territory. The substantial gaps between implied and actual interest rates needs to be explained, as they would seem to imply a rather compelling incentive to import capital into these countries. These gaps suggest that, for several of the transition countries, what has to be explained is not the tendency for capital inflows, but rather what has limited these inflows.

Of course, the interpretation of these interest differentials depends very much on the reasons for the real appreciations. One explanation is based on the assumption of product differentiation between goods produced in transition economies and those produced in industrialized countries. The tradable-producing industries in the transition countries started the transition with depressed demand and new competition in their traditional markets, and little if any reputation or brand recognition in western markets. To the extent that current account flows influenced starting exchange rates, therefore, it is not surprising that these rates were very depreciated. As reputations were established and penetration of western markets progressed, some real appreciation was warranted solely on the basis of the changing conditions for trade. This process has been protracted and, indeed, is still far from complete.

---

[6] This derivation uses the usual approximation $(1 + a)/(1 + b) \approx (a - b)$ when a, b are small.

[7] The reader is cautioned regarding the limitations of comparability of data. For instance, in Latvia yields on Treasury Bills are lower than other interest rates, reflecting their value to banks as collateral. (This would of course amplify the difference between actual and implied real interest rates highlighted in the table.)

A slightly more complex interpretation attributes the real appreciations to Balassa-Samuelson effects – i.e., rising *total factor productivity in tradable goods* relative to non-tradables. The gain in total factor productivity could reflect the efficiency gains of exposure to global markets, or the benefits of operating in an economy with increasingly more effective markets and institutions and a more stable macroeconomic setting. Rising output of traded goods and higher incomes are bound to put upward pressures on prices in the nontraded sectors – both through wage leadership and demand pressures.

## 2.2 Capital Scarcity

Another way of viewing the motivation for capital flows is the relative scarcity of capital in the transition economies. Based on imbalances in initial stocks of capital, the magnitude of potential capital flows to European transition economies can be estimated based on existing capital stocks.[8]

As a starting point, Table A2 highlights the large differences in output per worker between the European Union (EU) countries and the CEE countries at the onset of the transition. Output per worker in 1989 was between 23 and 79 percent of German levels when measured using WEO data that adjust for cross-country differences in purchasing power. In the decade that followed, some countries (Hungary, Poland, Slovenia, and to a lesser extent the Czech Republic) experienced real convergence, while others (Bulgaria, Latvia, Lithuania, and Romania) experienced real divergence and yet others (Estonia and Slovakia) kept their relative incomes constant.

Insofar as the large and persistent differences in output per worker reflect differences in capital-labor ratios, the process of growth and development should have entailed huge capital inflows. An indication of the potential magnitude of the flows that would be associated with capital scarcity alone, in the absence of differences in technology, can be gauged by the following calculations, which closely follow Lucas (1990).[9] The magnitude of the capital flows predicted by a simple model with identical Cobb-Douglas technologies in the two countries ranges from 147 to almost 800 percent of GDP in 1989 (Table A3). To put this in perspective, in a similar exercise for Spain's experience with capital flows following financial liberalization in 1986, Cordoba and Kehoe (1999) found that the capital flow required to equalize German and Spanish interest rates would be of the order of 86 percent of GDP.

Two points of reference emerge. First, it is clear that, given a trend real appreciation, the real interest rate in the transition country required for interest parity is substantially below that in the industrial countries. Second, from the analysis of domestic supply conditions it is clear that capital scarcity should make the rate of return on capital in European transition countries higher than that in advanced industrial countries. In many circumstances, these two phenomena may be inti-

[8] For a detailed analysis of supply conditions at the start of the transition see McDonald and Thumann 1990.

[9] For details, see Lipschitz, Lane, and Mourmouras, 2001.

mately related: rapid capital accumulation in areas of relative capital scarcity is often accompanied by rapid growth in TFP in tradables, as a result of exposure to modern technologies incorporated in imported, latest-vintage capital goods.[10] But both phenomena suggest that the puzzle is not so much why capital flows to transition economies have been so large, but why they have been so limited.

## 2.3 What Limits Capital Flows to Transition Economies?

While the European transition countries have received substantial amount of foreign financing in the decade following the transition, the current account deficits shown in Figure A2 above have not been anywhere close to those predicted by a simple model, as shown in Table A3. This raises the question of why capital flows have been so *small*, compared with what might be expected. Here, several factors will be mentioned briefly (although each could be analyzed in more detail).

a) *Differences in technology* may result in differences in the productivity of capital across countries. This could reduce the incentive for capital to move to the transition economies, especially to the extent that these gaps are not expected to close over the lifespan of the capital. Broadly interpreted, these technological differences reflect not just the state of knowledge but also aspects of the way production is organized. For instance, there may be inefficiencies in production even in advanced transition countries – corresponding to the observation that there is room for further progress in industrial restructuring (for instance, in the Czech Republic, Poland, and Slovenia) and in agriculture (e.g. in Poland).
b) *Externalities*, particularly those associated with human capital accumulation. Such externalities have been used, in particular by Lucas (1988, 1990), to analyze persistent cross-country differences in income per capita. They would also tend to imply a higher marginal product of capital in industrialized countries and thus a diminished incentive for capital to flow to developing and transition countries.
c) *Adjustment costs* of various kinds would tend to slow the adjustment of capital toward the levels of the industrialized countries.
d) *Immobile factors of production* such as suitable land or particular types of human capital may create bottlenecks that delay the adjustment of capital stocks.
e) *Institutional factors* may play an important role in limiting capital inflows. Foreign investors may be concerned that the rules of the game are uncertain, or may change – owing, in some cases, to concerns about the possibility of confiscatory taxation or exchange controls, as well as uneven application of laws and contracts.[11] Such concerns are not confined to transition countries, of course,

[10] The benefits of such technolology transfer would be attenuated by any locational disadvantages, such as those stemming from weaknesses in infrastructure, the legal system, or governance more generally.

[11] Recent findings by Garibaldi et al., 1999 that the distribution of FDI flows across countries is significantly influenced by investor perceptions of country risk as well as survey-

but are among the factors that limit the extent to which we operate in a truly global capital market.

f) Investors may be uncertain about the ability of the *financial system* to channel capital flows efficiently, and this would affect the risks and prospective returns on their investments. As a related point, there may be *credit market constraints* as access to credit may be limited by the availability of suitable domestic assets to serve as collateral.[12]

g) *Macroeconomic instability* may reduce the profitability of investment by making rational investment planning more difficult; uncertain or turbulent macroeconomic prospects tend to limit capital inflows and in some cases lead to capital flight. (The latter has been particularly important in the case of Russia.[13])

h) Finally, capital flows much larger than those actually witnessed would result in *increasing concerns about repayment*. Such concerns are reflected in the fact that current account deficits are regarded as warning indicators of a crisis.[14] Underlying market concerns over current account deficits – even if they, in fact, reflect real factors such as capital scarcity and productivity growth – are the institutional and financial considerations mentioned in the previous two points, together with the difficulty market participants face in ascertaining that capital inflows are in fact based on these real factors. For these reasons, larger current account deficits would tend to be associated with higher required risk premia and would serve to limit the capital flows in response to any given differential in returns.

## 2.4 Risks Associated with Capital Inflows

Although capital flows to transition economies may be associated mainly with real forces and although, as noted, there are some factors that tend to limit them, there are nevertheless some significant risks, associated with the possibility of sudden stops or reversals of these flows associated with changing market sentiment.

It is conceivable that movements in risk premia could help contain the size of capital inflows and allow for some natural speed limits on the pace of capital accumulation and the size of current account imbalances. The simplest ideal would be the case where the risk premium on the currency of the transition country was related in a smooth monotonic fashion to the size of the current account deficit. This would facilitate a smooth increase in domestic interest rates to the point where, at a certain level of the current account deficit, domestic interest rates would be high enough to balance real intertemporal forces – decisions on saving and consumption and the timing of investment – without eliciting overwhelming portfolio inflows. In practice, however, risk premia are unlikely to be so well behaved.

---

based indicators of the legal and political climate are consistent with the view that such factors are important limitations to capital flows.

[12] See Barro, Mankiw, and Sala-I-Martin, 1992; and Barro and Sala-I-Martin, 1995, p. 101.

[13] See for instance Abalkin and Whalley, 1999.

[14] Warning indicators have been discussed, for instance, by Berg and Patillo 1999. See also Keller et al., 2000, and McGettigan 2000.

They will be a function not only of the current account deficits, but also of a broad array of other variables – including political developments, bandwagon effects, and various elements of contagion from other emerging market countries – that may well be highly erratic and will certainly be beyond the control of the domestic policymakers.[15]

The problem for policy, therefore, is that macroeconomic developments will be hostage to capital account developments which will be highly sensitive to a vector of possibly erratic exogenous variables. There may thus be times when policymakers are trying to cope with overwhelming inflows that undermine any semblance of financial restraint. At other times, a sudden exogenous jump in risk premia may reverse capital flows and force a financing crisis and/or a major compression of demand.

The problem is a real one, and different nominal exchange rate regimes will not alter it fundamentally. It is true that floating exchange rates may be able to absorb shifting risk premia more smoothly. But they will not help stabilize the influence on domestic demand. Consider, for example, the case of a sudden drop in the risk premium from a seemingly settled domestic situation. Under a pegged exchange rate regime, the transition country may be overwhelmed with capital inflows resulting in inflation and a sharp deterioration in the competitiveness of the traded goods sector. Under a floating exchange rate regime where the domestic monetary authorities retain interest rate independence, the value of the domestic currency will jump to an over-appreciated level where some interest-equalizing depreciation is expected; and this appreciation could well be devastating for the traded goods sector of the economy.

## 3 Policy Responses to Capital Inflows

The previous section has stressed that in the absence of frictions, *real* factors, notably capital scarcity and productivity growth differentials, would account for capital flows to transition economies much larger than those actually observed. While these capital flows are limited by a variety of factors that were enumerated – and in particular by volatile risk premia associated with information and other frictions – they may nonetheless be huge. Certainly these capital flows are large enough to pose a challenge for economic policy and to lead to a buildup of vulnerabilities of the kind reflected in recent capital account crises.[16] The question is then what kinds of policy may be useful in tackling this challenge.

---

[15] See for instance Lane, 1992.

[16] A useful reference is Schadler et al., 1993, which considered the experience of 6 countries faced with surges of capital inflows: within the five years following the publication of this study, three of these countries had undergone major crises. The countries experiencing crises were Spain (1993), Mexico (1994–95), and Thailand (1997–98); Chile and Colombia weathered international financial crises; while in Egypt, the episode of capital inflows proved short-lived.

## 3.1 Exchange Rate Regime

The choice of exchange rate regime affects the channels through which capital inflows affect the economy, but no regime would by itself be sufficient to neutralize these effects.

Under a fixed exchange rate – either through a conventional peg or a currency board – inflows are associated with an increase in foreign exchange reserves and thence in the domestic money supply. The authorities then face a dilemma between monetary tightening, intended to restrain domestic monetary expansion and thus inflation, albeit at the cost of attracting more capital flows, versus monetary easing, aimed at restricting the capital inflows, albeit at the cost of fuelling domestic inflation. If real factors are driving the real exchange rate to appreciate, this appreciation will take place through an inflation differential if it does not take place through nominal currency appreciation. If capital is mobile, the use of sterilized intervention to maintain a peg is ultimately a losing game.

Under floating exchange rates, capital inflows typically result in a nominal (and real) appreciation that generates a current account deficit validating the capital inflow. To the extent that shifts in the capital account are much more rapid than changes in current account flows, there will almost certainly be some overshooting. This will entail distortions to competitive conditions that may persist for some time to the detriment of domestic resource allocation. Indeed, some producers of traded goods may face extremely difficult financial circumstances in the aftermath of a sudden rise in risk premia. As discussed above, even if the capital inflows are based on real productivity gains and capital scarcity, a very large current account deficit will make the country vulnerable to changes in market sentiment.

The exchange rate regime can influence market perceptions and thus opportunistic speculative flows. As is evident from the capital-account-based financial crises of the second half of the 1990s, a long-lived pegged exchange rate, with declining risk premia, increasing capital inflows, and a widening current account deficit, may be a recipe for disaster. A country with a fixed exchange rate may manage to hold onto the peg through substantial inflows by resorting to various sterilization mechanisms and accepting some real appreciation through inflation. As confidence in the nominal exchange rate grows, it is likely that more and more private foreign exchange positions will go unhedged, and that the vulnerability to – and the potential cost of – a change in market sentiment will increase.[17] In these circumstances, the authorities are likely to resist any downward pressure on the currency that may result from a sudden increase in the risk premium. To the extent that the market sees this resistance as ultimately futile, the central bank could be seen as a sitting duck for speculative market forces, and this perception of vulnerability will increase speculation against the currency to the point of its becoming

[17] On the other hand, to the extent that the exchange rate fluctuates in response to market forces, private agents may be induced to eschew unhedged financial exposure and even to hedge the risks in export earnings and import costs. The relatively benign reaction of Australia and New Zealand to the Asian crisis may be indicative of this sort of private behavior.

irresistible. Thus, whatever the underlying fundamentals, the exchange rate regime may itself serve to exacerbate volatility.[18]

In conclusion, the experience of recent crises suggests that a flexible exchange rate is likely to be the regime of choice for countries experiencing large capital inflows. But, if capital inflows have real origins, the authorities cannot look to their choice of nominal exchange rate regime alone to resolve their dilemma.

## 3.2 Fiscal Policy

In theory, contractionary fiscal policy can offset the expansionary influence of capital inflows.[19] In practice it makes sense to pursue contractionary fiscal policies during periods of large inflows. Moreover, a strong fiscal position should make it possible to adopt an expansionary stance in response to a sharp turnaround in the capital account.[20] But there are practical limits to what should be expected of fiscal policy: it is highly unlikely that any government will be able to change the stance of fiscal policy in the magnitudes and with the rapidity required to offset shifts in the capital account. Fiscal policy – which is constrained by multi-year governmental obligations and programs, and is subject to parliamentary debate and approval – is simply not a sufficiently flexible instrument.

## 3.3 Structural Reforms

Various aspects of structural reform may also be considered as part of the response to capital inflows. At the most basic level, the better the structure – labor market flexibility, enabling legal structure, absence of restrictive regulations, corporate governance, etc – the greater will be the supply response to capital inflows and the smaller the resultant imbalances (in the external current account and infla-

[18] There is a role for exchange rate based stabilizations, and in particular hard pegs – through currency boards or dollarization – and considerable evidence that they can deliver credibility benefits that translate into lower inflation without sacrificing growth performance (see Ghosh et al., 1998; Hamann 1999; Masson 1999; and Corker et al 2000). Nevertheless, the foregoing analysis suggests that the authorities would be wise to consider and embark on exit strategies before the onset of crisis.

[19] In a simple Mundell-Fleming model with fixed exchange rates and capital mobility monetary policy is irrelevant and only fiscal adjustment can be used to prevent overheating and reduce the current account deficit associated with capital inflows. In the same model with floating exchange rates, a combination of fiscal tightening and monetary easing can be used to reduce the current account deficit.

[20] The experience of the 1997–98 Asian crisis illustrates the importance of a sound fiscal position in providing room for the authorities to respond to a crisis in a way that served to cushion the macroeconomic consequences of a sharp reversal in the capital account. Once it became evident that the crisis was leading to a precipitous drop in private domestic demand, fiscal deficits were allowed to expand substantially (Lane et al., 1999).

tion). But the structure of the financial sector is particularly important. The crises in Asia and elsewhere have underscored the risks of liberalizing capital flows when the financial sector is weakly governed.[21] [22]

The circumstances analyzed in section II – where there are huge fundamental incentives to capital inflows and corresponding current account deficits – are bound to leave a country highly vulnerable to sharp changes in risk premia. Residents will already have incentives to borrow abroad, and any government guarantees (explicit, implicit or perceived) against exchange rate or illiquidity risk, any situation in which risks appear to be socialized without adequate regulation to limit institutions' exposures to such risks, will exacerbate this vulnerability.[23] Avoiding such risks requires both limiting the scope of guarantees to those that are essential to economic stability, and implementing adequate prudential regulations to ensure that excessively risky behavior does not result.[24]

## 3.4 Capital Controls

The conventional desiderata on the pace and sequencing of capital account liberalization[25] apply, and, indeed, some countries in Central and Eastern Europe – including Hungary, Poland, Slovenia, and Croatia – have retained some controls on short-term capital. Even though capital controls distort the intertemporal allocation of resources, are subject to evasion, and could be used as a pretext to relax macroeconomic discipline, they could provide emerging market countries a temporary shield from volatile short-term capital flows like interbank lending and portfolio investment.

---

[21] Also evident from recent crises, is the particular importance of the legal structure: without proper bankruptcy laws, for example, it may take years to unravel competing claims on assets after a crisis – and during this time assets will be underemployed, entrepreneurial activity misdirected, and growth reduced.

[22] Developing a sound financial system has been a priority for transition economies since the early days of transition (see for instance the volume edited by Caprio, Folkerts-Landau, and Lane (1994)). Many of the countries have made substantial progress, while in others there are evident weaknesses. For instance, among the Baltics, Estonia and Lithuania underwent considerable financial restructuring in the wake of serious banking problems in 1992–93 and 1995–96 respectively; in Latvia, in contrast, considerable vulnerabilities remain.

[23] See Dooley, 1998. Also, such guarantees are the basis of the so-called "Pangloss values" discussed by Krugman, 1998, whereby investments are undertaken on the basis of their prospective returns in the best possible state of the world.

[24] More generally, financial sector supervision and regulation in line with the Basel Core Principles is essential to ensuring that transition economies are adequately prepared to cope with capital inflows, and that these do not result in a buildup of vulnerabilities. See Folkerts-Landau et al. 1998.

[25] A key principle is to liberalize longer-term and more stable flows – e.g., direct investment – before shorter-term and less stable flows. If resorting to capital controls, price based controls à la Chile are better than quantitative restrictions and may well manage to lengthen the maturity structure of liabilities. See for instance Johnston et al., 1999.

What is the case for capital controls for a country where substantial inflows reflect capital scarcity and productivity gains? Such controls constitute an interference with market forces and, presumably, slow down the convergence of capital-labor ratios, productivity, and per capita income. An important rationale has to do with externalities. Clearly very large capital inflows increase current account imbalances, dependence on foreign capital, and thus vulnerabilities to international financial market conditions. To the extent that risk premia increase smoothly with current account deficits and other measures of vulnerability, there would probably be little justification for capital controls. However, to the extent that risk premia are erratic, or at least subject to influences unrelated to domestic economic developments, capital flows may impose enormous instability on an economy and overwhelm stabilization policy.

The conclusion is that, where there are existing restrictions on capital inflows, the authorities should proceed cautiously in liberalizing these restrictions. The sequencing of capital account liberalization should take into account the need to address domestic capital market imperfections and weaknesses in regulatory systems, with a view to taking advantage of the benefits of free capital mobility while minimizing the risks from short-term volatility. The situation is different for a country with a history of an open capital account: it may prove difficult to reintroduce capital controls successfully, particularly where there are numerous closely-held corporations and substantial intracorporate flows, requiring the authorities to run a race with the markets to keep up with the markets' ability to circumvent them.

## 3.5 Transparency

If the case for capital controls rests on erratic movements in risk premia, the case for transparency – assuming the sources of instability are not in domestic policy reversals – rests on providing markets with a continuous stream of accurate information so as to facilitate proper assessment. In circumstances of incomplete or asymmetric information, because some investors fear that others have more complete information, there will be herding, or bandwagon behavior, and, in extreme circumstances, investor panics. Contagion too is exacerbated by an insufficiency of information that makes it difficult for lenders to differentiate among borrowers on the basis of credit-worthiness.[26]

The benefits of transparency – or rather, the costs of opaqueness – were highlighted by some episodes in the Mexican and later the Asian financial crises as unpleasant information, particularly regarding the countries' usable reserve positions, became known to markets at the worst possible time, in the midst of a crisis. Had this information been made available all along, and had each of these countries maintained a dialogue with its international creditors aimed at keeping them fully informed, the information could have been priced into markets more smooth-

[26] This and other conditions for effective market discipline are discussed in Lane, 1992. Of course, there are several alternative explanations of contagion, only some of which reflect such informational imperfections. See for instance Masson et al., 1999.

ly. The recent initiatives, under the auspices of the IMF, to establish and monitor codes and standards in these areas, and to encourage the publication of IMF assessments reflects the international community's increasing awareness of the importance of these aspects of transparency as an element of crisis prevention.

## 4 Conclusion

Freed from controls, the development of the transition economies should be accompanied by very large capital inflows. The incentives for these flows are embedded in the initial conditions and the process of development. Such flows can be a useful servant – serving the purposes of development: financing investment, raising productivity, and increasing per capita incomes. But global capital markets can also be a cruel master: capital inflows and the corresponding current account deficits render countries vulnerable to global capital market conditions, and these can be both punishing of perceived domestic policy weaknesses and highly erratic (or at least highly responsive to events beyond the control of domestic policymakers). This reality requires that stabilization policy be cognizant of some nontraditional considerations related to exchange rate regimes, fiscal policy, structural and institutional factors, the rules governing capital flows, and the transparency of economic data and policy.

# Appendix: Figures and Tables

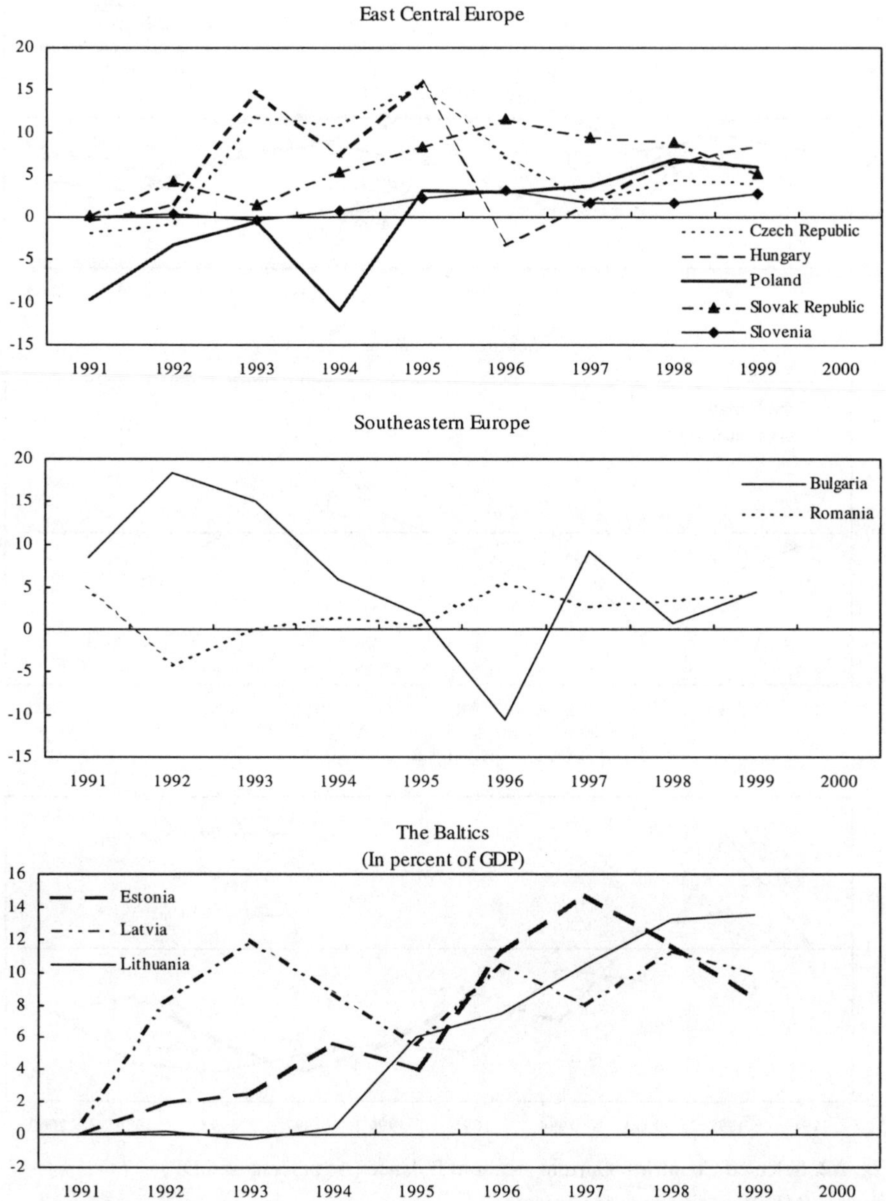


**Fig. A1.** Selected Countries: Net Private Capital Flows Excluding Change in Reserves (As percent of GDP)

*Source: IMF, World Economic Outlook*

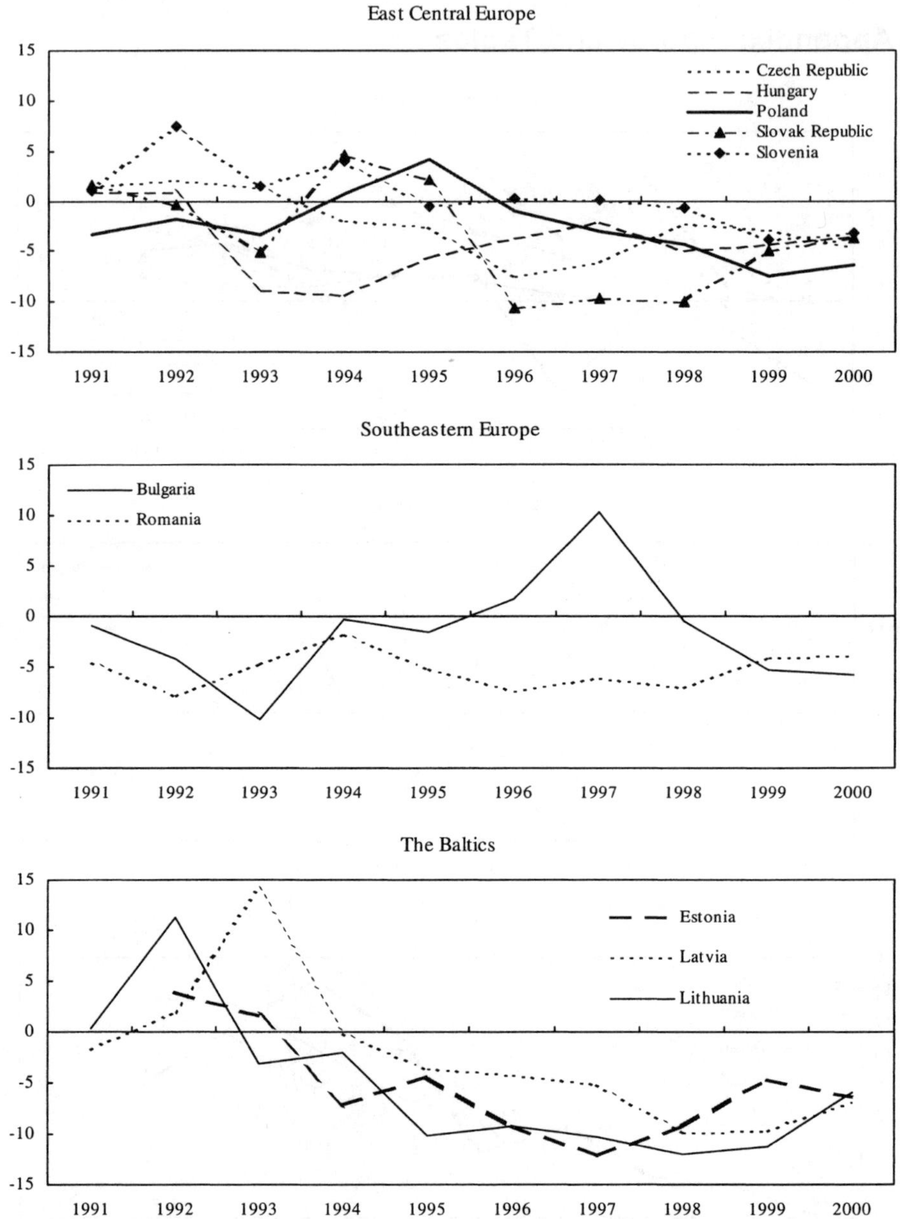


**Fig. A2.** Selected Countries: Current Account Balance (As percent of GDP)
*Source: IMF, World Economic Outlook.*

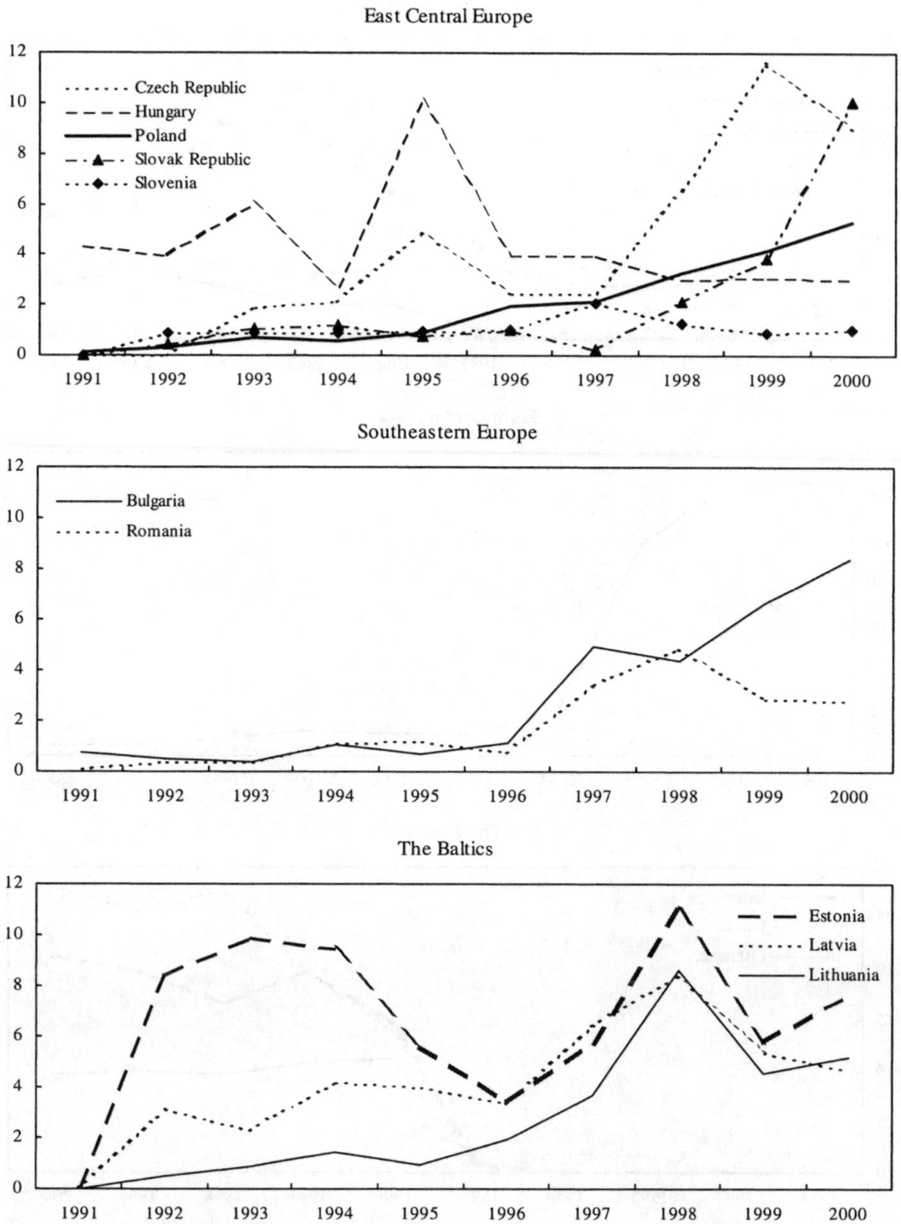


**Fig. A3.** Selected Countries: Foreign Direct Investment (As percent of GDP)
*Source: IMF, World Economic Outlook*

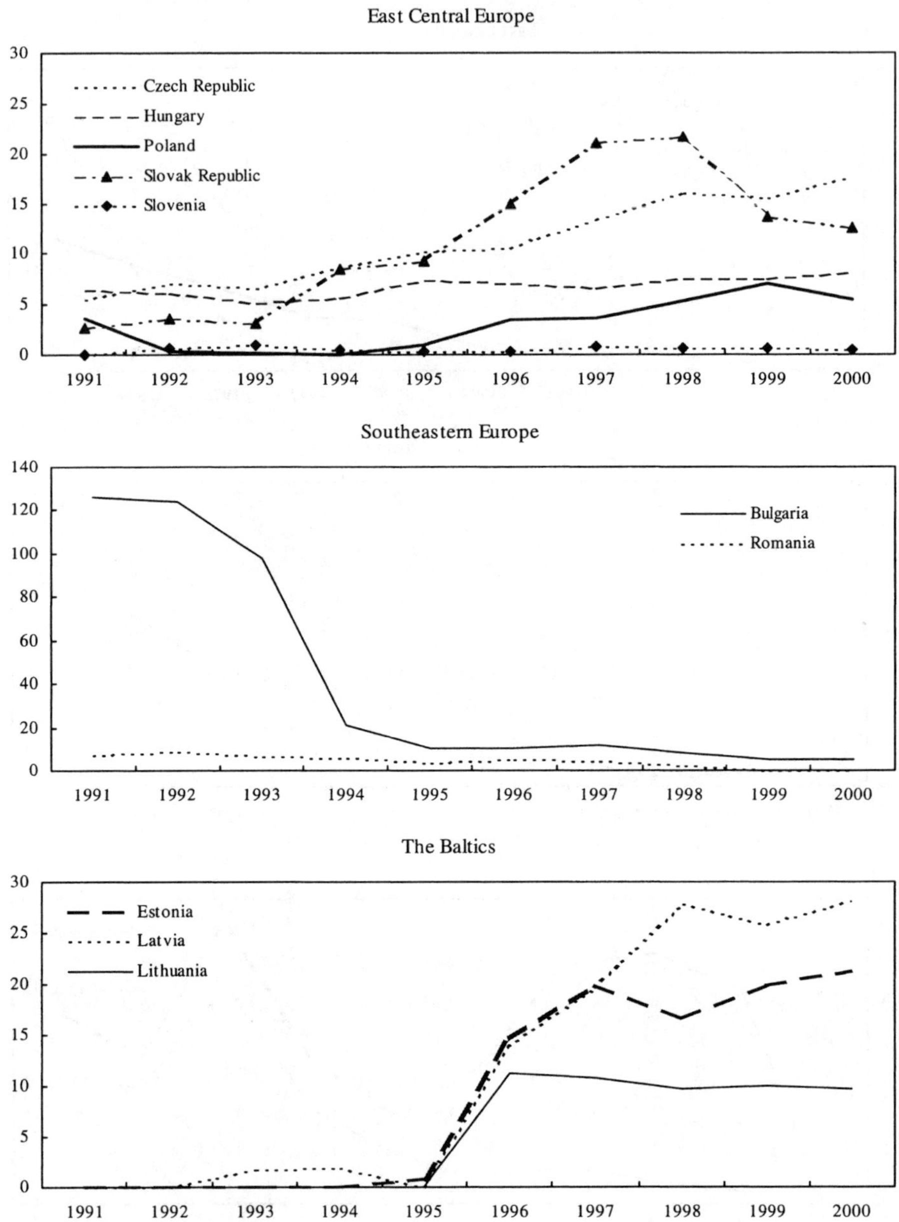


**Fig. A4.** Selected Countries: Short Term Debt (As percent of GDP)
*Source: IMF, World Economic Outlook*

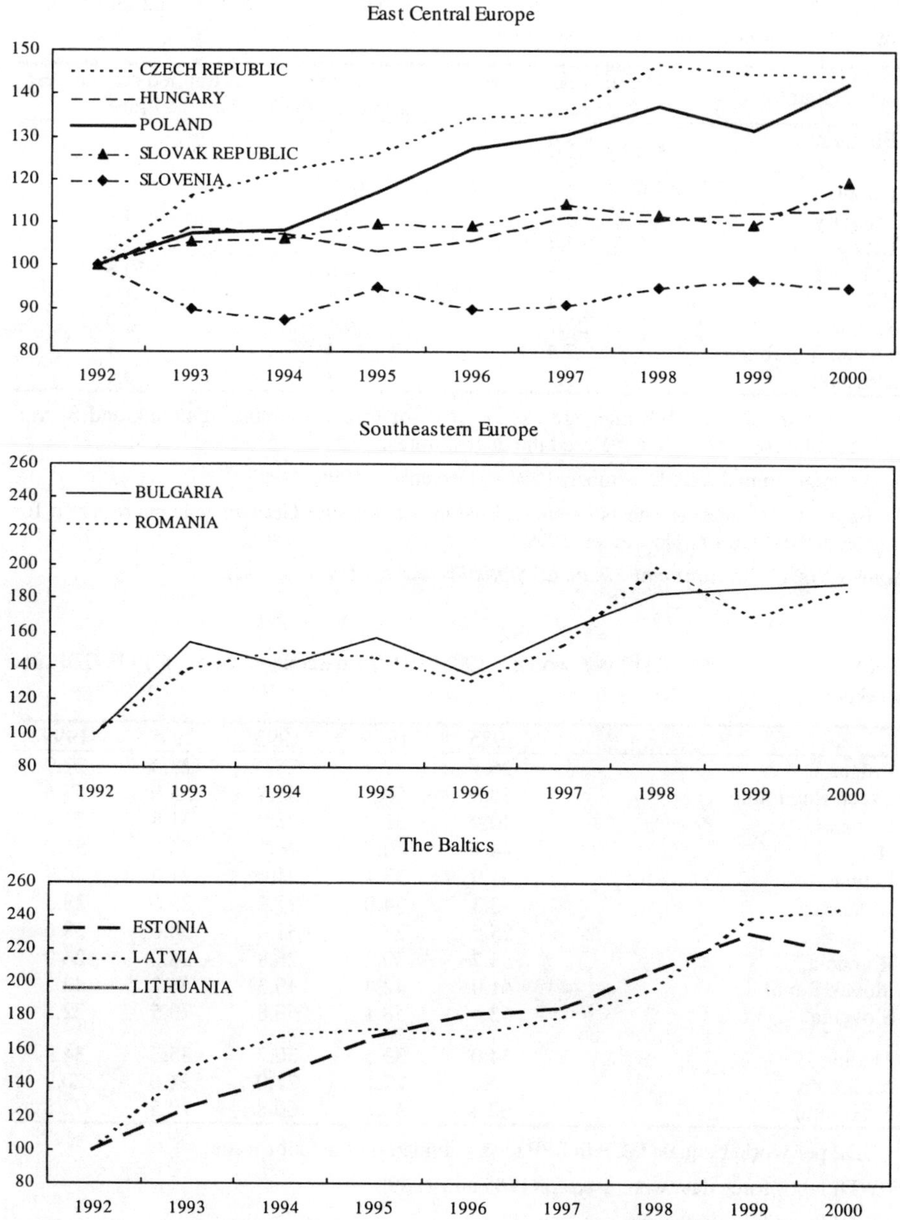


**Fig. A5.** Selected Countries: Real Effective Exchange Rate[1] (Based on consumer prices, 1992=100)

[1] Vis-à-vis US Dollar.

*Source: IMF, Information Notice System*

**Table A1.** Selected European Transition Countries, December, 1999: Actual and Implied Real Interest Rates

| Countries | Actual real interest rate[1] | Real currency appreciation[2] | Implied real interest rate[3] |
|---|---|---|---|
| Bulgaria | -10.4 | 8.5 | -5.8 |
| Czech Republic | -2.0 | 4.9 | -2.6 |
| Estonia | -6.2 | 10.1 | -7.2 |
| Hungary | 3.1 | 2.4 | -0.3 |
| Latvia | 3.4 | 11.4 | -8.3 |
| Lithuania | 8.8 | 14.5 | -10.8 |
| Poland | 4.4 | 5.8 | -3.4 |
| Romania | 21.7 | 4.1 | -1.9 |
| Slovak Republic | 7.4 | 4.4 | -2.1 |
| Slovenia | -5.1 | 2.3 | -0.1 |

[1] Short-term treasury bill rates are used except for Czech Republic, Estonia, and Slovak Republic for which we have used the deposit rates.

[2] Average annual rate, December, 1994 to December, 1999.

[3] Implied real interest rate is calculated using the average German real interest rate for December, 1994 to December, 1999.

*Source : IMF, International Financial Statistics and staff calculations.*

**Table A2.** CEE : PPP GDP per worker, 1985–99[1] (In percent of German PPP GDP per worker)

| | 1985 | 1989 | 1993 | 1998 | 1999 |
|---|---|---|---|---|---|
| Bulgaria | 26.1 | 29.4 | 28.0 | 23.3 | 22.9 |
| Czech Republic | 50.0 | 50.5 | 56.4 | 55.0 | 53.6 |
| Estonia[2] | 30.9 | 31.9 | 28.9 | 31.8 | 31.1 |
| Hungary[3] | 44.1 | 40.9 | 46.8 | 54.1 | 55.7 |
| Latvia[2] | 31.9 | 33.1 | 21.0 | 21.6 | 20.9 |
| Lithuania[2] | 33.3 | 34.0 | 27.6 | 29.0 | 28.5 |
| Poland[2] | 25.5 | 27.1 | 31.6 | 38.6 | 38.6 |
| Romania | 34.7 | 30.2 | 26.8 | 28.0 | 26.9 |
| Slovak Republic | 41.0 | 42.4 | 40.3 | 44.2 | 42.2 |
| Slovenia | 62.4 | 58.1 | 60.8 | 70.5 | 72.8 |
| Median | 34.0 | 33.5 | 30.2 | 35.2 | 34.9 |
| Minimum | 25.5 | 27.1 | 21.0 | 21.6 | 20.9 |
| Maximum | 62.4 | 58.1 | 60.8 | 70.5 | 72.8 |

[1] GDP per worker equals GDP in PPP terms divided by the labor force.

[2] WDI labor force data were used for 1985 and 1989.

[3] WDI labor force data were used for 1985.

*Sources: WEO; and World Bank, World Development Indicators (WDI).*

**Table A3.** CEE : Potential Capital Inflows, 1985–99 (In Percent of GDP)

| | 1985 | 1989 | 1993 | 1998 | 1999 |
|---|---|---|---|---|---|
| Bulgaria | 658 | 576 | 609 | 738 | 753 |
| Czech Republic | 306 | 300 | 253 | 264 | 275 |
| Estonia | 550 | 527 | 589 | 530 | 543 |
| Hungary | 363 | 396 | 334 | 271 | 259 |
| Latvia | 532 | 507 | 823 | 797 | 825 |
| Lithuania | 506 | 492 | 616 | 585 | 596 |
| Poland | 676 | 628 | 533 | 425 | 425 |
| Romania | 483 | 560 | 638 | 609 | 634 |
| Slovak Republic | 397 | 379 | 403 | 360 | 381 |
| Slovenia | 212 | 240 | 222 | 160 | 147 |
| Median | 495 | 499 | 561 | 477 | 484 |
| Minimum | 212 | 240 | 222 | 160 | 147 |
| Maximum | 676 | 628 | 823 | 797 | 825 |

*Source: Authors' calculations based on WEO and WDI data.*

## References


Abalkin A, Whalley J (1999) The Problem of Capital Flight from Russia. World Economy (May)

Barro RJ., Mankiw GN, Sala-I-Martin X (1992) Capital Mobility in Neoclassical Models of Growth. NBER Working Paper No. 4206 (November)

Barro RJ., Sala-I-Martin X (1995). Economic Growth. McGraw-Hill, New York

Boorman J, Lane T, Schulze-Ghattas M, Bulí• A, Ghosh AR, Hamann J, Mourmouras A, Phillips St (2001) Managing Financial Crises: The Experience in East Asia. Carnegie-Rochester Conference Series on Public Policy 53 (2000) 1–67

Berg A, Patillo C (1999) Are Currency Crises Predictable? A Test. IMF Staff Papers 46 (June): 107–138

Caprio G, Folkerts-Landau D, Lane TD (eds) (1994) Building Sound Finance in Emerging Market Economies. IMF and World Bank

Cordoba GF, Kehoe TJ (1999) Capital Flows and Real Exchange Rate Fluctuations Following Spain's Entry into the European Community. Working Paper, Federal Reserve Bank of Minneapolis (May)

Corker R, Beaumont C, van Elkan R, and Iakova D (2000) Exchange Rate Regimes in Selected Advanced Transition Economies – Coping with Transition, Capital Inflows, and EU Accession. IMF Policy Discussion Paper

Dooley MP (1998) A Model of Crises in Emerging Markets. NBER Working Paper No. 6300

Dooley MP, Fernandez-Arias E, Kletzer K (1994) Recent Private Capital Flows to Developing Countries: Is the Debt Crisis History? NBER Working Paper no. 4792

EBRD (1997) Transition Report 1997. (London; European Bank for Reconstruction and Development)

Folkerts-Landau D, LindgrenC-J, et al. (1998) Toward a Framework for Financial Stability. IMF World Economic and Financial Surveys

Garibaldi P, Mora N, Sahay R, Zettelmeyer J (1999) What Moves Capital to Transition Economies? Paper presented at IMF Conference A Decade of Transition: Achievements and Challenges

Ghosh AR, Gulde A-M, and Wolf HC (1998) Currency Boards: The Ultimate Fix? IMF Working Paper WP/98/8

Goldstein M, Mathieson DJ, and Lane T (1989) Determinants and Systemic Consequences of International Capital Flows. IMF Occasional Paper No. 77

Hamann AJ (1999) Exchange-Rate-Based Stabilization: A Critical Look at the Stylized Facts. IMF Working Paper WP/99/132

Johnston RB, Darbar SM, Echeverria C (1999) Sequencing Capital Account Liberalization: Lessons from the Experience in Chile, Indonesia, Korea, and Thailand. IMF Working Ppaer WP/97/157

Keller PM., Gulde A-M, and Kähkönen J (2000) Pros and Cons of Currency Board Arrangements in the Lead-Up to EU Accession and Participation in the Euro Zone. IMF Policy Discussion Paper PDP/00/1/

Keller PM et al. (2000) The Baltics: Exchange Rate Regimes and External Sustainability. Draft, IMF

Krajnyak K, Zettelmeyer J (1998) Competitiveness in Transition Economies: What Scope for Real Appreciation? IMF Staff Papers 45 (June)

Krugman PA (1998) What Happened to Asia? Unpublished: MIT

Lane, Timothy (1992) Market Discipline. IMF Staff Papers 40 (March)

Lane T, Ghosh AR, Hamann AJ, Phillips St, Schulze-Ghattas M, and Tsikata T (1999) IMF-Supported Programs in Indonesia, Korea, and Thailand: A Preliminary Assessment. IMF Occasional Paper 178

Lipschitz L, Lane T, Mourmouras A (2001) Capital Flows to Transition Economies: Master or Servant? IMF Working Paper (forthcoming)

Lipschitz L, McDonald D (1992) Real Exchange Rates and Competitiveness: A Clarification of Concepts, and Some Measurements for Europe. Empirica – Austrian Economic Papers 19, no. 1: 37–69

Lucas RE (1988) On the Mechanics of Economic Development. Journal of Monetary Economics 22: 3–32

Lucas RE (1990) Why Doesn't Capital Flow from Rich to Poor Countries? American Economic Review, Papers and Proceedings 80 (May): 92–96

Masson P (1999) Monetary and Exhange Rate Policies of Transition Economies of Central and Eastern Europe After the Launch of EMU. IMF Policy Discussion Paper 99/5

McDonald, D, Thumann G (1990) Investment Needs in East Germany. In: Lipschitz L, McDonald D (eds) German Unification – Economic Issues. IMF Occasional Paper 75.

McGettigan D (2000) Current Account and External Sustainabiliti in the Baltics, Russia, and Other Countries of the Former Soviet Union. IMF Occasional Paper 189

Obstfeld M, and Rogoff K, 1996, Foundations of International Macroeconomics. MIT Press, Cambridge, Massachusetts

Schadler S, Carkovic M, Bennett A, Kahn R (1993) Recent Experiences with Surges in Capital Flows. IMF Occasional Paper 108

# B. Long Term Structural Change and Productivity Growth in Russia

Evgeny Gavrilenkov

## 1 Point of Reference

The results for 1999 turned out to be the most promising figures not only of the entire reform period, but also of the 1990s as a whole. According to the State Statistics Committee, the gross domestic product increased by 3.2 percent in 1999. Growth in GDP was due primarily to growth in industrial output (which increased by 8.1 percent according to the official data). There was also an increase in production output in agriculture (by 2.4 percent), and investments in fixed capital grew as well (by 4.5 percent). In 2000 Russian economy is going to deliver even higher growth rates with GDP probably increasing over 6 percent and investment rising somewhere around 15 percent.

Taking it at face value, one can speak of substantial qualitative shifts in the economy – industrial output hasn't grown by 8 percent since the early 1970s. The last time there was an increase in investments was in the late 1980s (in 1990 investments grew by the statistically insignificant amount of 0.1 percent). It should be mentioned that in contrast to 1997, the resurgence, signs of which have emerged in the Russian economy in 1999–2000 after the prolonged slump tied to transformation processes and the profound investment crisis of the 1990s, is more sustained in nature and is due to a significant extent to the influence of internal factors, particularly the correction of the exchange rate of the national currency, which after the devaluation of 1998 corresponds more closely to the level of production efficiency that was reached in the late 1990s. In the long run, however, it will not be possible to count on the devaluation effect. Growth should be tied to a reduction in costs, and an increase in production efficiency, which has not yet happened.

Although private consumption fell substantially after the crisis according to the 1999 results (retail trade turnover dropped by 7.3 percent), this was the result of the sharp post-devaluation contraction of effective demand in 1998 – starting in the second quarter of 1999 real income and consumer demand started to rebound steadily, creating the potential for positive dynamics in 2000. In January-September of 2000 retail sales increased 8.3 percent relative to the first quarter of 1999. The level of aggregate consumption potentially could have been higher (both before and after devaluation) if there had been a more even structure for the distribution of income; however the reforms, in the form in which they were implemented, led to a situation in which approximately half of all current income was accumulated and is still being accumulated by the wealthiest 20 percent of the population in the highest income bracket. The concentration of a significant proportion of income in the hands of a relatively small group of Russian citizens substantially reduces the potential of mass consumer demand.

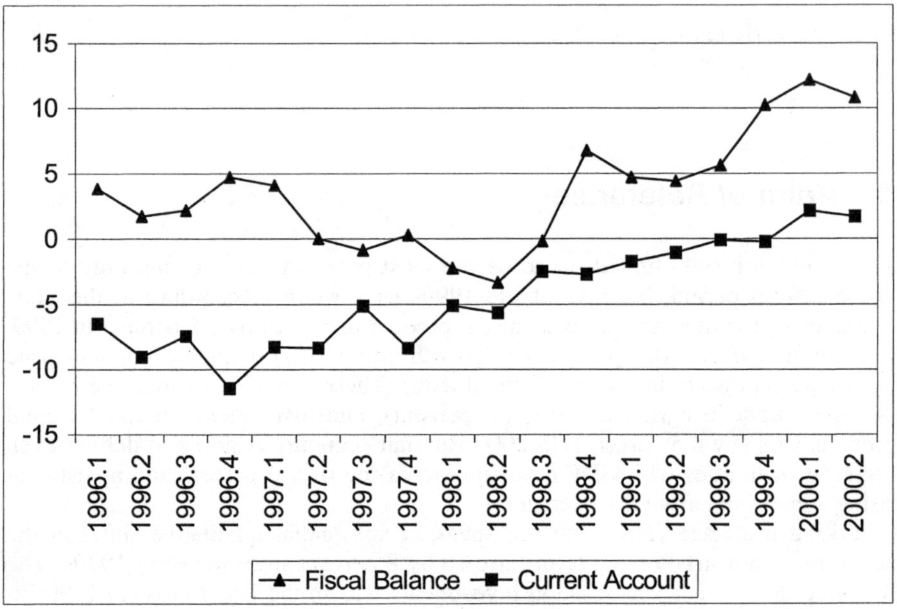


**Fig. B1.** Fiscal Deficit and Current Account in 1996–2000 (Billion US Dollars)

To some extent Russia was lucky in 1999–2000 as high oil prices resulted in additional fiscal revenues that could help the authorities run the budget almost without foreign borrowing. At the same time Russia fulfilled most of its foreign debt obligations. Despite substantial debt payments in 1999 and early 2000 international reserves remained stable in 1999 and increased more than twice in January-October 2000 reaching the highest level since the beginning of transition. This happened in the background of high trade surplus, which in 1999 reached 35.3 billion dollars and is going to approach 60 billion dollars in 2000. Current account in 1999 reached nearly 25 billions dollars and it had already reached the same level in the first half of 2000. Monthly trade surplus in 2000 varied about 5 billion dollars, while in 1995-1996 it was at its quarterly level. High trade and current account surpluses contributed to real appreciation of the ruble. Due to moderate inflation in 2000, the ruble remained stable in nominal terms fluctuating around 28 rubles per dollar. From a macroeconomic standpoint some strengthening of the ruble was in favor among fiscal authorities. So it looks quite realistic that Russia will be able to pay over $10 billion to foreign creditors in 2000 as proposed in the budget.

Due to an improvement in the balance of payments and better fiscal performance, the macroeconomic situation seems to be quite stable. Figure B1 shows that in 1999, and especially in the fall of 1999, the sum of both external and internal current balances (current account and fiscal balance) was positive. It is also seen from this chart that in the past years this sum was negative and crisis of the 1998 occurred when both balances, external and internal, became steadily negative. In 1999 and early 2000 the situation appears to be quite different. Figure B1 also points out the links between the balance of payments and fiscal balance. The economy can not be stable if both balances are negative and in the case that it is not financed from abroad. Poor macroeconomic management and huge fiscal deficits in 1994–1996 were compensated for through a surplus in the current account. In 1999–2000 the situation seems to be the most stable relative to previous years.

Nevertheless, it is premature to offer an entirely positive assessment of the results for 1999, as well as the prospects for economic development in 2000 and subsequent years, since all of the quantitative improvements at present must be viewed in the context of the profound economic crisis and production slump of 1998. After all, in 1999, the country basically did not tackle a single one of the key economic problems, with the sole exception of the execution of the budget and shrinking the budget deficit. In 2000, largely due to high oil prices, Russia is able to run the budget even with a surplus, but it is important that this happens in the background of the absence of structural reforms[1]. Huge current account surplus is compensated for respective of capital flight since the investment climate had not yet substantially improved. High growth rates of investment can be largely treated as a side effect of high oil price.

There are some other warning signals, however, that may indicate that present macroeconomic stability may be fragile and all those relative improvements may be not sustainable due to the fact that the economy became heavily subsidized in 1999: the energy sector became the donor for the rest of the economy. Really, electricity tariffs, which are subject to administrative regulations, increased only 14 percent in 1999, while PPI for the entire industry grew 67 percent during the same period. Despite the fact that in 2000 electricity prices were growing faster than in the entire industry (37 percent and 25.3 percent respectively for January-September 2000) this was not enough to compensate for the 1999 gap. It means that all electricity consumers benefited from low costs, while electricity producers were drifting towards bankruptcy as the government prevented them from raising prices. In the fuel industry prices grew 135 percent. Given high oil prices on the world markets, Russian oil producers were not pressing electricity producers, who were limited in cash, to pay in return for heating oil. Price dynamics inside the fuel industry were quite uneven, leading to gas prices increasing 14 percent (the same as in electricity) with much higher increases in the oil sector. This shows that electricity and gas industries in fact subsidized the economy in 1999. In fact, an improvement in foreign trade conditions also made a substantial contribution to the positive production dynamics and the improved financial position of a number of sectors in the economy.

Another problem is related to a widening gap between producer and consumer prices. In September 2000 producer prices increased 25.4 percent relative to De-

---

[1] Despite that in 2000 the Russian government released rather liberal long-term economic strategy.

cember 1999, while consumer prices increased 14.1 percent only. Given that the gap in 1999 was rather substantial (producer prices increased 67 percent, while consumer prices grew 36.5 percent) inflation potential may be growing. This means that growth may slow down if no substantial cost reduction and increase in production efficiency occur. Really, as was said, all positive trends in 1999 and in early 2000 were accompanied by little visible structural transformation. As a result deterioration in the real sector may complicate fiscal performance and debt service respectively.

## 2 Strategy for Russia

Structural change and productivity growth can be considered key problems for Russia. Thus, Russia's economic strategy should be targeted towards stimulating efficiency of production and structural transformation. The general logic of the strategy for the country's development in the 21st century arises from the following postulates:

- The Russian economy is part of the global economy. In the 1990s the extent of Russia's involvement in global economic processes grew significantly, and this occurred, first and foremost, as a result of the formation and development of the Russian private sector. Indeed, it was at the private sector level and among certain population segments that Russia began to resemble the rest of the world in economic and cultural respects, even if this did express itself in such exotic forms as capital flight or the export of human capital. At the state level, though, the pace of integration lagged behind considerably. Following the collapse of CMEA [Council for Mutual Economic Assistance] and the Warsaw Pact, Russia, as a state, did not manage to define its place either politically or economically on an international level, remaining an exporter of energy and raw material resources and industrial semifinished goods, and an importer of goods and services with a high degree of value added (including consumer goods). What's more, despite the fact that the government released its long-term economic strategy, the most general guidelines for the country's development have not been clearly formulated to this day[2], and in effect the direction of the country's movement has not been identified—does the country intend to seek a place in the EU in the future, is Russia's goal revival as a politically independent superpower, and so on. In other words, there are no clearly defined principles for the country's development in both diplomatic and geopolitical respects. As a result, Russia, as a sovereign state, stands alone both politically and diplomatically—although it does not have any clearly identified antagonists at present, nor does it have any obvious allies (with the exception of Belarus). The country's authority in the world arena is steadily falling, which is creating certain threats not so much for the state as such, but for the development of private

[2] Hopefully this may be seen in the new long term government program which is due to be completed in the near future.

business, and its internationalization, and it is making things considerably more complicated for the country's average citizens, since as the country's authority declines, so does the state's ability to defend the interests of national business and private individuals at the diplomatic level[3]. The inverse correlation also holds, however. In a market environment the state cannot be strong without a strong national business sector.

- In addition to this, more and more of the Russian population is measuring its quality of life, and will continue in the future to compare its standard of living, the standards of everyday life, to the standards of more developed countries in the world (which, on top of all that, have by no means not stopped their development). This is an objective consequence of the openness of the economy, and not just economic globalization, but cultural globalization as well. Given the current level of openness in the Russian society and economy, the objective reality is that there will be further cultural and economic integration of Russian citizens and economic entities into the system of global cultural and economic ties. In this regard, the deepening isolation, the diplomatic "alienation" of the Russian state from the processes of making important decisions at the international level, the frequent disparity between the positions taken by the Russian state and those of the majority of countries around the world[4], the absence of a clearly formulated and at the same time realistic geopolitical doctrine that would be consistent not only with the country's potential level of development, but also its current level of development, runs counter to the trend mentioned above of increasing involvement by Russian private structures in global economic processes. An analysis of the trends in world development over recent decades, globalization, and the ever-increasing integration of the economies of sovereign states into a single system of global economic ties, offers evidence of steady growth in the role not only of private structures (transnational corporations in particular), but also supranational entities—the EU, NATO, WTO, OPEC, ASEAN, and the like. With the exception of the United Nations, Russia does not play an active part in any such structures—in any event its voice is far from decisive in the decision-making process.
- It is obvious that the problem of restoring the authority of the Russian state in the international arena, and improving the standard of living for the country's people with a view to bringing it gradually closer to the standard of living in the most developed countries in the world, can be resolved only if there is a strong, dynamically developing economy. Considering the current state of affairs, resolution of the problems facing the country will require rapid economic growth based on greater production efficiency, the creation of a qualitatively new economic structure, and modernization of the economy. This must occur against the backdrop of a progressive opening up of the country, since historical experience (including Russia's own experience) demonstrates that cultural

[3] Detention of a Russian ship by U.S. naval forces in the Persian gulf was yet another example providing confirmation of this.

[4] The striking disparity between Russia's positions and those of the G-7 countries, which are supported by the majority of European countries, regarding problems in the observance of human rights in Kosovo and Chechnya is a vivid example of this.

and economic isolation is a sure path toward degradation of the economy, the state, and society as a whole. Russian laws and the experience of enforcing these laws are such that at the present time the Russian economy is open at the exit points and remains fairly closed at the entry points, due to the fact that in practice the powerful limiting factor of arbitrary bureaucratic control and corruption plays a determining role. In this sense, the country can be considered closed to foreign capital to a certain extent – bureaucratic traditions that have been shaped over a period of decades, and corruption, which has in effect become the norm in the business world, are firm barriers blocking the penetration of foreign capital into the country. In addition, the exotic tax system and the high degree of influence wielded by criminal elements create the conditions for the export of capital out of the country – this is true both for money earned from criminal activities and for money that has been earned entirely legally. Decapitalization of the economy is the result. The gradual opening up of the economy should proceed not only through enhancement of the legislative base with a view to creating a state that is strong in legal respects and is capable of guaranteeing stability in the country, but also through the elimination of unnecessary bureaucratic hurdles, and efforts to combat corruption and criminal activity.

It is essential that the 1999–2000 period is also revealing because during this period the basic contradictions and dilemmas of how Russia operates were clearly exposed, and it became obvious to the majority of experts and the public that it is impossible to maintain steady economic growth within the framework of the system that developed during the previous period (this pertains primarily to the institutional and structural aspects), which means that it also impossible not only to resolve social and geopolitical issues, but even to formulate them adequately. One of these contradictions – the inconsistency between the depth of the private sector's integration into the global political and economic system on the one hand, and that of the state as such on the other, was mentioned above.

One can also point to the substantial gap between the market exchange rate and the purchasing power parity of the ruble as an example of another contradiction that characterizes the presence of profound structural problems in the Russian economy. It should be noted that a significant gap between the market exchange rate of the national currency and purchasing power parity is typical not only of Russia, but of many other transition economies as well. The same picture can also be seen in developing countries. In Russia, however, this gap is clearly hypertrophied – according to estimates, in 1999 in terms of purchasing power parity the ruble exceeded its market exchange rate by a factor of approximately 5.5 (i.e., the same as in 1993–1994). In Eastern European countries, which have made more progress in the direction of reform than Russia has (the Czech Republic, Poland, Hungary, Slovenia), these figures differ by a factor of approximately 2. At the same time, in the majority of developed countries of the world with stable, functioning market institutions, dynamic economies, and mature financial markets, the purchasing power parity and market exchange rates are close to one another, while in the most developed European countries the market exchange rate of the national currencies exceeds the purchasing power parity, as a rule (Figure B2). This is due in large part to heightened demand for the currencies and securities of these countries on the part of nonresidents.

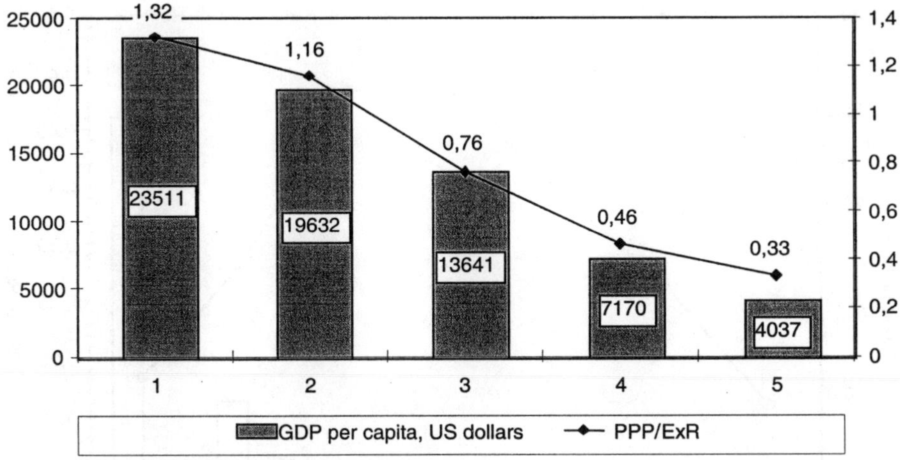


**Fig. B2.** Average per Capita GDP and Ratio of Parity to Exchange Rate by Groups of Countries

If the exchange rate of the national currency in nominal terms significantly exceeds the purchasing power parity, this is evidence of the presence of substantial price disparities and a distorted structure of comparative prices. In this situation prices for a number of goods and services may be comparable to world market prices, while for other groups of goods and services there is a substantial discrepancy (with regard to the Russian economy this applies, for example, to housing and municipal services or passenger transport services). This means that in effect this sort of economy is characterized by a high level of hidden subsidies, which in turn takes certain sectors of the economy beyond the boundaries of competitiveness, and deforms the structure of mass effective demand, since both consumers and producers receive distorted price signals.

A dynamically developing economy and effectively operating financial markets are the basis for stability of the national currency. Figure B2 provides an illustration of the connection between the level of a country's development, measured by the size of per capita GDP produced, and the ratio between the market exchange rate and purchasing power parity. In this regard Russia is confronted with a contradiction of the following sort: at the present time (in 1999), the country's average per capita GDP, calculated in terms of purchasing power parity, was on the order of US$ 6,725, that is, Russia could have been counted in the group of countries that were characterized by an approximately 2-fold gap (and not a 5- or 6-fold gap) between purchasing power parity and the market exchange rate. This approximate ratio was maintained in Russia before the 1998 crisis – in 1996–1997, when the gap between purchasing power parity and the market exchange rate was the smallest (Figure B3). It is typical that the highest level of activity on Russia's financial markets, which are an essential attribute of a market economy, occurred during this period, although the structure of Russia's financial markets during this period, although the structure of Russia's financial markets during this period was extremely distorted.

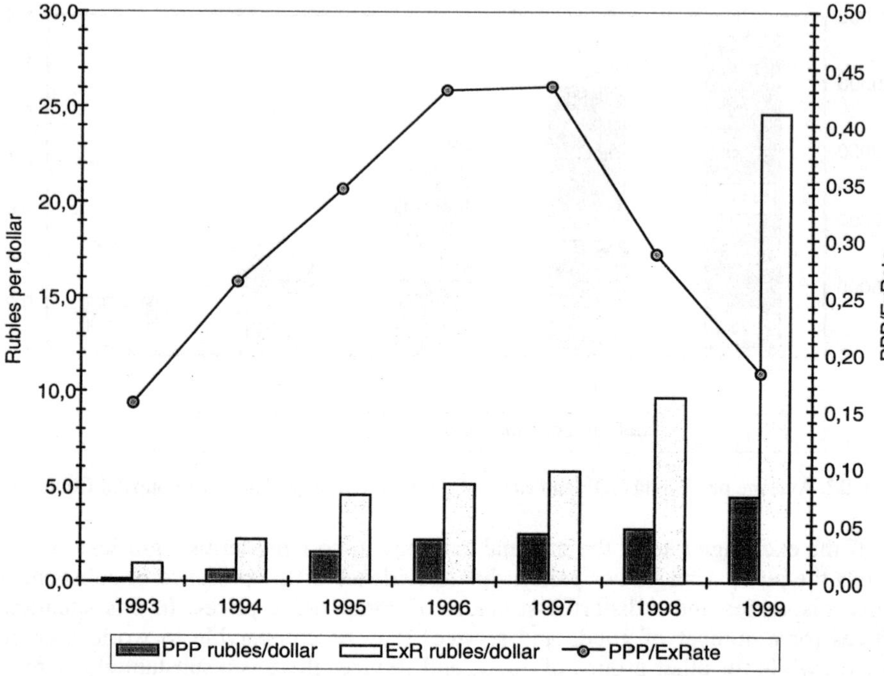


**Fig. B3.** Purchasing Power Parity and the Market Exchange Rate of the Ruble in 1993–1999

Thus, on the one hand, the ruble is clearly undervalued at the present time. On the other hand, given a stronger ruble, the real sector will not be competitive. Nevertheless, it is obvious that in the long run the ruble's exchange rate must rise in real terms, which will increase the level of competition between Russian and foreign producers of goods and services, with the greatest impact felt on the domestic market. In this sense it is entirely natural that in the context of continuing uncertainty regarding the prospects for economic policy and the potential for its implementation, and in the absence of structural reforms, the strengthening of the real exchange rate of the ruble from April through August of last year was not sustained – as soon as the growth in the money supply accelerated at the end of the year, excess liquidity appeared immediately on the exchange market, adjusting the market rate to bring it closer in line with the equilibrium rate.

The low cost of the ruble means that the volume of the ruble money supply is clearly not consistent with the scale of the economy of a country like Russia (at the end of 1999 the ruble M2 aggregate was slightly more than US$ 24 billion). A low level of monetization objectively means a low level of savings; it hinders development of the banking system, limits opportunities for lending to the real sector[5], and also limits opportunities for economic growth. A low level of monetization also makes the country extremely sensitive to external influences—the outflow from or inflow into the country of US$ 5–10 billion (which is negligible in global terms) could seriously destabilize Russia's financial system. On the other hand, it is obvious that currency emission in and of itself is not likely to revive the economy: the low level of financial and payment discipline, the lack of institutional reforms, the export of capital, and a number of other factors have created a situation in which a large proportion of settlements are effected in non-monetary form throughout the economy as a whole, there is a lower demand for money, and there has been widespread displacement of normal monetary settlements in economic practice. As a result, excess ruble liquidity has just one place to go – the exchange market.

Macroeconomic imbalances in the monetary sphere are aggravated by the fact that against the backdrop of a low level of monetization, the outflow of capital from the country has not been halted. According to estimates based on balance of payments data, the annual export of capital from the country is on the order of US$ 20–25 billion. Widespread discussion of this problem, which existed throughout the 1990s, began only in 1999, after the devaluation, when the negative impact of the process of Russia's lending to the rest of the world was aggravated by an increase in the relative scale of this phenomenon compared to the scale of the country's economy (using the market exchange rate of the ruble). The export of capital continued in 1999–2000 as well[6], which certainly does not reflect favorably on the government authorities that were responsible for the implementation of economic policy. Really, gross national savings in 1999 reached nearly 26 percent of GDP (Table B1), while gross fixed investments only reached 15.8 percent of GDP (inventory accumulation was negative: -0.7 percent of GDP). In 1999 growth in GDP occurred against the backdrop of a marked reduction in domestic consumption and a negligible increase in investments, which was compensated for by gigantic net exports. Nevertheless, the country did not manage to pay off everything it owed to creditors, or to build up reserves. The direction of capital flows (financial resources flow into a country or out of a country) is an accurate indicator of the effectiveness of a state's economic policies, and a way to measure the level of confidence in the authorities. It is important for Russia not only to halt (or curtail) the outflow of capital, which theoretically could be achieved through administrative methods (within the framework of another political system, of course), but also to see a voluntary return of Russian capital back into the country in the future. This, however, will be possible only within the framework of a liberal economy and stable state authority under the conditions when rule of law is fully introduced in Russia, which will be attractive for foreign investors as well.

[5] Of course, there are also other, more significant causes hindering the process of development of the financial system.

[6] It looks as if relative to the past years capital flight decreased in 1999 in dollar terms, but increased as a percentage of GDP.

**Table B1.** Savings, Investments and Capital Flight

| | 1994 | 1995 | 1996 | 1997 | 1998 | 1999 | 2000 |
|---|---|---|---|---|---|---|---|
| % of GDP: | | | | | | | |
| Savings | 30,2 | 28,0 | 26,8 | 21,6 | 17,4 | 25,5 | 32,7 |
| Gross Capital Formation | 25,5 | 25,4 | 24,6 | 22,8 | 15,7 | 15,5 | 16,7 |
| Gross Fixed Capital Formation | 21,8 | 21,3 | 21,2 | 19,5 | 17,6 | 16,3 | 17,3 |
| Capital Flight | -2,76 | -1,62 | -5,95 | -6,36 | -8,37 | -10,4 | -10,0 |

As a consequence, the crisis of authority and the economic crisis meant that the country's economy remained oriented toward the fuel and raw materials sectors, an orientation that had developed over previous decades. Rapid privatization of the mineral-raw materials and fuel and energy sectors of the economy allowed for the accumulation of significant material and financial assets in private hands, although as a consequence of the virtual impossibility of investing[7] in other, potentially promising sectors of the economy, its structure steadily deteriorated.

Another contradiction of the economic reforms of the 1990s was the fact that a significant number of restrictions on economic activity within the country, including administrative ones[8], actually remained in place, while many of the restrictions on capital flows were lifted in a relatively short period of time. This led to a situation in which not only the import of capital into the country, but also investment in the Russian economy from domestic sources, did not make any sense; it made more sense to export capital out of Russia, which is what happened throughout the 1990s. To a significant extent this was due to the fact that as a result of the constantly smoldering internal conflict among the various branches of power[9], by the end of the 20th century the Russian state was unable to perform its primary function – to serve as a guarantor of the rule of law and stability (in one form or another), and to devise a predictable economic policy.

In spite of the failure to resolve a number of key problems, in a number of areas Russian reforms went further than in a number of other countries with transition economies. This is true for privatization and openness of the economy, in particular. Thus, the major dilemma at this point is how to eliminate the contradiction referred to above between excessive regulation of the economy, on the one hand, and its liberalization, on the other. Theoretically, this can be achieved by employing two methods: a) increasing the degree of state intervention, and b) further liberalization of the economy, eliminating the remaining barriers blocking access to markets, creating a genuinely competitive environment, simplifying the "rules of the game," and easing the conditions for economic activity.

---

[7] The Russian economy absorbed the minimum volume of investments required, which allowed it to meet the current needs of the fuel and raw materials sector of the economy, one that is oriented predominantly toward export.

[8] In addition to the administrative restrictions, one should also take into account restrictions related to the activities of criminal elements, which in effect increase the tax burden on the producer, as well as corruption, the weak legislative base, and so on.

[9] Including the regional aspect of the problem.

The first of the options (which is, in effect, adoption of the concept of a mobilization economy) is not discussed in this paper, since its implementation would mean new large-scale reforms not only of the economic mechanism, but the state's political system as well, which goes beyond the limits of the authors' knowledge. Proceeding from the realities that characterize the situation in the country and the world at the turn of the century, and also proceeding from historical experience, an orientation toward the creation of a liberal economic model with a fairly high level of competition, in which the state's intervention in economic life is reduced to a minimum, seems more reasonable. In this case the state has an even greater role to play as a guarantor of legal and political stability.

So far at least, the existence of these and a number of other contradictions is giving rise with increasing frequency to a desire to strengthen administrative control over economic processes – to impose administrative barriers to protect the domestic commodity producer from competition, to require exporters to surrender all of their foreign exchange earnings, to increase the ruble money supply at a faster pace in an administrative effort to cut it off from the exchange market, and so on. One should understand, however, that if such measures do produce a positive effect, it can only be short-lived. It is not possible to lay the foundation for sustained economic growth that will continue for decades using tricks such as these. Sustained growth of the Russian economy, in the form in which its market principles were created in the 1990s, is possible only given the formation and development of all the attributes inherent in capitalism – a diversified financial market, legal and political stability, functioning legislation that provides reliable protection for shareholders' rights (including minority shareholders' rights), and so on.

Thus, an essential condition for resolving the tasks facing the country is to provide for accelerated growth of the economy, achieved on the basis of:

- increasing the efficiency of the economy, building a market infrastructure, providing equal conditions for competition, establishing all-encompassing market relations;
- ensuring political stability and constant conditions for economic activity – stable and predictable economic policy; this applies in particular to macroeconomic policy, which should be transparent and comprehensible to all economic agents;
- fundamental improvement of the investment climate, assigning priority to the development of sectors that are capable of realizing Russia's competitive advantages (this applies in particular to sectors that are not capital-intensive, as well as production facilities where innovation potential could possibly be realized);
- balanced openness of the Russian economy and the utilization of its foreign economic potential, integration into the global economic system (including at the level of individual production facilities, which could join the system of international cooperation);
- creation of the social foundation for long-term, stable economic development – a middle class.

At the beginning of the 21st century, the country is truly faced with the real threat of ending up on the periphery of the civilized world as a consequence of its falling farther and farther behind technologically. The only way to avoid this is to move from stagnation to economic growth, which must be sustainable, and must continue to be so over a prolonged interval of time. On the other hand, the level of individual consumption (in terms of purchasing power parity) in Russia is one third of what it is in European countries, and one-fifth of the level in the United States[10]. The strategic goal of narrowing the technological gap must be set between Russia and the developed countries of Europe and America. An especially important factor here is that over the long term, the growth rates need to exceed the average world rates, otherwise it will not be possible to narrow the gap either in terms of the overall level of consumption or total GDP, which will limit prospects for future development.

## 3 Economic Growth and the Investment Climate

In light of the above, from a macroeconomic standpoint the conditions were objectively created in the transformation process which make it necessary for further economic development in the near future to follow the path of accelerated growth in private investments, since the concentration of high income levels among a relatively small segment of the population creates the conditions for the formation of investment potential. The concentration of property, which also ended up in the hands of a relatively narrow segment of the population, also points to the fact that as a result of the transformation period in the 1990s, conditions were created so that in the future, at least at the initial stage, economic development would proceed primarily along the "investment" path of development, and not along the path of more rapid growth in mass demand. Bearing in mind that one should not expect a rapid transformation of the existing structure of income and property in the direction of their more even distribution, *investments, rather than expanded mass consumer demand, are becoming the catalyst of economic growth.*

From another standpoint, the objective need for investments arises from the fact that by the late 1990s the country's aging production apparatus was not just obsolete, but was also showing signs of physical wear. According to data from the State Statistics Committee, the average age of Russian industry manufacturing equipment in late 1998 (table B2) was nearly 18 years (as opposed to 8.4 years in 1970), while the proportion of deteriorating fixed capital throughout industry as a whole reached almost 53 percent (compared to 25.7 percent in 1970). It should be stressed that deteriorating fixed capital was distributed quite evenly throughout almost all sectors (with the exception of the food industry, where this figure was somewhat lower at 44 percent). This means that without investments and large-scale updating of fixed capital one can hardly expect sustained growth in industrial production over the long term. Things are not any better in other sectors of the economy that produce goods. Realization of the accumulated investment potential

[10] This gap is even greater when evaluated in terms of the current exchange rate.

based on the state's recognition of the inalienable right of ownership, and the provision of guarantees to protect this right, should result in a sharp *increase in production efficiency, even if this is achieved, as it might seem now, at the expense of "equality and fairness."* One can expect a transformation of the structure of the Russian economy against the backdrop of just such an investment boom. One should also realize that at the initial stage in the realization of this particular concept of development, the relative gap between the rich and the poor is not going to shrink. This will occur, however, when there is overall growth in income and consumption.

**Table B2.** Age Structure of Fixed Capital in Industry in 1970–1996 (in Percent)

| total (end of period) | | of which aged (years): under 5 | 6–10 | 11–15 | 16–20 | over 20 | average age |
|---|---|---|---|---|---|---|---|
| 1970 | 100 | 40.8 | 30.0 | 14.0 | 6.9 | 8.3 | 8.42 |
| 1975 | 100 | 37.5 | 29.7 | 14.8 | 9.0 | 9.0 | 8.34 |
| 1980 | 100 | 35.5 | 28.7 | 15.6 | 9.5 | 10.7 | 9.47 |
| 1985 | 100 | 33.1 | 28.2 | 16.0 | 9.8 | 12.9 | 10.11 |
| 1990 | 100 | 29.4 | 28.3 | 16.5 | 10.8 | 15.0 | 10.80 |
| 1991 | 100 | 26.6 | 28.9 | 17.1 | 11.3 | 16.1 | 11.30 |
| 1992 | 100 | 22.8 | 29.4 | 18.2 | 12.0 | 17.6 | 11.98 |
| 1993 | 100 | 19.0 | 29.5 | 19.5 | 12.8 | 19.2 | 12.60 |
| 1994 | 100 | 14.7 | 29.8 | 20.7 | 13.8 | 21.0 | 13.41 |
| 1995 | 100 | 10.9 | 29.5 | 21.7 | 14.9 | 23.0 | 14.13 |
| 1996 | 100 | 8.0 | 27.4 | 23.2 | 15.9 | 25.5 | 14.98 |
| 1997 | 100 | 5.4 | 24.0 | 24.6 | 17.5 | 28.5 | 15.88 |
| 1998 | 100 | 4.1 | 20.1 | 25.6 | 18.6 | 31.6 | 16.09 |
| 1999 | 100 | 3.9 | 15.3 | 45.9 | | 34.9 | 17.92 |

In connection with this, one of the most important ideological tasks at the present moment is the need to dispel the illusions surrounding the Russian mentality, namely the idea that the country's population is committed to collectivist, public-spirited values. The spirit of collectivism was artificially implanted in the country in the 20th century, while the results of the country's development in the 1990s, as well as the experience of previous centuries, provides more convincing evidence that individualism, private property, reliance on one's own energies, and the entrepreneurial spirit are more consistent with the mentality of Russian society. In both agriculture and industry in the late 19th and early 20th centuries, for example, the driving force behind production was a relatively little segment of hard-working, industrious entrepreneurs. Contemporary economic policy should be devised with these realities in mind as well. In order to realize the creative potential of Russian citizens, which is incomparably greater than in the majority of developing countries, and to spur commercial initiative, there need to be simpler rules for entering the market, bureaucratic barriers need to be broken down, and unnecessary obstacles in the form of various types of licensing and controls need to be removed. These measures will automatically help reduce the level of corruption.

Another myth, the roots of which are intertwined with the myth of the "collectivist consciousness" of the Russian public, is the myth of the need to expand and strengthen state authority. If the thesis of the strengthening of the state, understood as the strengthening of state institutions, does not raise objections from virtually any of the groups of specialists, then we categorically need to reject intentions to expand the state's sphere of influence in both the economy and the life of society. The development of the global economy in the late 20$^{th}$ century points to an increase in the role of non-governmental organizations and the strengthening of transnational companies. It is predicted that in the next few decades the process of internationalization of economic relations will continue, although the result of this sort of development is not just overall growth of the global economy, including growth in poor countries, but also a widening of the gap between poor and rich states. With its highly educated human capital, however, Russia has every opportunity to pull itself out of the group of poor countries. Thus, Russia is faced with a choice: either follow the flow of the key trends in the global economy, enjoying the advantages of integration and reducing its political and economic costs, or orient itself toward a more closed, separate type of development.

If the first course is followed, Russia will have to make significant strides in expanding its membership in various international organizations, which will allow it not only to successfully adopt the generally accepted "rules of the game," but also to change the mentality of economic agents and Russian society as a whole. This should help achieve the main goal of Russia's economic development, which is not simply to bring about a *substantial rise in the living standards in the Russian Federation, but also to advance to a qualitatively new level.*

Bearing in mind the structure of the distribution of property that developed over the years, the very uneven distribution of the Russian population in terms of income level (with the richest 20 percent of the population regularly receiving approximately half of total income), as well as the overall low level of income and consumption, conditions have been created in the country in which just a small group of citizens are able to become investors. Under these conditions, the priorities for the country's economic development will be determined predominantly by large (by Russian standards) investors. Thus, the state either needs to recognize the status quo as it applies to the current distribution of property, the legality of capital accumulated in the 1990s, and provide reliable guarantees to protect private property, or it will run up against a lack of confidence on the part of investors in the future. The chances of increasing investment activity are much higher under the first scenario. Under the second scenario, the threat of a new, non-market redistribution of property could slow down the country's development for many years to come.

An analysis shows that in an environment of political stability and given fulfillment of the conditions referred to above with regard to building more reliable legal foundations for a market economy, after the 2000 elections one can expect steady growth in investments. The rate of growth in investments may substantially exceed the rate of growth in consumption over a fairly prolonged period of time. The demand for investments in the country may remain fairly high as a consequence of the prolonged period of underinvestment and, in effect, the lack of structural changes in the economy over a period of decades. The capital-intensive structure of the Russian economy that was inherited from the past also points to the potentially high demand for investment: investment will be needed not only to create and develop new production operations, but also to keep Russia's traditional sectors – the extractive industries, power engineering, metallurgy, and chemistry – in working order, which should include their modernization as well. On the other hand, the supply of investment resources could grow substantially given greater certainty about the country's political future. As mentioned above, the potential for this does exist – in particular with regard to a reduction in the outflow of capital and its potential return back into the country (both under the guise of "foreign" capital, and in the form of voluntarily repatriated domestic capital).

According to estimates, in 1999 the overall accumulation of fixed capital totaled US$ 27 billion, which at the current exchange rate is comparable to the annual outflow of capital from the country. Even a slight improvement in the investment climate, and a reduction in the volume of export earnings not returned and other sources of money flows that can be interpreted as an outflow of financial resources from the Russian economy, could result in a significant increase in the volume of funds invested in the Russian economy. Starting in 2002, and possibly even in 2001, the annual growth in fixed capital investment could be at least 10–20 percent. The period of heightened investment activity will last for 6–8 years. A period of high growth rates for investment and high growth rates for GDP was characteristic of many countries, from Japan in the 1960s to Poland in recent years.

## 4 Efficiency, Competition, Institutions

Over the long term, the need to provide for economic growth and raise the standard of living not through the application of extensive factors, which was how things were done under the administrative system, but as a result of greater production efficiency, is of critical importance to Russia. This assumes, first of all, a restoration of financial responsibility for the results of economic activity, which is correspondingly not possible without an improvement in payment discipline (including on the state's part), activation of the bankruptcy mechanism, development of the judicial system, recovery of financial markets, particularly the corporate securities market, and so on. In other words, without development of the entire market infrastructure.

The main factor behind the need for reforms in the Russian economy is the critical drop in the efficiency of social production under centralized management and the lack of incentives for productive labor. Objectively speaking, the rejection of total directive regulation in the context of a virtual lack of economic incentives, and the move toward creating a system of production relations in Russia based on economic interest, was the key decision that could have helped to improve production efficiency. The existence of private property in the production sphere is an initial condition for the creation of such a system. Simply recognizing that the right of private property ownership is inalienable is not enough, however. Another *key condition is a competitive environment, and the creation of equal conditions for competition for all economic entities throughout the entire country.* It is competition, and the threat of losing one's place in the market, that is the driving force behind improving production efficiency. The drafting and adoption of progressive anti-monopoly legislation is a high priority in economic policy.

Special importance should also be assigned to a policy of supporting small and mid-sized business, the essence of which should not be reduced to state financing and concessional lending to this sector, which cannot realistically be expected under Russian conditions; what this policy should do is help eliminate barriers to gaining access to the markets. This is the sector of the economy that promotes the rapid creation of jobs, that serves as a "school" in the market economy for beginning participants in the market, and it practices natural selection of the most successful entrepreneurs.

The country needs institutional reform in order to realize the potential for growth within the market system. A market economy is not possible without banks and capital markets. The restructuring of the banking system and creation of a system of successfully operating banks, which would truly perform the role of intermediaries between savings and investments, must be carried out at an accelerated pace, and this effort needs to be started immediately.

If the restructuring of the banking system and development of the government securities market serves the redistribution of financial resources, the functioning of the corporate securities market also serves the redistribution of property – from one owner to another, more effectively. In this connection, the protection of shareholders' rights is one of the state's most important tasks. The development of the insurance system, which is still in the embryonic stage in Russia, should proceed in this direction.

The state's tax policy should serve as a crucial factor in the stable functioning of the economic system. A substantial simplification of the tax system needs to be carried out in the near future, with a view to reducing the total number of taxes, primarily through the elimination of taxes that have a low collection rate, and assigning a greater role to indirect taxes compared to direct taxes. Changes in the tax system in the immediate future should be accompanied later on by efforts to maintain its essential stability, stricter requirements, and the orderly passage of tax legislation at all levels of government authority. Transparent and responsible budget policy is one of the fundamental principles of state regulation of the economy. It must be realized against the backdrop of improved tax administration.

Under the current conditions, the task of *reviving the financial markets* (both the government debt instruments market and the corporate securities market) remains extremely urgent; one can hardly imagine a normally functioning market economy without these markets. Furthermore, considering the significant quantity of ruble funds that are essentially frozen in various accounts (correspondent accounts with the Central Bank, type C accounts), these resources could be brought into circulation, and if necessary, they could be used as borrowed funds for the financing of the budget deficit. It is unlikely that we can expect a repeat of the GKO [government short-term bond] story now, since the budget deficit is substantially smaller than it was in 1995–1998. New government securities could, on the one hand, replace the so-called non-market government bonds (OGNZ) that were issued in 1998, for example. On the other hand, they would make it possible to track more clearly the level of market interest rates, which is extremely important to investors.

A revival of financial markets is also important because they are supposed to function on a continuing basis, redistributing available resources among sectors of the economy. During an economic upturn, in the event of a potential influx of foreign currency (as a result of a halt in the export of capital or the influx of foreign investments), monetary authorities are faced with the task of sterilizing this flow by issuing Central Bank financial instruments.

## 5 Macroeconomics

In the broad spectrum of issues in macroeconomic policy, the interdependence of budget policy, which is determined to a great extent by the problem of servicing foreign debt, and monetary and exchange rate policies, is of special importance. The general outlines of budget policy are obvious: the state is not supposed to spend more than it is capable of collecting in taxes, and the state should refrain from taking on excess obligations (at the level of regional budgets), so as not to increase the tax burden on the economy; it should also strive for a balanced budget, with no deficit (this possibility will depend, however, on prospects for restructuring the foreign debt). Consequently, the foreign debt-servicing schedule is an exogenous factor. At the present time, the size of the foreign debt is practically the same as the GDP. As a result, every year for the next ten years the country is supposed to pay between US$ 15 billion and US$ 20 billion to its creditors. This task is clearly beyond the ability of the Russian economy. Therefore, resolution of the problems referred to above, and a predictable and consistent liberal economic policy, should also help settle the problem of the foreign debt, its restructuring, or even forgiveness of part of the debt. Forgiveness of part of the debt will make it possible to achieve a corresponding reduction in the tax burden in the economy, it will stimulate production and economic growth, and it will make it possible to increase non-interest income.

In addition to capital flight, the unavoidable outflow of money from the country tied to the need to service the foreign debt, remains and will continue to be an important limiting factor in the country's development. While a radical improvement in the investment climate aimed at creating more favorable conditions for investment in Russia than in other countries is a matter for domestic policy alone, the settlement of the foreign debt problem requires consideration of international factors as well. Figure B4 provides an illustration of the foreign debt schedule of the federal government and the country's monetary authorities in 2000–2010 after London Club debt restructuring.

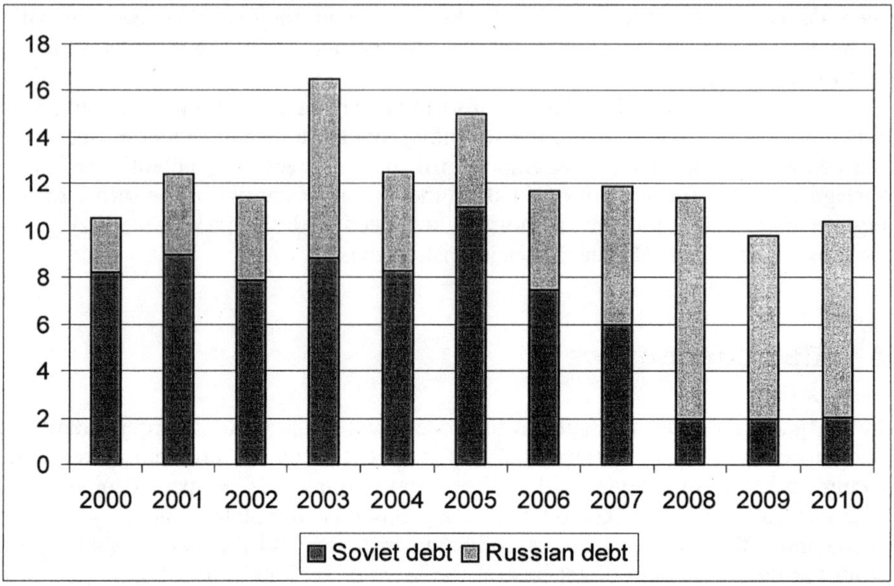


**Fig. B4.** Schedule of Foreign Debt Payments by the Federal Government and Monetary Authorities in 2000–2010

As one can see from the available data, annual payments on the foreign debt are supposed to be approximately one-tenth of the GDP. These quantities are comparable in scale to capital flight[11] from the country (which is still somewhat higher: in 1998 estimated legal and illegal export of capital from Russia exceeded US$ 23 billion and US$ 18 billion in 1999. It is likely that there will be further decrease in this figure in 2000. These resources (or even just a portion of them) could potentially be used within the country for investments that could provide for economic growth in the future. An economy cannot survive under the conditions of such massive export of capital by the private sector and such a heavy debt burden.

It is also important that the servicing of Soviet-era debt accounts for the bulk of the debt burden on the Russian economy, as one can see from Figure B6. The problem of servicing and repayment of the Russian share of the debt is most critical up to 2005. In connection with this, one of the highest priorities in the government's economic policy should be to reach agreements with creditors. Clearly, Russia will be most likely to succeed in reaching this type of agreement if: a) Russia lives up to its claims to be called a democratic country by preserving democratic freedoms; b) a long-range strategy is proposed that is based on the principles of a free market economy; c) the first steps, even small ones, are taken to implement the above mentioned program. The problem of restructuring the

[11] The estimated volume of capital flight is based on balance of payments data and includes the change in arrears on foreign exchange and ruble export earnings not received on time for outstanding import advances, the volume of trade credits and advances granted, and net errors and omissions.

foreign debt should be addressed in a comprehensive manner, involving all groups of creditors, taking into consideration not just budgetary limitations, but balance of payments limitations as well. As calculations have shown, *the country's realistic potential capacity for servicing debt over the next decade is no more than US$ 10–13 billion per year.*

The path to a balanced budget also lies in the improvement of tax administration and a certain redistribution of financial flows between the federal center and regions. Specifically, there should be a sharp increase in the income tax collection rate; income tax collections measured as a percentage of GDP could be increased by a factor of 2.5–3 compared to the current level. This can be achieved mainly through better compliance with tax payment requirements on the part of the more affluent segments of the population, where the level of tax evasion is the highest. Income tax (at least the bulk of it) should become a federal tax, which could increase the revenue side of the budget by 2–3 percent of GDP. Introducing the practice of making large purchases only by means of non-cash settlements, using plastic cards, could be one of the measures aimed at fighting income tax evasion (as well as the evasion of other taxes).

Table B3 shows that the structure of the revenue side of the extended government budget in Russia differs substantially from the state revenue structure in developed countries of the world. The main difference is not the state's relatively small share in GDP (this share is substantially lower in a whole group of countries), but the fact that the proportion of taxes paid on the basis of household income (income tax and payments to social funds) is much lower. Throughout the EU, on average, this figure is more than 52 percent, while in Russia in 1998 it was a little more than 35 percent.

It is more likely that the tax collection problem in Russia is due to ineffectual tax administration, rather than "incorrect" tax rates. For example, in spite of the fact that there is a fairly wide range of tax rates among various countries (in Switzerland the lowest rate is 1 percent and the highest rate is 13.2 percent, while in Holland the lowest and highest rates are 13 and 60 percent, respectively), the income tax accounts for the most important part of the revenue side of the budget. It hardly makes sense to lower the income tax rates to 10–20 percent, or to introduce a single income tax rate, as a number of specialists are proposing. It seems more reasonable to maintain the existing income tax rates, although the income bracket taxed at the highest rates should be raised substantially. Wealthy people, whose incomes are comparable to incomes in developed countries of the world, should pay the same amount of taxes as people pay in the rest of the world. The state should improve tax administration in regard to key taxes (the income tax, VAT and excise taxes, social funds), by concentrating the efforts of tax services on these taxes in particular. At the same time, the majority of less significant taxes, which still represent a large share of the Russian budget should be eliminated (other taxes, as one can see from Table B1, account for almost one-fourth of total tax revenues). It would also be advisable to make some reductions in contributions to the social insurance fund – those contributions which are earmarked for the maintenance (or the mothballing, in effect) of the aging sanatorium-health resort infrastructure, and are hindering the development of a competitive tourism business in Russia.

**Table B3.** Structure of Extended Government Tax Revenues in Russia and Certain Countries of the World (as a Percentage of Total Tax Revenues)

| | For reference: total taxes (as % of GDP) | Income tax | Profit tax | Taxes on goods and services | Other taxes | State funds of a social nature |
|---|---|---|---|---|---|---|
| Russia (1998) | 32.8 | 8.1 | 10.9 | 30.4 | 23.4 | 27.2 |
| OECD average | 38.5 | 29.3 | 6.9 | 30.2 | 10.8 | 22.8 |
| EU average | 41.0 | 25.8 | 6.8 | 31.5 | 9.5 | 26.4 |
| United States | 29.7 | 34.5 | 7.9 | 17.2 | 12.4 | 28.0 |
| France | 43.9 | 13.9 | 3.4 | 26.7 | 15.0 | 40.9 |
| Japan | 29.1 | 25.6 | 14.9 | 14.4 | 14.8 | 30.1 |
| Greece | 41.2 | 9.3 | 5.0 | 43.9 | 12.6 | 29.2 |
| Denmark | 49.9 | 52.1 | 4.4 | 31.7 | 8.6 | 3.1 |
| Turkey | 23.5 | 27.1 | 4.9 | 31.8 | 17.6 | 18.6 |
| Switzerland | 23.5 | 32.8 | 5.8 | 16.7 | 21.8 | 22.9 |

One of the major problems for wealthy individual taxpayers in Russia is the social tax. Really, suppose, some businessman is able to pay himself 10,000 dollars net per month. If he were honest he would pay approximately 40 hundred dollars to social funds (pension, medical insurance etc.) plus 35 hundred dollars of income tax. Social security contributions really look too big and unjust for him, as the state can guarantee him a negligible pension (relative to his current incomes) after he retires. The same applies to medical and social security guaranteed by the state. Thus, the general approach to taxation of the wage bill should be as follows. The sum of the social security and personal income tax rates should be flat for each of income groups and should not exceed 35 percent: the personal income tax scale should be progressive, while social security tax scale should be regressive. Really, wealthy people may build their own social safety net, while they need more direct services from the government (courts, police, etc) than poor. It is also important to equalize tax rates for individuals and corporations in order to avoid various schemes of tax evasion. By no means is strengthening tax administration of great importance as well.

Shifting the emphasis toward the income tax and the sales tax (which is paid by the final user, in effect, and wealthier people pay more) will follow the long-range trend in the growth of personal income, as it is determined by the reform of housing and municipal services and the elimination of inefficient subsidies for housing and municipal services.

A balanced budget will help limit the money supply and, in effect, will help reduce the inflationary tax, which leads to the depreciation of ruble savings and encourages flight from the ruble. In connection with this, the role of monetary policy will grow as execution of the budget improves. The channeling of money into the economy will occur not as a result of government lending at concessional rates, but through the mechanism of lending at market rates by commercial banks, which in turn, sooner or later, will have to take up their primary activity – lending to the real sector, performing the role of serving as intermediary between savings and investments, and turning short money into long money, small deposits into large credits. Furthermore, growth in the money supply, and correspondingly the inflation rate, will be determined by growth in international reserves, as well as the ability of monetary authorities to sterilize excess ruble liquidity.

One way or another, the expected expansion of the money supply and the effect of macroeconomic factors that have come into play now give one reason to believe that the trend toward devaluation of the ruble in nominal terms will continue. Over the short term, the most reasonable situation appears to be one in which the real exchange rate of the ruble will remain stable, while over the long term, as the economy grows, the ruble will become stronger. In both cases, two different models of exchange rate dynamics are possible: steady growth or "stepped" growth. In the first case, the Central Bank should operate fairly cautiously in the foreign exchange market, buying foreign exchange to build up reserves and smoothing out only major deviations from the established trend. In the second case, in the event of the "stepped" version, the Central Bank will pursue more active interventions to keep the exchange rate at the prescribed level. It will be forced to spend foreign exchange more freely, which will aggravate the problem of servicing the foreign debt. What's more, the "stepped" version is burdened with problems tied to a shift to a higher exchange rate. At the time of such a shift, economic agents may have false expectations of a stable exchange rate, and the movement to a new level could cause panic in the market, which would have a corresponding negative impact on the entire economy. Overall, the smooth growth version is preferable, since it makes exchange rate dynamics more predictable, it does not create illusions among economic agents, and it provides for greater stability in the development of the economy.

The state should ensure the stability and transparency of monetary policy. Practical experience around the world shows that the "desired" inflation rate (and not the dynamics of the money supply or the exchange rate of the national currency, for example) is being chosen as a target indicator for monetary authorities in more and more countries. Thus, the primary task of monetary policy is to provide for the corresponding price dynamics and to create predictable macroeconomic conditions, which should facilitate decision-making not only in the area of budget planning, but by economic agents at the microeconomic level as well. At the same time, monetary authorities are relatively free with regard to employing the available instruments of monetary policy (changing interest rates, reserve requirements, expansion or contraction of the money supply, and so on).

## 6 Domestic Demand and Demographics

Considering that investments are supposed to become a catalyst for sustained growth at the beginning of the new century, they will help create new jobs at new, more efficient production facilities. In the future, this should make it possible to *bring into play another engine of growth, such as steadily expanding mass domestic demand.* In the 1970s and 1980s the middle three quintiles of the Russian population accounted for around 56–58 percent of current income (see table B4), while the wealthiest 20 percent of the population accounted for just 33–37 percent. Incidentally, approximately the same structure of income distribution is also typical of highly developed countries with a high overall level of income, including the United States and European countries. In these states, however, this income distribution was shaped under the conditions of a market system of economic management and serves as a guarantor of social and political stability and a driving force for growth. In the Soviet era, on the other hand, stability and a similar income distribution were achieved by entirely different methods.

**Table B4.** Distribution of Monetary Income among the Population (as a Percentage)

| | 1970 | 1975 –1990 average | 1991 | 1992 | 1993 | 1994 | 1995 | 1996 | 1997 | 1998 | 1999 | for reference Madagascar | for reference USA |
|---|---|---|---|---|---|---|---|---|---|---|---|---|---|
| Total monetary income | 100 | 100 | 100 | 100 | 100 | 100 | 100 | 100 | 100 | 100 | 100 | 100 | 100 |
| of which, by 20% groups: | | | | | | | | | | | | | |
| first | 7.8 | 9.8 | 11.9 | 6.0 | 5.8 | 5.3 | 5.5 | 6.2 | 6.0 | 6.2 | 6.2 | 5.8 | 4.7 |
| second | 14.8 | 14.8 | 15.8 | 11.6 | 11.1 | 10.2 | 10.2 | 10.7 | 10.2 | 10.5 | 10.6 | 9.9 | 11.0 |
| third | 18.0 | 18.6 | 18.8 | 17.6 | 16.7 | 15.2 | 15.0 | 15.2 | 14.8 | 14.9 | 14.9 | 14.0 | 17.4 |
| fourth | 22.6 | 22.3 | 22.8 | 26.5 | 24.8 | 23.0 | 22.4 | 21.5 | 21.6 | 21.0 | 21.0 | 20.3 | 25.0 |
| fifth (with highest income) | 36.8 | 33.5 | 30.7 | 38.3 | 41.6 | 46.3 | 46.9 | 46.4 | 47.4 | 47.4 | 47.4 | 50.0 | 41.9 |

*Sources: State Statistics Committee, World Bank*

During the reforms in the 1990s the structure of income distribution among the population changed so that the middle three quintiles began to account for around 46 percent of total income, while the wealthiest 20 percent account for about 47 percent of income, which is the same. This sort of income distribution curve is typical of poor, developing, and politically unstable countries. Thus, *one of the key tasks of economic policy over the long term is to make the existing income distribution more even.* This task will become most pressing in several years, when the economy could be affected by a certain amount of inertia in its growth. From the standpoint of the social orientation of reforms, the results of the transition from socialism to capitalism should lead to a situation in which the advantages of the market structure of the economy are felt by the majority of the population, rather the minority, which was the case throughout the 1990s. This will strengthen stimuli for productive labor, while providing for a stable connection between production and consumption.

Over the long term, in the implementation of its economic strategy Russia may run up against a number of objective limitations and problems. A number of these limitations and threats are the result of strictly demographic processes. From Figures B5 and B6 one can see that according to the inertial demographic forecast in several years Russia is going to encounter serious problems related to the aging of the population. The shrinking of the total population that began in the early 1990s will continue and after 2005 it will be due to a decline in the working-age population, while the level of dependents under the age of 15 will remain relatively stable. At the same time, there will be a sharp rise in the number of pensioners, and there will a corresponding increase in the so-called "demographic burden" on the working members of the population.

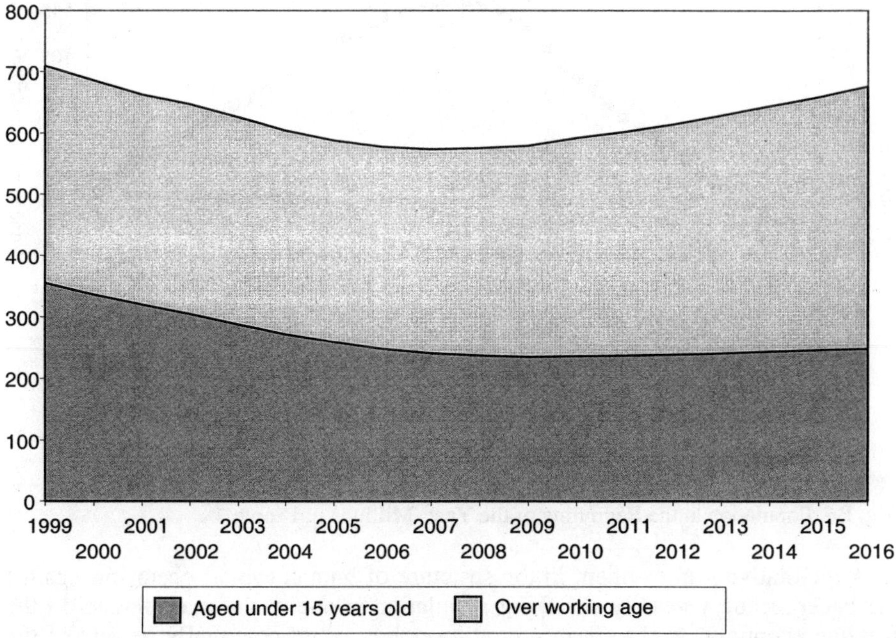


**Fig. B5.** The "Demographic Burden" on 1,000 Working-age People, at the Beginning of the Year

At the same time, the growth in the number of working-age people will continue up to 2005–2006, which will increase the burden on the labor market and aggravate the unemployment problem. The labor surplus will increase over the next 5–6 years, and the economy is not going to experience a shortage of manpower resources. On the other hand, the appearance in the labor market of a new generation of manpower, whose mentality and education have already been oriented toward market conditions, will mean tougher competition on the labor market, which will certainly have a positive impact on the quality of manpower resources employed in production. This is particularly important, considering that in the 1990s skilled personnel, who could not find a place for themselves in the new Russia, were lost to migration (primarily to the United States, Germany, and Israel, with approximately 80,000 people leaving to establish permanent residence there in the 1990s). In addition to those who acquired foreign citizenship, the Russian economy also lost and is continuing to lose skilled specialists who are able to compete successfully in the global labor markets and are leaving to work under contractual arrangements. Growth in the Russian population resulting from migration is due primarily to the influx of less-skilled manpower from the CIS and Baltic countries.

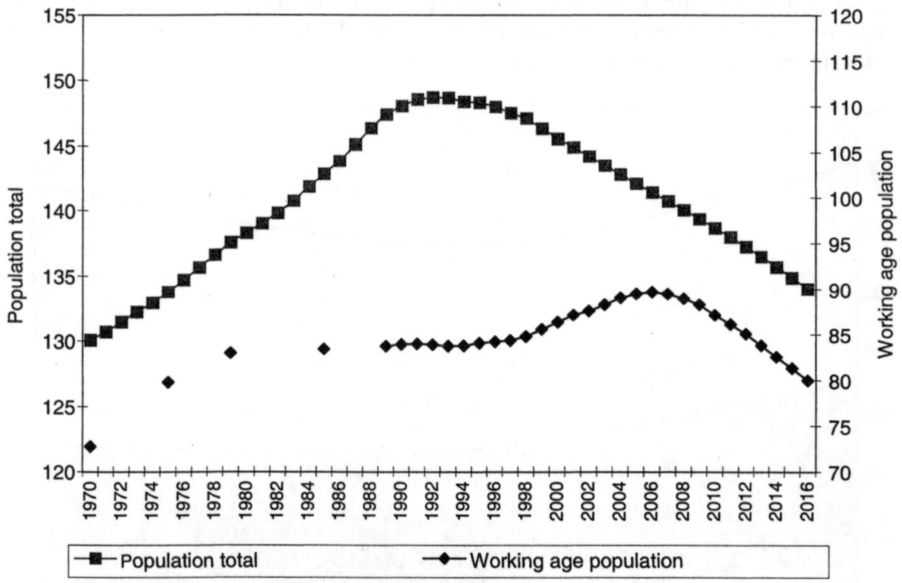


**Fig. B6.** Population at the Beginning of the Year, Millions of People

A qualitative improvement in the structure of human capital occurring against the backdrop of a steadily shrinking population is one of the main threats to the Russian economy. A change in migration policy could potentially be one of the conditions for moving into a trajectory of sustained economic growth. Historical experience shows that Russia made the most pronounced spurts forward in its cultural and economic development during those periods when it was open to the rest of the world. In previous centuries German, French, and Dutch people served the Russian state. Later on many of them became Russian citizens. This meant much more than an influx of capital; it also meant an influx of culture and knowledge, which are particularly lacking in Russia today. The business culture vacuum, which was created in the country over past decades as a result of the genocide of the intelligentsia that began in the 1920s, needs to be filled. Conditions need to be created to keep people from leaving Russia, and on the contrary, to encourage them to come here. Russian citizenship should become just as desirable for investors and foreign hired workers as Canadian, American, Argentine, and other citizenship is for today's Russians. Many countries around the world offer concessions to investors and grant the right to obtain a residency permit or citizenship when candidates meet certain requirements. Strategically speaking, Russia should follow this same course.

The resolution of demographic and migration issues should not be delayed, since the influx of an industrious labor force into the country's economy will help to regenerate the segment of the population that earns a steady income, and it will help increase mass demand. In the event of a passive demographic policy, starting in 2005–2006 the rise in the number of pensioners, and particularly among the low-income segment of the population, will aggravate the problem of mass demand, and the formation of a middle class, and it will hinder the formation of a more even structure of income distribution, which means it will also limit opportunities for economic growth.

## 7 The Widening Technological Gap is a Threat to Russia's Future

As noted above, the country is going to have to resolve a number of problems and it is going to encounter a number of factors restricting its freedom to maneuver. A wide range of limiting factors will be the result of external conditions– the expected dynamics of the development of the world economy, the demand for traditional Russian export goods, and prices for these goods. From this standpoint, it is extremely desirable not to drag out the reforms and to take advantage of favorable world market conditions, since a decline in world oil prices is expected as early as 2001, as a consequence of the fact that world oil production will exceed demand. It may be expected that in 2001–2003 oil prices may stabilize at much lower level than was in 2000, which will significantly reduce the potential foreign exchange earnings entering the country. The economic system that evolved in Russia, based on exports of natural resources, will finally exhaust itself.

In the short- and medium-term, development of the domestic market is one of the priorities of economic policy. Another priority of state policy should be to promote the development of sectors and production facilities that have the potential to gain competitive advantages over foreign producers. The world's experience in economic development shows that the most successful development occurs in those countries in which something new is created, in which new production operations appear. Of the world's ten largest companies, more than half belong to relatively new sectors of the economy, which didn't even really exist three or four decades ago. These are telecommunications, computer technologies, and so on. Russia's main path of development does not lie in the utilization of its natural resources and existing fixed capital, but in innovation. Creation of the conditions needed for this and elimination of a number of barriers preventing new business from entering the markets are at the top of the agenda for the new millennium. In all likelihood, however, the state will be able to devote the proper attention to the country's innovation potential no sooner than several years from now, after a period of economic growth has begun, and as execution of the budget stabilizes. Up until that time, and in the future as well, it is important for Russia to integrate itself into global cooperative relations, so that Russian producers of certain components and assemblies cooperate in the production of more sophisticated products of companies that are known around the world. This sort of cooperation will encourage the development of a new business ethic, and it will promote the formation of contract law in Russia.

Efforts aimed at the accelerated development of "breakthrough" sectors should be directed at the utilization of Russian potential in high-tech areas related to the defense industry. Two main areas of emphasis can be identified in this effort.

First, the development of the relevant exports as the basis for expanding demand for products and strengthening the financial position of sectors in the defense complex. Second, realization of the scientific potential that still exists in this area should be based not only on direct state support for military production, but also on expanding the application of advanced scientific achievements in open sectors of the economy on a market basis. The unsatisfactory results of the conversion of the Russian defense industry are due primarily to the fact that the effort was reduced in large part to misguided measures to change the production orientation of high-tech production facilities. This meant double losses: the strictly technological losses, as well as the attempt to switch to a production operation that they knew was going to be unsuccessful, since in reality a substantial reconstruction of enterprises in the defense industry, which requires substantial investments, is needed to ensure the profitability of new products.

* * *

Given the pursuit of a liberal economic strategy, by the end of the decade some structural shifts should be clearly evident in the country's economy. At the present time the Russian economy is characterized by an extremely deformed structure of the GDP (see tables B5 and B6 for comparison), reflected in net exports, which are clearly too high, and a low level of consumption.

As one can see from Table B5, the proportion of net exports in Russia is more than 16 percent, while the proportion of final consumption remains extremely low. Although data on the Russian GDP presented in Table B5 are based on calculations at the current exchange rate of the ruble, and due to the much larger gap between the ruble's current exchange rate and its purchasing power parity they are not entirely comparable to the data for other countries presented in Table B6, one can nonetheless track the general trends in the change of the structure of the GDP. Calculations show that in 8–10 years, given the implementation of a liberal reform strategy, which means the implementation of structural reforms, the transformation of budget expenditures, the implementation of housing and municipal services reform, pension reform, the development of financial markets, restructuring of the banking system, and so forth, the gap between the ruble's purchasing power parity and current exchange rate could shrink substantially.

**Table B5.** Structure of Use of GDP in Russia (as a Percentage)

| | 1990 | 1991 | 1992 | 1993 | 1994 | 1995 | 1996 | 1997 | 1998 | 1999 |
|---|---|---|---|---|---|---|---|---|---|---|
| GDP | 100.0 | 100.0 | 100.0 | 100.0 | 100.0 | 100.0 | 100.0 | 100.0 | 100.0 | 100.0 |
| Expenditures on final consumption | 69.4 | 62.6 | 49.9 | 64.2 | 69.7 | 72.8 | 72.9 | 74.7 | 77.1 | 68.6 |
| by households (including private nonprofit institutions serving households) | 48.6 | 45.7 | 35.5 | 46.3 | 47.1 | 52.9 | 52.1 | 53.1 | 57.9 | 53.2 |
| by general government | 20.9 | 16.9 | 14.3 | 17.9 | 22.6 | 19.9 | 20.7 | 21.6 | 19.2 | 15.4 |
| Gross accumulation | 30.3 | 37.1 | 35.7 | 27.9 | 25.7 | 23.8 | 23.1 | 22.6 | 15.4 | 15.1 |
| of fixed capital | 28.9 | 23.8 | 24.7 | 21.0 | 22.0 | 21.4 | 20.9 | 19.8 | 17.5 | 15.8 |
| of inventory | 1.4 | 13.3 | 11.0 | 6.8 | 3.8 | 2.3 | 2.2 | 2.8 | -2.1 | -0.7 |
| Net exports | 0.2 | 0.3 | 14.5 | 8.0 | 4.6 | 3.4 | 4.0 | 2.7 | 7.5 | 16.3 |

**Table B6.** Structure of Use of GDP in Certain Countries (Data for 1997, as a Percentage)

| | United States | Germany | Greece | Mexico | Turkey | Poland |
|---|---|---|---|---|---|---|
| GDP | 100.0 | 100.0 | 100.0 | 100.0 | 100.0 | 100.0 |
| Expenditures on final consumption | 83.1 | 76.6 | 88.2 | 73.6 | 81.0 | 82.5 |
| by households (including private nonprofit institutions serving households) | 67.7 | 57.2 | 73.4 | 65.3 | 68.8 | 65.3 |
| by general government | 15.4 | 19.3 | 14.8 | 8.4 | 12.1 | 17.3 |
| Gross accumulation | 18.1 | 22.6 | 20.1 | 26.4 | 24.8 | 22.4 |
| of fixed capital | 17.2 | 20.1 | 20.0 | 19.5 | 26.1 | 21.2 |
| of inventory | 0.8 | 2.5 | 0.0 | 6.9 | -1.3 | 1.3 |
| Net exports | -1.2 | 0.9 | -8.3 | 0.0 | -5.7 | -5.0 |

An average GDP growth rate of 5–6 percent per year over a 20-year period could be entirely realistic for the country. In some years growth could speed up to 8–10 percent. Over 20 years GDP could triple, while over the coming 10 years it can increase somewhat 70 percent. This growth will be uneven among various sectors of the economy, which, together with the change in the price structure, would substantially change the nominal structure of GDP. By the end of the period (20 years), the proportion of consumption could exceed 80 percent, net exports would fall, and could even become negative, if Russia becomes a reliable recipient of capital.

A failure to take quick action to normalize the economic situation in the country and to create the conditions for sustained economic growth will threaten not only social stability, but Russia's survival as a state. The sluggish demographic projection speaks to the fact that in 40 years Russia's population could shrink to 90 million people. This will occur against the backdrop of rapid population growth in relatively poor non-European countries, which could have far-reaching geopolitical consequences, including a threat to the country's territorial integrity. The projected decline in population could have much more serious consequences for Russia than for Europe[12], due to its much lower level of development and its political isolation from developed countries of the West.

## References

Barro RJ, Sala-i-Martin X (1995) Economic Growth. McGraw-Hill

Fisher S and Sahay R (2000) The Transition Economies After Ten Years. IMF Working paper, WP/00/30, International Monetary Fund, Washington

DeBroek M, Koen V (2000) The "Soaring Eagle": Anatomy of the Polish Take-Off in the 1990es. IMF Working paper, WP/00/6, International Monetary Fund, Washington

Jovanovich B (2000) Growth Theory. NBER Working paper 7468, January 2000

Growth Experience in Transition Economies. IMF mimeo, September 1998

Begg D, Wyplosz Ch (1999) How Big a Government? Transition Economy Forecasts Based on OECD History, September1999, paper presented at the 5th Dubrovnik Conference on Transition Economies

Tybout J (1998) Manufacturing Firms in Developing Countries: How Well Do They Do, and Why? Georgetown University, August 1998

Dollar D, Kraay A (2000) Growth is Good for the Poor. The World Bank, mimeo, March 2000

Jones ChI (1997) Introduction to Economic Growth, New York and London

Setterfeld M (1997) Rapid Growth and Relative Decline. Modelling Macroeconomic Dynamics with Hysteresis. Macmillan Press Ltd

[12] The threat of a decline in the native-born population in European countries also poses a serious problem for the region's economic development.

# C. Innovation, Growth and Wage Structure in Transforming Economies

Andre Jungmittag and Paul J.J. Welfens

## 1 Introduction

Today it is commonplace to argue that technological change and innovation have a positive impact on economic growth. However, the mechanisms translating innovations into broad-based economic effects remain at least partly unknown. This holds especially for transition countries where innovations play only a very subordinated role. For these countries it is more important to achieve technological capabilities which allow them to imitate processes and products. Innovation theory, development theory and many recent success stories, e.g. the South East Asian NICs, show that these capabilities don't fall from heaven but rather are mainly a result of own efforts. These efforts comprise not only scientific and technological inputs and outputs but also the building-up of an adequate institutional framework, as it is through institutions that innovation and imitation processes are mediated. A theoretical concept in which technical and institutional change is explicitly linked is that of systems of innovation (Lundvall, 1992): meaning the overlapping networks of R&D institutions in the business community and the public sector. We will discuss these aspects more comprehensively in section 2, where we will present some indicators describing the technological capabilities and performance of the transition countries. Furthermore we will cast a glance at the former institutional framework which can be considered as the national innovation system of the former socialistic countries.

Our second point concerns the importance of trade as a determinant of economic growth. From basic textbook models and from empirical analysis one expects that economic opening-up and growing trade can contribute to output growth. The expansion of the tradables sector is crucial because productivity growth in this sector is typically higher than in the nontradables sector such that the relative price of tradables in terms of nontradables will fall with economic development and per capita income (Balassa-Samuelson hypothesis). In regards to the link between trade and growth, a strong impulse comes from rising exports of manufacturing goods as is argued by Ito (1998, p. 196). His argument and findings lack sufficient justification – the finding is that both Indonesia and Nigeria had a share of manufactures in export earnings of about 1% in 1975, however by 1992 the share had risen to 48% in Indonesia whose per capita figures surpassed Nigeria in the 1980s where the proportions had remained almost unchanged. In section 3 we will develop some ideas about the "Learning by Exporting Hypothesis". Furthermore we will present some empirical evidence for this hypothesis.

For Russia and Visegrad countries economic catching up and sustained growth are natural policy priorities at the beginning of the 21st century. The achievement of economic catching up can be approached from several analytical viewpoints – one could draw on historical case studies, on economic theory or on simulation studies – the alternative being to muddle through, an option which is predestined to failure in the long run.

Facing high unemployment rates of close to 10% and low wages in Russia there should be room for the expansion of labor intensive production. Given the relatively large endowment with human capital there could also be some long-term scope for rising output and exports in knowledge-intensive sectors. However, the EBRD's (1999) export analysis of Russia has shown that Russia's share of those products going to OECD countries has fallen to almost zero in the 1990s.

Product quality remains a major problem in post-socialist Russia encouraging Russian exporters of capital-intensive and knowledge-intensive production to largely orient products towards developing countries where only low unit export values can be obtained. If Russia's OECD-exports of skill-intensive manufacturing product were to increase, the respective Russian firms would in many cases have to adopt Western quality standards and to more heavily rely on imports of high quality intermediate products. The strong real devaluation after the collapse of the Ruble in 1998 is encouraging exports, but it is unlikely to stimulate imports of intermediate high quality products which would be used in the production of high quality exports. To some extent it seems that OECD countries are not unhappy to see that Russia's exports have declined in the 1990s and that especially the share of exports to Western Europe is small. This raises the question, however, whether the EU and the US really have a natural interest in Russian stagnation and the shift of its regional export focus towards developing countries – if Russia, facing unattractive alternatives in a rather protectionist (enlarged) EU, would restore its formerly leading role as one of the worlds top arms exporters this would hardly contribute to global stability and prosperity.

Concerning theory, the new growth theory and the new international trade theory offer interesting ingredients for a potential catching-up strategy. Knowledge accumulation and national plus international productivity spillover effects are emphasized in these new approaches. This does not mean to overlook the traditional benefits from trade which come both on the import and the export side (plus the option of recording temporary current account deficits). With respect to learning from experience it is natural to focus mainly on Asian NICs – and perhaps on Mexico - which were quite successful in economic catching-up. We will consider this learning by Asian Nics perspective in section 4. In section 5 we will discuss the impact of these catching-up processes on structural change and the wage structures in transition countries. Finally, we will draw some conclusions in section 6.

## 2 Innovation and Growth: Where do the Transition Countries Stand?

With the start of the transformation process in the early nineties the R&D intensities in the Central and Eastern European countries were reduced dramatically (BMBF, 1999). The actual average R&D intensities of most transition countries from 1987 to 1997 (or the most recent year available) are displayed in figure C1. Nearly all of these countries show R&D intensities below 1 % which is in the range of the R&D intensities of low to medium income countries. The only countries which show slightly higher R&D intensities are the Czech Republic, Slovak Republic and Slovenia.

This poor position of the transition countries is also obvious when the comparative disadvantages in R&D personnel are considered (figure C2). The measure used here is the relative technological capability share (*RTS*) calculated as

$$(1)\quad RTS = 100 \cdot \log\left(\frac{\textit{Scientists and engineers in R \& D in country i}}{\textit{Scientists and engineers in R \& D worldwide}}\right) \text{ respectively}$$

$$(2)\quad RTS = 100 \cdot \log\left(\frac{\textit{Technicians in R \& D in country i}}{\textit{Technicians in R \& D worldwide}}\right).$$

Nearly all transition countries show strong relative disadvantages i.e. negative *RTS* values for both, scientists and engineers as well as technicians in R&D. Concerning scientists and engineers only Azerbaijan and the Russian Federation show slight positive values. The situation is of particular concern as disadvantages in the sector of technicians, a profoundly important element in imitation and incremental innovation, are extraordinarily low. If it holds true that native national technological capabilities are an essential ingredient for technological imitation and catching-up, national policy must aim at improving their absolute as well as relative technological capabilities. It is well known from the South East Asian NICs that these countries invested a lot in their capabilities to imitate before they became innovators on a world market level (Jungmittag et al., 1998).

R&D is normally associated with the input side of the science and technology process (or innovation process if innovation is on the agenda of the development process) whereas patents are an indicator for the output of this process when a country moves from merely imitation to innovation. Figure C3 shows that most if not all transition countries have not reached this threshold in terms of international marketable innovations. It displays the patent applications per one million inhabitants at the US Patent and Trademark Office. With the exception of Slovenia, Hungary and perhaps the Czech Republic these numbers are infinitely small. This again points out that the role of nearly all transition countries is imitation and not innovation.

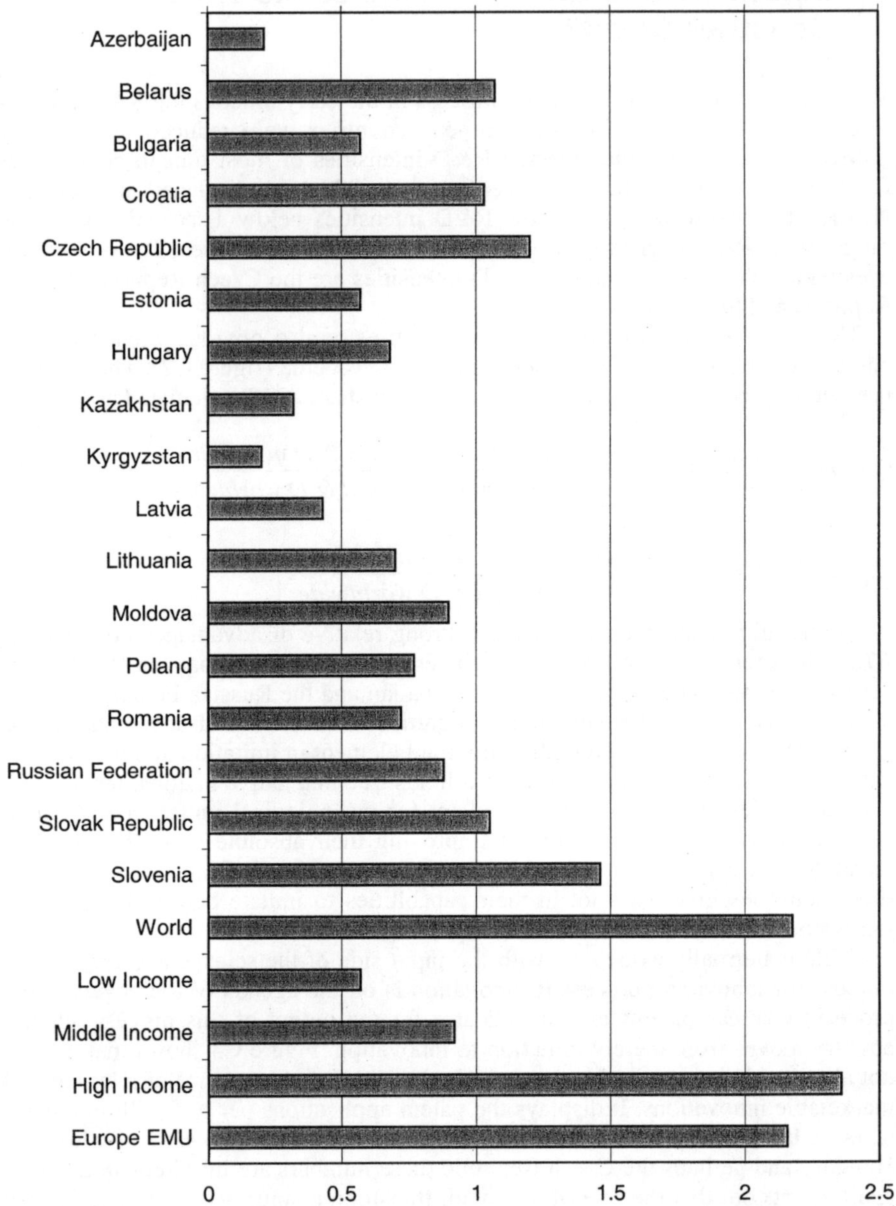


**Fig. C1.** Average R&D Intensity of Transition Countries 1987–1997 (or latest year available)

*Source: World Development Report (2000), Table 5.12, p 306–308*

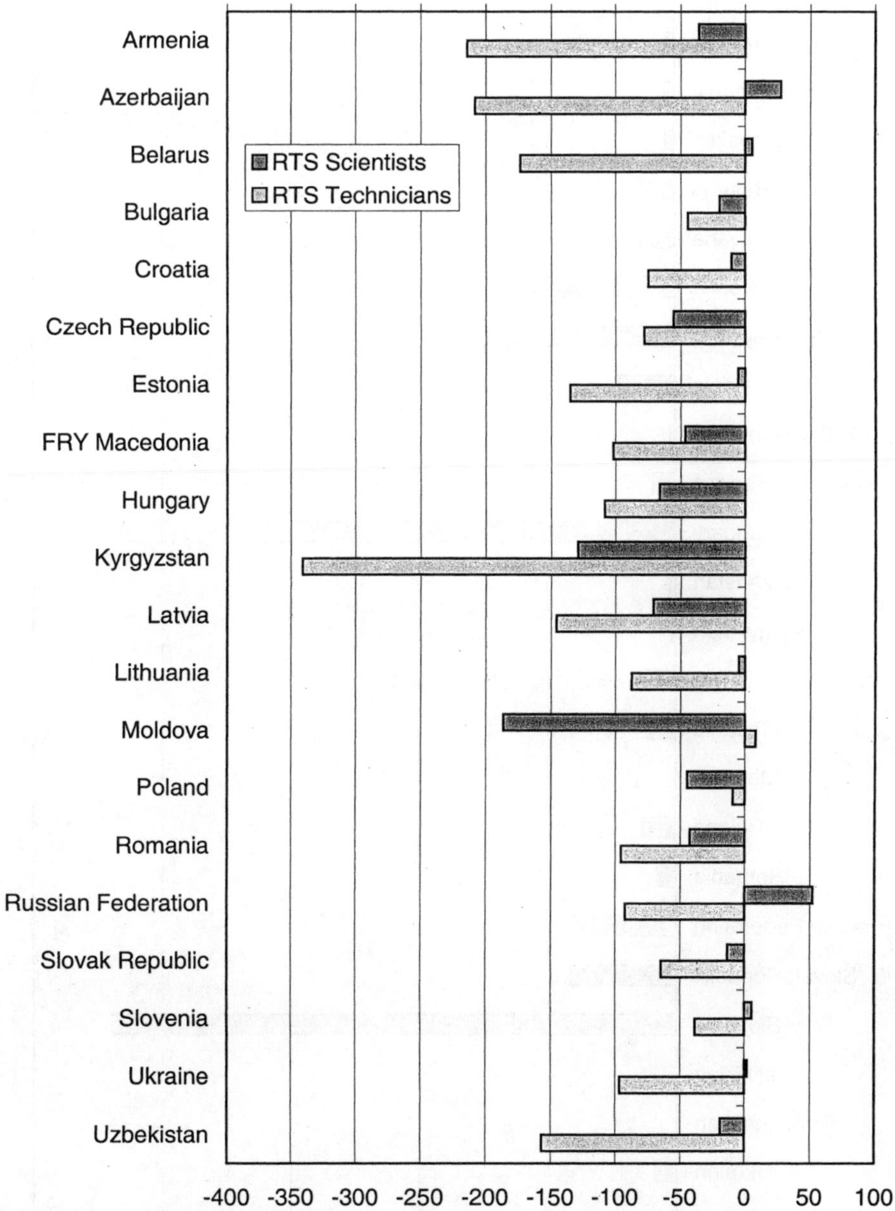


**Fig. C2.** Comparative Disadvantages in R&D Personnel of Transition Countries 1987–1997 (or latest year available)

*Source: World Development Report (2000), Table 5.12, p 306–308, own calculations*

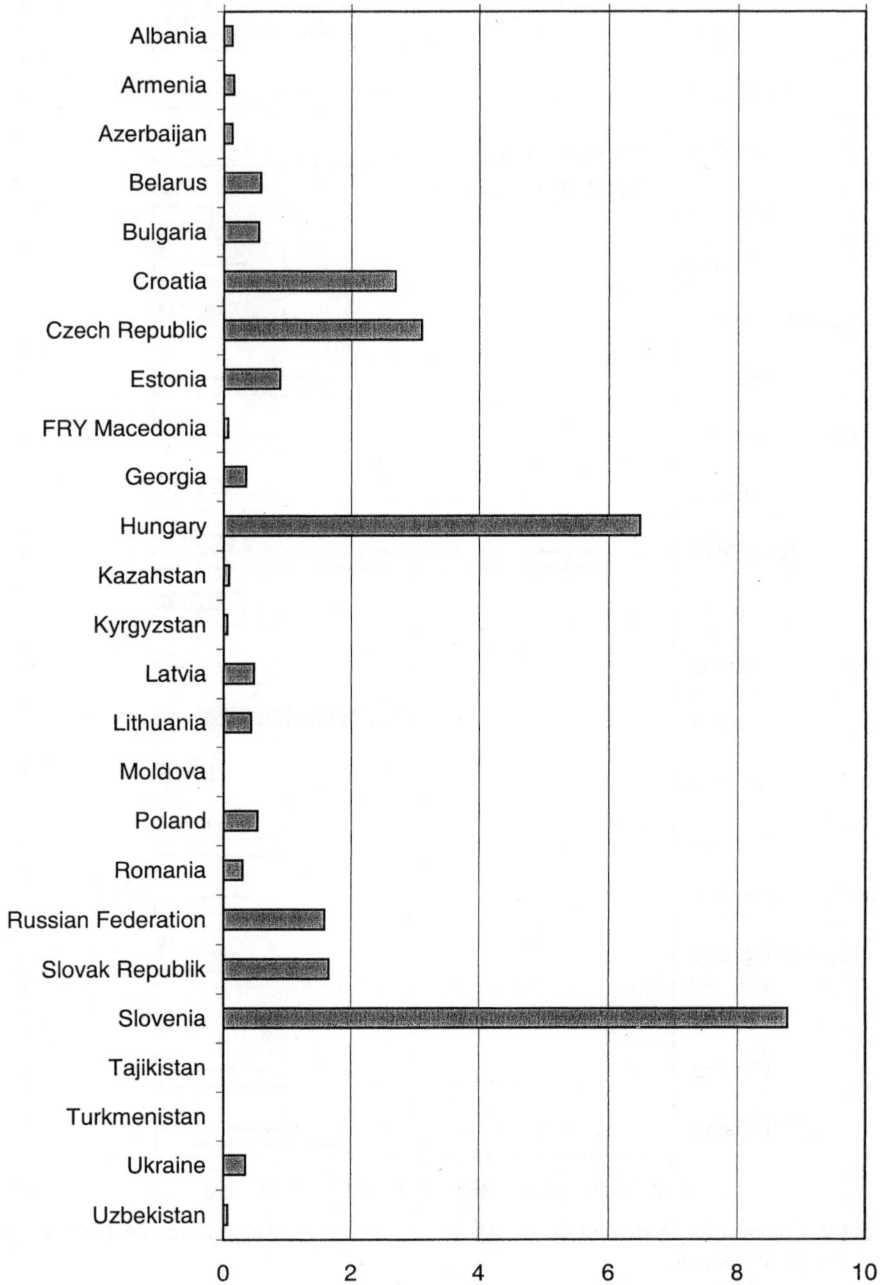


**Fig. C3.** Patent Applications at the USPTO (per one Million Inhabitants) 1992–1998 of the Transition Countries

*Source: USPTO (2000), EBRD (1999), own calculations*

The question which naturally arises at this stage of the discussion is whether there is actually a link between R&D and growth performance in the transition countries. For answering this question we considered the correlations between these two measures. For a careful interpretation of these correlations it must be mentioned that they imply no causality either from R&D to growth nor vice versa but simply show the situation at a taken moment for a cross section of countries. Based on their rough character they can be labeled as "back on the envelope calculations". Figure C4 displays the relationship between R&D intensity 1987–1997 and growth of GDP 1992–1998. Both, the linear specification as well as the specification with R&D intensity in logs are statistically significant at, at least, the 5 % level.

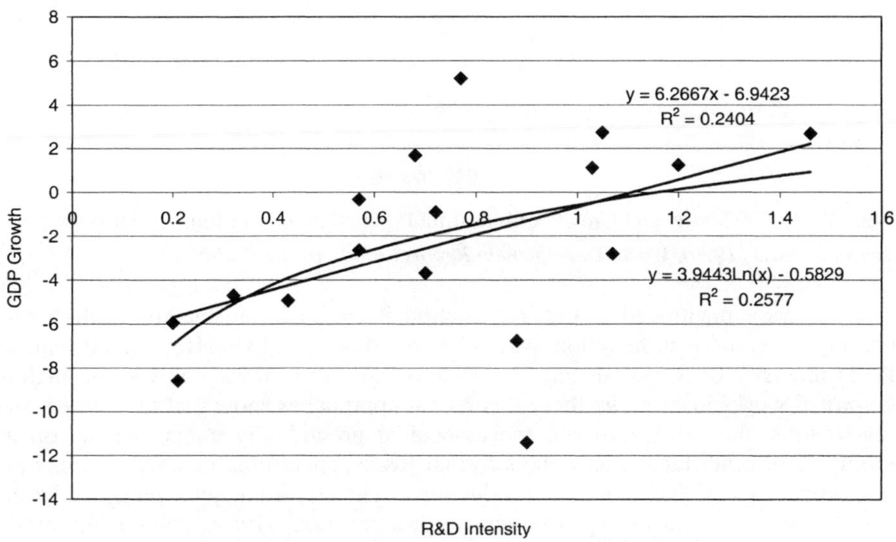


**Fig. C4.** R&D Intensity and Growth of GDP in Transition Countries
*Source: EBRD (1999), World Development Report (2000), own calculations*

The link between R&D and growth becomes even more obvious when growth of industrial production from 1992 to 1998 is considered. Now both correlations – the linear specification as well as the specification with R&D intensity in logs – are statistically significant at the 1 % level (figure C5). The better fitting of the specification with R&D intensity in logs points to the fact that R&D intensity tends towards a certain limit or shows at least – like other inputs – diminishing marginal returns.

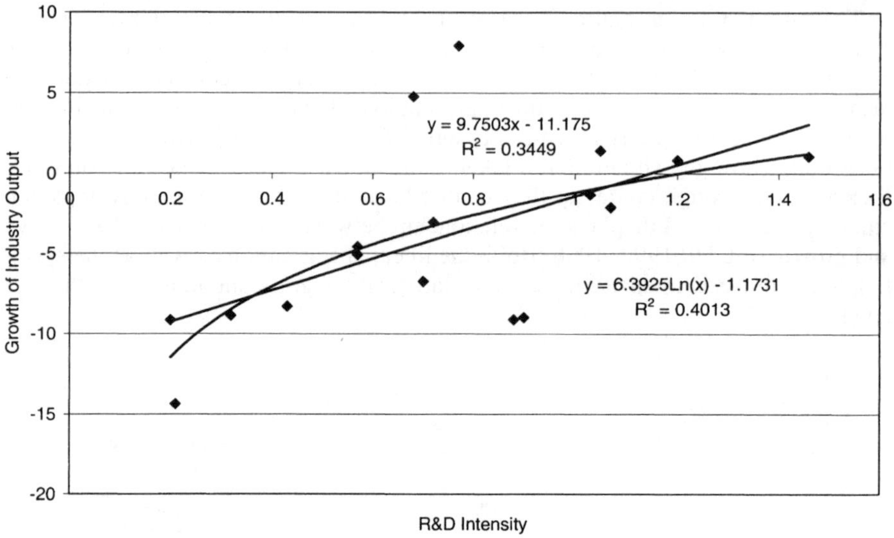


**Fig. C5.** R&D Intensity and Growth of Industrial Production in Transition Countries
*Source: EBRD (1999), World Development Report (2000), own calculations*

As already mentioned in the introduction it would be misleading if the capabilities of an innovation system would be only described by its R&D input (either R&D intensity or R&D personnel). Modern innovation theory as well as major empirical works inspired by these theoretical approaches show that the success of innovations, their diffusion and the associated productivity gains, depend on a multitude of other factors as well as formal R&D. Therefore, incremental innovations come to a large extent from production engineers, from technicians and from the shop floor and many improvements to products and services come from interaction with the markets and with related firms (e.g. subcontractors or suppliers).

All this points to the fact that qualitative factors affecting innovation systems should be taken into account as well as quantitative indicators (Freeman/Soete, 1997). This interplay between the institutional framework (the qualitative part) and purely R&D measures can be best highlighted by a comparison of the national innovation systems of Japan and the USSR in the seventies (see table C1). Although the USSR had a much higher R&D intensity in this period its performance was much lower due to unprofitable frame conditions. One reason was the concentration of R&D on military and space applications with little direct or indirect spillovers into the civil economy. Another reason was the failure to develop R&D at the enterprise level. The Soviet system was based on separate research institutes within the academic sector (for basic research), for each industry sector (for applied research and development) and for the design of plant and the import of technologies and the links between these institutions and the modest R&D on the enterprise level were rather weak.

**Table C1.** An Example for Different National Innovation Systems in the 1970s

| Japan | USSR |
|---|---|
| High GERD*/GNP ratio (2.5 %). Very low proportion of military/ space R&D (< 2 % of R&D). | Very high GERD/GNP ratio (c. 4 %). Extremely high proportion of military/ space R&D (> 70 %). |
| High proportion of total R&D at enterprise level and company financed (approx. two thirds). | Low proportion of total R&D at enterprise level and company financed (< 10 %). |
| Strong integration of R&D, production and import of technology at enterprise level. | Separation of R&D, production and import of technology and weak institutional linkages. |
| Strong user-producer and subcontractor network linkages. | Weak or non-existent linkages between marketing, production and procurement. |
| Strong incentives to innovate at enterprise level involving both management and workforce. | Some incentives to innovate made increasingly strong in the 1960s and 1970s but offset by other negative disincentives affecting both management and workforce. |
| Intensive experience of competition in international markets. | Relatively weak exposure to international competition except in arms race. |

*GERD= gross expenditures on R&D

*Source: Freeman/Soete (1997), p 303*

Furthermore, from the theoretical viewpoint of a "technological gap" approach we have to differentiate between three possible scenarios with respect to technological catching-up (Stehrer/Wörz, 2001). In his seminal work Gerschenkron (1962) developed the idea of an "advantage of backwardness" which results from the fact that backward countries can choose for their imitation processes between different technological possibilities. With regards to the choice of technologies, he concludes for successful catching-up countries:

> The advantages inherent in the use of technologically superior equipment were not counteracted but reinforced by its labor-saving effect. This seems to explain the tendency on the part of the backward countries to concentrate at a relatively early point of their industrialization on promotion of those branches of industrial activities in which recent technological progress had been particularly rapid;...

Such a scenario can be labeled a "jumping-up scenario". However, an opposite scenario is also imaginable where technological catching-up will first take place in low-tech industries, and only when the initial gap has reached a certain threshold will the backward country start to close its gap in the next more technology-intensive industries. This kind of asymmetric technological diffusion is considered in a variant of a formal model in Gries/Jungblut (1997) and the respective scenario can be labeled as "climbing up the ladder scenario".

In a third scenario it is assumed that backward countries improve their technology at such a rate that their gaps are reduced in all industries at the same speed. This kind of symmetric technological diffusion is considered in the first variant of the previously noted model of Gries/Jungblut (1997) and within the context of international trade in a model in Krugman (1985). It can be labeled as "continuous convergence scenario".

Based on these theoretical scenarios Stehrer/Wörz (2001) investigated the catching-up process of OECD-North countries, OECD-South countries (Greece, Iceland, Portugal and Spain) and East Asian countries (Hong Kong, Indonesia, Korea, Malaysia, Singapore and Thailand) relative to the USA. Their results, which due to data problems (e.g. the data are expressed at current prices and current PPP) have to be considered with some cautions, show that productivities in the OECD-North and –South countries converge towards the US level in low-tech and medium-low-tech industries but not in medium-high-tech and high-tech industries, while East Asian countries' productivities converge towards the US level in low-, medium-low- and medium-high- industries but not in high-tech industries. Considering also the behavior of wages and unit labor costs the authors conclude that East Asian countries realized a competitive advantage in the medium-high-tech industries and that their catching-up behavior better fits the first scenario ("jumping-up") whereas the catching-up behavior of the OECD-South countries fits more into the second scenario ("climbing the ladder"). However, they also mentioned "... that catching-up patterns ... do not always follow the patterns implicitly assumed or proposed by the models...".

## 3 Learning by Exports: A Feasible Perspective?

In this section we will develop some ideas about the link between export growth, productivity gains and economic growth (cf. also Welfens, 1999 and Welfens/Gavrilenkov, 2001). Economic opening-up will normally stimulate economic specialization in line with comparative economic advantage which raises economic welfare as consumption can be increased. This standard textbook argument, however, does not explain why rising exports of manufacturing products go along with relatively strong productivity gains. Six effects could indeed be important for this link, namely with respect to producing manufacturing products:

- Manufacturing production requires combining various suppliers' inputs – buying from the market – and value-added of the respective firm in the export sector. Learning to organize a complex production process for production with a focus on world markets generates important know-how which can then be applied in other sectors. Moreover, there should be feedback effects on domestic suppliers in the sense that firms looking for competitive domestic suppliers (and for imported inputs) will push for restructuring and modernization among prospective suppliers. This could generate network effects in the sense that if more firms are familiar with the grammar and syntax of the market economy language, the scope of market transactions could increase.

- Manufacturing production offers many opportunities for product differentiation and imitation which thus creates options for raising value-added over time; in the export sector there is also a continuous change in the structure of demand which stimulates learning, flexibility and structural change.
- Exporting manufacturing products naturally encourages looking for cheap foreign inputs and thereby helps to transfer foreign technology via imported intermediate products (for empirical evidence of the impact of import weighted foreign R&D stocks on total factor productivities see Coe/Helpman, 1995). Productivity gains indeed can often be achieved by intelligent importing. Singapore and Hong Kong are well-known examples in this respect.
- Exporting manufacturing products will be stimulated if neighboring countries also engage in export promotion and thereby stimulate economic growth. Following the logic of the gravity equation which emphasizes that economic geography matters, the simultaneous liberalization of trade in neighboring countries can be expected to bring higher growth effects than isolated liberalization.
- Exporting manufacturing products brings one into contact with potential foreign investors in the manufacturing industry who will acquire competitive firms or engage in greenfield investment in the long term. As such foreign investors typically enjoy technological advantages and produce a broader variety of products in various subsidiaries, such investors will often find it rather easy to define an efficient technological graduation strategy for the new subsidiary.
- Finally, we add a well-known aspect but modify it in an important way. The (manufacturing) tradables sector is quite competitive meaning that inefficient specialization will result in high losses and bankruptcy. The pressure of world market competition thus helps avoiding the trap of inefficient specialization with no or poor productivity gains. This in turn could stimulate FDI inflows because foreign investors will anticipate that a high degree of manufacturing openness will reduce the risk of inconsistent government intervention.

The above reasoning is consistent with the empirical findings of Sachs (1996) and Sachs/Warner (1995) whereby in a convergence regression model natural resource abundance is found to negatively affect growth. In the convergence model the hypothesis is that the lower the income level the higher the growth rate. The growth rate is influenced by the gap between the equilibrium income level and current income where the equilibrium income level is affected by structural variables and policy variables. Such policy variables include openness to trade, market efficiency, and the national savings rate.

However, the question is whether there is empirical evidence which could confirm the prospects for success of such an export led growth strategy for the transition countries, even if they showed in the period from 1992 to 1998 no tendency toward a convergence of per capita incomes. Moreover there is a positive correlation between initial per capita income in 1992 and the average growth rate from 1992 to 1998. If we look at the shares of manufactures in the exports of these countries in 1998, we find in a lot of cases shares slightly below or at the world average of 80 % (figure C6). Only Kazakhstan, Moldova and the Russian Federation have rather small shares. In the case of Kazakhstan and the Russian Federation the small proportion of manufactures in exports is replaced with a large proportion of commodity exports including fuels, ores and metals, and in the case of Moldova mainly the export of food. Only the Czech Republic and Slovenia have small comparative advantages in exporting manufactures. Considering the structure of the manufactures exports of the transition countries, it is clear that they must have comparative advantages in the group of low and medium technology products as they have clear comparative disadvantages in the group of high technology products (figure C7). The only exception relevant to Euroland is Hungary whose share of high technology products in manufacturing exports coincides with the world average.

Now, the natural question is again, whether countries with a large share of manufactures in exports show better growth performance (or a smaller shrinkage performance). Figure C8 shows that there exists a strong positive correlation between the share of manufactures in exports 1998 and the average growth of GDP from 1992 to 1998, which is statistically significant at the 1 % level. Even if such cross section correlation allow no conclusions about causality between exports in manufactures and growth, it however does not contradict the theoretical reasoning about the links between exports and growth. Combining the results from section 2 and 3, the analysis shows furthermore that the technological capabilities of the transition countries are roughly in line with their export performance.

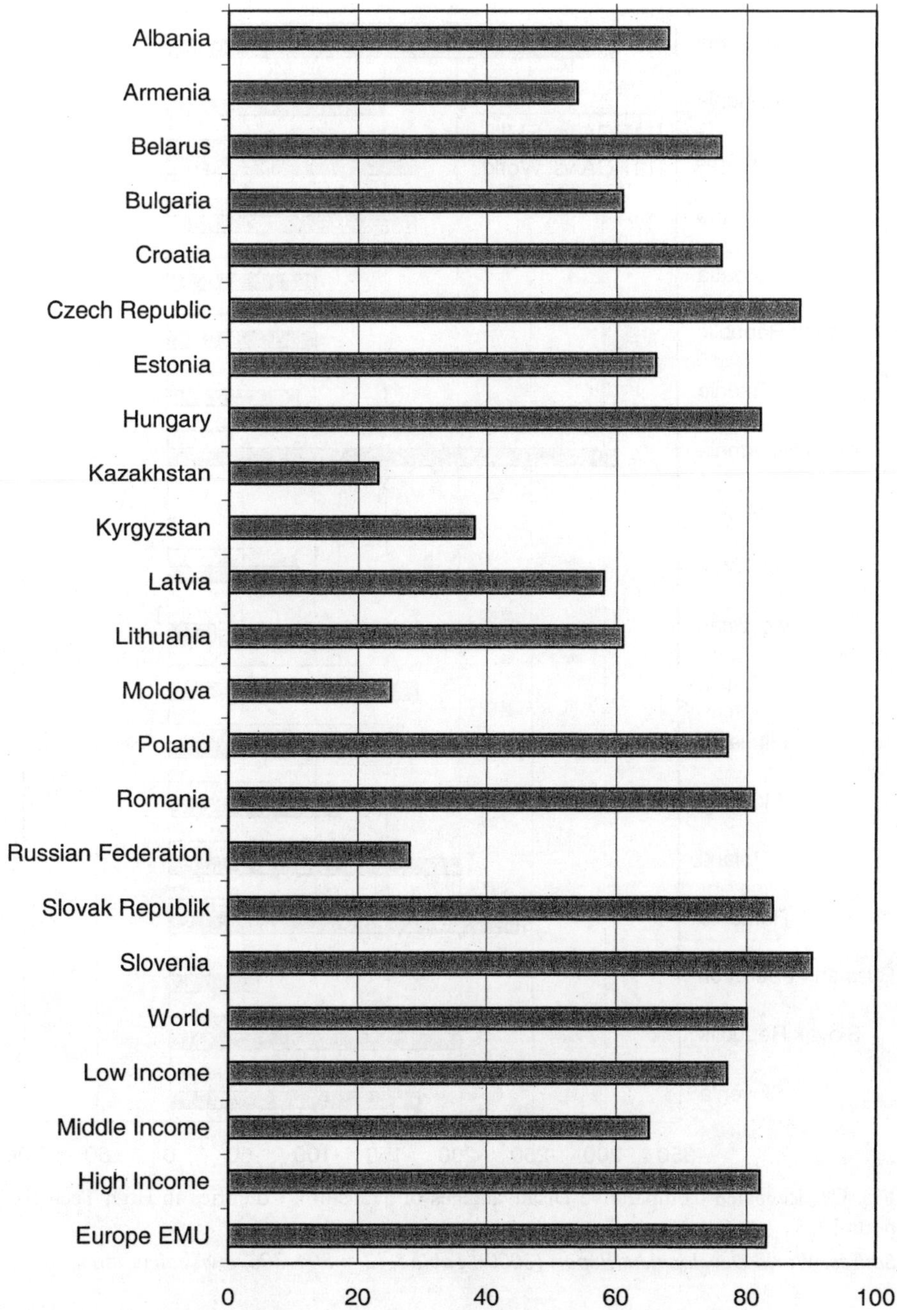


**Fig. C6.** Shares of Manufactures in Exports 1998 of the Transition Countries

*Source: World Development Report (2000), Table 4.5, p. 198–200*

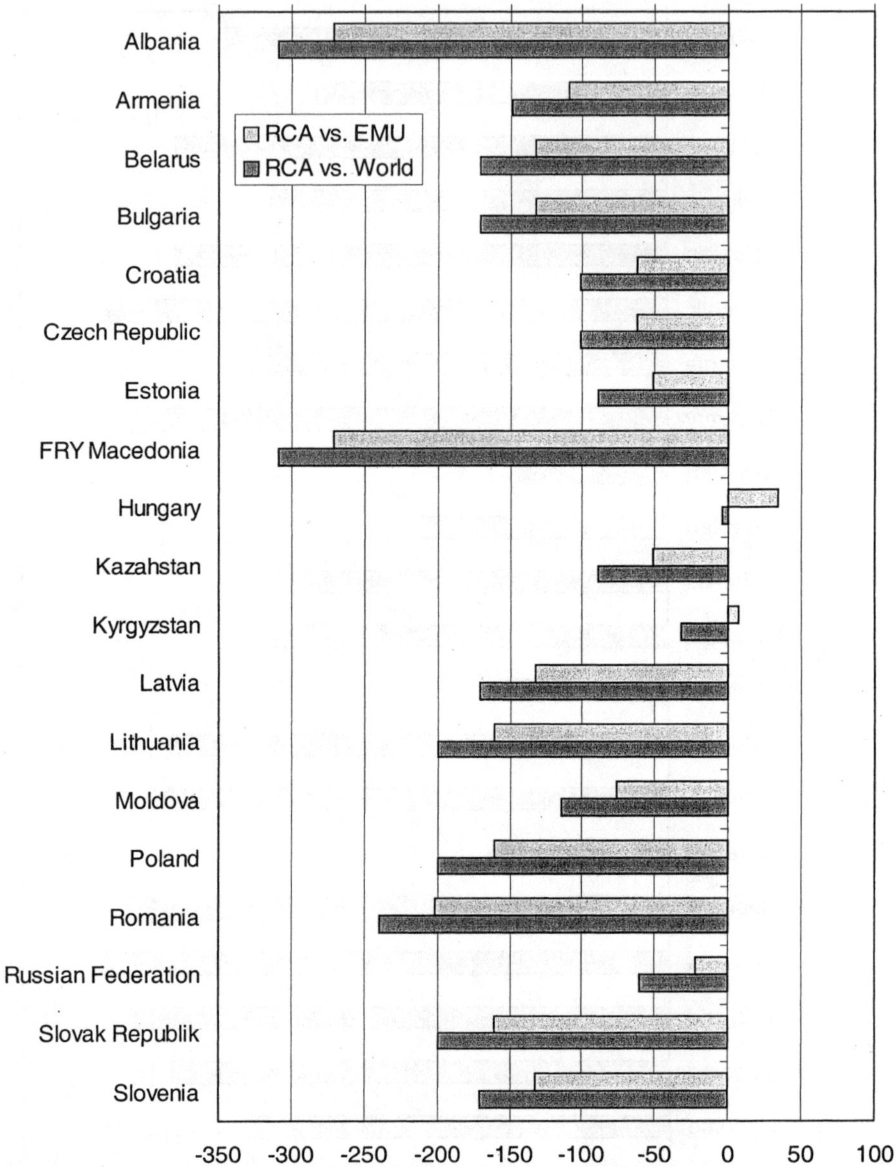


**Fig. C7.** Revealed Comparative Disadvantages of Transition Countries in High Tech Exports 1998

*Source: World Development Report (2000), Table 5.12, p 304–306, own calculations*

**Fig. C8.** Shares of Manufactures in Exports and Growth of GDP in Transition Countries
*Source: World Development Report (2000), Table 4.5, p 198–200, EBRD (1999), own calculations*

# 4 Learning from Asian NICs

Asian Newly Industrializing Countries were able to successfully integrate into the world economy in the 1970s and 1980s. It is useful to take a look at the success story of the Republic of Korea (SONG, 1990). Rapid growth in Korea was achieved through a strategy which emphasized structural change, raising exports and increasing the number of firms. The number of manufacturing firms with over 5 employees nearly tripled in the period 1973–85. Growth rates in 1986–88 reached 12% in each year and inflation was in the range of 2–3%, 1990 per capita income reached about $ 4500. The main ingredient of Korea's growth in the 1960s and 1970s were labor inputs which mainly came from agricultural surplus labor. As regards total factor productivity growth this explained slightly less than ½ of overall growth rates in 1962–73 and 1973–86; advances in knowledge played a larger role than improved resource allocation. The fact that economies of scale played a considerable role in Korea, they accounted namely for about 1/5 of the growth rate, can only be explained on the basis of high export growth – the Korean market itself would often be too small to exploit scale economies optimally on a pure domestic market basis. West Germany's period of rapid catching-up is also strongly explained by a rise of total factor productivity and of economies of scale.

**Table C2.** Supply-side Sources of Growth (in % p.a.): Korea, Japan, Germany (W.), USA

| | Korea | | Japan | West Germany | USA |
|---|---|---|---|---|---|
| | 1963–73 | 1973–86 | 1953–71 | 1950–62 | 1948–86 |
| Real GNP growth rate | 9.54 | 7.82 | 8.81 | 6.27 | 3.2 |
| 1. Contribution of inputs | 5.41 | 4.07 | 3.95 | 2.78 | 1.8 |
| Labor | 3.24 | 2.16 | 1.85 | 1.37 | 0.9 |
| Capital | 2.17 | 1.91 | 2.10 | 1.41 | 0.9 |
| 2. Total factor productivity | 4.13 | 3.75 | 4.86 | 3.49 | 1.4 |
| Advances in knowledge | 1.36 | 1.67 | 1.97 | 0.87 | 1.0 |
| Improved resource allocation | 0.98 | 0.62 | 0.95 | 1.01 | 0.4 |
| Economies of scale | 1.78 | 1.46 | 1.94 | 1.61 | |

Note: Kwang Suk Kim and Joon Kyung Park, 1985, estimated the sources of growth of the Korean economy for the period 1963–82. The results show that out of an income growth rate of 7.61 percent, total factor input explains 5.12 percent and total factor productivity (TFP) 2.49 percent. Their estimate of TFP appears to be much lower than my estimates here.

*Source: Song (1990), p 68*

In Korea the development pattern largely followed Japan's catching-up process: The predominant exports of manufactured products shifted over time from (1) labor intensive goods to (2) other capital intensive goods, (3) capital-intensive and skill-intensive goods, (4) capital- and-technology intensive and high wage goods, and (5) research-, capital- and high skill-intensive goods. Thus there were stages of development and integration into the world market, and it is unclear whether one could leapfrog some of the stages mentioned. To the extent that optimal technological and economic catching-up implies a lexicographical order of technologies, industrial policy which would aim at leapfrogging could come at high costs and could even result in temporary stagnation.

It is doubtful whether the Korean government's strategy of promoting fast-growing firms and giving them preferential access to credit and other incentives was adequate since concentration in major markets increased over time. This contributed to a rather inefficient banking system whose weakness was heavily exposed in the Asian crisis in the late 1990s. Interestingly, the number of state-owned firms increased in the 1970s and 1980s; during the first Five-Year Plan (1962–66) there were 52 public enterprises, however in 1988 there were 103, and if local public enterprises are included the figure climbs to 222 firms – mainly in infrastructure services and tourism. There was also a Korea Development Bank and a Korea Land Promotion Corporation, among others. Public enterprises reached a share of 9.1% of GDP in the 1980s, up from 7% in 1963. Since the 1980s Korea has adopted a gradual policy of privatization. Being pragmatic, one may conclude that public enterprises should not exceed 10% of GDP. Efficiency of public enterprises can be improved by the disclosure of a broad set of accounting and balance-sheet data. The creation of a publicly owned joint stock company is advisable – the disclosure rules of stock companies will then apply to state-owned firms.

An important question concerns the role of industrial policy which naturally would focus on industries with productivity-enhancing backward and forward linkages. While industrial policy is almost certainly inefficient in a leading industrialized country there may be some role for industrial policy in countries with a medium per capita income. While it might be difficult to pick winner industries, it could be more easy to identify the losers, provided that the economy is largely an open one, forcing firms and sectors to exploit competitive advantages – the apparent comparative advantages between these sectors typically provides relatively clear signals. There are certain exceptions, e.g. the case of Ireland's catching-up process where government relied on a strategy which focused on the improving the country's human capital basis, recognizing the need to take the geographic location of Ireland into account. Ireland is on the absolute periphery of Europe – hence government emphasized the development of a human-capital intensive sector with „weightless“ electronics products for which transportation costs played a minor role (Görg/Ruane, 1999).

Government interference in the process of growth and structural change is bound to be rather inefficient if government itself – for various reasons – is inefficient. Weak political competition and a weak constitutional consensus are typical reasons for policy failure. While limited industrial policy could be useful to some extent in Russia, it is clear that the main force shaping decisions on investment and innovation must come from a functional capital market and an efficient banking system. Given the many distortions in this area there is much to be done in these two fields.

Asian NICs successfully combined export expansion and domestic growth after 1960. Outward oriented economic policy was often combined with restrictions on imports and investment inflows, although long-term international subcontracting in the Republic of Korea and other Asian countries was equivalent to foreign investment inflows. These inflows indeed increased in the 1980s and 1990s. High savings rates and an elastic labor supply from agriculture supported, respectively, the growth of industry and exports.

In several studies on Singapore, Korea and Taiwan – for the 1970s and 1980s – Young (1992; 1994; 1995) along with Krugman (1994) and Kim/Lau (1994) argued that the Asian NIC's rapid growth is mainly attributable to factor accumulation rather than a miracle. The basic message of these studies has been that total factor productivity growth played only a small role in growth in Asia. This means that these high growth levels will not be sustainable once there is no longer an elastic excess labor supply from agriculture.

However, as emphasized by Ito (1998), the studies of Sarel (1995; 1996) and Bosworth/Collins (1996) who focus on the more recent decades – the 1980s and 1990s – saw rather high estimates for total factor productivity growth in Indonesia, Malaysia and Thailand and higher estimates for Korea, Singapore and Taiwan. Therefore technological progress might come with sequencing and the stage of economic development. In Asia, Singapore, Thailand and Indonesia were able to attract high FDI inflows in the 1980s and 1990s; in the 1990s Taiwan and Korea also increasingly relied on FDI inflows while becoming successful foreign investors themselves. According to Ito (1998) stages of development and economic catching-up should be distinguished (modified Rostow approach).

Applying this reasoning to Russia and other transforming economies, successful catching-up will depend upon a prudent sequence of growth-enhancing steps which must include adequate policy impulses. Achieving sustained export growth of manufacturing goods seems to be a medium-term key element for catching-up. As output per capita starts to increase, the opportunities to produce and export diversified products as well as products based on economies of scale improve. This should finally provide the opportunity for high profits, enabling increased R&D expenditures (relative to value-added) and then skill-intensive export expansion in the next growth stage.

As regards export and economic growth, the Asian NIC's progress is partly in line with the new growth theory (Romer, 1986; 1990) which emphasizes economies of scale and human capital formation as ingredients of sustained growth. To the extent that foreign investors invest more in training of employees than domestic firms, FDI inflows have a higher growth effect than the simple aspect of capital accumulation would suggest.

## 5 Structural Change and Wage Structure in a Period of Economic Opening up and Growth

Economic opening up typically will go along with high productivity growth in the tradables (T-)sector; productivity growth in the nontradables (N-)sector will be relatively low. In an economy with mobile and homogenous labor there will be a uniform nominal wage W in both sectors (point $E_0$ with wage rate in terms of tradables being $w_0$). As the growth rate of marginal (and average) labor productivity in the N-sector is lower than in the T-sector application of the marginal productivity rule for factor rewards implies that the relative nontradables price $P^N/P^T$ will increase; this also will reflect consumer's preferences if one assumes that the income elasticity of the N-demand is higher than for the T-demand. Assume that productivity in the T-sector rises so that the marginal product schedule for this sector shifts upwards (see $T_L$'). With productivity in the N-sector unchanged there will be an expansion of the T-sector not only because of technological progress but also because of workers moving from the N-sector to the T-sector. If the relative price of nontradables should increase adequately the initial sectoral labor allocation would be restored (point $E_2$). Real income measured in terms of tradables has increased. Note that in the case of technology spillovers from the T-sector to the N-sector, the rise of the relative nontradables price – consistent with restoring the initial labor allocation – would be smaller than considered in the previous case. An import empirical issue (not explored here) is the size of technology spillovers and the determinants of the spillover effects.

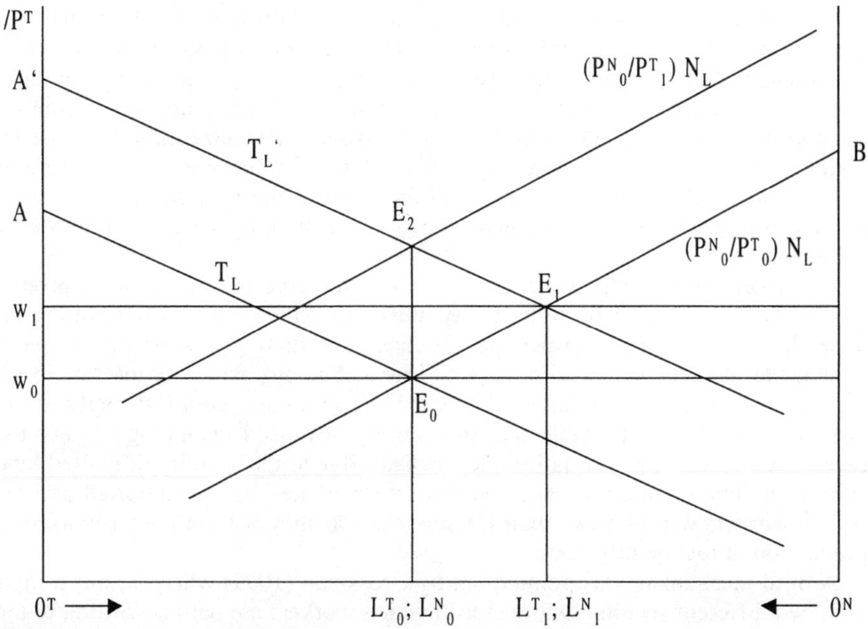


**Fig. C9.** Structural Equilibrium and Technological Progress

To the extent that entrepreneurship has to be encouraged transition countries will face rising inequalities since the discrepancy between owners of real capital – the winners in the privatization game – plus the nouveaux riches entrepreneurs and workers, especially unskilled workers will increase. Opening up itself could already raise the wage differential between skilled and unskilled workers as recent theoretical analysis has shown.

Trade has a direct effect on growth, but it might also have important effects on the choice of technology and thereby can be more important than the direct effects would suggest. Clearly, exports facilitate exploitation of scale economies and imports support economic catching-up by given the country access to high quality intermediate imports, but also by exposing the import-competing firms to the pressure from the world market. Moreover, with rising per capita income there will be more intra-industry trade which in turn is partly related to vertical intra-industry trade which means trading in products of different qualities.

While neoclassical theory suggest that economic opening up will lead to international convergence of factor price ratios and of absolute factor rewards, reality often has shown – at least temporarily – that international income differentials have increased and that income differentials within the country that opened up have increased. International differences in capital intensity are only one relevant aspect explaining income differentials. Heterogeneity of labor is also important.

Recent analysis (survey: Jansen, 2002) has shed light on the issue of wage dispersion in the sense of the wage ratio of skilled to that of unskilled labor. Manasse/Turrini (1999) focus on a model with intra-industry trade, including vertical intra-industry trade which means trading of different product qualitities. The model assumes that in order to export, firms have to pay some fixed costs. As the country opens up for trade those companies producing high quality can afford to pay the fixed costs. Thus only the high skilled workers employed in the production of high quality products will benefit from trade. Intra-industry trade thus could lead to increasing wage inequality. This is, of course, not an argument against trade rather it points to the need for training and retraining plus some redistributive activities of government aimed at maintaining some minimum social cohesion.

Duranton (1999) emphasizes in his model the role of intermediate products which can be of low or of high quality, but only skilled workers are able to produce the high quality intermediate products. As final goods producers decide whether to use advanced technology or low technology which is inferior in productivity the decision in favor of advanced technology could strongly benefit skilled workers. It is possible that in autarchy advanced technology is not used because of a lack of high quality intermediates due to the scarcity of skilled labor. With economic opening up, high quality intermediates can be imported and high skilled workers will improve their relative wage as they will no longer work in the production of low quality goods.

A third mechanism was pointed out by Grossman (1999) who presents a model with two different sectors: One sector in which workers are paid according to their individual marginal product (e.g. the software industry) while the other sector is unable to technically distinguish individual marginal products and therefore pays according to the average worker's talent in this sector (e.g. automotive industry). In this setting we will see the most talented workers being active in the software industry. When two countries with different distributions of the workforce start trading we will observe that in the country with the more heterogeneous workforce more people will be working in the software sector. When the two countries start trading the country with the more heterogeneous workforce will specialize in software and export software products, while the other country will export cars. This tends to increase the inequality in the „software country“ while the opposite holds for the country with the more homogenous workforce.

Taking into account a macroeconomic production function and adopting a growth perspective it holds that overall economic growth (with g denoting a growth rate) can be written as

$$(3)\quad g_Y = b_1 g_L + b_2 g_H + b_3 g_K + b_4 g_Z - b_5 V$$

where $L$ is unskilled labor, $H$ is skilled labor, $K$ the stock of capital and $Z$ the rate of technological progress which itself is influenced by various variables, including government R&D support, the trade volume and foreign direct investment inflows. $V$ is the degree of political instability which negatively affects growth. Kormendi/McGuire (1985) have focused on a broader set of variables to explain growth in a cross-country regression.

An interesting hypothesis (Welfens, 2002) for explaining the growth rate of technological progress is to assume- within a hybrid neoclassical-new growth theory model- that $g_z$ of country I is positively related to the export-GDP ratios of country I and country II (or the export-GDP ratio and the import-GDP ratio) and to the ratio of researches to the population.

## 6 Conclusions

In this paper we investigated the technological capabilities of transition countries, showing that the role of these countries at a world market level is imitation and not innovation. This finding has important negative implications for their growth prospects. Furthermore we present some theoretical reasoning and empirical evidence that these technological capabilities fit well with a learning by exports strategy which fosters exports of manufactures. Transition countries with an already high proportion of manufactures also show better growth performance. However, again in line with their technological capabilities, all transition countries revealed comparative advantage in the export of low and medium technology products.

When the results are considered together, the evidence shows that successful catching-up will depend upon a prudent sequence of growth-enhancing steps which must include adequate policy impulses. These policy impulses must on the one hand take into consideration the momentary and actual situation in transition countries and on the other need to include the building-up of an adequate institutional frameworks which can form the basis for an efficient national system of innovation. Achieving sustained export growth of manufacturing goods seems to be a medium-term key element for catching-up. As output per capita starts to increase, the opportunities to produce and export diversified products as well as products based on economies of scale improve, which finally should lay the ground for high profits and increasing R&D expenditures (relative to value-added) as well as skill-intensive export expansion in the next growth stage.

Besides the conclusions based on the empirical findings, some more general conclusion concerning restructuring, structural change and exports of manufacturing products can be drawn. Therefore, basic theory and experience suggest several crucial ingredients for sustained economic growth. As regards the process of economic catching-up in Russia, within the context of market economy and democracy there are some prerequisites which partly relate to the political system, the rule of law and competition. A market economy will generate high productivity growth only

- if economic freedom,
- entrepreneurship and innovation
- the rule of law
- competition and liberal trade and
- political stability in a democratic framework

can be combined. Freedom is the basis for entrepreneurial creativity and innovativeness, as well as a critical media which raises the level of information on the side of voters and political competitors. The rule of law is necessary because market transactions are based on contracts and contracts are useful only if contracts can be enforced by the legal system. Competition and liberal trade are needed to bring about static efficiency in the sense of price = marginal costs on the one hand, on the other hand competition will encourage Schumpeterian processes, that is process innovations which cut costs, and product innovations which allow firms to fetch higher prices in markets. Catching-up goes along with trade and technological progress however, it is unclear whether sustainable growth can be achieved as there is often the problem of political instability. Moreover, economic opening up and growth may go along with a rise of social inequalities which could create social and political tensions.

Improving education is important for medium term catching up because attracting FDI in technology intensive sectors and creation of new dynamic firms will be stimulated by a broadening of human capital investment. Human capital will also help to accelerate the imitation process and to raise per capita income which in turn will accelerate structural change. With rising exports of manufacturing- and a rise of the share of scale-intensive goods- not only will per capita income rise but there will be improved prospects for growth stimulating high FDI inflows which will strengthen innovation dynamics in the long. While we do not suggest a strict lexicographical order of the elements of catching-up there are good arguments that intelligent-sequencing can spur growth, trade and catching-up.

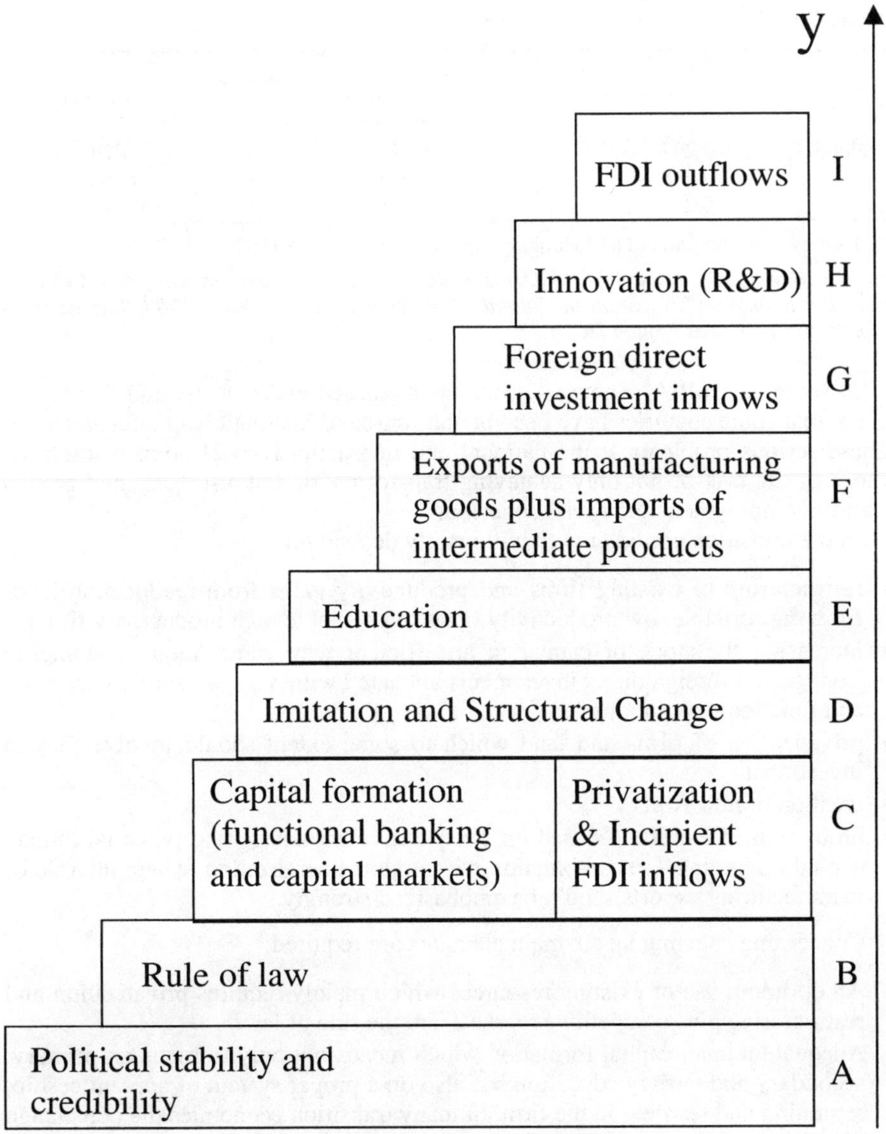


**Fig. C10.** Requirements for Catching-up (y = per capita GDP)

Most former socialist countries – except for Hungary (and the Czech Republic) – suffer from high transitional unemployment and large income discrepancies. The Gini coefficient has increased dramatically in some countries, most noticeably in Russia.

**Table C3.** Gini Coefficient in Transition Countries

| | Gini Coefficient | | |
|---|---|---|---|
| | prior to reform* | at end of first reform stage* | difference |
| Poland | 0,272 | 0,301 | 0,029 |
| Hungary | 0,248 | 0,308 | 0,060 |
| Russia | 0,238 | 0,380 | 0,142 |

*reform periods for Poland and Hungary: 1990–95, for Russia 1992–1995.

*Source: Keane MP, Prasad ES (2000), Inequality, Transfers and Growth: New Evidence from the Economic Transition in Poland. IMF Working Paper No. 117/00, International Monetary Fund, Washington DC, p 37*

In some ex-CMEA countries crime has increased enormously, and there is no doubt that some countries have become the source of international mafia activities. These serious problems at the national and international level point to the relevance of the task of not only achieving transformation but also sustained growth cum full employment and social cohesion.

In the transition period growth will mainly depend on

- restructuring of existing firms and productivity gains from reallocating labor from unprofitable low productivity firms to profitable high productivity firms;
- increasing the stock of capital in an efficient way which requires domestic savings and foreign direct investments allocated within a system of competition and functional capital markets.
- privatization of firms and land which to some extent should involve foreign investment
- creation of new firms
- promotion of exports – based on comparative advantage and potential human capital upgrading - in combination with import liberalization, where the role of manufacturing exports should be emphasized strongly.

Concerning catching up six main elements are required:

- An optimum use of existing resources which mainly requires privatization and restructuring plus competitive markets and the rule of law.
- Adequate human capital formation which means not only to focus on primary, secondary and tertiary education but also on a proper system of apprenticeship, retraining and learning in the firm. In many transition economies the percentage of young people not attending school has achieved high levels, and this will impair long term growth.
- Optimal specialization and opening up in order to fully exploit the benefits of „geographical and technological proximity“: As the gravity equation model of trade suggests that a high share of trade will normally be with neighboring countries it is crucial that regional trade liberalization initiatives successfully develop. Moreover, as trade is likely to be more intensive between countries with similar levels of technology (Jungmittag, 2000) it is in the interest of countries with a medium per capita income to develop a technology position

which is slightly above the level normally recorded at this income level: Thus there is a natural technological basis to intensify trade with slightly more advance countries which in turn should stimulate exports and economic growth.
- Availability of cheap infrastructure service which in turn requires privatization and adequate regulation of infrastructure. A broad and cheap network of infrastructure stimulates capital formation and encourages networking among firms. It also stimulates competition and a fortiori innovation.
- Functional banks and capital markets which help to price risk adequately.
- Active membership in main international organizations.

From a pragmatic point of view it would be important that Russia plays a more active role in the relevant international organizations. One can only hope that Russia will quickly adopt an observer status at the European Patent Agency; and that Russia will join the World Trade Organization. Moreover, Russia should become a full member of the OECD, giving Russia a voice in all the important policy committees but at the same time forcing her to collect and publish data in all relevant policy fields. This would mean that policymakers in Russia could identify much easier weak policy areas and recognize fields of rapid improvement. With Mexico, Korea and some Visegrad countries already being a member of the OECD, Russia could find interesting benchmarks for herself and potential partners in „club decision-making“ in Paris. The OECD – and the EU – also could be an important partner when it comes to imposing strict competition policy in Russia.

However, especially in Russia, there exist a lot of impediments to economic catching up. The most basic steps upwards in the per capita income league have not been realized in Russia in the 1990s. According to a global survey of the World Bank (1997), policy instability and lack of the rule of law (crime and corruption problems) – both of which may be summarized under political stability and credibility – are a serious impediment for foreign investment.

Most of FDI in Eastern Europe was found to be market-seeking so that cost motives are not of prime importance at first sight. However, an EBRD survey has shown that the type of FDI varies strongly according to the host country's progress in economic transition. FDI projects in postsocialist countries which are more advanced in transition show three characteristics (Lankes/Stern, 1997):

- FDI projects are more export-oriented
- FDI projects are more integrated into the foreign parent's multinational production process
- FDI projects are more likely to exploit the host country's comparative advantage.

Finally considering the prospects for convergence in the former CMEA countries, it must be emphasized that high and sustained growth is crucial for sustainable transformation. High investment-GDP ratios, a high marginal product of capital, growth-enhancing trade dynamics and accumulation of R&D capital plus human capital are crucial for high growth. Governments facing consolidation problems and capital flight are unlikely to be able to adequately support research and development expenditures in the business community and to finance high expenditures for education; if such unfavorable development is combined with peripheral geographical location the prospects for high growth are unfavorable. Poland, Hungary, the Czech Republic, Slovenia and the Baltic Countries face rather favorable medium term growth prospects, while most other transition economies stand to grow rather slowly.

The Pantarhei III model for Germany has shown that the output multiplier for raising the R&D capital stock is much higher than for investment, where a main channel is the rise of exports as a consequence of faster accumulation of R&D capital. This suggests – in line with the new growth theory - that in the course of economic catching-up the role of R&D expenditures (and of human capital formation) will become increasingly important in all of central Europe.

If eastern Europe should be unable to avoid long term divergence there is much risk that massive migration and political conflicts will create further and sustained regional imbalances which undermine growth and prosperity for the whole of Europe. International organizations such as the IMF; the EBRD and the EU should positively contribute to avoiding strong divergence in eastern Europe. Naturally, the main task of achieving growth lies with national governments. The success stories of the leading postsocialist countries should be studied carefully; this plus taking into account modern economic theory should help to achieve high growth in all transition economies in the long run.

## References


BMBF (ed) (1999) Zur technologischen Leistungsfähigkeit Deutschlands. Zusammenfassender Endbericht 1998, Bonn

Bosworth B, Collins SM (1996) Economic Growth in East Asia: Accumulation versus Assimilation. Brooking Papers on Economic Activity 2, Brookings Institution, Washington DC

Coe DT, Helpman E (1995) International R&D spillovers. European Economic Review39: 859–887

De Mello (1999) Foreign Direct Investment-led Growth: Evidence from Time Series and Panel Data. Oxford Economic Papers 51: 133–151

Duranton G (1999) The Future of the High-Skill Equilibrium in Germany. Oxford Review of Economic Policy 15: 43–59

EBRD (1999) Transition Report 1999. London

EBRD (2000) Transition Report update. London

Freeman C, Soete L (1997) The Economics of Industrial Innovation. 3. edition, London/Washington

Gerschenkron A (1962) Economic Backwardness in historical perspective. In: Gerschenkron A (1962) Economic Backwardness in historical perspective. A Book of Essays, Cambridge MA, pp 5–30

Görg H, Ruane F (1999) European Integration and Peripherality: Are There Lessons from Ireland. Trinity Economic Papers Series 1999/10

Gries T, Jungblut S (1997) Catching up of Economies in Transformation. In: Welfens PJJ; Wolf HC (eds) Banking, international capital flows and growth in Europe. Berlin et al, pp 297–313

Grossman GM (1999) Imperfect Labour Contracts and International Trade. CEPR Discussion Paper 2240, London

Ito T (1998) What Can Developing Countries Learn from East Asia's Economic Growth? In: Pleskovic B, Stiglitz JE (eds) Annual World Bank Conference on Development Economics. The World Bank, Washington DC, pp 139–166

Jansen M (2002) International Trade and the Position of European Low-skilled Labour. In: Addison J, Welfens PJJ (eds) Labor Markets and Social Security. 2nd revised and enlarged edition, Springer, Heidelberg and New York (forthcoming)

Jungmittag A (2000) Internationale Innovationsdynamik und Spezialisierungsstruktur: Empirische Befunde und wirtschaftspolitische Implikationen. Paper presented at the workshop "Growth and Innovation Policy in Germany and Europe", Potsdam

Jungmittag et al (1998) Berichterstattung zur technologischen Leistungsfähigkeit Deutschlands 1977 - Materialien des FhG-ISI. Karlsruhe

Kim J-I, Lau LJ (1994) The Sources of Economic Growth of the East Asian Newly Industrialized Countries. Journal of Japanese and International Economies 8 (3): 235–271

Kormendi RC, McGuire PG (1985) Macroeconomic Determinants of Growth. Journal of Monetary Economics 16: 141–163

Krugman P (1985) A 'Technological GAP' Model of International Trade. In: Jungenfelt K, Hague D (eds) Structural Adjustment in Advanced Economies. Houndsmill et al., pp 35–61

Krugman P (1994) The Myth of Asia's Miracle. Foreign Affairs, November-December: 62–78

Lankes HP, Stern N (1997) Capital Flows to Eastern Europe and the Former Soviet Union. EBRD Working Paper No. 27, London

Lundvall BA (ed) (1992) The National System of Innovation. London

Manasse P, Turrini A (1999) Trade, Wages and Superstars. CEPR Discussion Paper 2262

Rodrigo GC (2001) Technology, Economic Growth and Crises in East Asia. Edward Elgar Publishing, Cheltenham, UK, Northampton, MA

Romer PM (1986) Increasing Returns and Long-Run Growth. Journal of Political Economy 98: 71–102

Romer PM (1990) Endogenous Technological Change. Journal of Political Economy 94: 1002–1037

Sachs JD (1996) Sources of Slow Growth in African Economies. HIID Development Paper, Harvard University, Cambridge, Mass.

Sachs JD, Warner AM (1995) Economic Reform and the Process of Global Integration. Brookings Papers on Economic Activity 1, Brookings Institution, Washington DC

Sarel M (1995) Growth in East Asia: What We Can and What We Cannot Infer from It. IMF Working Paper 95/98, International Monetary Fund, Washington DC

Sarel M (1996) Growth and Productivity in ASEAN Economies. Paper presented at the conference sponsored by the IMF on macroeconomic issues facing ASEAN countries, 6–8 November, Jakarta

Song B-N (1990) The Rise of the Korean Economy. Oxford University Press, Oxford

Stehrer R, Wörz J (2001) Technological Convergence and Trade Patterns. WIIW Working Papers No. 19, Vienna

Welfens PJJ (1999) Eastern EU Enlargement and the Russian Transformation Crisis. Springer, Heidelberg and New York

Welfens PJJ Gavrilenkov E (eds) (2001) Restructuring, Stabilizing and Modernizing the New Russia. Springer, Heidelberg and New York

Welfens PJJ (2002) Information & Communication Technology and Growth: Some Neglected Dynamic Aspects in Open Digital Economies. In: Audretsch D, Welfens PJJ (eds) The New Economy and Economic Growth in Europe and the US. Springer, Heidelberg and New York, pp 29–52

World Bank (1997) Improving the Environment for Business and Investment in the CIS and Baltic Countries: Views from Entrepreneurs and the World Bank Country Economists. Background paper presented at the EBRD Annual Meeting

World Bank (2000) World Development Report. Washington DC

Young A (1992) A Tale of Two Cities: Factor Accumulation and Technological Change in Hong Kong and Singapore. NBER Macroeconomic Annual 1992, MIT Press, Cambridge, Mass.

Young A (1994) Lessons from East Asian NICS: A Contrarian View. European Economic Review 38: 964–973

Young A (1995) The Tyranny of Numbers: Confronting the Statistical Realities of the East Asian Growth Experience. Quarterly Journal of Economics 110: 641–680

# Appendix

**Table C4.** Growth in Real GDP in Selected Transition Countries, Forecast for 2000 (%)

| | Forecast | Projected Level of per-capita GDP as % of 1989 |
|---|---|---|
| Bulgaria | 3,5 | 70 |
| Czech Republic | 2 | *95 |
| Hungary | 4,5 | 104 |
| Poland | 5 | 128 |
| Romania | 0,5 | 76 |
| Central & eastern Europe & Baltic States | 3,6 | 100 |
| Kazakhstan | 3,5 | 65 |
| Russia | 4 | 59 |
| Ukraine | 2 | 37 |
| CIS | 3,6 | 57 |

* equals 50% of EU average

*Source: EBRD (2000), Transition Report update*

**Table C5.** Average GDP/capita/year growth for selected economies

| Period | 1960–73 | 1973–85 | 1985–97 | 1960–97 |
|---|---|---|---|---|
| Japan | 8,5 | 2,7 | 2,6 | 4,7 |
| Singapore | 8,4 | 5,1 | 6,2 | 6,6 |
| Hong Kong | 7,5 | 5,2 | 5,3 | 6,0 |
| Taiwan | 6,7 | 5,4 | 6,6 | 6,2 |
| South Korea | 6,6 | 6,1 | 7,7 | 6,8 |
| Indonesia | 2,1 | 5,9 | 4,3 | 4,0 |
| Malaysia | 4,6 | 4,1 | 5,3 | 4,7 |
| Thailand | 4,4 | 3,4 | 6,1 | 4,6 |
| China | 2,1 | 4,5 | 5,5 | 4,0 |
| India | 0,2 | 2,4 | 3,6 | 2,0 |
| Sri Lanka | 0,0 | 4,2 | 2,2 | 2,0 |

*Source: Rodrigo (2001), p 5*

**Table C6.** Collins and Bosworth decomposition of the sources of growth (percentage growth rates per year for the period 1960–94)

| Country or region | Output per worker | Contribution of each component: Physical capital per worker | Education per worker | TFP |
|---|---|---|---|---|
| Taiwan | 5,8 | 3,1 | 0,6 | 2,0 |
| South Korea | 5,7 | 3,3 | 0,8 | 1,5 |
| Singapore | 5,4 | 3,4 | 0,4 | 1,5 |
| Indonesia | 3,4 | 2,1 | 0,5 | 0,8 |
| Thailand | 5,0 | 2,7 | 0,4 | 1,8 |
| Malaysia | 3,8 | 2,3 | 0,5 | 0,9 |
| Philippines | 1,2 | 1,2 | 0,5 | -0,4 |
| East Asia (all of above) | 4,2 | 2,5 | 0,6 | 1,1 |
| China | 4,5 | 1,5 | 0,4 | 2,6 |
| South Asia | 2,3 | 1,1 | 0,3 | 0,8 |
| Africa | 0,3 | 0,8 | 0,2 | -0,6 |
| Middle East | 1,6 | 1,5 | 0,5 | -0,3 |
| Latin America | 1,5 | 0,9 | 0,4 | 0,2 |
| USA | 1,1 | 0,4 | 0,4 | 0,3 |
| Other industrial | 2,9 | 1,5 | 0,4 | 1,1 |

*Source: Bosworth/Collins (1996)*

# D. Financial Sector and Human Capital in a Long-Term Growth Perspective: The Case of Russia

Ralf Wiegert

## 1 Introduction

Russia has failed to adopt a transition strategy for nearly a decade, which may lead to high economic growth and a long-term catching-up process in relation to the average per capita-income of the OECD countries. The transformation from plan to market, which began in 1992 under the assumption that these reform efforts would turn around the country's economic decline, proved to be rather costly from the beginning. Only since 1999 is there some economic recovery, partly due to the large depreciation of the Ruble after the financial crisis in 1998, and partly to the rise of the price for crude oil on the world market.

Political distress in the context of ongoing disputes between the presidential administration and the left-dominated Parliament, and the consequences of the break-up of the Soviet Union, as well as other influential factors like the wars in Chechnya, have contributed to this bad performance. In comparison to other transition countries, one of the main distinctive features of Russia is the rather unfavourable initial conditions which the country had to face some ten years ago. There has been, after yet another financial crisis in August 1998 which once again dashed hopes for economic recovery, a turnaround in economic development in the past two years which has set an end to a decade of recession (Sutela, 2000). With the inauguration of Vladimir Putin as Russian president came a new group of economic reformers which joined the federal government and developed a transition strategy, which, despite the fact that its targets and priorities are still rather vague, provides a guideline to economic reforms which might lead the country to a long-term oriented sustainable growth path (Gavrilenkov, 2001; Yasin et al., 2000).

There is broad consensus among politicians and scholars that progress in institutional reform, which still lags behind, and the restoration of the rule of law and the tackling of widespread corruption, together with political and administrational arbitrariness, are top priorities for the Russian government on the way to a long term-oriented economic catching up-process (see e.g. EBRD, 1999; IMF, 1999; OECD, 2000). Recent contributions and empirical research suggest that Russia is caught in a kind of reform trap where major influential institutions, public as well as private, are more interested in maximizing short term profits and rents than accelerating economic and political reform which might lead to a more market-oriented business environment with a higher degree of transparency and competition, and thus more efficient use of the available resources. Public institutions are often seen as an actor reflecting a kind of grabbing hand which deals with private firms and creates laws and regulations only to extract rents and maximize their additional unofficial income (Shleifer/Vishny, 1997; Zaostrovtsev, 2000). Contrary to this, private firms are supposed to shape their business environment in an increasingly sophisticated manner; acting as so called state captors, such as groups with particular political influence able to set their own "rules of the game" by bribing public institutions and thereby eliminating competitors and maximizing their rents (Hellman/Jones/Kaufmann (2000). Other firms in the respective sector are forced to compete with these state captors and to act in a similar manner. Consequently, the rule of law as set by governmental authorities is undermined in exchange for public goods like legal protection, which are sold through "private offers" by corrupt politicians and bureaucrats.

The fight against corruption and the restoration of the rule of law seems to be the most crucial problem for Russian policymakers these days, yet there are, as regards a long term oriented catching up-strategy, more aspects than institutional development and removing obstacles to implement proper market-oriented reform measures. Progress in economic growth theory in the past two decades has considerably expanded the range of factors associated with and important for sustained economic growth. The question, however, remains which and to what extent particular factors are relevant for the catching up process of the European transition countries, and especially for Russia. This paper wants to take heed of the economic factors which are supposed to be relevant in a long-term oriented perspective. Current developments in Russia, taking on theoretical (mainly based on the standard neoclassical model and extensions) and empirical considerations concerning the role of the financial sector and the stock of human capital for economic growth, are compared with recent results, and conclusions as regards future growth prospects as well as some basic policy options for elements of a growth strategy for Russia are drawn.

## *Recent findings on economic perspectives of transition countries*

A large number of studies focus on the performance of the transition countries since the introduction of market reforms and try to link these two features together in order to identify certain policy successes and failures (Aslund/Boone/Johnson, 1996; Sachs/Warner, 1995; Brenton/Gros/Vandille, 1997; De Melo/Gelb, 1997). De Melo/Gelb construct an index on market liberalization issues and compare it with the economic development of the respective transition countries. Fischer/Sahay/Vegh (1996a, b) further develop this method and expand the perspective on 20 and 25, transition countries, respectively. All this analysis concludes that the degree of market liberalization is positively correlated with the economic performance of these countries. Heybey/Murrell (1997), however, stress another important aspect. They analyse the initial conditions in various transition countries. According to their results, initial conditions were more important for the economic performance than differences in policy decisions in the early transition stage. With ongoing transition efforts, however, initial conditions should play a minor role and policy failures are the main causes for economic crisis.

Forecasting economic growth and analysing economic development of the transition countries has been difficult to address and produced much disputed results.

One attempt to analyse growth prospects for transition countries was done by the World Bank (1996) in its Development Report. They used an equation originally developed by Barro (1991) and Levine/Renelt (1992). Their approach included several factors which had a statistically robust impact on economic growth, such as the initial level of per capita-GDP, population growth rate, investment, government consumption, and primary and secondary school enrolment. They derived parameters, with which they linked the influence of the respective factor on economic growth, by using data from a series of developing countries. The World Bank (1996) and various other authors (Denizer; 1997; Fischer/Sahay/Vegh, 1998) applied this approach with some specifications on the transition countries. They obtained, however, for Russia rather high and in retrospective slightly unrealistic results, e.g. Fischer/Sahay/Vegh (1998) got 6,18% (according to the Barro-approach) and 4,83% (Levine/Renelt-approach) as the average annual growth rate for per-capita-GDP. The difference is explained by the fact that the first approach lays relatively more weight on the role of human capital whereas the second one emphasizes the role of macroeconomic investment.

These approaches, and especially their application on transition countries, have been subject to criticism. Of course something must be wrong since the predictions simply did not match reality in Russia (or only when given extreme favourable global conditions). An alternative study on the basis of institutional indicators was developed by the EBRD (1997). The bank obtained far lower growth rates for Russia than the Barro/Levine/Renelt-approach because of the significant institutional underdevelopment in the Russian Federation and other countries of the former Soviet Union. Campos (1999) also criticizes this approach and takes it the other way round; he runs a regression analysis on the impact of the factors mentioned in the Barro/Levine/Renelt-equations on per-capita-growth of GDP in the countries of the former Soviet Union and comes to different results as to their overall influence. He concludes that government expenditures had a positive and human capital a negative impact on the average annual growth rate. The reason for the negative impact of human capital is the high level of human capital – and thus the high relative importance compared to other factors – which exists in the countries of the former Soviet Union, while the actual rate of economic growth is comparably low or even negative. This at least shows that several factors are still missing for long-term growth analysis of transition countries. Above all, it should be clear that transition countries in Eastern Europe cannot be that easily compared with developing countries.

The most influential factor leading to the high growth rates from Fischer/Sahay/Vegh (1998) is the amount of human capital available in the Eastern European transition countries and especially in Russia, but this approach seems to be highly questionable since they measure human capital as the quantity of primary and secondary school enrolment, and there are other shortcomings like the omission of other factors like institutional development. It is a quite common view that the transition countries in Eastern Europe have rather comfortable prospects for economic catching-up when their amount of human capital is considered (World Bank, 1995; Balzer, 1993). This should certainly be a major advantage and quite a distinctive feature separating them from the analysis of developing countries, but one has to acknowledge that the human capital acquired in Eastern Europe was, for the most part, accumulated under the socialist system. Russia today still clearly shows a lack of the human capital needed to run a market economy. This begs the question to what extent the Russian education, in particular its vocational system, has been restructured in order to cover the needs and the skills demanded in a market economy. As will be shown later, Russia's educational sector appears to be in precarious shape, reflecting the overall economic situation and transitional decline, which might endanger Russia's ability for economic recovery in the medium to long term.

As regards Russia in particular comparably few publications are dedicated to the exploration of growth differences between its various regions. This seems to be a clear lack of research activities since Russia is itself a large and economically heterogeneous country, as was pointed out by McIntyre (1998). He takes a closer look at the effects of both national and sub-national (on the regional and local level) policies on regional economic performance. National policy decisions, due to a considerable lack of control by the federal government and therefore increasing political power within the regional and local governments themselves, somehow played only a minor role for regional economic development and/or could have been counteracted to some degree by regional authorities. The division of the economic sphere in Russia into several separated units is also mentioned by Kirkow (1997) and especially by Berkovitz/DeJong (1998a), who identified certain internal economic borders within Russia due to large price differences according to different price regulations across various regions. The same authors (1998b) develop an empirical model with which they try to identify policy areas where regional governments play a major role compared to the influence of the national policy level on economic development in the respective region. A basic conclusion from all these publications is that regional authorities have extensive influence on the implementation of policy decisions at the national level.

As the rest of the paper deals with Russia on the national level, these considerations should make clear that economic development and conditions in Russia's regions vary greatly (see both maps overleaf for the gross regional product per capita and for the total education expenses per capita). Thus, reasons for policy problems and possible solutions are different as well. Yet, theoretical considerations can develop results which are equally important to various kinds of surrounding conditions. Hence the following chapters will try to yield insights into which priorities for a growth strategy standard growth theory as well as recent results in growth research suggests. We focus on two aspects in particular, that is the importance of financial markets as institutions for capital allocation and of education as a way to improve the stock of human capital and hence the efficiency of labour and the quality of the workforce to be employed in the economy.

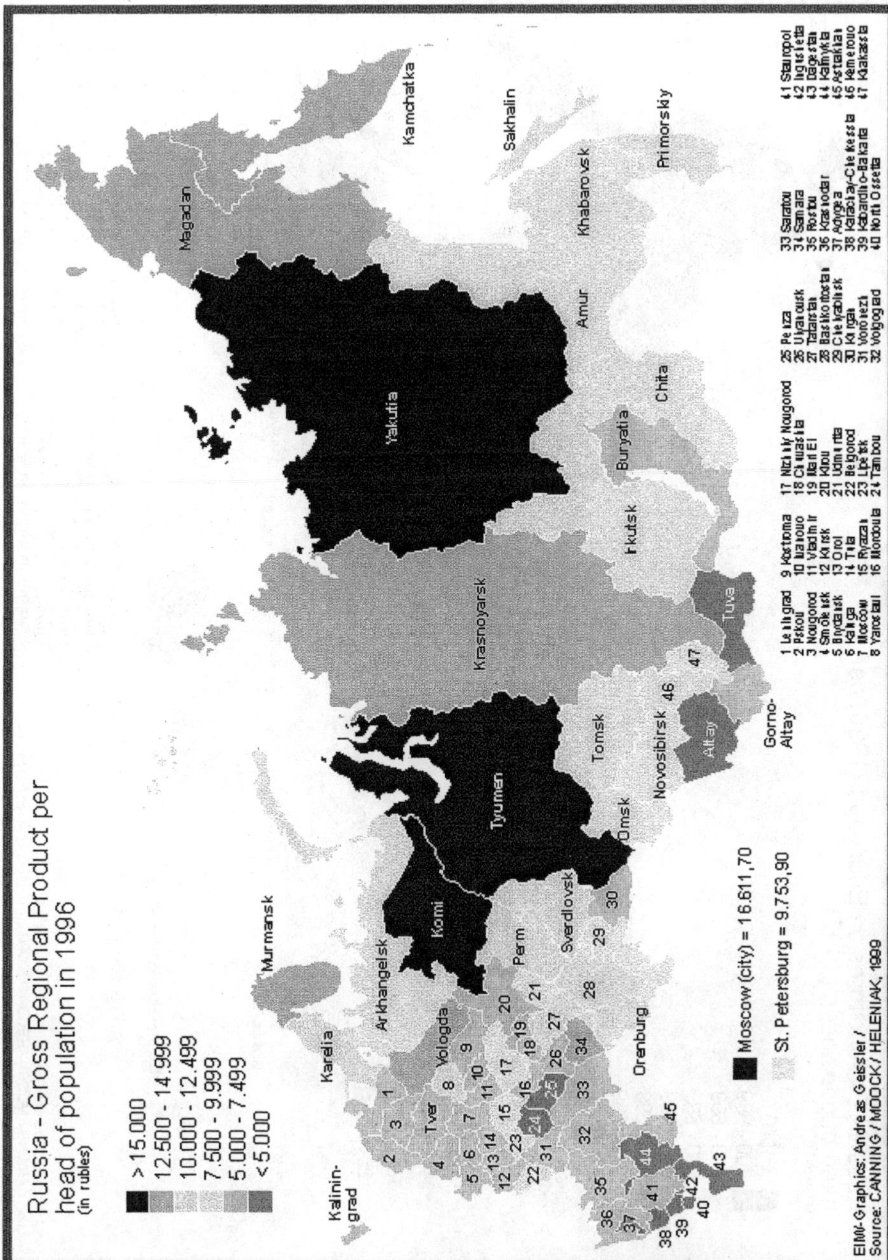


**Fig. D1.** Russia – Gross Regional Product per Head of Population in 1996

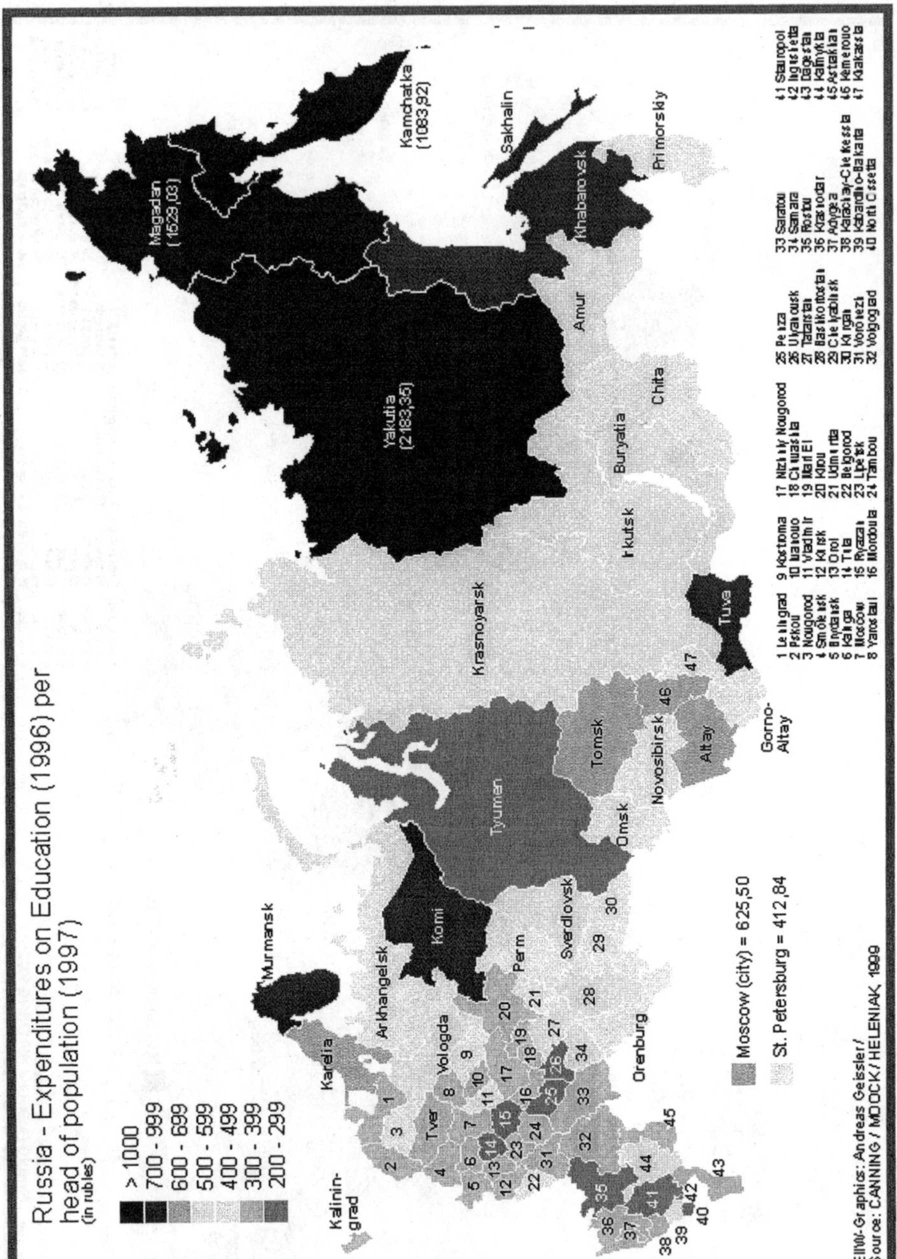


**Fig. D2.** Russia – Expenditures on Education (1996) per Head of Population (1997)

# 2 The Importance of Financial Markets and Human Capital from Growth Theory Perspectives and Empirical Evidence

The role of human capital and of financial markets for economic development has attracted interest from a broad variety of scholars in recent years (see e.g. Tsuru (2000) or Levine (1997) for financial markets and Lopez/Thomas/Wang (1998) for human capital). Despite some mixed empirical evidence, consensus among the literature is growing that both are of crucial importance for economic development and sustainable long term growth. Still, one rather simple but also comprehensive theoretical method to show the importance of both human capital and financial markets is the neoclassical growth model originally developed by Solow (1956). Albeit the model consists of a neoclassical production function with two homogenous factors, labour L and capital K, where the allocation of capital as well as labour and its different skill levels are disregarded, financial markets are the allocating institutions of physical capital, and the creation of human capital can be integrated in the model through modifications.

## 2.1 Financial Sector and Growth

The neoclassical growth model with two input factors, labour (L) and (physical) capital (K), and a constant ratio for saving (s), depreciation of (physical) capital (•) and growth of the labour force (n), and the growth of capital intensity k = K/L, that is k', is governed by:

(1) $s f(k) - (n + \delta) k = k'$

Therefore, by considering the per-capita-production function

(2) $y = f(k)$

with y as per-capita-income one can see that growth of y is determined by the development of k (see Mankiw (1995) for model specifications). Without technological progress, growth of per-capita-income can only occur if (for n = 0 and s and • held constant) k is growing. As long as physical capital as input factor exhibits diminishing returns per additional unit capital employed, there exists an equilibrium value of k (the so called steady state), where the economy is converging to and where, when it finally reaches that level, k, as well as y, will not grow any longer. Like in the standard literature (e.g. Barro/Sala-i-Martin, 1995), one can show that under the given assumptions of the Solow-model every economy converges to a particular level of k and y, and that during this process of convergence the economy exhibits growth rates in y higher than other countries which have already progressed further to their long-term equilibrium or even reached their steady state.

Disregarding the development of the labour force n, which is assumed to remain constant at zero growth, s and $\delta$ have special importance for both the speed with which the economy converges and for the steady state level of k and y, respectively. Fig. D3, which draws upon the relationship between k and the growth rates of k and y, shows this theoretical argument by using the per-capita-production function f(k) and the related savings function $s_0$ f(k), which equals gross investment. Growth of capital stock per capita $k'_0$ is determined by the difference between gross investment $s_0f(k)$ and the depreciation of capital (and the growth of the labour force n) $(n + \delta_0)$ k. The steady state level of per-capita capital stock, to which the economy converges, is $k_0*$; in case of an economy with a lower per-capita capital stock net investment per capita k' is positive and output growth per capita will exhibit positive growth until the steady state is reached. Transition countries are believed to be in such a process of convergence and should produce temporarily higher growth in y than the OECD average.

Saving ratios and capital depreciation may differ between countries due to household behaviour, environmental conditions, and other factors, but one may also show herewith the impact of a more or less efficient financial sector of an economy, regarding its role as a financial intermediary between savers and investors and as the allocating mechanism for the country's financial resources. If the financial sector of an economy (and in the case of the transition countries the banking part of it) has a poor record in attracting savings like in Russia with its crisis-ridden banks (and also low degree of competition), savings which are channelled through the financial sector to satisfy investment needs are significantly lower than in countries with a more efficient banking sector. Therefore one may argue that gross investment shrinks from $s_0$ f(k) to $s_1$ f(k) with $s_1 < s_0$.

What often goes in line with poor savings conditions is a malfunctioning of the financial sector as a capital allocating mechanism. By choosing inefficient investment decisions, and therefore producing less valuable productive capital than possible, the depreciation of capital increases. The problem can be aggravated e.g. by labour regulation (or bureaucratic obstacles) which is too strict in a sense that the capital stock cannot be used efficiently and depreciates therefore over time (through e.g. technological progress) without making full use of it. With an increasing capital deprecation $\delta$ the graph $(n + \delta_0)$ k also goes up to $[(n + \delta_1)$ k] leading together with a lower savings ratio ($s_1$) to a significantly lower equilibrium level of k ($k_1*$), which corresponds with a lower steady state-level of per-capita output $y_1*$.

These simple theoretical considerations underline the importance of the efficient functioning of the financial sector in a market economy; a well-functioning financial sector as an intermediary between savers and investors can help boost savings on the one hand and provide for efficient investment decisions on the other. Russia as a country with a deeply depressed and uncompetitive banking sector should be able to realize large gains from restructuring its banking sector by introducing and enforcing sound rules of banking and bringing in more competition.

Openness to the world as regards capital account transactions may alter these theoretical results both positively or negatively. On the one hand capital flight, like in Russia, worsens the already low "internal" savings ratio (meaning those savings which are in effect reinvested in the country itself) and inflowing FDI on the other, can enable the country to achieve a higher "internal" savings ratio and therefore a higher growth path with a faster catching-up process relative to more advanced countries.

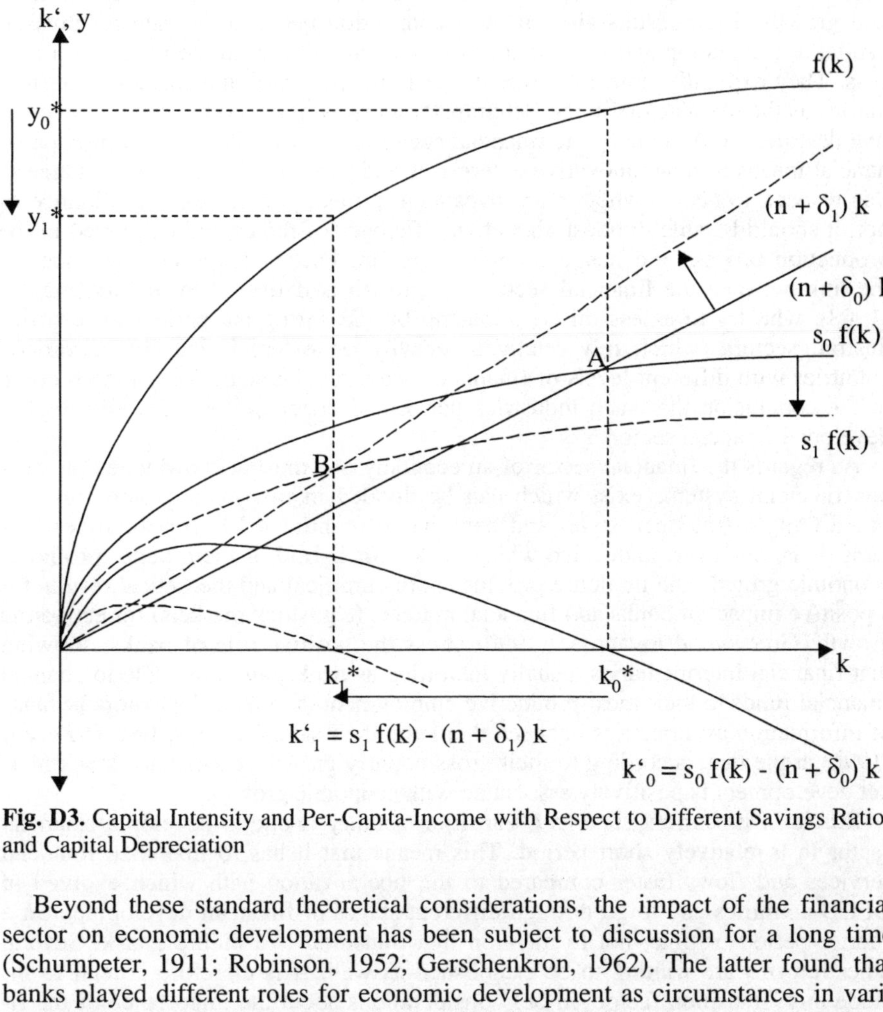


**Fig. D3.** Capital Intensity and Per-Capita-Income with Respect to Different Savings Ratios and Capital Depreciation

Beyond these standard theoretical considerations, the impact of the financial sector on economic development has been subject to discussion for a long time (Schumpeter, 1911; Robinson, 1952; Gerschenkron, 1962). The latter found that banks played different roles for economic development as circumstances in various countries were not the same; e.g. as Britain on the one hand had a entrepreneurial class which almost induced industrialization, banks merely facilitated that process, Germany on the other hand had a different socio-economic structure which lead to a more important role for banks in propelling industrialization of the country. Lucas (1988) stated that the role of the financial sector for economic development has been overemphasized. But, as will be discussed briefly in the following section, recent theoretical and empirical evidence suggests that there is indeed a significant positive relationship between the level of development of the financial sector (including financial markets as well as the banking sector) and overall economic performance.

King/Levine (1993) collected data from a survey covering 80 countries in order to analyse the impact of the countries' financial sector on their growth performance. They concluded that there is indeed a positive relationship between finance and growth. Their results also stated a connection between the rate of physical capital accumulation and the efficiency of the capital used in the production process. They explicitly linked the role of the financial sector and financial intermediaries as the main actors in the Schumpeterian view of economic growth by creative destruction. As long as the financial sector is developed enough to provide financial means to new innovative enterprises and, what is of crucial importance in this respect, to decide whether an investment project justifies external finance or not, it should be able to boost allocative efficiency of the capital employed in the production process and hence economic growth. Further empirical evidence for the link between the financial sector and growth is delivered by Rajan/Zingales (1998), who try to assess this relationship by measuring the performance of industrial sectors (which rely relatively heavily on external finance) in various countries with different levels of financial sector development. They indeed come to the conclusion that such industries performed better in countries with higher developed financial sectors.

As regards the financial sector of an economy one must acknowledge that various financial systems exist which can be divided in two main groups: market-based (Anglo-American style) and bank-based (continental-European style) systems. It is, however, undecided which system or hybrid of them better promotes economic growth; the literature provides both empirical and theoretical results for a positive impact of banks and financial markets (e.g. stock markets) for economic growth. Greenwood/Jovanovic (1990) stress the positive role of banks, showing that financial intermediaries, usually identified as banks, are more able to channel financial funds to their most productive employment than their depositors because of information asymmetries between them and their saving clients. Levine/Zervos (1996) argue that, according to their cross-country growth regressions, stock market development is positively associated with economic growth.

Russia in its current state as a transition country is due to develop a financial sector in a relatively short period. This means that it has to liberalize financial services and flows faster compared to the liberalization path which evolved in OECD countries and to go through different stages of financial development in a shorter period of time, not to mention that transition is a multiple task. Several other reforms are waiting to be established as well. It is therefore crucial to include this "transition factor" in our considerations about the importance of the financial sector for economic growth. Bossone (1999) argues that according to different levels of financial liberalization different types of financial systems become important for the efficiency of the financial sector in promoting growth. In particular, he stresses via a theoretical model the superior results of the market solution against financial intermediaries like banks from a certain level of financial development onwards. He admits, however, that during the early stages of financial liberalization banks are undoubtedly necessary for collecting private households' savings and intermediating those funds to the enterprise sector, since financial markets like stock markets require a highly sophisticated institutional setting and surrounding infrastructure. Earlier publications (e.g. McKinnon, 1993) were even sceptical about the role of banks in the early stages of liberalization and argued for massive restrictions in order to avoid banking failures and huge losses by private households. In some way, however, he proved to be right as regards the current financial situation in Russia.

### *The financial sector in Russia*

Given the largely accepted view that there is a positive link between financial sector development and economic growth, the question arises how the financial sector affected economic growth in Russia. However, this questions has recently been answered and the economic development in the aftermath of the *financial* crisis proves these answers to be correct.

The importance of the financial sector for overall economic development in Russia is best shown by the performance of industrial output and growth of GDP in the follow-up of the financial crisis in 1998. Before that, the financial sector had only negligible, if any, positive impact on the economy at all, since it played a minor role due to various strategic failures since the very beginning of financial liberalization in the Russian transformation process and, above all, to mounting fiscal debts which were covered by the private capital market since 1995 to a largely increasing extent. The real sector recovered relatively quickly given the sudden downturn which left the financial sector in deep distress immediately after the crisis broke out, mostly thanks to the huge devaluation of the Ruble and thus the improved position of Russian producers against their foreign competitors. In addition, the price increase for crude oil on the world market left Russia and its banking system awash with foreign currency. Russian reserves in foreign currencies increased nearly twofold from 1999 to 2000 (from USD 12,6 billion in 1999 to USD 21,2 billion) and the increase of the monetary base from January to June 2000 was due to a large extent to growing net foreign currency reserves (the monetary base increased from the end of 1999 to June 2000 at a rate of 22,5%, whereas net foreign currency reserves growth was 51,5%; DIW et al., 2000). Despite this high cash inflow, the Russian banking system still simply lacks opportunities to reinvest the money due to the largely underdeveloped capital market and the institutional and technical prerequisites for evaluating the standing of a borrower. Only now are there some signs that more sophisticated capital market mechanisms like syndicated loans are gaining ground in the Russian capital market. Russia seems to have not yet reached a certain threshold level where commercial banking is attractive with respect to the creation of large diversified loan portfolios in order to fulfil its function in overcoming financial restrictions when restructuring the transition economy (Buiter/Lago/Rey, 1998).

Regarding the previous theoretical considerations on the relationship between the functioning of the financial sector and economic growth, one may argue that Russia's investment performance in recent years, which showed a large backdrop similar to the development of GDP (see table D1 and D2), means that the country has or is about to lose a huge part of its capital stock (only now do recent figures point to a double-digit increase in gross fixed investment in Russia in 2000, DIW et al., 2000). The share of gross fixed capital accumulation steadily declined from 37,1% in 1991 to 15,1% in 1999, whereas Poland exhibited a share of 22,4% in 1997 (Gavrilenkov, 2001), which seems to be closer to the level needed to be able to initiate a catching up process. In terms of the neoclassical model this means that Russia is further slipping away from its steady state value k* rather than catching up with high investment and GDP growth rates. If one takes into account the large share of the shadow economy in Russia and its related investment efforts, the overall drop in investment and also in GDP should not be that deep (Schneider, 2000; or for further considerations on the output collapse see Aslund, 2001). But that does not change the critical point which is addressed by this paper very much, that from a long term perspective investment and GDP will more or less recover as soon as investment conditions improve. But, as the theoretical considerations suggest, without an efficiently functioning financial sector the prospects for the catching up process are more limited than for countries with similar initial conditions but a more efficient financial sector.

**Table D1.** Saving and Investment in Russia (all data as % of GDP)

| | Gross National Saving | | | Gross Fixed Capital Formation | | | | Current Account Surplus |
|---|---|---|---|---|---|---|---|---|
| | Total | Private | Public | Total | Private | Public | Depre-ciation | |
| 1989 | 35.0 | na | na | 33.0 | 10.0 | 23.0 | 10.6 | 2.0 |
| 1990 | 30.0 | na | na | 29.0 | 15.0 | 14.0 | 9.0 | 1.0 |
| 1991 | 37.0 | na | na | 24.0 | 20.0 | 4.0 | 9.0 | 13.0 |
| 1992 | 33. | na | na | 24.0 | 22.0 | 2.0 | 9.6 | 9.0 |
| 1993 | 28.0 | na | na | 20.0 | 21.0 | 1.0 | 9.5 | 8.0 |
| 1994 | 29.0 | na | na | 22.0 | 22.0 | 0.0 | 9.2 | 7.0 |
| 1995 | 27.0 | na | na | 21.0 | 9.0 | 12.0 | 9.6 | 6.0 |
| 1996 | 26.0 | na | na | 21.0 | 9.0 | 12.0 | 9.8 | 5.0 |
| 1997 | 22.2 | 16.8 | 5.4 | 22.9 | 9.6 | 13.3 | 9.9 | -0.7 |
| 1998 | 16.8 | 13.0 | 3.8 | 16.2 | 4.4 | 11.8 | 9.3 | 0.6 |
| 1999 | 28.0 | na | na | 17.0 | 6.0 | 11.0 | na | 9.0 |

*Source: Buiter WH (2000) From Predation to Accumulation? The second Transition Decade in Russia. Economics of Transition 8 (3): 603–622*

**Table D2.** Gross Fixed Investment in Selected Transition Countries (Percentage change in real terms)

| | 1992 | 1993 | 1994 | 1995 | 1996 | 1997 | 1998 | 1999 Estimate |
|---|---|---|---|---|---|---|---|---|
| Czech Republic | 16,5 | 0,2 | 9,1 | 19,8 | 8,2 | -2,9 | -3,9 | -5,5 |
| Hungary | -2,6 | 2,0 | 12,5 | -4.3 | 6.7 | 9.2 | 13,3 | 6,6 |
| Poland | 2,3 | 2,9 | 9,2 | 16,9 | 20,6 | 21,9 | 14,5 | 5,0 |
| Russia | -41,5 | -25,8 | -26,0 | -7,5 | -19,3 | -5,7 | -8,6 | 1,4 |

*Source: EBRD (2000) Transition report 2000. London*

In the model two variables, the savings ratio and the depreciation of the capital stock, were considered as crucial indicators for the functioning of the financial sector. The functioning of the financial sector as regards the savings ratio and, what is more important, its capability in collecting these financial means on its accounts can be measured by the ratio of broad money (M2) to GDP, which includes circulating money as well as demand and time deposits. Beneath this indicator, Beck/Demirgüc-Kunt/Levine (1999) present a comprehensive set of indicators for the efficiency of the financial sector which they derived from a broad based cross-country survey. During the transition years until now, the ratio M2 to GDP has not exceeded the 0,16 level in Russia (table D3), whereas in more advanced countries like Poland or Hungary this ratio has already reached the 0,4 level (EBRD, 1998; in bank-based financial systems like Germany or France this figure stands at around 0,75). One must note that this ratio has to be regarded with respect to the financial system of a country. During the transition to a system with higher sophisticated financial markets this ratio should diminish again as savers tend to shift their portfolio towards other financial instruments which are not included in M2.

The low ratio of M2 to GDP in Russia and the ratio of claims on the private sector to total assets of the banking sector, which shows a similar development (table D3), point to the fact that the Russian banking system was not able to fulfil one of its core functions in a market economy in recent years, to collect savings and to reinvest these means in the enterprise sector. The financial crisis of 1998 still aggravated the problem (Kashin, 2000; Olenev, 2000). Regarding this inability of the financial sector and the corresponding low effective savings ratio (at least according to the official data), the growth prospects of Russia seem to be more restricted than those of other transition countries with a higher effective savings ratio. As confidence and hence the amount of financial funds available for Russian banks is low, the same holds for the their own activities as regards extending loans and granting credits to both enterprises and private customers. Almost non-existent data on the standing of potential clients (there are no track records available for private customers and there is a lack of comprehensive data on the financial situation of enterprises often related to the unwillingness of managers to reveal business data to the public) creates large information asymmetries which cannot be overcome. Thus, until now, the core income source of banks consists of foreign currency transactions (around 1/3 of their aggregate income; furthermore, they spend nearly half of their expenses on such transactions). Interest income and spending amounts only to around 10% and 5%, respectively, of the total figure (RECEP, 2000, p. 60). This shows that most banks still serve merely as a kind of corporate treasury for their owners, rather than working as a financial intermediary.

There is a good point in arguing that a large portion of savings are invested without using the official financial sector and bank accounts, and that therefore the functioning of the financial sector is of minor importance compared to the security of property rights (Johnson/Macmillan/Woodruff, 1999). Above all, small enterprises seem to be more constrained by weak property rights than the unavailability of external financial assistance, at least in the early stages of transition. The share of output which is reinvested in the economy should therefore be higher than the above mentioned indicators suggest. But that does not really change the picture. Since these forms of investment (through internal financial means like current cash flow) are limited by their nature, forms of external finance become more important than expanding the business. And if an economy lacks a system which is able to provide such instruments of external finance it is restricted to a certain level of economic development. What is even more important, such a grey capital market cannot provide the transparency and variety of investment opportunities which is needed in theory to be able to choose the most profitable investment projects, which is at the same time associated with minimizing the depreciation of capital.

As regards capital depreciation there appears to be a feature for the Russian financial system, which is suspected to considerably increase the respective rate because of its lack of capability to choose efficient investment decisions. This is the still low level of competition in the banking market (e.g. Sberbank still owns around 80% of the market share of retail clients; its position in the banking market is guaranteed by a unique network of around 1500 district offices and many smaller branches). The total number of bank branches in Russia stood in October 2000 at around 3850 according to Central Bank data (CBR, 2000). The distribution of total assets among Russia's banks are also highly concentrated; the top 20 banks in Russia account for more than 60% of total assets in the banking sector, leaving the smallest 325 banks (in October 2000, 1325 banks were registered at the Central Bank) with only 0,29%, meaning that these banks are merely empty shells with virtually no assets (see fig. D4).

A low level of competition leads to the suspicion that investment projects are not decided according to their profitability. Rather they force borrowers out of the capital market via too high interest rates due to the quasi-monopolistic setting of interest rates. The spread between deposit and lending rates may serve as an indicator for the degree of competition in the banking sector, since a higher degree in competition should go in line with lower interest rate spreads ( the price for the financial intermediation service). In Russia this spread is still rather high, well above 15% in 2000 (see fig. D4). One must acknowledge, however, that this figure at least partly reflects the large obstacles and high costs due to lack of comprehensive data Russian banks face when trying to engage in the credits and loans business. Thus, resolving the data problem via improving accounting rules and practice is one of the crucial elements for financial reform.

One way to overcome such financial restrictions is currently shown by the newly built holding structures around commodity companies (e.g. Gazprom) which have emerged as cash-rich investors in line with the latest oil price boom and combined with the currency devaluation (ready to buy companies in various kinds of sectors, at home and abroad) are channelling funds through their own financial network. On the one hadn, this may be a cheap method of fuelling investment means to large parts of the economy, but on the other this leads to a heavy reliance on insider financing without efficient outside control, which should ideally prevent structural imbalances. In case of worse economic conditions, especially low oil prices, these large conglomerates may turn out to be large failures. Consider the case of South Korean "chaebols" in the aftermath of the Asian crisis in 1997 (however, as regards capital formation, they worked quite well in previous decades, albeit under different circumstances than Russia, see Rodrik, 1994 or 1996, 17–21; Young, 1993). All in all, one may argue that without proper control by markets the depreciation of capital may go up, leading to a lower steady state level of capital intensity and per-capita-income in the long run.

It seems reasonable that by drawing conclusions on these issues governed by theoretical considerations, that the growth perspectives of the Russian economy are constrained by an underdeveloped financial sector, which leads first to lower investment as a result of a lower effective savings ratio and, second, to a higher macroeconomic depreciation of capital. Both effects are supposed to lower the steady state-value of per-capita-income. C.p. this may result in a slower and not that far-reaching catching up-process compared to transition countries with more advanced financial sectors.

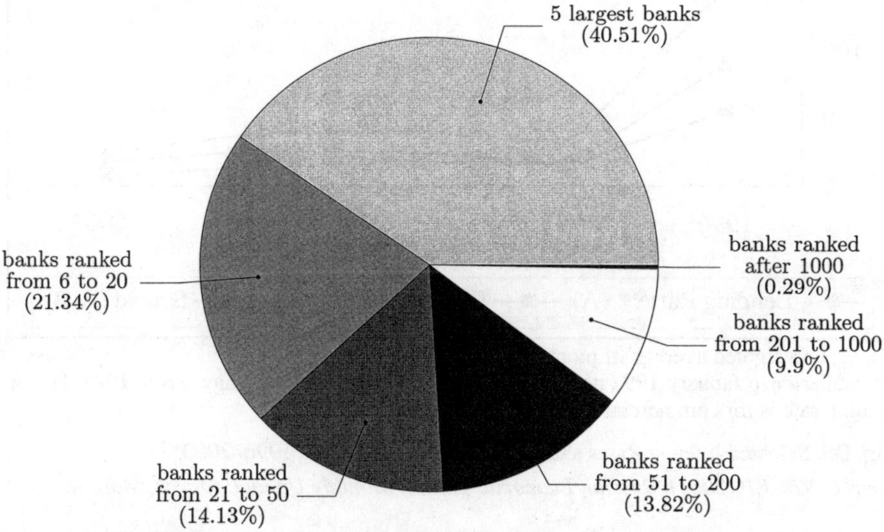


**Fig. D4.** Concentration of Assets in Banking Industry in % of total assets, bank ranking according to asset value
*Source: CBR (2000) Bulletin of Banking Statistics No. 10, Moscow; own calculations.*

**Table D3.** Selected Indicators for the Performance of Banks as Financial Intermediaries in Russia

| | 1995 | 1996* | 1997 | 1998 | 1999 | 2000 |
|---|---|---|---|---|---|---|
| M2 (Broad Money Supply) | 220,8 | 288,3 | 374,1 | 448,3 | 704,7 | 1144,3 |
| GDP (in bn Rb) | 1540,5 | 2145,7 | 2478,6 | 2725,8 | 4607 | 6946,5 |
| Ratio of M2 to GDP | 0,14 | 0,13 | 0,15 | 0,16 | 0,15 | 0,16 |
| Total Assets of Banking Sector (A) | 342,3 | 497,7 | 622,7 | 933,1 | 1549,7 | 2259,4 |
| Claims on the Private Sector (B) | 133,8 | 157,3 | 225,9 | 346 | 521,6 | 867,1 |
| (B)/(A) | 0,39 | 0,32 | 0,36 | 0,37 | 0,34 | 0,38 |
| Rouble Deposits by Russian Citizens (C) | 70,6 | 118,4 | 148,2 | 149,5 | 211,1 | 308,9 |
| Foreign Currency Deposits (D) | 55,3 | 69,4 | 80,5 | 190,9 | 290,2 | 420,1 |
| (C)/(D) | 1,28 | 1,71 | 1,84 | 0,78 | 0,73 | 0,74 |

* There is a break in the series from December 1996 onwards, from then it includes only deposits at banks with active licences.

*Source: RECEP (2000) Russian Economic Trends. Monthly Update: March, Moscow*

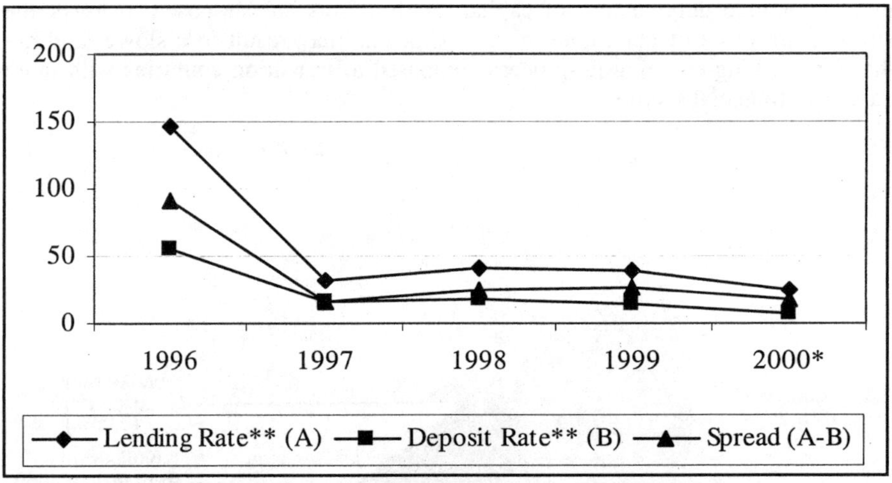


*In %; unweighted average of monthly data.
**Data prior to January 1997 not compatible with current methodology. From 1998 data on lending rate is for commercial banks excluding Sberbank.

**Fig. D5.** Selected Interest Rates and Related Spread in Russia 1996–2000*

*Source: RECEP (2001), Russian Economic Trends, Monthly Update: March, Moscow.*

## 2.2 Human Capital and Growth

As our focus shifts from the financial sector to the relationship between the stock and skill structure of human capital of an economy to economic development, our view on the neoclassical model is distracted from the process of convergence, which the savings ratio and capital depreciation is supposed to govern as regards to speed and target value of k and y. In standard neoclassical terms, long-term growth of per-capita-income (when the steady state-level is finally reached) can only occur if an exogenous, factor-efficiency enhancing element is integrated into the model. This is usually done by technological progress, which enhances either the efficiency of capital (Hicks) or labour (Harrod) or the total factor productivity (Solow).

Education as human capital stock accumulation is viewed as a factor to improve labour efficiency; to integrate this, the per-capita production function is thus modified to

(3) $y = f(k)$, with $k = K/(L\ h)$

with h representing a factor to measure the efficiency of labour employed, or, to put it in terms of human capital, h represent the average value of human capital per unit labour L employed. According to the Lucas (1988; see also Lucas, 1993) and Uzawa (1965) models, one may endogenize h by introducing a second sector to the economy which 'produces' education leading to an enhancement of human capital stock. People can choose to use their labour force (their working hours) L either in the goods-producing sector of the economy or in the educational sector, in the sense that they increase their personal stock of human capital and their labour efficiency, with u representing the share of labour force used in the y-sector and (1–u) the share used in the h-sector. The growth rate (dh) of the labour efficiency factor h is therefore governed by gross human capital accumulation A(1–u) hL, from which the depreciation of human capital •H, similar to the depreciation of physical capital, is subtracted:

(4) $dh = A(1-u)\ hL - \bullet H$

with A as an efficiency factor for the education sector of a country. As Lucas (1988) shows, this modification of the Solow-model is able to explain theoretically positive growth rates of per-capita income of an economy even after it has reached its long term equilibrium in an endogenous way rather than simply resorting to an exogenous factor. Usually, this effect of human capital on economic development is explained by a special property of knowledge as human capital. Since it can be viewed ate least partial as a non-rival good, knowledge can be used, once it is acquired, as often as necessary, until it becomes outdated by further technological development or structural shifts in production. Romer (1986, 1990) argues that knowledge creates spill-over effects which lead to higher returns on capital and hence to endogenous growth via human capital accumulation.

The Uzawa-Lucas-model provides a first, albeit rather simple theoretical explanation on how education and human capital might influence economic development. Human capital in this model is a homogenous good, but the skills and structure of human capital is what really matters. The complementary relationship between technological progress and its adaptation in the form of human capital and hence in the production process is of crucial importance in this respect. Sorensen (1999) takes heed of both factors and their complementarity by constructing a growth model similar to Romer's (1990), adding to the latter an educational sector. Sorensen distinguishes in his model two different stages of economic development as regards to a particular threshold level of human capital stock; first a stage with a low level of human capital, a level below a critical value (and a related low level of per-capita-income), and second a stage with human capital stock above that threshold level. The difference between these two stages is shown as regards the driving forces of economic growth: an economy below the critical level is only able to sustain long-term growth of per-capita-income if investment in human capital per period is high enough, which points to the importance of the educational sector in adapting and coping with technologies from abroad, so that these can be applied in the countries production sector. Enhancing human capital and innovation activities is what matters here for sustained growth. One may argue that openness of a country with respect to trade and foreign direct investment, with which innovative technologies are often related (Saggi, 2000), is of crucial importance for economic development in the earlier stage. As the economy reaches the threshold level of human capital, research and development of new technologies sets in within the country itself. Sorensen (1999) argues that due to its already accumulated knowledge and the related capabilities of applying technological progress in production, the marginal product of research and development within the country is now high enough to attract investment in the R&D-sector, and self-generated technological progress together with further enhancement of human capital stock become the driving forces of growth in per-capita-income.

There is empirical evidence for a positive relationship between the accumulation of human capital and economic growth, too (Barro, 1992; Mankiw/Romer/Weil, 1992), but a respectable amount of studies also exist which attribute a negative impact of particular forms of human capital accumulation on economic growth (Pritchett, 1996; Benhabib/Spiegel, 1994). One explanation for the latter may be that schooling as an indicator for the stock of human capital, measured by the primary or secondary school enrolment rate, does not or only up to a certain level create human capital suitable for further productivity and economic growth (see for further considerations Lopez/Thomas/Wang, 1999). However, it seems clear that human capital does not by itself create more efficient use of production factors. What is much more important is the structure of human capital: who gets educated, what is learned, and when. Only when acknowledging this may one conclude that human capital indeed plays a crucial role for the growth prospects of a country.

Surprisingly, the role of human capital has been neglected somehow in the scholarly literature when considering economic strategies for Russia (one major Russian contribution to the issue comes from Dobrynin/Dyatlov/Tsyrenoba, 1999); a theoretical analysis on this issue contribute Fan/Overland/Spagat (1999) who develop a multi-generation model on the impact of human capital accumulation for Russia. On the one hand, they argue that Russia's human capital is currently in a rather precarious position, because incentives to acquire human capital (first of all private returns on education) have fallen sharply during transition. This seems to be not quite reasonable given the distorted socialist wage structure created to equalize wages according to different skill levels on a broad scale. On the other hand, Russia has a rather solid stock of human capital which should enable the country to overcome an intergenerational education gap in case of prolonged incentive failures for the acquisition of human capital. However, as they argue, this might hold only if the educational infrastructure is soon restructured and better equipped. A low-budget educational sector and high unequal income structures among the population may therefore lead to a deterioration of the stock of human capital and hence to shrinking long-term growth prospects. Empirical evidence on how private returns to human capital have developed in Russia during the transition period is provided by Nesterova/Sabirianova (1999). Contrary to Fan/Overland/Spagat (1999), they show that private returns on education increased during transition. However, this increase must be seen before the background of the former socialist centralized wage setting system, which did not provide much incentives for accumulating human capital as rates of return for education were comparably low due to centralized wage-setting, which had to satisfy political goals rather than skill levels.

As regards unemployment among different skill levels, one may argue that incentives to enhance qualifications and broaden skills have somehow improved. Table D4 shows that in Russia unemployment figures have risen with all kinds of educational levels. However, the increase for tertiary and vocational level was lower compared to the two lowest levels. But compared to transition countries like Hungary or the Czech Republic, where unemployment among the higher educated levels (tertiary and vocational) remained broadly constant, this rising disparity, which suggests a lower probability for unemployment by increasing skill level, is much less impressive.

**Table D4.** Unemployment by Educational Level in Selected Transition Countries (percentage of corresponding labour force)

| Country | Education level | 1992 | 1993 | 1994 | 1995 | 1996 | 1997 |
|---|---|---|---|---|---|---|---|
| Czech | Total | - | 3.9 | 3.7 | 3.6 | 3.7 | 4.3 |
| Republic | Primary or less | - | 8.8 | 8.1 | 10.3 | 11.2 | 13.4 |
| | General | - | 2.7 | 2.6 | 2.0 | 2.1 | 2.8 |
| | Vocational | - | 3.6 | 3.7 | 3.4 | 3.5 | 3.9 |
| | Tertiary | - | 1.9 | 1.4 | 1.1 | 0.6 | 1.2 |
| Hungary | Total | 9.7 | 12.0 | 10.8 | 10.2 | 10.5 | 9.3 |
| | Primary or less | 14.3 | 17.4 | 16.0 | 16.0 | 16.3 | 16.0 |
| | General | 6.7 | 8.6 | 7.8 | 6.8 | 7.2 | 6.1 |
| | Vocational | 11.3 | 14.5 | 12.8 | 12.2 | 12.7 | 10.6 |
| | Tertiary | 2.3 | 2.9 | 2.9 | 2.7 | 3.1 | 1.9 |
| Poland | Total | 12.9 | 13.8 | 14.0 | 12.6 | 12.4 | 11.3 |
| | Primary or less | 12.0 | 14.0 | 15.0 | 13.8 | 13.7 | 14.3 |
| | General | 13.8 | 13.0 | 13.1 | 12.0 | 11.8 | 10.4 |
| | Vocational | 15.5 | 17.4 | 17.4 | 15.7 | 15.4 | 13.5 |
| | Tertiary | 6.6 | 6.0 | 5.2 | 4.1 | 3.6 | 3.7 |
| Russian Federation | Total * | 4.9 | 5.6 | 7.9 | 9.2 | 9.5 | - |
| | Primary or less | 5.8 | 6.7 | 9.8 | 11.6 | 13.0 | - |
| | General | 5.8 | 6.6 | 9.8 | 11.5 | 11.6 | - |
| | Vocational | 4.3 | 5.1 | 6.8 | 8.1 | 8.5 | - |
| | Tertiary | 3.2 | 3.4 | 4.7 | 4.8 | 4.4 | - |

Data are second quarter labour force survey data.
*1992–1995 data is for fourth quarter; 1996 data is for first quarter.

*Source: Berryman SE (2000) Hidden Challenges to Education Systems in Transition Economies. World Bank, Washington DC, p 121*

During Russia's transition and in particular among its major economic problems (decreasing income levels in line with increasing inequality and poverty) the maintenance of the level of human capital is of special importance and should not be neglected, especially if there are other important requirements (e.g. austerity of public budgets) which must be met. Cutting education expenditures seems to be rather easy (in contrast to expenditures related to political pressure groups like miners, pensioners, or the business lobby), but welfare costs in terms of lower future growth prospects might be even higher. Total public expenditures on education as percentage of GDP have remained on a low level, especially when compared to other transition countries (see table D5; see also table D7 in the appendix for more detailed data on educational aspects, note in particular the sharp contraction of new school construction). The slowdown as regards quantity and quality by public educational institutions has been partially offset by private institutions (private primary and secondary schools as well as universities) which emerged to an increasing extent during the 1990s (see table D6). However, only the share of students in private universities (6,2% of the total in 1996) is of considerable importance for the educational sector, whereas the number of pupils in private schools remains neglectable. But this picture might change as the quality of public provision of educational services further decreases. Since private schools and universities usually charge a high fee from pupils and students, this development will lead to growing disparities regarding qualification levels between different income groups of the Russian population. This situation is aggravated by an already high income inequality in Russia, which may have further adverse effects for overall economic development (Welfens/Wiegert, 2001).

**Table D5.** Total Public Expenditures on Education (percentage of GDP)

| Country | 1989 | 1990 | 1991 | 1992 | 1993 | 1994 | 1995 | 1996 | 1997 |
|---|---|---|---|---|---|---|---|---|---|
| Czech Republic | 4.0 | 4.1 | 4.1 | 4.5 | 5.2 | 5.4 | 5.3 | 5.3 | 4.7 |
| Hungary | 5.7 | 5.8 | 6.3 | 6.6 | 6.5 | 6.4 | 5.5 | 4.9 | 4.3 |
| Poland | - | 4.8 | 5.1 | 5.4 | 5.4 | 5.3 | 5.2 | 5.4 | 5.5 |
| Russian Federation | - | 3.7 | 3.6 | 3.6 | 4.0 | 4.5 | 3.6 | 3.8 | 4.2 |

- Not available

*Source: Berryman SE (2000), Hidden Challenges to Education Systems in Transition Economies. World Bank, Washington DC, p 123*

**Table D6.** Selected Data on Private Schools in Russia (share of total in percent)

| | 1993 | 1994 | 1995 | 1996 | 1997 |
|---|---|---|---|---|---|
| Pre-schools | | | | | |
| 0Number of private pre-schools | 13,9 | 11 | 9,1 | 7,7 | .. |
| Capacity in private pre-schools | 8,5 | 4,4 | 5,7 | 5,2 | .. |
| Primary education (classes 1–4) | | | | | |
| Number of private schools | 0,6 | 0,7 | 0,8 | 0,7 | .. |
| Students in private schools | 0,2 | 0,3 | 0,3 | 0,3 | .. |
| Lower secondary (classes 5–9) | | | | | |
| Number of private schools | 0,3 | 0,2 | 0,6 | 0,8 | .. |
| Students in private schools | 0,1 | 0,1 | 0,2 | 0,2 | .. |
| Upper secondary (classes 10–12) | | | | | |
| Number of private schools | 0,6 | 0,8 | 0,8 | 0,9 | .. |
| Students in private schools | 0,2 | 0,3 | 0,3 | 0,3 | .. |
| Upper secondary, vocational | | | | | |
| Students in private schools | 0,2 | 0,2 | 0,2 | 0,2 | 0,2 |
| Tertiary, non-university degree | | | | | |
| Students in private schools | .. | .. | 0,3 | 0,5 | 0,8 |
| Tertiary, university degree | | | | | |
| 1Students in private schools | 2,7 | 4,2 | 4,9 | 5,5 | 6,2 |

*Source: Canning M; Heleniak T; Moock P (1999) Reforming Education in the Regions of Russia. World Bank Technical Paper No. 457: 54*

As regards the reform of the educational system in Russia two major challenges arise: first, the level of human capital already achieved (from literacy to technological capabilities) has to be preserved and, second, the system should be brought in accordance with market requirements. It seems fairly clear that, like the production structure of the economy itself, the education system of the socialist period was distorted and designed to fulfil the respective requirements, which are not in line with those of a modern market economy. Therefore, ensuring flexibility among various kinds of occupations through retraining efforts is a key factor in decreasing the risk of unemployment among the former socialist workforce. As Sabirianova (2000) shows, occupational mobility has risen considerably during the transition period in Russia. However, occupational mobility has increased, which points to a growing degree of flexibility among Russia's working population (but also to increasing depreciation of earlier acquired human capital which was related to the former occupation). Friebel/Guriev (1999) state that worker mobility remained comparably low in Russia due to various kinds of labour market regulations and non-monetary benefits which workers are supposed to loose when leaving their current job.

Lopez/Thomas/Wang (1999) derive, among other aspects, three important features about the link between human capital and growth. First, the higher the level of human capital already achieved the better its owner is able to acquire more; second, the broader the educational base (starting with literacy) among the population, the higher the growth potential and, third, the more open a country, the stronger the link between human capital and growth. As regards the second point, the decreasing share of total enrolment rates in primary and secondary schools in Russia is particularly worrying (see table D8 in the appendix).

Given its broad educational and intellectual base, Russia surely has rather good prospects in relation to the first two points, far better than those of Korea in the 1960s, for example, which had to start with a primary school campaign to create educational conditions for a highly developed economy. As regards Russia's openness, it still seems to be rather difficult for foreigners to do business in Russia. Of course, Russia is not the closed economy to the West that it was a decade ago, but there is a substantial lack of foreign participation in the country's business sectors, considering the rather large potentials in this respect. Thus one may conclude that educational and knowledge exchange between Russia and its neighbours, first of all the western ones, seems to be rather poorly developed. The business and educational environment for staff exchange on the scientific level must therefore be improved.

Beneath financial issues, the efficiency of the educational sector in creating human capital and enhancing skills (factor A in the human capital function dh) with given resources is of course of crucial importance. According to a case study of the University of Tomsk, Hare/Lugachyov (1997) raise four aspects which influence the efficiency of the education system, in particular universities and research institutions:

- ownership, property rights, and governance issues
- funding issues and the state budget
- tax regime
- non-functioning of the market economy (demonetization and barter problems)

These aspects are almost directly related to the federal government's policy decisions, reflecting nearly all necessary reforms usually claimed to implemented. Some additional factors arise when considering the state of the Russian educational system. Hare/Lugachyov (1997) show the consequences of these problems by studying the case of the University of Tomsk:

- the educational system is rather diversified and its higher institutions (e.g. universities) are related to and guided by various federal ministries or by the State Committee for Higher Education, which is largely responsible for coordination between the various actors,
- the use of the assets of educational institutions is not at their disposal or at the disposal of related ministries/ committees, but at the government's agency for the administration of state properties.

One must note that universities and other scientific institutions face almost the same problems as other economic actors, i.e. private enterprises. Their environment is therefore similarly distorted and hence they are required to act beneath their core activities. The diversified structure and the various and somehow arbitrarily given responsibilities lead to a highly intransparent organization of the Russian higher education system. This refers first of all to the funding process, which seems to be highly inefficient due to a lack of feedback information between the educational institution and its responsible ministry/committee. Also the centralized property of most of the universities' assets is a major roadblock for a critical minimum of flexibility which an educational institution needs.

## 3 Conclusion and Policy Options

Theoretical and empirical results acknowledge that both human capital and the efficiency of financial markets play an important role for economic development. Transition countries and Russia in particular are no exception in this case. Whereas the differences in output since the beginning of the transition process are almost due to other factors like adverse initial conditions, institutional shortcomings, and fiscal and monetary policy failures, the relative importance of these two factors examined here will increase in the future after a certain level of stability is achieved.

As regards the development of human capital stock, three main aspects are important:

- incentives to improve skills and qualifications among the labour force,
- efficiency of the education system,
- broad-ranged access to basic and higher education with respect to different social groups.

Russia faces problems as regards to all of these main aspects. However, returns to human capital and hence incentives for acquisition of skills and qualifications have improved during the transition period. This also holds for the flexibility of the labour force. More severe restrictions for human capital development are set by the inefficiencies of the educational system in Russia. First of all, when disregarding shrinking financial resources provided to the public educational institutions, the low degree of transparency among the budgetary process and the distribution of funds to the educational institutions makes addressing the efficiency problem virtually impossible. More transparent decision-making procedures and funding as well as clearer rules for the sources and distribution of funds to educational institutions are required. Furthermore, indicators for the efficiency of educational services have to be developed (e.g. according to Canning/Moock/ Heleniak, 1999) before reforms in the educational sector can be seriously discussed. The maintenance of the public educational services at a high level is also important as income inequality has risen considerable during transition. Usually, private schools provide on the one hand more efficient and market-oriented educational services, but on the other hand their rising importance bears the danger of excluding large groups of the population from high-qualified educational services as long as there is no adequate funding mechanism for members of lower income groups in place.

Russia's financial sector has not yet overcome the tensions from the past financial crisis in 1998; many problems related to bankrupt and debt-ridden banks still remain unresolved. So there is no wonder that trust in banks and hence their ability to act as financial intermediaries is quite low. When considering policy options, numerous suggestions and proposals for financial sector reform already exist, including honest bank restructuring efforts, the introduction of accounting principles for an honest and fair view of enterprises performance, the withdrawal of the state out of the banking sector in the sense that political and economic goals should be separated (the federal government was unable to provide a list of all public shares in the Russian banking sector, i.e. as the handling of public accounts is a major income source for Russian banks, this business is subject to huge lobbying efforts and to a political/economic relationship between government and related private banks), and the general issue of bringing a higher degree of competition to the banking sector (EBRD, 2000; OECD, 2000; Buch/Heinrich, 2000). Foreign banks, although their role is limited mainly due to political reasons, can play an important role in the Russian market in regards to the provision of financial services and even consultants for foreign direct investment. With increasing economic stability they should be willing to engage there with enhanced effort.

According to its functions in a market economy (allocating physical capital resources and raising funds for financing investment), the influence of the Russian financial sector on economic development is neglectable in the sense of the explanations attributed to the neoclassical model in chapter 2.1. Reflecting these theoretical considerations, in the long-term Russia may lag behind other transition countries with a higher developed financial sector and a healthier banking system without using its entire growth potential. Capital resources are wasted due to malfunctioning allocation and a low ability of banks in raising financial funds, and in addition, the banking sector in Russia appears to be rather costly with respect to the still high interest rate-spreads. Russia should therefore be able to realize large gains from financial sector reform as regards its future growth potential.

# Appendix

**Table D7.** Selected Data on Education Finance in Russia, 1989–1997

| | 1989 | 1990 | 1991 | 1992 | 1993 | 1994 | 1995 | 1996 | 1997 |
|---|---|---|---|---|---|---|---|---|---|
| Education expenditures | | | | | | | | | |
| as a share of GDP (in %) | na | na | na | 3.58 | 4.03 | 4.36 | 3.51 | 3.75 | 4.07 |
| as share of total federal budget expenditures (in %) | na | na | na | 5.90 | 3.80 | 3.57 | 3.28 | 2.80 | 3.51 |
| as share of total regional budget expenditures (in %) | na | na | na | 14.89 | 15.31 | 19.83 | 19.80 | 21.11 | 21.14 |
| Average wage in education, total[1] | 183.6 | 202.9 | 338.8 | 3.7 | 40.1 | 152.2 | 309.2 | 551.5 | 587.4 |
| in higher educational institutions[1] | 202.6 | 236.0 | 472.3 | 4.5 | 41.8 | 186.2 | 365.1 | 610.6 | na |
| in specialized secondary institutions[1] | 206.4 | 221.8 | 410.0 | 3.9 | 46.3 | 176.0 | 358.0 | 639.2 | na |
| in compulsory schools[1] | 175.5 | 193.4 | 374.9 | 3.6 | 44.5 | 163.4 | 359.5 | 587.5 | 592.2 |
| Average wage in education compared to average wage in economy in % | 71.0 | 68.4 | 61.4 | 60.5 | 68.3 | 69.1 | 65.5 | 69.8 | 62.8 |
| in higher educational institutions[4] | 78.3 | 79.5 | 85.6 | 73.5 | 71.2 | 84.5 | 77.3 | 77.3 | na |
| in specialized secondary institutions[4] | 79.8 | 74.7 | 74.3 | 63.9 | 78.9 | 79.9 | 75.8 | 80.9 | na |
| in compulsory schools[4] | 67.9 | 65.2 | 67.9 | 58.4 | 75.8 | 74.1 | 76.1 | 74.3 | 63.3 |
| New school construction | | | | | | | | | |
| Pre-schools[2] | 284.0 | 225.0 | 147.0 | 95.7 | 60.3 | 42.1 | 28.2 | 20.0 | na |
| Compulsory schools[2] | 645.0 | 545.0 | 396.0 | 303.1 | 296.3 | 194.0 | 218.0 | 152.2 | na |
| Primary-professional institutions[2] | na | 14.3 | na | 8.4 | 12.0 | 8.4 | 3.0 | 3.0 | na |
| Specialized secondary institutions[3] | na | 67.8 | na | 22.8 | 11.0 | 45.4 | 13.6 | 11.5 | na |
| Higher educational institutions[3] | na | 204.0 | na | 139.3 | 84.6 | 61.1 | 62.7 | 63.9 | na |
| Number of compulsory schools needing capital repair | na | na | 19637 | na | 21821 | na | 23176 | 23600 | 24100 |
| As a share of all compulsory schools which are condemned | na | na | 28.1 | na | 31.1 | na | 32.1 | 34.6 | 35.0 |
| Number of compulsory schools which are condemned | na | na | 4014 | na | 4086 | na | 4153 | 4200 | na |
| As a share of all compulsory schools | na | na | 5.7 | na | 5.8 | na | 5.9 | 6.0 | na |

[1] 1989–91 Rubles, 1992–97 thd. Rubles.
[2] thousand places.
[3] thousand sq. meters.
[4] average wage of respective educational institutions compared to average wage in economy in %.

*Source: Canning M, Moock P, Heleniak T (1999) Reforming Education in the Regions of Russia. World Bank Technical Paper No. 457, Washington DC, p 50*

**Table D8.** Selected Data on Vocational and Professional Schools in Russia, 1989–1997

| | 1989 | 1990 | 1991 | 1992 | 1993 | 1994 | 1995 | 1996 | 1997 |
|---|---|---|---|---|---|---|---|---|---|
| Number of primary professional institutions (PTUs) | na | 4328 | 4321 | 4269 | 4273 | 4203 | 4166 | 4114 | na |
| Number of Students in PTUs[1] | na | 1867 | 1841 | 1773 | 1742 | 1699 | 1689 | 1670 | na |
| Number of Students accepted to PTUs[1] | na | 1252 | 1234 | 1096 | 1007 | 949 | 928 | 899 | na |
| Number of graduates from PTUs[1] | na | 1272 | 1141 | 1039 | 922 | 878 | 841 | 821 | na |
| Number of teachers in PTUs | na | na | 166 | 155 | 154 | 154 | 151 | 151 | 157 |
| Number of specialized secondary institutions | 2595 | 2603 | 2605 | 2609 | 2607 | 2574 | 2612 | 2608 | na |
| Students in specialized secondary institutions[1] | 2338 | 2270 | 2202 | 2090 | 1994 | 1871 | 1923 | 1976 | na |
| Number of students accepted[1] | 768 | 754 | 732 | 652 | 644 | 630 | 665 | 662 | na |
| Number of graduates[1] | 640 | 637 | 623 | 585 | 546 | 532 | 473 | 494 | na |
| By speciality: | | | | | | | | | |
| Industry and construction | 907 | 865 | 813 | 764 | 746 | 724 | 771 | 812 | na |
| Agriculture | 317 | 302 | 296 | 290 | 287 | 260 | 254 | 253 | na |
| Transport and communications | 196 | 188 | 178 | 169 | 165 | 157 | 166 | 170 | na |
| Economics and law | 224 | 216 | 210 | 215 | 206 | 188 | 195 | 196 | na |
| Healthcare, physical culture and sport | 306 | 309 | 312 | 277 | 239 | 210 | 214 | 224 | na |
| Education | 338 | 341 | 343 | 322 | 301 | 283 | 269 | 267 | na |
| Art and cinematography | 51 | 50 | 51 | 53 | 50 | 49 | 55 | 53 | na |

[1] in thousands.

*Source: Canning M, Moock P, Heleniak T (1999) Reforming Education in the Regions of Russia. World Bank Technical Paper No. 457, Washington DC, p 53*

**Table D9.** Selected Data on Higher Educational Institutions in Russia, 1989–1997

| | 1989 | 1990 | 1991 | 1992 | 1993 | 1994 | 1995 | 1996 |
|---|---|---|---|---|---|---|---|---|
| Number of higher educational institutions (HEIs) | 512 | 514 | 519 | 535 | 548 | 553 | 569 | 573 |
| Number of students in HEIs, total[1] | 2861 | 2824 | 2763 | 2638 | 2543 | 2543 | 2655 | 2801 |
| By field of study: | | | | | | | | |
| Humanities | na | na | na | na | 242 | 231 | 265 | 284 |
| Social and behavioural sciences | na | na | na | na | 270 | 248 | 321 | 373 |
| Natural sciences | na | na | na | na | 152 | 140 | 138 | 140 |
| Medical science | na | na | na | na | 180 | 167 | 163 | 157 |
| Engineering | na | na | na | na | 830 | 787 | 781 | 799 |
| Other | na | na | na | na | 869 | 960 | 1122 | 1212 |
| Number of universities | 40 | 42 | 48 | 52 | 57 | 72 | 75 | 81 |
| Number of students in universities | 309 | 328 | 382 | 390 | 393 | 508 | 522 | 590 |
| Number of students accepted into HEIs (thousands) | 603 | 584 | 566 | 521 | 544 | 568 | 629 | 674 |
| Number of graduates from HEIs[1] | 433 | 401 | 407 | 425 | 444 | 407 | 396 | 415 |
| By speciality: | | | | | | | | |
| Industry and construction[1] | 162 | 145 | 145 | 155 | 164 | 145 | 133 | 137 |
| Agriculture[1] | 38 | 36 | 36 | 35 | 41 | 31 | 31 | 34 |
| Transport and communications[1] | 22 | 19 | 21 | 22 | 22 | 19 | 17 | 18 |
| Economics and law[1] | 38 | 38 | 39 | 35 | 30 | 33 | 36 | 39 |
| Healthcare, physical culture and sport[1] | 32 | 28 | 29 | 34 | 33 | 34 | 31 | 33 |
| Education[1] | 138 | 132 | 134 | 141 | 149 | 142 | 143 | 150 |
| Art and cinematography[1] | 4 | 4 | 4 | 4 | 4 | 3 | 5 | 5 |
| Number of private HEIs | na | na | na | na | na | 157 | 193 | 244 |
| Number of students in private HEIs[1] | na | na | na | na | na | 111 | 136 | 163 |
| As share of all students in HEIs | na | na | na | na | na | 4,2 | 4,9 | 5,5 |

[1] in thousands

*Source: Canning M, Moock P, Heleniak T (1999) Reforming Education in the Regions of Russia. World Bank Technical Paper No. 457, Washington DC, p 53*

**Table D10.** School Enrolment Rates in Selected Transition Countries

| Country | 1989 | 1990 | 1991 | 1992 | 1993 | 1994 | 1995 | 1996 | 1997 |
|---|---|---|---|---|---|---|---|---|---|
| Basic Education Enrolment Rates (gross rates, percentage of 6/7–14/15 age group) | | | | | | | | | |
| Czech Republic[1] | 97.6 | 98.6 | 98.7 | 99.2 | 99.1 | 99.5 | 99.4 | 99.2 | 99.1 |
| Hungary[2] | 99.0 | 99.2 | 99.2 | 99.2 | 99.1 | 99.1 | 99.1 | 99.2 | 99.2 |
| Poland[3] | 97.9 | 97.5 | 97.3 | 97.1 | 97.2 | 97.1 | 97.2 | 97.4 | 98.0 |
| Russian Federation[4] | 93.0 | 93.6 | 94.4 | 93.3 | 91.9 | 90.7 | 91.3 | 91.4 | 90.8 |
| General Upper Secondary Enrolment Rates (gross rates, percentage of 15–18 age group) | | | | | | | | | |
| Czech Republic | 15.9 | 16.1 | 15.6 | 15.9 | 16.5 | 17.6 | 18.8 | 18.8 | - |
| Hungary | 19.7 | 19.8 | 19.5 | 19.5 | 19.2 | 20.0 | 21.2 | 22.3 | 23.6 |
| Poland | 21.0 | 21.7 | 23.3 | 24.9 | 26.4 | 28.1 | 29.7 | 30.5 | 32.3 |
| Russian Federation | 24.7 | 22.5 | 33.9 | 22.9 | 22.6 | 23.7 | 24.6 | 26.0 | 27.7 |
| Vocational/Technical Upper Secondary Enrolment Rates (gross rates, percentage of 15–18 age group) | | | | | | | | | |
| Czech Republic | 73.6 | 69.2 | 62.9 | 60.6 | 62.7 | 78.2 | 81.0 | 66.2 | 65.3 |
| Hungary | 62.7 | 62.7 | 59.8 | 56.8 | 54.3 | 54.6 | 57.2 | 60.0 | 62.0 |
| Poland | 72.2 | 70.9 | 69.0 | 67.8 | 67.7 | 68.0 | 67.6 | 67.5 | 67.4 |
| Russian Federation | 54.1 | 50.8 | 49.0 | 46.4 | 44.2 | 41.7 | 41.8 | 41.9 | 41.9 |
| Overall Upper Secondary Enrolment Rates (academic and vocational/technical secondary education) | | | | | | | | | |
| Czech Republic | 89.5 | 85.3 | 78.5 | 76.5 | 79.2 | 95.8 | 99.8 | 85.0 | 65.3 |
| Hungary | 82.4 | 82.5 | 79.2 | 76.3 | 73.4 | 74.6 | 78.4 | 82.3 | 85.7 |
| Poland | 93.2 | 92.5 | 92.2 | 92.7 | 94.2 | 96.1 | 97.3 | 98.1 | 99.6 |
| Russian Federation | 78.8 | 75.8 | 72.9 | 69.3 | 66.9 | 65.4 | 66.4 | 67.9 | 69.5 |
| Tertiary Enrolment Rates (gross rates, percentage of 18–22 age group) | | | | | | | | | |
| Czech Republic | 12.7 | 13.6 | 13.1 | 13.3 | 13.6 | 14.2 | 15.0 | 16.6 | 17.3 |
| Hungary[5] | 13.9 | 14.2 | 14.8 | 15.7 | 16.8 | 18.5 | 20.7 | 22.9 | 23.8 |
| Poland[6] | 11.6 | 12.4 | 13.0 | 14.3 | 15.7 | 17.0 | 18.1 | 19.7 | 20.6 |
| Russian Federation | 16.7 | 17.0 | 17.1 | 16.9 | 16.4 | 16.1 | 16.9 | 17.6 | 18.7 |

[1] 6–14 year olds.
[2] 6–13 year olds.
[3] 7–14 year olds.
[4] 7–15 year olds.
[5] Net rate.
[6] Based on 19–24 age group.

*Source: Berryman SE (2000) Hidden Challenges to Education Systems in Transition Economies. The World Bank, Washington DC, p 111–114, 117*

## References


Aslund A (2001) The Myth of Output Collapse after Communism.Washington D.C.: Carnegie Endowment for International Peace, mimeo

Aslund A, Boone P, Johnson S (1996) How to Stabilize: Lessons from Post-communist Countries.Brookings Papers on Economic Activity 1: 217–291

Balzer H (1993) Science, Technology and Education in the Former USSR. In: Sharpe ME, Kaufman R, Hardt JP (eds) The Former Soviet Union in Transition. Armonk, NY, pp 889–908

Barro R (1991) Economic Growth in a Cross-Section of Countries. Quarterly Journal Economics 106(2): 407–444

Barro RJ (1992) Human Capital and Economic Growth. In: Federal Reserve Bank of Kansas City (ed) Policies for Long-Run Economic Growth. Symposium Series, Kansas City, pp 199–216

Barro RJ, Sala-I-Martin X (1995) Economic Growth. New York

Beck Th, Demirgüc-Kunt A, Levine R (1999) A New Database on Financial Development and Structure. World Bank Working Paper No. 2146, Washington D.C.

Benhabib J, Spiegel M (1994) The Role of Human Capital in Economic Development: Evidence from Cross-National Aggregate Data. Journal of Monetary Economics

Berkovitz D, De Jong DN (1998a) Russia's Internal Border. Regional Science and Urban Economics 29: 633–649

Berkovitz D, De Jong DN (1998b) Accounting for Growth in Post-Soviet Russia.

Berryman SE (2000) Hidden Challenges to Education Systems in Transition Economies.: The World Bank, Washington D.C.

Bossone B (1999) Financial Development and Industrial Capital Accumulation. World Bank Working Paper No. 2201, Washington D.C.

Brenton P, Gros D, Vandille G (1997) Output Decline and Recovery in Transition Economies: Causes and Social Consequences. Economics of Transition 5 (1): 113–129

Buch CM, Heinrich RP (1999) Handling Banking Crisis: The Case of Russia. Economic Systems 23: 349–380

Buiter WH (2000) From Predation to Accumulation? The second Transition Decade in Russia. Economics of Transition 8: 603–622

Buiter WH, Lago R, Rey H (1998) Financing Transition: Investing in Enterprises during Transition. EBRD Working Paper No. 35, London

Campos NF (1999) Back to the Future: The Growth Prospects of Transition Economies Reconsidered. Working Paper No. 229, April, The William Davidson Institute

Canning M, Moock P, Heleniak T (1999) Reforming Education in the Regions of Russia. World Bank Technical Paper No. 457, Washington D.C.

CBR - Central Bank of Russia (2000) Bulletin of Banking Statistics: October, Moscow

De Melo M, Gelb A (1997) Transition to Date: A Comparative Overview. In: Zecchini S (ed) Lessons from Economic Transition: Central and Eastern Europe in the 1990s. Kluwer Publishers, Dordrecht

Denizer C (1997) Stabilisation, Adjustment and Growth Prospect in Transition Economies. World Bank Working Paper No. 1855, November, Washington D.C.

DIW/IFW (2000) Rußlands Aufschwung in Gefahr. DIW Wochenbericht Nr. 50/2000: 843–864

Dobrynin AI, Dyatlov SA, Tsyrenoba ED (1999) Chelovecheskij Kapital v Transitivnoj Ekonomike: Formirovanie, Otsenka, Effektivnoct' Ispol'zoovaniya. Nauka , St. Petersburg

EBRD (1997) Transition Report 1997. EBRD, London

EBRD (1998) Transition Report 1998. EBRD, London

EBRD (1999) Transition Report 1999. EBRD, London

EBRD (2000) Transition Report 2000. EBRD, London

Fan CS, Overland J, Spagat M (1999) Human Capital, Growth and Inequality in Russia. Journal of Comparative Economics 27: 618–643

Fischer S, Sahay R, Vegh C (1996a) Economies in Transition: the Beginnings of Growth. American Economic Review Papers and Proceedings 86 (2): 229–233

Fischer S, Sahay R, Vegh C (1996b) Stabilization and Growth in Transition Economies: The Early Experience. Journal of Economic Perspectives: 45–66

Fischer S, Sahay R, Vegh C (1998) From Transition to Market: Evidence and Growth Prospects. IMF Working Paper No. 52, Washington D.C.

Friebel G, Guriev S (1999) Why Russian Worker Do not Move: Attachment of Workers Through In-Kind Payments. William Davidson Institute Working Paper No. 283

Gavrilenkov E (2001) Long Term Structural Change and Productivity Growth in Russia (Notes on Basic Premises of Russia's Economic Strategy). In: Lane T, Gavrilenkov E, Oding N, Welfens PJJ (eds) Economic Development and Modernization in Russia and Eastern Europe. Springer, Heidelberg and New York

Gerschenkron A (1962) Economic Backwardness in Historical Perspective: A Book of Essays. Praeger, New York and London

Greenwood J, Jovanovic B (1990) Financial Development, Growth and the Distribution of Income. Journal of Political Economy 98 (5): 1076–1107

Hare PG, Lugachyov M (1997) Higher Education in Transition to a Market Economy: A Case Study. CERT Discussion Paper 1997/17, Edinburgh

Hellman JS, Jones G, Kaufmann D (2000) "Seize the State, Seize the Day". State Capture, Corruption and Influence in Transition. World Bank Policy Research Working paper No. 2444, Washington D.C.

Heybey B, Murrell P (1997) The Relationship between Economic Growth and the Speed of Liberalization During Transition.

IMF (1999) Russian Federation: Recent Economic Developments. IMF Staff Country Report No. 99/100, Washington D.C.

Johnson S, Macmillan J, Woodruff C (1999) Property Rights, Finance and Entrepreneurship. SITE Working Paper No. 152, Stockholm

Kashin Yu (2000) Sberegatel'nyj Protsess i Sberegatel'nyj Bank, in: Voprosy Ekonomike, 5/2000, 120–131.

King RG, Levine R (1993) Finance and Growth: Schumpeter Might Be Right. Quarterly Journal of Economics108: 719–737

Kirkow P (1997) Russia's Regional Puzzle: Institutional Change and Economic Adaptation. Communist Economies & Economic Transformation 9: 261–287

Levine R (1997) Financial Development and Economic Growth: Views and Agenda. Journal of Economic Literature 35: 688–726

Levine R, Renelt D (1992) A Sensitive Analysis of Cross-Country Growth Regressions. American Economic Review 82: 942–963

Levine R, Zervos S (1996) Stock Market Development and Long-Run Growth. World Bank Economic Review 10: 323–339

Lopez R, Thomas V, Wang Y (1998) Addressing the Education Puzzle: The Distribution of Education and Economic Reforms. World Bank Working Paper No. 2031, Washington D.C.

Lucas RE (1988) On the Mechanics of Economic Development. Journal of Monetary Economics 22: 3–42

Lucas RE (1993) Making a Miracle. Econometrica 61: 251–272

Mankiw GN (1995) The Growth of Nations. Brookings Papers on Economic Activity: 275–326

Mankiw NG, Romer D, Weil D (1992) A Contribution to the Empirics of Economic Growth. Quarterly Journal of Economics 107: 407–437

McIntyre R (1998) Regional Stabilisation Policy under Transitional Period Conditions in Russia: Price Control, Regional Trade Barriers and Other Local-Level Measures. Europe-Asia Studies 50: 859–871

McKinnon RI (1993) The Order of Economic Liberalization. 2nd ed., The Johns Hopkins University Press, Baltimore, London

Nesterova DV, Sabirianova KZ (1999) Investment in Human Capital Under Economic Transformation in Russia. EERC Working Paper No. 1999/04, Economics Education and Research Consortium, Moskau

OECD (2000) Country Reports: The Russian Federation. Paris

Olenev A (2000) Bankovskaya Sistema v Rossii posle Krizisa: Promezhutochnye Itogi, Tendentsii i Perspektivy. Investitsii v Rossii, Nr. 6: 30–31

Pritchett L (1996) Where Has All the Education Gone? World Bank Policy Research Working Paper No. 1581, Washington D.C.

Rajan RG, Zingales L (1998) Financial Dependence and Growth. The American Economic Review 88: 559–586

RECEP (2000) Russian Economic Trends, Quarterly Issue, Vol. 9, No. 3: 59–65

Robinson J (1952) The Rate of Interest, and other Essays. MacMillan, London

Rodrik D (1995) Getting Interventions Right: How South Korea and Taiwan Grew Rich. Economic Policy 20: 55–107

Rodrik D (1996) Understanding Economic Policy Reform. Journal of Economic Literature 24: 9–41

Romer PM (1986) Increasing Returns and Long-Run Growth. Journal of Political Economy 94: 1002–1037

Romer PM (1990) Endogenous Technological Change. Journal of Political Economy 98 No. 5: 71–102

Sabirianova KZ (2000) The Great Human Capital Reallocation: An Empirical Analysis of Occupational Mobility in Transitional Russia. William Davidson Institute Working Paper No. 309

Sachs JD, Warner AM (1995) Economic Reform and the Process of Global Integration. Brookings Papers on Economic Activity 1: 1–118

Saggi K (2000) Trade, Foreign Direct Investment and International Technology Transfer: A Survey. World Bank Working Paper No. 2349, Washington D.C.

Schneider F, Enste D (2000) Shadow Economies Around the World: Size, Causes and Consequences. IMF Working Paper No. 26/2000, Washington D.C.

Schumpeter JA (1911) The Theory of Economic Development. Harvard University Press, Cambridge, MA

Shleifer A, Vishny R (1999) The Grabbing Hand. Government Pathologies and Their Cures. Harvard UP, Cambridge, Mass.

Solow RM (1956) A Contribution to the Theory of Economic Growth. Quarterly Journal of Economics 70: 65–94

Sorensen A (1999) R&D, Learning, and Phases of Economic Growth. Journal of Economic Growth 4: 429–445

Sutela P (2000) Überwindung der russischen Transformationskrise: Ausgewählte Aspekte und Politikoptionen. In: Welfens PJJ, Wiegert R (eds) Überwindung der Transformationskrise in Rußland. Forthcoming

Tsuru K (2000) Finance and Growth: Some Theoretical Considerations, and a Review of the Empirical Literature: OECD Economics Department Working Paper No. 228, OECD, Paris

Uzawa H (1965) Optimum Technical Change in an Aggregative Model of Economic Growth. International Economic Review 6: 18–31

Welfens PJJ, Wiegert R (2001) Überwindung der Wirtschaftskrise in Rußland. Springer, Heidelberg and New York

World Bank (1995) Russia: Education in Transition. Washington D.C.

World Bank (1996) From Plan to Market. World Development Report 1996. Washington D.C.

Yasin E, Aleksashenko S, Gavrilenkov E, Dvorkovich A (2000) Realizatsiya Liberal'noj Strategii pri Sushchestvuyushchikh Ekonomicheskikh Ogranicheniyakh. Voprosy Ekonomike 7/2000: 4–20

Young A (1993) Lessons from the East Asian NICs: A Contrarian View. NBER Working Paper No. 4482

Zaostrovtsev A (2000), Rent Extraction in a Rent-Seeking Society. Spider Working Paper Series No. 10, St. Petersburg State University, St. Petersburg

# E. Structure and Growth of Private Consumption in Russia and East Germany

Cathleen Faber and Hans Gerhard Strohe

## 1 Introduction

Private consumption is a main part of national accounts. Often private consumption is taken as an early or parallel indicator of economic growth. Data on private consumption is also needed in many other fields of official statistics. Data on private consumption help in forecasting effects of changed tax systems, it is essential in statistics of consumer prices for measuring weighting structures etc. Furthermore, private consumption is an indicator of social welfare and standard of living.

After the collapse of the communist world system at the beginning of the 90s private consumption totally changed in both East Germany and Russia. There were changes in the consumer's preferences, and consumer's behavior, in the assortments of retail outlets as well as in supplies and demands. There were totally different necessities to satisfy.

This paper analyzes structure and growth of private consumption in Russia and East Germany comparatively. The analysis of growth is determined to be a quantitative analysis of data on private consumption. The analysis of structure is a rather quality-orientated analysis. Private consumption is determined by two factors: the price of goods and services on one hand and their volume on the other. The following three examples demonstrate that unchanged figures of total value of private consumption can be caused by extremely different situations:

1. People buy the same goods and services as before in the same volume or,
2. They buy cheaper goods and services by a higher volume or,
3. They buy more expensive goods and services but by a lower volume.

All three different situations lead to the same result concerning the value of private consumption.

An important problem concerning the measurement of real private consumption is the fact that, especially in Russia, many transactions are not conventional monetary transactions. They are made by barter and shadow economy. The question is, how to measure this part of private consumption in official statistics. This leads to the not yet answered question of the effects of barter and shadow economy to other economic indicators.

The availability of statistical data on GDP is a general problem in both East Germany and Russia. On one hand, there is a time lag between measuring and publishing this data. On the other hand, official statisticians collect data more quickly on the origin of GDP than data on the use of GDP.

## 2 Statistical Definitions of Private Consumption

The term "consumption" on its own can be ambiguous and misleading. Sometimes it is used by economists to refer to consumption expenditures, sometimes to designate acquisitions of goods and services and sometimes consumption means the physical use of goods and services for the direct satisfaction of human needs or wants.

In economics the word consumption means using up goods and services. In modern economic terms it means, specifically, "final" consumption as distinguished from using up goods to produce other goods in manufacturing industry.

There are conceptual differences between the main consumption aggregates for the three sectors in which final consumption takes place, namely

- the household sector
- the non-profit institutions serving households sector (NPISH)
- the general government sector.

This paper focuses on final consumption of households. It is measured by the value of all individual consumption goods and services acquired by resident households. Statistical Offices in both East Germany and Russia more or less took the definitions of the United Nations System of National Accounts (United Nations, 1993). Russia tried to reform her accounting and statistical system and, simultaneously, her approach to international standards. East Germany used previous definitions of the former Federal Territory based on recommendations of EUROSTAT (the European Statistical Office) and the United Nations.

Finally, three sets of goods and services enter into household final consumption (United Nations, 1993, p.216):

1. Goods and services acquired through expenditure by households themselves. Their value is given by the household final consumption expenditure. This consists of expenditure, including imputed expenditure, incurred by households on individual consumption goods and services, including those sold at prices that are not economically significant.
2. Goods and services acquired as social transfers in kind from non-profit institutions serving households. Their value is given by expenditure, including imputed expenditure, incurred by resident non-profit institutions serving households.
3. Goods and services acquired as social transfers in kind from general government. Their value is given by government expenditure on individual consumption of goods and services.

Total final consumption in the economy may be considered from two angles:

- the expenditure side or
- in terms of final consumption.

It may be defined from the expenditure side as the total value of all expenditures on individual and collective consumption such as goods and services incurred by resident households. Or, it may be defined in terms of actual final consumption as the value of all individual goods and services acquired by resident households plus the value of collective services provided by general government or NPISH to the resident households.

By distinguishing between consumption expenditure and actual final consumption, ambiguity can be avoided. When consumption is recorded on an expenditure basis, the purpose is to identify the institutional units that incur the expenditures and hence control and finance the amounts of such expenditures. When consumption is recorded on an acquisition base, the purpose is to identify the units that actually acquire the goods and services and benefit from their use, either immediately or subsequently. The value of total final consumption is the same, whichever base is used.

## 3 General Factors Influencing Private Consumption

It is necessary to separate the main economic variables influencing consumer behavior – that is income and prices – from all the remaining influencing factors such as individual preferences, social pressures, customs, and habits. Furthermore, economic models usually assume a rational person and complete information regarding the market situation.

### *Spending in relation to incomes*

The theory points to the income of consumers as the most important single determinant of consumption patterns (Keynes, 1936; Friedman, 1957). From this follows that in any community both the average income level and the distribution of incomes have an important influence on total final consumption.

Therefore, the expected average level of further income influences consumption habits as much as actual present income.

In times of transition the income expectations are usually uncertain.

### *Prices*

Often the price of a good or service very strongly influences the consumption behavior. Increasing prices could lead to the effect that the consumer would buy other (comparatively cheaper) goods or services. He/she could buy a lower volume than before. It is also possible that the consumer buys the same product as before, but therefore he/she has to spend less money on other goods. Furthermore, the consumer could buy the same as before increasing its household's expenditure. The opposite occurs with decreasing prices.

The impact of price changes depends on the kind of goods and services and the existence of substitutes. It is more or less difficult to substitute staple food. Replacement gets easier for consumer goods like toothpaste or durable goods such as furnishings. The effects also depend on the level of income. Normally, price variation has a stronger influence on the poorer layers of society.

### *Market situation*

Furthermore, the preferences and the market situation have an impact on consumption. After long lines and sometimes blank shelves in post-communist super markets, now modern shops, outlets, and super markets have been developing. Totally new branches occurred. Consumption behavior totally changed in market economies (for the Polish case see Lofman, 1994, pp 30–31).

### *Exchange rates*

The transition process leads to a high amount of foreign imports in former post-communist countries. Prices of these goods and services strongly depend on foreign exchange rates. (Faber/Strohe, 2000)

### *Non-rational factors*

To be fully rational and consistent, consumers need to have access to sufficient information on goods and prices so that they can choose those with the lowest unit price for a given quality. But consumers do not always behave this way. To some extent this is due to the desire for conspicuous consumption: part of the attraction of the good simply is its high price. Consumers show non-rational attitudes toward necessities and luxuries. Generally, people from post-communist countries had a lot to catch up to play in the ways of western living standards and consumption behavior. It is obvious that the younger generation in particular tried to imitate western ideals and idols.

### *Effects of massive advertisements*

The influence of modern advertising techniques must also be considered. Advertising may raise the demand for the group of competing products as a whole.

This has changed the standards of consumption. Before the collapse of the communist countries, public consumption was treated as more important than private luxury. Then the consumer suddenly found himself in the center of advertisement for private consumption. Private consumption was no longer a vice, but a virtue.

This fact especially influences consumers in transition countries. Big American companies – such as Coca Cola for example – temptingly show large displays and many people buy the new product instead of former Russian or East German soft drinks. There was no longer a demand for former brands. Citizens of post-communist countries had not yet grown immune to the influence of colorfully alluring advertisement.

In addition, it can be stated that the total effect of modern advertising is to shift the preferences of consumers in favor of luxury goods rather than necessities, in favor of consumption rather than saving, and in favor of employment rather than leisure.

This has changed standards of consumption. Before the collapse of the communist countries, public consumption had been treated as more important than private luxury.

## 4 Structure and Growth of Private Consumption in East Germany

State Statistical Offices for Statistics (Statistische Landesämter) of East Germany started compiling data on GDP, private consumption, and other economic indicators on the base of individual states in 1991.

They used the system of national accounts from the Western part of Germany, but with methodological corrections according to the East German market situation.

Since 1995, the State Statistical Office for Statistics of Berlin has been offering data for Berlin as a whole only. From that time on it was not completely possible to compare the different development of GDP and other economic indicators for the former German Democratic Republic (the new states of Germany) and the old states of Germany.

In addition, a lot of methodological changes in GDP compilation were started approaching the European System of Nation Accounts in 1995 (Statistisches Bundesamt, 1999b, 1999c). The newly based data for individual states was expected to be published before January 2000. Unfortunately the Federal Statistical Office of Germany (Statistisches Bundesamt) could not solve the problems connected with this production and so they will be published as late as in July 2000. Therefore, at the moment, it is difficult to get detailed data for the last two or three years, especially for individual federal states.

However, figure E1 shows the development of GDP, total consumption and consumption in different sectors for all of Germany.

The German GDP slowly went up from 3500 billion German Marks in 1995 to 3900 billion German Marks in 1999. Total final consumption took approximately 75 percent of GDP. Total consumption by private households was one half of German GDP, governmental consumption around 20 percent and consumption of non-profit institution serving households (NPISH) less than 2 percent. These ratios did not significantly vary during the last decade.

Private consumption also went up from 1900 billion German Marks in 1995 to 2100 billion in 1999. Governmental consumption and consumption by non-profit institutions serving households were more or less constant.

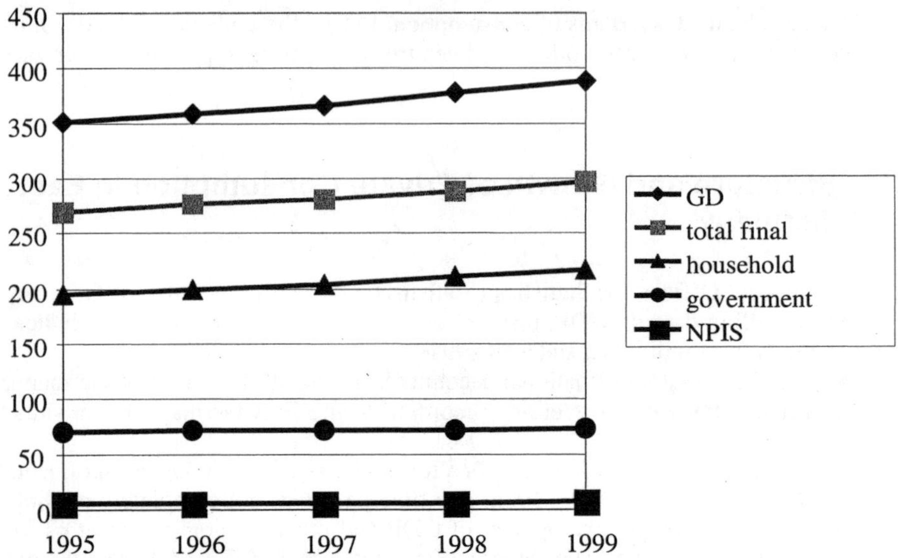


**Fig. E1.** Gross domestic product and final consumption of Germany (in billion German Marks and current prices)

*Source: Statistisches Bundesamt (2000) p 34/38*

Figure E2 compares the same indicators for the state of Brandenburg. Only Brandenburg represents the new states of Germany here. There was no data on final consumption available in 1991. The State Office for Statistics and Data Processing in Brandenburg does not publish data on consumption of non-profit institutions serving households. Furthermore, there is no data on governmental consumption in 1997. Due to the restructuring process in compiling data on GDP on the base of states new data will be available in July 2000.

Nevertheless, figure E2 shows that GDP of Brandenburg increased from 35800 million German Marks in 1991 to 77800 million in 1998. It has to be emphasized, that in East Germany the ratio of private consumption to GDP and also of governmental consumption to GDP seem to be very high. The ratio of private consumption to GDP took around 80 percent in 1992 and went down to 60 percent in 1997. One can imagine two reasons for that. On the one hand, the people in East Germany really spent a lot of money during the time immediately after the reunification of Germany. Millions wanted to have a new car, a new TV-set, travel tours and so on. On the other hand there were many transfers and "imports" from West Germany reducing the GDP figure of Brandenburg.

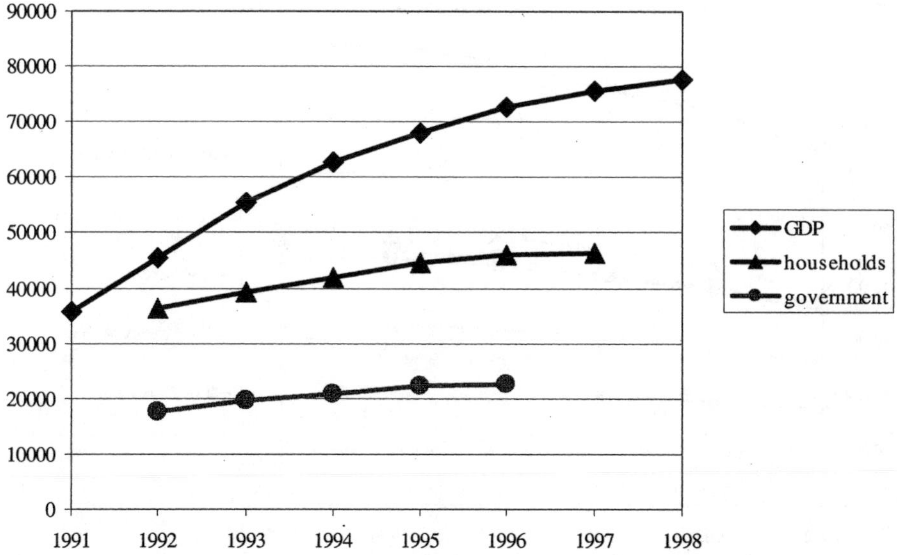


**Fig. E2.** Gross domestic product and final consumption in Brandenburg (in million German Marks and current prices)

*Source: Landesamt für Datenverarbeitung und Statistik Brandenburg (1999) p 26/44*

The growth rate of GDP in Brandenburg was much higher than the development of final consumption. Consequently, the ratio of total consumption to GDP has been falling since 1992.

Figure E3 compares the development of final consumption by private households for all five new states of East Germany. It is obvious that the graphs are more or less similar. There are differences in the level of final consumption of private households only. The state Saxony (the richest of the five) has a comparatively high final consumption of private households, whereas Mecklenburg-West Pomerania (the poorest) has the lowest. Final private consumption of Brandenburg lies between these figures.

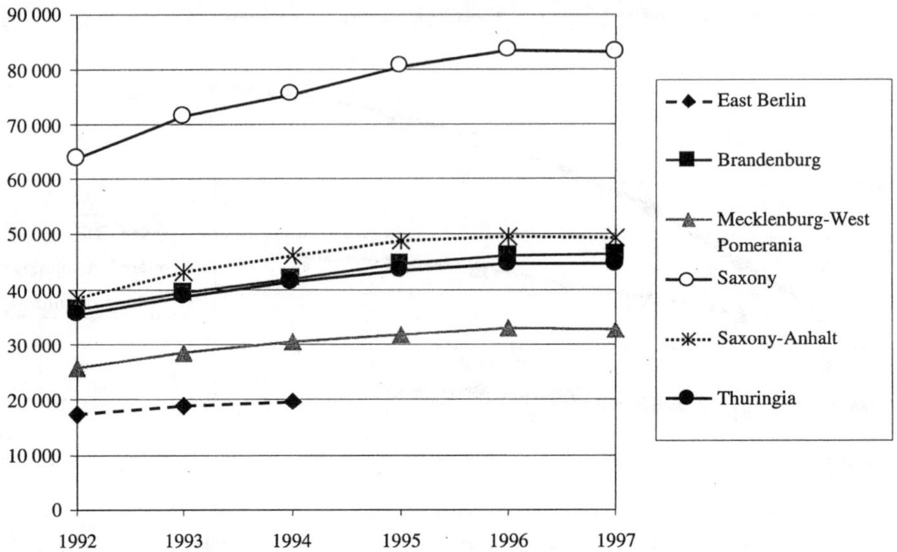


**Fig. E3.** Final consumption of private households in East Germany (in million German Marks and current prices)

*Source: Statistisches Landesamt Baden-Württemberg (1999)*

A comparison of changes in final consumption of private households would deliver a unique figure for all five states. Furthermore, it would also be interesting to analyze private consumption per capita, but there is no data available at the moment.

The expenditure shares of private households are to be compared for a more detailed analysis of structural changes in private consumption. Data on household's expenditure is based on two sources in East Germany: current economic accounts of a few individual households and the so-called Microcensus (a survey of households conducted every 5 years) of more households. Inquiries for the Microcensus of East Germany took place in 1991 and 1995. Therefore, such a comparison of household's expenditure is possible for these two periods only.

Figure E4 shows the expenditure shares for 1991 and 1995. The data is equal to the weighting structure for the compilation of consumer price indices in East Germany.

In 1991 the highest expenditure share of consumption in the new states and East Berlin was that of food and non-alcoholic beverages (20 percent), followed by transportation (19 percent) and rent, water, power, gas, and fuel (together 12,5 percent). In 1995, the expenditures shares of foods and non-alcoholic beverages and of transportation fell to 15 percent; the expenditures for housing services increased to one quarter of the total final expenditures of private households.

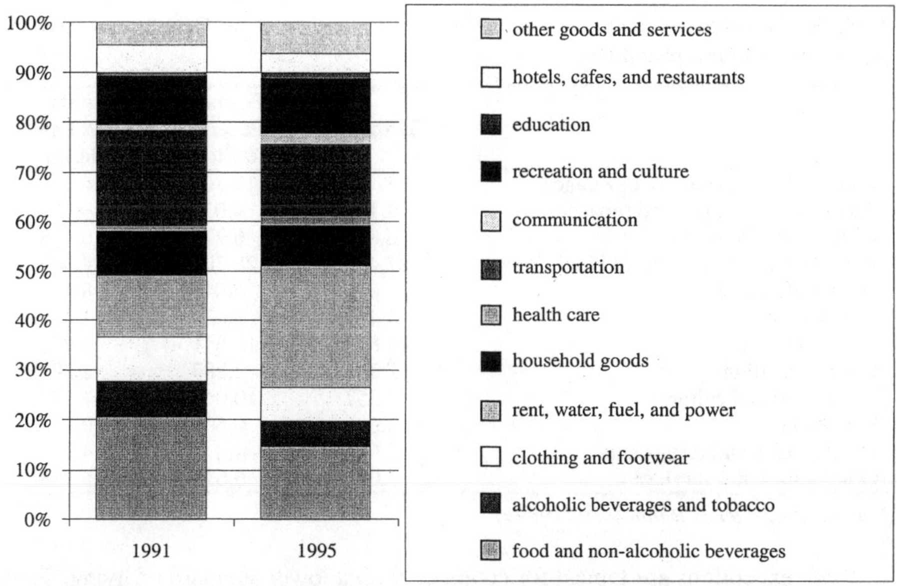


**Fig. E4.** Structure of final consumption by private households in East Germany (as percentage of total households expenditures)
*Source: Statistisches Bundesamt (1999a)*

For comparison, table E1 displays the expenditure shares of private households for all of Germany, West Germany and East Germany including East Berlin in 1995.

It is easy to see that, by 1995, the structure of private consumption in East Germany approximated that of West Germany with the exception of higher food consumption and lower consumption of health care.

**Table E1.** Structure of final consumption by private households in Germany in 1995 (as percentage of total expenditures)

| | Germany | Former Federal Territory | New states and East Berlin |
|---|---|---|---|
| Food and non-alcoholic beverages | 13,126 | 12,705 | 14,706 |
| Alcoholic beverages and tobacco | 4,167 | 4,039 | 4,899 |
| Clothes and footwear | 6,876 | 6,772 | 6,998 |
| Rent, water, power, gas, and fuel | 27,477 | 28,702 | 24,307 |
| Household goods | 7,056 | 6,648 | 8,468 |
| Health care | 3,439 | 3,636 | 1,879 |
| Transportation | 13,882 | 13,658 | 14,473 |
| Communication | 2,266 | 2,287 | 2,208 |
| Recreation and culture | 10,357 | 10,064 | 11,133 |
| Education | 0,651 | 0,600 | 0,857 |
| Hotels, cafes and restaurants | 4,608 | 4,875 | 4,114 |
| Other goods and services | 6,095 | 6,014 | 5,958 |

*Source: Statistisches Bundesamt (1999a)*

These exceptions are typical for countries with a lower standard of living. Thus there are obvious tendencies on convergence in the field of these remaining consumption differences between East and West. Already in 1998, the share of food, beverages and tobacco in East Germany had decreased to 15.9 percent from 19.6 percent in 1995.

## 5 Final Consumption in Russia

The State Office for Statistics of Russia GOSKOMSTAT started very early in 1991 with the implementation of the United Nations System of National Accounts.

The Russian System of National Accounts is strongly influenced by two factors:

- hidden economic activities
- informal economic activities

"Hidden economic activities, in the majority of cases, include legal economic activities, which are not reported or are under-reported by the economic units with the purpose of tax and social charges evasion, avoiding some administrative and social responsibilities in all sectors of the economy. Informal economic activity is mainly undertaken on legal grounds by individual producers or by the so-called un-incorporated enterprises that is by enterprises owned by individuals or households, which often are not registered according to the prescribed order. Their activities are based on the informal relationship among the participants; they may produce goods and services (in full or partially) for their own consumption. Often, the informal activity assumes a secondary employment; often it is a non-professional activity." (GOSKOMSTAT, 2000, p. 5)

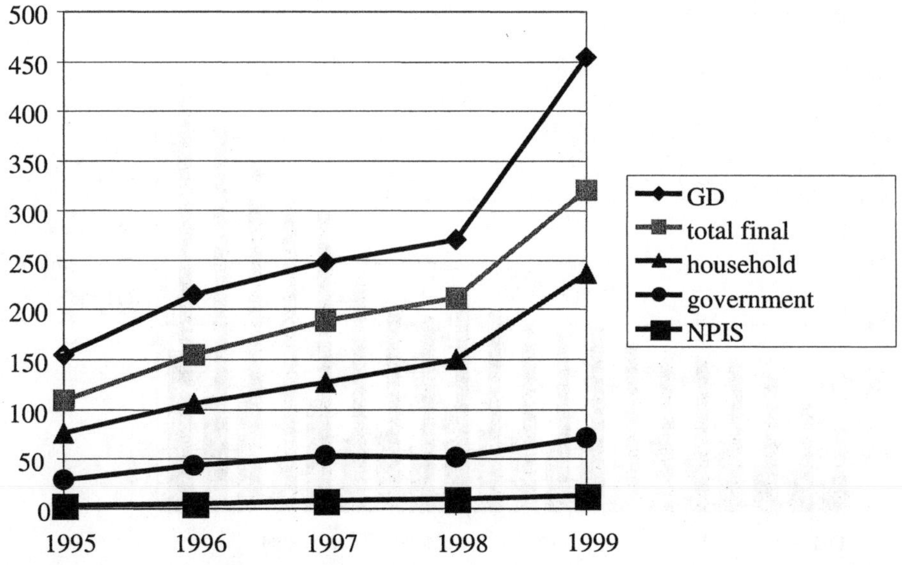


**Fig. E5.** Gross domestic product and final consumption in Russia (in billion Russian Roubles and current prices)
*Source: data from GOSKOMSTAT*

Therefore, the economy cannot be fully observed by direct statistical methods. Using indirect data, by applying the balancing methods, and using expert estimates help to obtain estimates of hidden and informal economy. These adjustments are done for the GDP produced, for the GDP used and for the GDP calculated from the income side.

"The total adjustment for the various types of hidden and informal activities and economic transactions unaccounted by usual methods amounted in production account for 1998 to 22 percent of total GDP in current prices." (GOSKOMSTAT, 2000, p. 5)

Until now there are only estimations of GDP in current prices available. Figure E5 shows the development of Russian GDP and final consumption by sectors.

Similar to East Germany, the ratio of total final consumption to GDP was very high in Russia. The ratio of private final consumption to GDP varied from 49 percent in 1995 and 1996 to 55 percent in 1998. In contrast to East Germany, there was no tendency for a reduction of this ratio before 1999. The ratio of governmental consumption to Russian GDP was comparatively constant at a level of around 20 percent from 1995 till 1998. In 1999 it decreased a little.

Figure E6 gives a more detailed view to the development of final consumption by sectors. Here quarterly data are used.

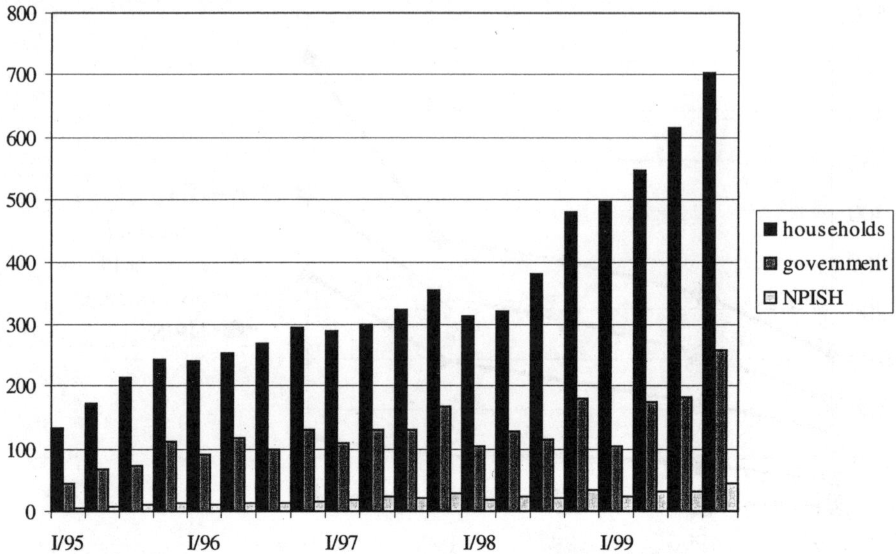


**Fig. E6.** Final consumption in Russia by different sectors (in billion Russian Rubles and current prices)
*Source: data from GOSKOMSTAT*

Seasonal variation in this figure is obvious. Usually final consumption of private households was low in the first quarter of a year and went up until the fourth quarter. Since the financial crisis in 1998 final consumption of private households has been growing almost monotonously without significant seasonal variations.

There were more variations in final consumption of the governmental sector. Its consumption expenditures were comparatively low in the first and third quarter of a year and higher in the other two quarters.

For an analysis of the development of consumption it is necessary to abstract from the fast growing trend in these figures. Its origins lie in the high rate of inflation and the presentation of the data in current prices.

However, under the assumption that all sectors of consumption were equally influenced by inflation, it would be possible to examine at least the changes in the structure of consumption.

Figure E7 displays calculations by the authors excluding the effects of inflation on final consumption of private households. The figures of final consumption by households were deflated using the corresponding index of consumer prices. The base period is the fourth quarter of 1997 looking for a period before the transition crisis in 1998.

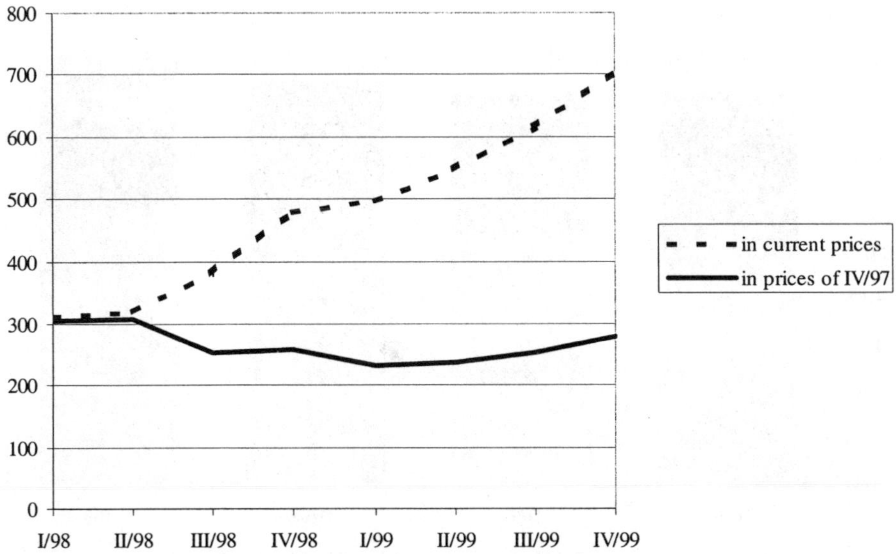


**Fig. E7.** Growth of final consumption by private households in Russia from 1998 till 1999 (in constant and actual prices)
*Source: calculations by the authors with data from GOSKOMSTAT (1999)*

Final consumption of households in current and in constant prices spread apart from each other after the financial crisis and the lope in consumer prices in the third quarter of 1998. Final consumption in current prices has been going up due to higher consumer prices since that time. Whereas final consumption of households in constant prices developed on a comparatively low level and has been increasing since 1999.

The analogous calculations for governmental consumption and consumption of non-profit institutions serving households would be more difficult, because of the need for specific deflators. Similar problems would arise with deflating total figures of GDP.

Deflating the data of other sectors by using the index of consumer prices would not change the structure and ratios of the corresponding figures given above.

More detailed data are needed for analyzing the structure of private consumption in Russia. GOSKOMSTAT publishes data related to structural analysis only rarely and irregularly. Figure E8 shows the structure of household's expenditures in 1998.

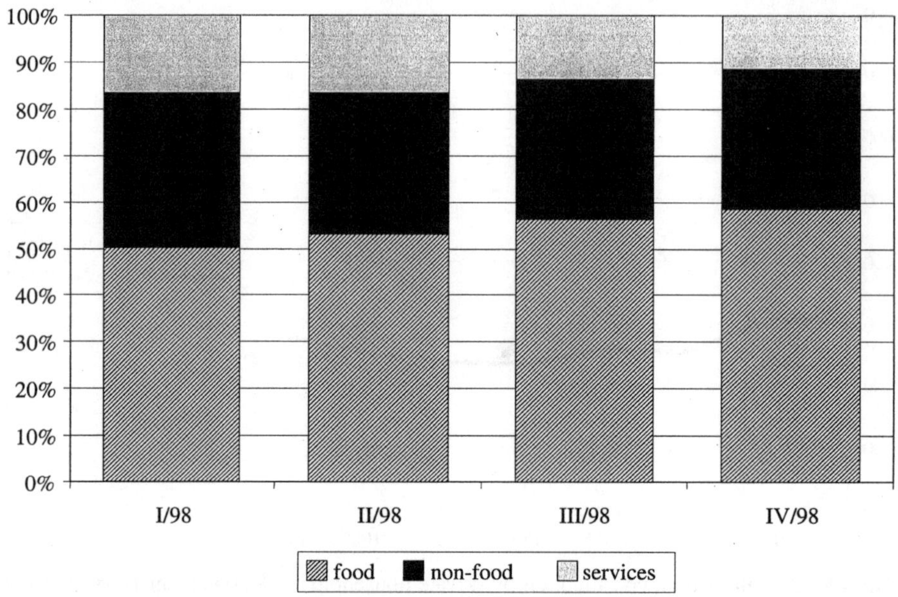


**Fig. E8.** Structure of final consumption by private households in Russia in 1998 (as percentage of total expenditure)

*Source: Faber/Strohe (1999), p. 19; data from GOSKOMSTAT (1999)*

It is obvious that food took a share of one half of total households expenditures at the beginning of 1998. Its share used to increase quarter by quarter. The ratio of expenditure for non-food to total household's expenditure was more or less constant at a level of approximately 30 percent, whereas the share of services decreased from 17 percent in the first quarter of 1998 to 12 percent at the end of the year.

# 6 Conclusions

Especially in transformation countries, there is a high ratio of final consumption by private households to national gross domestic product. Perhaps this is caused by the following two facts:

- really high spending of private households due to totally changed consumer needs and preferences, partially due to new prestige attitudes and the desire for luxury;
- high transfers and imports from foreign countries and low domestic production, reducing the national gross domestic product.

However, this ratio has been decreased during the transformation process in both East Germany and Russia.

Furthermore, there were high expenditure shares on food and beverages and low shares for services at the beginning of the transition period. Reasons are

- low income
- unpaid salaries and wages (in Russia)
- higher rate of unemployment.

The figures of Russia are largely influenced by high inflation. Surprisingly, they seem to be rather constant after eliminating this price effect.

Nevertheless, many other factors have massive effects on total consumption too. Most important ones are income, prices, advertisement and attitudes towards necessities and luxury.

Hidden economy and informal activities have an important influence on the economic indicators in Russia. Thus GDP estimations cannot be provided by direct statistical methods only. Indirect collection of data, balancing methods and expert estimates must be taken into consideration. The development and execution of such methods is a large potential research field for both theoretical and official statistics.

## References

Faber C, Strohe HG (2000) Consumer Prices in Russia and Transforming Official Statistics. In: Welfens PJJ, Gavrilenkov E (eds) Restructuring, Stabilizing and Modernizing the New Russia: Economic and Institutional Issues. Springer, Berlin Heidelberg

Faber C, Strohe HG (1999) Price and Income Statistics – main components of measuring a standard of living. Paper presented at the Conference "Restructuring, Stabilizing and Modernizing Russia", Dec. 1999, Moscow

Friedman M (1957) A Theory of the Consumption Function. Princeton

GOSKOMSTAT (2000) Implementing SNA-93 in the Russian Statistical Practice. Problems and Possible Solutions. Paper presented at the JOINT ECE/Eurostat/OECD Meeting on National Accounts. Geneva, April 2000

GOSKOMSTAT (1999) Statistical Bulletin No. 1(51), March 1999

Keynes JM (1936) The General Theory of Employment, Interest and Money. New York London

Landesamt für Datenverarbeitung und Statistik Brandenburg (1999) Statistische Berichte: Entstehung, Verteilung und Verwendung des Sozialprodukts im Land Brandenburg 1992 bis 1998

Lofman B (1994) Polish Society in Transformation: The Impact of Marketization on Business, Consumption, and Education. In: Schultz CJ, Belk RW, Ger G (eds) Research in Consumption Behaviour – Consumption in Marketizing Economies. Vol. 7, Greenwich, Connecticut, pp 29–55

Statistisches Bundesamt (1999a) Pressekonferenz zur Umstellung des Preisindex für die Lebenshaltung auf Basis 1995=100. Warenkorb und Wägungsschema

Statistisches Bundesamt (1999b) Revision der Volkswirtschaftlichen Gesamtrechnungen 1999 – Anlass, Konzeptänderungen und neue Begriffe. Wirtschaft und Statistik 4/1999: 257–281

Statistische Bundesamt (1999c) Revision der Volkswirtschaftlichen Gesamtrechnungen 1991 bis 1998. Wirtschaft und Statistik 6/1999: 449–478

Statistisches Bundesamt (2000) Volkswirtschaftliche Gesamtrechnungen, Fachserie 18, Reihe 3: Vierteljahresergebnisse der Inlandsproduktberechnung, 4. Vierteljahr 1999

Statistisches Landesamt Baden-Württemberg (1999) Privater Verbrauch in jeweiligen Preisen 1970 bis 1997. Arbeitskreis "Volkswirtschaftliche Gesamtrechnung der Länder". Stand: 22.09.1999

United Nations (1993) System of National Accounts

# F. Labor Market Transformation and Hidden Unemployment in Russia

Nina Oding

## 1 Introduction

The need for economic reform in Russia was dictated by the country's low labor productivity levels and the absence of a mechanism for rational resource management. However, its actual implementation has been far from perfect and is still to be completed.

In this situation, a study intended to analyze past changes in Russia's economy and identify efficient ways to complete structural reconstruction and generate economic recovery has a special value.

Currently, Russian economy is a scene of deep controversies that eventually pushed it to a systemic crisis. On the one hand, Russia has moved along the path of economic transition, but on the other hand, it finds itself in a deep slump despite a number of healthy developments that might lead to growth. Market watchers offer different assessments of Russian economic reforms. During earlier stages of the transition, battles were fought between the proponents of "shock therapy" and gradualists, while at present researchers discuss the character and types of economic transformations. Optimists believe that de-politization of the resource distribution process signifies the advent of a free market (Aslund, 1995), while pessimists maintain that the current domination of leasehold relations in the country and the lack of competition speak to the contrary (Samson,1998). A number of writers (Illarionov,1996; Gaidar,1998) believe that the current lull results from the excessive state-control load on the economy.

In our opinion, the most crucial challenge facing Russian economic transition stems from uncompleted or non-existent market-wise institutional transformations that could pave the way for true market relations.

The EBRD report (EBRD,1997) notes that privatization has failed to provide for economic growth, and therefore new laws and market institutions should be put in place to stimulate competition and stamp out corruption. In addition, the country has yet to both realize the imperfection of its market transformations and actually press forward with a number of reforms (administrative, budget, pension, etc.).

One of the paramount goals of any market transition is to efficiently overhaul the country's employment strategies. In this connection, the labor market study is of special pragmatic and theoretical value, as it addresses the current status and development trends in the Russian labor market, employment evolution and the character of unemployment, as well as employees' behavior in the labor market, and the government's employment policies.

Currently, Russia's labor market is haunted by multiple challenges carried over from those times when labor was proclaimed to be both "honor and duty" for every soviet citizen, and anyone without a job automatically became a sponger subject to criminal prosecution. The soviet constitution guaranteed the right of labor to everyone; complete employment was viewed as a natural state of things, and unemployment, as the scourge of Western economies. In 1990, almost 90 percent of able-bodied soviet citizens were among the economically active population, and women accounted for 52 percent of all blue, and white collar personnel. The bulk of social benefits (housing, healthcare, recreation, etc.) was distributed through enterprises, and the soviet social strategies formally looked similar to those of a Welfare State. There existed, however, a fundamental difference: the USSR lacked relevant civil society institutions through which anyone seeking help could enforce the provision of benefits due to her/him by law. We side with the view that in actual reality, the USSR's social policies were designed to protect the interests of the *nomenklatura* who were, unlike the rest of the population, the real focus of social privileges (Shkaratan, 1998. p.6). However, on the surface this appeared as a policy intended to guarantee the welfare of every employee, mother, child, or pensioner, and it is the persistence of the soviet myth about guaranteed social protection to everyone that currently blocks the formation of a social basis for economic and political reform.

The economy of labor was one of the most heavily ideologized branches in the soviet economic science that developed within the framework of Marx's political economy and ignored the applied issues of actual labor relations. These were aggravated by officially imposed constraints on options for a person to select a profession or job that suited her/his abilities best; as a result, the mobility of labor was extremely low. In the course of many years, the social structure in the country practically did not change, while hidden unemployment reached impressive levels and took the form of enterprises underutilizing their labor force. Open unemployment was growing as well, concurrently with the growing numbers of excessive jobs. At the same time, the economy suffered significant work-time losses due to irregular materials supply, poor organization of labor, low production discipline, and frequent stoppages within working shifts. Some estimates put the then army of excessive labor at 15% to 20% of total the labor force (A. Nespopova, 1996. p. 43).

The mobility of professions was restricted by rigid professional orientation and the lack of opportunities to retrain, while geographic mobility was held back by the system of compulsory domicile registration, currently still in place. Instead, the state encouraged migration to outlying raw-material supplying districts with harsh climates. At the same time, internal migration of labor within separate industries and regions reached significant levels (in 1990, it accounted for 14 percent of total manufacturing work force).

## 2 The Main Features of the Labor Market

The actual labor market formation began after the system of complete (and often forced) employment was demolished. As indicated in (Zaslavsky, 1998, p 77), the key reason behind the demise of the soviet (pre-planned) system of pseudo-employed labor was the uncompetitiveness of large manufacturing enterprises. Divestiture and institutional transformations set off restructuring in the sphere of employment and led to the emergence of new types of jobs and the exodus of excessive labor from still operating enterprises. At the same time these developments expanded the labor market and opened up opportunities for moving into new professions. In 1997, the share of those employed in the non-state sector amounted to 74 percent.

Before the reforms the state was practically the only employer in the country where excessive employment was a rule. Now, with private and mixed economic sectors in place and the state sector substantially commercialized, the ranks of employers have expanded. However, due to a combination of new ownership relations, production relations, work motivation, and specific policies by Russian enterprises to be reviewed below, there has been no direct connection between the output dynamics and the numbers of employees, which resulted in a considerable growth of hidden unemployment. For example, some industries (power engineering, oil and gas industries, and metallurgy) accepted new labor even though their production volumes were falling. The process of new-jobs creation was developing in these industries at a higher pace than that of eliminating old and inefficient jobs.

One should also bear in mind that the share of the employed continued to fall in both absolute and relative terms (Appendix: Table F2). The average age of the Russian employed declined, and the countrywide share of the employed in the 15–49 year old bracket increased.

This took place against a background of a significant redistribution of labor between economic sectors and industries of the country. There was a surge in the share of those employed in the private sector from 8.8 percent in 1980, to 12.5 percent in 1990, to 36.9 percent of the total employed in 1995. The share of employed at state and municipal enterprises fell 2.4 times from 1980, while the share of those at mixed ownership units jumped 6.2 times (Appendix: Table F3).

Employment is currently on the rise in trade and catering, municipal services, education, health care, banking, and public administration, while it is falling in industry, construction, and transportation (Appendix: Table F4).

Among manufacturing industries labor force contraction is characteristic for mechanical engineering, forestry, wood processing, and wood-and-pulp industry, and light industry, while food, gas, petrochemical, non-ferrous metallurgy, and power engineering post a reverse process. However, despite all these rather substantial changes, Russia's employment structure reveals features characteristic of averaged economies.

However, the dwindling production outputs jacked up both open and hidden unemployment. Budget cuts in spending on the social sector, science, and culture, as well as bad wage arrears countrywide depressed the population's real incomes.

Thus we can see that structural adjustment in Russia has produced fairly controversial and unexpected results. The reformers had hoped that divestiture in the economy and the emergence of a new private sector would open new horizons and bring about radical changes. What they actually got were controversial developments in the economy and glaring labor market disproportion. In this connection it is important to find answers to the following questions:

What has in reality happened to the labor market?

Do these developments naturally follow from the reform at hand, or do they represent its total failure?

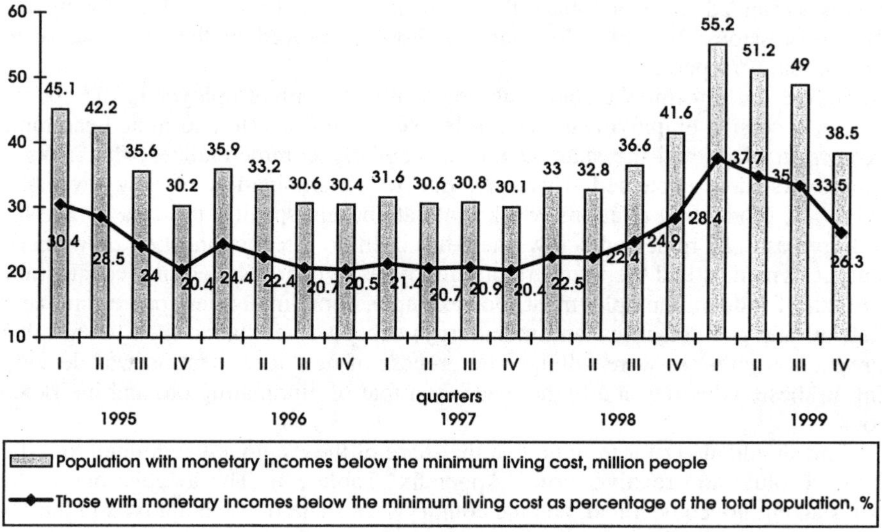


**Fig. F1.** Poverty level evolution*

*Source: RF State Statistics Committee. Rossijskij statisticheskij ezhegodnik, 1999 RF State Statistics Committee. Rossijskij statisticheskij ezhegodnik, 2000*

These issues were in the focus of a number of macro-economic studies and overall reviews of labor markets, labor fluctuation, and labor market flexibility (see for example Commander and Corricelli 1995; Clarke 1996; Godfrey, 1995; OECD 1994, Pfau-Effinger, 1995; Samoradov, 1993; Standing, 1995).

The scope of change in the Russian labor market has been assessed in a number of studies based on an optimistic view of the factors of labor turnover and the existing ratio between the size of wages and the general market situation (cf. OECD, 1996.; Layard and Richter, 1994). Other authors dispute the validity of these factors and describe the factor of wage flexibility as "the price of continued employment security". They focus their attention on the problem of "remaining labor market rigidity sustained by labor hoarding by worker-controlled state enterprises" (Commadner, et al., 1995). Guy Standing believes that Russia is suffering from excessive labor market flexibility manifesting itself in super-low wages (see

Standing, 1994). S. Clarke summed up various views and identified three major approaches.

«Within the liberal camp there are two sharply contrasting interpretations which declare Russia to be the ultimate negative or positive example. On the one hand, it is argued that Russia is plumbing the depths of recession as a result of labor market rigidities which impede structural adjustment On the other hand, it is argued that Russia has developed a perfectly flexible labor market which is the key to structural adjustment without mass unemployment. The third, skeptical position, combines the latter view that Russia has an extremely flexible labor market with the former view that Russia has undergone little structural adjustment, while contesting the position common to both that Russia has avoided mass unemployment. (Clarke, 1996, p.4–5)

In our opinion, the variety of approaches to the problem, and the different degrees of optimism in assessing Russian labor market developments do not stem from the difficulty to obtain trustworthy information about labor market processes alone. Here we should take into account a very interesting viewpoint suggested by S. Clarke who maintains that in reality we ought to distinguish three separate labor markets: the internal labor market, the informal labor market, and the external labor market.

The "internal" labor market operates within large enterprises and is based on the redeployment of the labor force within the enterprise. The “informal” labor market is the principal channel for job-to-job transition between enterprises and the main segment of the labor market through personal connection for acquire secondary employment. The “external” labor market is the principal channel for job transition through unemployment, through which people seek jobs using advertisements or through public and private employment services (Clarke, 1996, p.8).

It should be noted that behind the modest figures of the official unemployment is hidden the peculiar feature of the Russian labor market – the regionalization (Appendix: Table F5). As pointed out by T.Maleva (Maleva , 1998, p.14), unemployment is varied from 1–2% in several central regions to`7% in the 9 depressive regions. There is a group of regions with critical labor market conditions. Its used to having underdeveloped infrastructure and a low supply of new jobs, and as a result there is a tendency to reproduce the crisis on the labor market. These are Vladimirskaja, Ivanovskaja, Kirovskaja oblasti (to the East from Moscow), Mordovija,Shuvashija, Udmurtija ( with structural crisis of the economy), and the North-Caucasus republics Kalmykija and Dagestan with the labor force excess (Garsija-Iser, Golodetz, Smirnov, 1997, p.114).

I. Zaslavsky suggests that, in a situation of increasing autarky which leads to the isolation of regional labor markets, researchers should address various types of regional markets, among which he identifies the following: a) asymmetric markets, b) balanced markets, and c) diversified markets ( Zaslavsky, 1998, p. 84).

Despite profound economic and institutional transformations, Russia's full-scale economic development is still hampered by a variety of factors comprising:

- vaguely determined property rights
- markets' low information transparency

- constantly changing framework conditions for economic activity
- financial uncertainty
- political instability
- non-existence of an independent judicial system
- non-existence of bureaucracy

Both positive and negative developments occurred practically simultaneously as a single compound of events, which made it difficult for the population to find their bearings and accommodate to the new environment. The current situation in the labor market is a fantastic mixture of old and new standards of behavior, targets, and motives both inherited from the soviet experience, and newly acquired ones (Chachulina, 1996. p. 14).

However, the scope of transformations that have taken place since the beginning of the reform, and the volume of collected statistics enable us to undertake an analysis of the changes that have occurred in the country by paying special attention to the following:

- peculiarities of enterprise behavior in the market that largely depends on the legal status of a given enterprise and varies between state enterprises, privatized businesses, and newly established units.
- labor force stratification that determines different patterns of behavior in the labor market.

## 3 Employment/ Unemployment Statistics in Russia

Statistics on the total number of the unemployed and their composition are built on the results of regular employment surveys undertaken by Russian statistics bodies since 1992, and on data supplied by state employment services.

By the ILO standards, the unemployed are persons over 16 years of age who, during the reviewed period:

- had no job (or other work that brings income)
- were looking for a job (approached state or private employment agencies, put their notice in the media, directly approached enterprise management or other employers, tried to use their personal connections for this purpose, or tried to organize a business of their own
- were prepared to take a job.

Thus, the ILO gives the term "unemployment" a very broad interpretation which allows one to get a true picture of the actual scale of unemployment in the country. At the same time, their criteria also defines as unemployed individuals who do not want any job at all, or only simulate that they are looking for one.

According to the ILO, the number of unemployed in the RF in 1997 was 8.1 million and in 1998 stood at 8.9 million (11.2% and 12.3% of EAP, respectively).

According to the RF State Statistics Committee, the number of officially registered unemployed in 1997 stood at 1.99 million (2.8% of the EAP) and in 1998 was 1.93 million (2.7% of the EAP) (Appendix: Table F6).

Currently, the statistical study of the unemployed is based on employment surveys and information supplied by state employment agencies. Official unemployment data are based on the registers kept by state employment agencies. Employment agencies' statistics come to state statistics bodies in a consolidated form.[1]:

According to studies by the RF State Statistics Committee, actual unemployment levels are much higher than those captured by state employment services.

Representative nationwide surveys that were staged within the 1992–1996 Program for Monitoring the Economic Situation and Health of the Population (RMEZ) and took into account data on forced leaves put the actual unemployment figure at 12 percent ( Sabirijanova, 1998, p. 42).

State statistics allow one to forecast movements fairly precisely, but only in the official sector of the open labor market and mostly with regards to the state enterprise labor force (Appendix: Table F7). The Federal Employment Service only covers a part of the actual universe of labor supply and demand, and it does not take into account the whole array of new developments in the sphere of employment arising from the peculiarities of market relations in Russia.

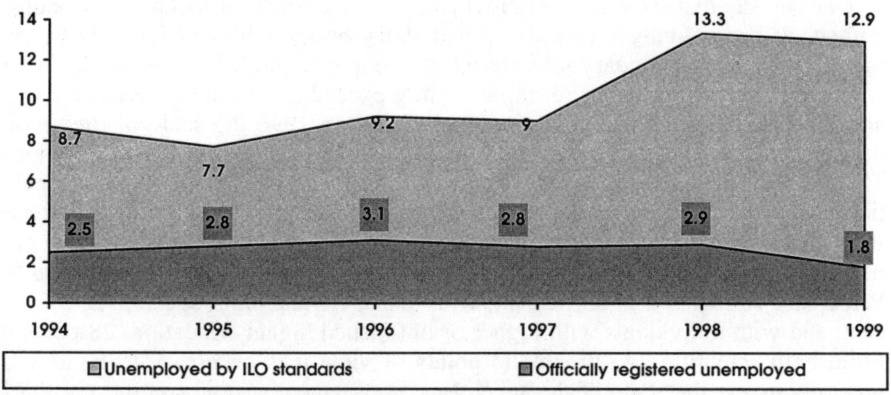


**Fig. F2.** Unemployed by ILO standards and officially registered

As noted in papers by Moscow Carnegie Center, both open and latent unemployment have significant destructive bearing on the currently existing labor market. At the same time, one should not overestimate the actual force of this negative influence. More detailed studies show that there exists, concurrently with the widely spread latent unemployment, a cushioning phenomenon of hidden employment.

Notably, current Russian practices do not reveal any significant amount of flexibility between wage, and employment evolutions. Wages became a sort of a

[1] Officially, unemployment has been measured from the second half of 1991, and statistics reports were introduced in the first quarter of 1991.

social allowance, and their average share (across the years of reform) in the population's incomes fell to 40 percent. As the result, the major factor behind the unheard-of (in the soviet times) workforce mobility, unconnected to any structural changes in the jobs distribution pattern, is the widely used practice of secondary employment, including in the "gray" and shadow economies[2].

The bulk of those partly employed also have permanent or temporary secondary employment. By Goscomstat data, in mid-1995, 4.7 million people in manufacturing alone had additional sources of income from secondary employment. In 1996, the numbers of individuals with secondary employment amounted to 10 to 12 million. This was against a background of shrinking employment in the official sector of the economy, which is most probably a sign of employment spilling over into "shadowy quarters".

The secondary employment of those on part-time jobs or administrative leave (these people have their primary employment at state enterprises) differs from the secondary employment of those in the private sector by its irregular character. The key motive for obtaining a secondary job is larger income. Currently, the overwhelming majority of employed Russian citizens (64 percent) assess their jobs only from the point of view of income, although at least 53 percent of them would prefer jobs with smaller but guaranteed incomes.

One can say that secondary employment plays the role of a social and economic damper. It keeps living standards up and stalls the growth of official unemployment. Those with secondary jobs are mostly people employed in the public sector, where average wages either reach or slightly exceed the minimum cost of living, and individuals on part-time working schedules. In 1996 the scale of the secondary employment sector was reported to cover at least 10 to 15 million people (or 15 to 20% of the total employed). These data were obtained through mass population surveys. In certain social groups the share of those with additional incomes was 1.5 to 2 times over the average second-employment levels. With those employed by private businesses this share stands at 42 percent, with Moscow and St. Petersburg residents it is 33 percent, with managers and chief specialists, 32 percent, and with individuals with higher or unfinished higher education, 28 percent. From both scientific and pragmatic points of view it is necessary to be able to precisely assess the scale of the secondary employment sector, and the peculiarities of secondary labor supply and remuneration as compared to those at main jobs. However, at present it cannot be done with a sufficient degree of reliability.

Traditionally, the unemployment index is taken as a signaling device to assess an economy's restructuring levels. However, the budding Russian labor market (despite a few fairly stable trends) is too volatile in terms of changes and mobility inside the employed category. This makes a *simultaneous* measuring of both unemployment rates and the rates of job supply (workforce inflow/outflow figures) reflecting the workforce turnover a more reliable instrument to understand struc-

---

[2] Within the informal sector, one can distinguish two major types of employment by the employees' qualification, and incomes levels: highly-qualified and well-paid jobs (private lessons, medical services, construction works, etc.) and low-qualified activities (small retailing, various types of individual services, the "shuttle-trade" business, etc).

tural changes in the Russian labor market. This should also be compared with current job turnover (a sum of created/killed jobs)[3].

The results of annual surveys by the Russian Economic Barometer (coinciding with Goscomstat figures) show that the average annual coefficient of workforce hiring was within the range of 16 to 19 percent, the coefficient of job leaving, 24 to 32 percent; and the average annual rate of employment contraction, 8 to 15 percent. Job liquidation in Russia peaked in 1994, the period of a record deep production slump. R. Kapelushnikov (Kapelushnikov,1998: p. 111) maintains that Russia exceeds most Central European and East European countries with its intensity of workforce redistribution and can be compared to many West European economies. At the same time, in terms of job-turnover intensity it falls below those transitional economies that opted for a “shock therapy” strategy. Thus he defines the Russian type of a labor market as a system of "running on the spot", where despite outwardly energetic developments the market does not move at all or crawls too slowly towards a new, more efficient structure of employment.

All currently employed can be conventionally divided into three categories: those employed in the formal state sector, in the formal non-state sector, and in the informal sector.

The informal sector in Russia can be largely defined as a source of secondary (additional) employment for those engaged in the formal sector. The International Labor Organization describes the informal sector as a totality of very small units, mainly independent businesses, producing and selling goods and services. Some of them use the labor of their family members while others employ hired hands. According to international recommendations on labor statistics, the lack of official registration is not regarded as a universal compulsory distinctive feature of an informal economy unit, but it may be regarded as such depending on the conditions of the country.

The Russian informal sector is extremely variegated. The borderline between the informal and formal sectors, between the informal sector and economic inactivity, or between the informal sector and the "shadow" economy is fairly vague.

*The shadow economy* (i.e. registered businesses dodging taxes or engaged in any prohibited types of economic activity) can be found in every sector recognized by the Russian national accounting system (these include non-finance enterprises, finance enterprises, state management, etc). Therefore, to come up with a credible analysis of the informal sector, one should cover a broad range of economic activities.

---

[3] For example, the 1998 workforce turnover (workforce inflow/outflow figures) in St. Petersburg stood at 49.3%. This was much more than in the Soviet Union, where labor turnover never exceeded 14%, and significantly more than in East and West Europe. In Poland during “shock therapy” this index was 42%, and in Bulgaria and Hungary, 32 and 22%, respectively. A more detailed analysis reveals discrepancies between the two methods of workforce-turnover assessment, one measuring the sum of those newly accepted and those who left jobs, and the other measuring the sum of job turnover. It turns out that job turnover is a much slower process in both Russia and St. Petersburg compared to that in Poland in the first years of economic reform (1990–1991).

Both the informal sector and the shadow economy existed in Russia before the present reform, but during recent years the composition, scale, and character of the informal sector has drastically changed. The numbers of those engaged in it have soared manyfold, and the share of trade in its activities has drastically increased.

Official statistics provide no quantitative indices of employment in the informal sector. These can only be established with a great degree of approximation on the basis of the available labor market statistics, socio-economic studies, and studies of employment dynamics in the sector of private individual gardening and private household activities.

Employment in the informal sector keeps down the numbers of officially registered unemployed and pushes up the numbers of those who find themselves in an intermediate position between the officially recognized unemployed and individuals with full-time jobs.

## 4 Hidden Unemployment

"Open" unemployment covers the officially registered unemployed and those who are not registered with state employment agencies and whose average per capita family incomes are below or on the level of the minimum cost of living. The criterion of the minimum living cost allows to exclude those individuals who do not need to work for their subsistence.

In Russia, however, there has emerged a large-scale hidden (potential) unemployment.

Hidden (potential) unemployment is the index of a latent production-slump related contraction of demand for labor that has not yet materialized in the form of open labor shedding by depressed enterprises.

Any production slump produces a relative excess of workforce normally followed by either a reduction of economically unfeasible jobs or compressed work schedules. Consequently a part of the workforce is made redundant, and the other part find themselves in an "under-employed" mode having to work shorter hours. However, if enterprises shy from redundancy cuts under a GDP decline, their productivity inevitably goes down, followed by wages. Expenditures on the upkeep of excessive workforce keep the recovery of productivity levels at bay.

To keep productivity on the same level after a decline in the GDP, one must cut one's workforce to a level conforming to existing demand. Excessive workforce is practically equal to open unemployment. A decline in the GDP followed by lower productivity is a sign of economically unfeasible employment accumulated within the company.

Thus hidden unemployment exists in the form of excessive jobs maintained by enterprises (Appendix: Table F8).

Those hit by hidden unemployment continue to work their regular hours without additional income, with the average per capita income in their families falling below or staying on the level of the minimum living cost (this is happening for instance to those in public industries). The International Labor Organization describes this sector as a category of *invisible part-time employment.* The reluctance or inability of their employers to provide them with normal pay indicates either that their jobs are excessive for the given enterprise, or that their labor potential is underused for other reasons.

Economic restructuring and the deteriorating financial situation of a significant proportion of enterprises forces them to shed labor, thus transforming hidden unemployment to open unemployment.

To determine the actual scale of hidden unemployment is not an easy task, impossible without a wide-scale selective survey of households.

There is another newly emerged phenomenon in the Russian labor market, that of *visible part-time employment.*

Visible part-time employment is defined as a situation where a certain number of employees are forced to work shorter hours or shorter weeks, or are sent on administrative leave with or without partial compensation. Normally it is forced onto the employees, which is confirmed by the fact that their average family per capita incomes are below or equal to the minimum living cost.

All the above challenges facing a researcher of the employment situation can be met only after a series of specialized sociological surveys and additional selective studies. When organizing such selective studies, it seems feasible to concentrate on households. Answers to a questionnaire obtained at a working place can never be as sincere as at home. A household is an elementary consumer unit where wages and other family incomes undergo redistribution. Under the conditions of an economic crisis and sharply contracted social guarantees provided by the state, households (families) were forced to shoulder the burden of a multitude of social and economic problems. A household is also a more lucrative object of study than a separate individual because such a study allows the classification of families by the share of their non-working dependents. And this, in turn, will help to more precisely determine the numbers of those in extreme poverty who need special targeted social protection.

## 5 Enterprise Behavior and Employment Policy

In the course of the reform, state and industrial bodies' ownership rights have been decentralized and handed over to enterprises and other legal and physical entities. Privatization as the key element of Russian economic reform is reviving the institute of private ownership as a basis for an efficient economy. Undoubtedly, a large-scale overhaul of property relations is the best way to boost competition and the economic efficiency of enterprises (Vsemirnyj Bank, 1996, p. 8), as in a market environment the newly acquired economic independence will inevitably lead privatized enterprises to choose the most efficient path for resource utilization.

Initially, the concept of privatization in Russia was aimed at creating a structure of divested property that would automatically lead to its further redistribution in favor of independent responsible owner, but a system of politically biased privileges, associated with the first phase of privatization, produced an inefficient structure of charter capital. The majority of shareholders in each enterprise were its employees, with a significant proportion of the stock belonging to management. According to P. Sutela, "one should characterize the immediate post-privatization property relations in Russia as managerial, not employee ownership" (Sutela, 1996). All later changes in the charter capital structure consisted of a further redistribution of shares in favor of enterprises' administration and consolidated large-stake owners. (Simachev, 1997). A survey by the Institute for Strategic Analysis and Entrepreneurship showed that the bulk of shares in the majority of jsc's was owned by the members of their administration. Notably, executive officers in joint-stock companies formed during the initial stage of privatization own more stock (over 40 percent) than managers of recently formed companies (over 20 percent) (Komarov, Simachev, Klimenko, 1996).

By the end of the voucher phase of privatization, about half of divested enterprises had no outside stockholders, and two-thirds of such enterprises had no stockholder representatives on their boards of directors. Stock market control over enterprises is insignificant, as shares outstanding belong to very few enterprises and their liquidity is low. Thus the expected positive effect of the decentralization of the decision-making procedure has failed to materialize in full, because decisions made by enterprises completely depend on their directors' own goals and methods.

As a result of all the above, the economic policies of transitional-period enterprises is characterized by an urge to maintain production at any cost, which makes them fundamentally different from both market-oriented companies with their drive towards profit maximization, and deficit-economy enterprises which normally strive to maximize their resources.

The new structure of ownership that emerged after the first phase of privatization failed to result in an efficient management structure or in the modernization and development of production. These objectives could have been achieved (as reformers had planned) through property right redistribution, involvement of new (outside) owners, adjustment in the management structure and replacement of old managers, as well as through the partial sale of assets. Yet this required certain macroeconomic conditions including stable legal regulations and strict financial rules for enterprises, which unfortunately did not exist (Dolgopiatova, 1995, pp 11–14). Further plans included luring substantial investment in the course of the monetary stage of privatization by selling state-owned stakes and real properties, and by implementing investment programs.

In this situation most enterprises concentrated on mere survival. In Russia, the adjustment strategies of an enterprise consisted in preserving existing structures: the unit's integrity, including all its personnel, the administration's authority of supervision, and ties with major counteragents, as well as traditional sources of development and traditional types of activity. When the government tried to impose financial (though fairly incoherent) constraints, enterprises either responded with market adjustment strategies or resorted to various means designed to mitigate these constraints (Dolgopiatova, 1995). At the same time, enterprises based their survival strategies on the easiest options open to them, on the obtainment of state support and/or the sale of their own resources. Two other options available were shadowy financial turnover and (broadly used) barter trade.

In a transitional economy, the basic pattern of efficient enterprise strategies undergoes various modifications. In her study of active and passive enterprise strategies, Inkeri Hirvensalo distinguishes between five types of enterprise behavior and classifies enterprises accordingly into *strategic restructurers, traders, lobbyists, asset strippers and downsizers,* and *footdraggers* (Hirvensalo, 1996, p 55). Differences in their economic behavior are determined by the interests, mentality, and qualification of the most active groups of owners, which may include both enterprise managers and outside investors.

However, other features of enterprise behavior that reflect their attempts to introduce market adjustment and cost-cutting policies have recently transpired. At the same time, these changes often coexist with old strategies of tax dodging and social payments. Internal restructuring is increasingly becoming one of the most important elements of enterprise strategies. During the initial phase of privatization it occurred at a half-hearted pace and only concerned labor shedding, whereas now, with the acute lack of current funds and investment resources, restructuring measures will be extended to social facilities, production areas, and sites.

This situation specifically affects employment policies by enterprises which

- shed labor only insignificantly despite a significant production decline, and
- reduce net work-time by resorting to partial employment and administrative-leave practices.

The ultimate result of these developments is a situation where excessive employment is a blessing to administrations because it insures their enterprises' survival and allows them to continue the economically inefficient utilization of resources which nevertheless brings them additional income (rent). This conclusion can also be supported by the fact that labor intensity and production efficiency at such enterprises go down.

Excessive workforce (i.e. personnel numbers exceeding the existing production requirements) is one of the characteristic features of a modern Russian enterprise. The scale of over-employment at Russian enterprises has been *significant and practically stable* throughout the period of reform (that is why open unemployment figures remain fairly moderate). Regular countrywide surveys of the situation at manufacturing enterprises, undertaken by the "Russian Economic Barometer" (REB)[4] in 1995–1997, show that fluctuations of excessive workforce during that period were insignificant. The proportion of manufacturing enterprises with excessive workforce increased from 58% in 1995 to 63% in 1996, but then it bounced back again, practically to the initial level. The last REB survey shows that the share of "extra hands" stood at about one-fifth (18%) of the total personnel at overstaffed enterprises. As mentioned, official statistics only cover two types of overstaffing, when personnel either 1) works a part-time schedule, or 2) is sent on administrative leave, which is evidently insufficient for a comprehensive analysis of this phenomenon.

---

[4] The monthly sample of these surveys contains about 200 enterprises of all major manufacturing industries from all Russian regions. The last survey was held in November 1997 with the financial support of the Ford Foundation.

A number of employment studies have shown that part-time working schedules and administrative leaves produce different effects. A part-time schedule gives enterprise management some breathing time to stall redundancy cuts, and the higher the number of part-time employees, the lower are redundancy rates at these enterprises. Administrative leaves, on the contrary, speed up extra hands' exodus.

To get the true picture, one has to focus on other manifestations of excessive labor as well. These are lower working loads with certain personnel categories, differentiation of various personnel categories by the intensity of labor, higher wage differentiation between various personnel categories when certain categories see their wages jump while other's have to suffer not only lower wages, but wage arrears as well, and in some cases production by some groups of the personnel (whose work load may be fairly extensive) of unprofitable products (some enterprises resort to this method to keep "extra hands" occupied).

Some studies completed in St. Petersburg and Russia-wide show that there are three major reasons why enterprise management hold on to excessive labor:

1. Their feeling of social responsibility or paternalism with regard to their personnel that are supported, in many cases, by expectations of higher demand on their production.
2. Prohibitive organizational and financial costs of the redundancy procedure.
3. Aspirations to maintain the status of the enterprise (the power, influence, and authority of a director often depend on the size of the enterprise).

Enterprises' capacity to hold on to their excessive workforce is limited by their reserve of liquid monetary resources.

When financial difficulties persist for a long time redundancy levels at the most vulnerable enterprises begin to rise quickly. A policy of budget constraints leads to a bi-polar concentration of loss-generating and prospering enterprises and thus to growing "open" unemployment.

The most thriving enterprises are those who export their products (ferrous and non-ferrous metallurgy), produce goods or services enjoying strong domestic market demand (e.g. food industry), those with a special strategic importance for the country or region and therefore heavily subsidized by the state and enjoying tax benefits, and at last companies with thriving financial or commercial affiliates. In mechanical engineering the best financial situation is enjoyed by power engineering, shipbuilding, the aircraft industry, and spaceship-and-missile industries. These enterprises are radically restructuring their systems of management by eliminating or bringing down the status of those divisions that used to play a central role under the conditions of a deficit economy, and by establishing or expanding those divisions that are of crucial importance in a market environment. As a rule this restructuring is taking place in a situation of a dual structure of management. Production management is concentrated in the hands of the chief engineer and shop superintendents, staunch proponents of a command economy system, while the joint-stock company management is dominated by market-oriented financial and economic units.

All the above may trigger certain changes in enterprises' employment strategies in the nearest future. The restructuring of property rights is nearing completion and the excessive-payroll tax has been revoked. Given a careful economic policy by the government, all these factors cannot but lead to massive redundancies.

## 6 The Case of St. Petersburg

St. Petersburg is second only to Moscow in relation to its share of research institutes, scientists and people with higher education within Russia. A third (32.6%) of St. Petersburg's employable age population has university or equivalent degrees, compared to less than a fifth (18.4%) of the total working population in Russia. St. Petersburg is the home of more than one in ten of Russia's research institutions and of one in seven of all Russian scientists. This concentration of highly qualified workers is due to the predominance of university and research institutions but is also a reflection of the historically high share of the military industrial complex in the city. These are sectors highly dependent on direct state expenditure and rather exposed to the political, economic, and social changes that have taken place since the early 1990s. The ability of the highly skilled and scientifically educated workforce of St. Petersburg to adjust to the new economic circumstances is key to St. Petersburgs ability to adjust to the new more open and competitive economic environment.

In St. Petersburg, because of the economic crisis and insolvency of the former major customer, the state, there occurred a substantial redistribution of employment between manufacturing industries and public industries and services. The exodus of labor from manufacturing was concurrent with a significant increase of workforce in the latter two sectors. Within manufacturing industries, employment grew in natural monopolies, in the food industry, and in metallurgy.

Another direction of labor spillover was between large, medium, and small businesses, with the latter taking the upper hand. The strongest outflow from large and medium enterprises was registered in 1994, when new economic sectors and small businesses, in contrast to the rest of the economy, had an upsurge in their demand for labor. More mobile and flexible small enterprises (units with under 100 employees in manufacturing and construction, and under 50 employees in other industries) substantially increased their personnel (see Table).

According to the St. Petersburg Statistics Committee, in 1996–1997 the bulk of individuals combining jobs or working on contract at large and medium enterprises in St. Petersburg fell on education (42%), healthcare (15%), culture and science (17%), and manufacturing (6%).

At the same time, according to regular surveys by VTCIOM, a strong urge for additional employment is also characteristic of management personnel and chief specialists at enterprises. In 1997 and 1999, the quantity of officially registered part-time employment went down. By the end of 1997, St. Petersburg had 51 500 people (3.8% of the average registered employees) working part-time schedules, or 40% down from the end of 1996. During each month of 1997, between 3% and 4% of large and medium enterprise employees were either on administrative leave or worked part-time. In 1999 about 88.6 thousand people worked part-time, and 83.4 thousand people were on administrative leave.

The total figure of those on forced leaves in 1997 is 133 600 employees, or 10% of their average registered number. The average duration of administrative leaves was 44 days per person, and 28% of those on administrative leave got no monetary compensation.

**Table F1.** The average number of registered personnel at enterprises of different size ('000 people)

| | 1992 | 1993 | 1994 | 1995 | 1996 | 1997 | 1998* | 1999* |
|---|---|---|---|---|---|---|---|---|
| Personnel at large and medium enterprises | 1936.3 | 1785.6 | 1652.2 | 1545.3 | 1418.8 | 1322.1 | 1325.6 | 1284.6 |
| As share of the economically active population | 75.5 | 69.8 | 63.9 | 59.4 | 55.1 | 47.9 | 51.2 | 49.0 |
| Personnel at small enterprises | 450.3 | 583.0 | 700.5 | 821.5 | 911.2 | 1089.3 | 591.2 | 671.9 |
| As share of the economically active population | 17.6 | 22.8 | 27.1 | 31.6 | 35.4 | 42.4 | 22.8 | 25.6 |

* *Rossijskij statisticheskij ezhegodnik. RF State Statistics Committee. 2000*
*Sources: Sankt-Peterburg i Leningradskya Oblast' in 1996, Peterburgcomstat, 1997; Social'naya i Economicheskaya Situatsiya v Sankt-Peterburge i Leningradskoy Oblasty v Janvare-Dekabre 1997, Peterburgcomstat, 1998;*
*Social'naya Sfera v Sankt-Peterburge i Leningradskoy Oblasty, Peterburgcomstat, 1997.*
*Social'naya Sfera v Sankt-Peterburge i Leningradskoy Oblasty, Peterburgcomstat, 1998*
*Social'naya Sfera v Sankt-Peterburge i Leningradskoy Oblasty, Peterburgcomstat, 1999*
*Social'naya Sfera v Sankt-Peterburge i Leningradskoy Oblasty, Peterburgcomstat, 2000*

In St. Petersburg, secondary jobs are held mostly by engineering and technical personnel (24% of total secondary jobs), managers (28%), and professionals in the humanities (doctors, teachers, lawyers, etc.) (18%). The bulk of those with secondary jobs are men (56%) and persons in the 31–40 age bracket (37%).

On par with manufacturing, the second major home of those seeking secondary jobs is education (22% of respondents from each of the two industries). The majority of those wishing to have a secondary job (57%) work at large and medium sized state enterprises.

The understanding of the experiences and behavior of a highly educated workforce is significant for the understanding of the success of the labor market transformation. This is especially true in St. Petersburg, were this group makes up a significant proportion of the labor force. Therefore the goal of the Tacis/ACE project is to get information on job-seekers behavior and the ability of the highly skilled and scientifically educated workforce of St. Petersburg to adjust to the new economic circumstances.*

* A study completed in 1997–1998 by TACIS ACE, Leontief Centre (St. Petersburg), Cranfield School of Economics (the UK), PSB Partners (London/Berlin), and the VNG (Netherlands)

The study of job seekers is based on a survey of highly educated people visiting the Molodezhnaja Birzha Truda (MBT or Youth Employment Exchange). A a stratified sample was developed based on the general database of clients held by the MBT. Its database represents different categories of job-seekers, the unemployed and people wanting to change their job or to obtain second job. Its company client base includes both older enterprises, public services (health, education), and particularly enterprises in the new service sector.

Case studies, based on interviews with the most senior manager responsible for personnel issues, were conducted in 21 enterprises. The enterprises represent a cross section of employers in St. Petersburg, including smaller and larger employers, and organizations with Russian, foreign, and mixed ownership. The review of the enterprise case studies show a varied picture of demand for labor and of practices for dealing with recruitment and retention. Interestingly, the survey shows that recruitment and retention is not a major problem for the majority of enterprises, suggesting that the labor market has perhaps somewhat stabilized. While the companies were not specifically selected for their reliance on highly educated labor, the majority of the workforce in the majority of the companies falls under this category. There was a clear bias towards employees under the age of 45, especially in the more recently established enterprises. The skill shortages that are perceived by companies concern as much market related skills as broader motivational and attitudinal deficits among current and potential employees. Examples are initiative, motivation, and flexibility, coupled with formal qualifications and experience.

Informal practices such as reliance on existing employees, relatives and business contacts were clearly seen as the most efficient way of attracting new employees. All other methods, including recruitment agencies, advertisements, or state agencies, were only used by a minority of enterprises. The high level of discontent with private recruitment agencies, seen in principle as an appropriate channel for specialists in managers, suggests that users are becoming more critical and that this pressure might add to the development of the new industry.

In relation to personnel policies, be it remuneration, training, or development, the survey suggests that financial constraints as well as ownership and size are major factors. The majority of enterprises pursue active training policies. Larger foreign owned / joint venture companies tend to have the most developed personnel policies, including incentive policies, training and development, personnel planning, and recruitment and selection procedures. The 'old' Russian enterprises were often hindered both by a lack of financial resources and by a fragmented and planning related approach to personnel decisions, a heritage from previous times. The 'new' Russian enterprises were often too small to warrant internal specialist support for personnel issues. Nevertheless, respondents showed considerable awareness of the need for professionalism in this area, even if this mainly took the form of being aware of their lack of expertise.

As said, labor turnover appears to have been reduced with the exception of some of the 'new' Russian enterprises which seem to be the focus for high labor turnover as well as for temporary and fixed term employment. These enterprises also put the greatest emphasis on variable earnings and 'flexibility' in the sense of having employees available for as long as they are needed. Other enterprises, particularly foreign owned ones, were more interested in creating stability.

## 7 Concluding Remarks

The Russian labor market attracts researchers' attention as both an important element of social challenges facing the country, and a crucial macroeconomic aspect of economic transformation. Economic transition has produced a specific, controversial impact on the labor market in Russia.

The current stringency of the labor market stems from depleted economic activity and a drastic contraction of employment. At the same time, official unemployment figures fail to capture the actual scale of unemployment in the country.

There is an evident discrepancy between the depth of the economic slump and employment figures evolution. Enterprises face a dilemma of either shedding excessive labor or keeping all their personnel at any cost. Employment undergoes diversification and falls into several types, full-time employment, part-time employment, temporary employment, and secondary employment. "Grey" employment is expanding.

Unemployment in Russia is held at comparatively low levels due to specific forms of labor market flexibility. The current level of unemployment reflects the existence of variegated options to find a job beyond the formal sector of economy. There is no definite answer to the question to what the actual extent of private sector's influence on unemployment is, or whether unemployment can be considered an instrument for market restructuring.

The current practices by enterprises, which establish shortened work weeks or send their personnel on administrative leave, is of special interest for market watchers. They define this situation as either part-time employment or a form of latent unemployment.

The still persisting political and economic instability in the country influences both enterprises' policies and the character of employment.

## References

Aslund A (1995) How Russia Became a Market Economy. Brookings

Chachulina L (1996) Povedenie rabotnikov na rinke truda v uslovijach perechoda k rinochnoy ekonomike. In: Sotsial'naja politika v period perechoda k rinku. Problemi i reshenija. Sbornik statey Mosk, Tsentr, Karnegi

Clarke S(1996) Structural adjustment without mass unemployment? Lessons from Russia. In: The Restructuring of Employment and the Formation of a Labor Market in Russia. Centre for Comparative Labor Studies, University of Warwick, pp 4–5

Clarke S et al (1996) The restructuring of unemployment and the formation of a labour market in Russia. ISITO, Moscow, Centre for Comparative Labour Studies, University of Warwick

Commander S, Coricelli F (1995) Unemployment, Restructuring and the Labour Market in Eastern Europe and Russia. In: Commander S et al, Russia. N.Y.

Dolgopiatova T (1995) Rossiyskiye promyshlennye predpriyatiya: osobennosti perekhodnoy modeli povedeniya. Predprinimatelstvo v Rossii 1: 11–14

EBRD (1997) Transition Report.

Gaidar E (1998) Taktika reform i uroven' gosudarstvennoi nagruzki na ekonomiku. Voprosi ekonomiki 5

Garsija-Iser M, Golodetz O, Smirnov S (1997) Kriticheskie situazii na regional'nykh rynkakh tryda. Voprosi ekonomiki 2: 114–124

Hinversalo I (1996) Strategic Adaptation of Enterprises to Turbulent Transitionary Markets. Operative Strategies of Finnish Firms in Russia and the Baltic States during 1991–1995, ETLA, Helsinki

Illarionov A (1996) Bremja gosudarstva. Voprosi ekonomiki No. 9

Kapelushnikov R (1998) Dvizhenije rabochej sily i rabochix mest v promyshlennosti. Voprosy Ekonomiki No 2

Komarov A, Simachev Yu, Klimenko A (1996) Ustavnoy kapital: vazhen ne razmer, a struktura. Ekonomika i zhizn No 47

Layard R, Richter A (1994) Labour market adjustment in Russia. Russian Economic Trends 3/2

Maleva T (1998) Rossiiskij rynok nruda i politika zanjatosti: paradigmy i paradoksy. Gosydarstvennaja i korporativnaja politika zanjatosti/ Moskovskij Tzentr, Karnegi

Nesporova A (1996) Tendentsii i politika na rossiiskom pinke truda. Problemi teorii i praktiki upravlenija No 1

OECD (1996) Labour Resrtuctering in Russian Enterprises: a case study.

Samson I (1998) Will Russia Come to a market Economy? Voprosi ekonomiki No 8

Sabirjanova K (1998) Mikroekonomicheskij analiz dinamicheskix izmenenij na rossijskon rynke truda. Voprosy Ekonomiki No 1

Shkaratan O (1998) Sozial'naja politika v kontekste postsovetskoi ekonomiki. Mir Rossii, 1\2

Simachev Y. (1997) Struktura stoimosti chastnogo biznesa kak pokazatel urovnia ego razvitiya. Voprosy ekonomiki No 6

Standing G (1994) Employment Restructuring in Russian Industry. World Development 22(2)

Sotzial'naja politika v period perekhoda k rynky: problemy i reshenija (1996) Moskovskij Tzentr Karmegi.

Sutela P (1995) But Does Mr. Coase Go to Russia? Review of Economies in Transition No 4

Vsemirniy Bank (1996) Ot plana k rinku. Otchet o mirovom razvitii.

Zaslavskiy I. (1998) K charakteristike truda v sovremennoy Rossii. Voprosi ekonomiki No 2

Zaslavskiy I. (1998) K novoy paradigme rinka truda. Voprosi ekonomiki No 2

## Appendix

**Table F2.** Labor market dynamics

| | 1992 | 1993 | 1994 | 1995 | 1996 | 1997 | 1998 |
|---|---|---|---|---|---|---|---|
| Economically active population (million people) | 76.0 | 75.4 | 74.1 | 73.0 | 73.2 | 72.8 | 72.6 |
| Including: | | | | | | | |
| Employed | | | | | | | |
| - as millions of people | 72.1 | 70.9 | 68.5 | 66.5 | 65.9 | 64.7 | 63.7 |
| - as percent of the total | 94.8 | 94.0 | 92.3 | 91.0 | 90.1 | 88.8 | 87.7 |
| Unemployed | | | | | | | |
| - as millions of people | 3.9 | 4.5 | 5.6 | 6.5 | 7.3 | 8.1 | 8.9 |
| - as percent of the total | 5.2 | 6.0 | 7.7 | 9.0 | 9.9 | 11.2 | 12.3 |

*Sources: Rossija v tsifrax . Kratkij stat. sbornik/ Goskomstat Rossii, 1999*

**Table F3.** Distribution of employed people by sector of economy (million people)

| | 1992 | 1993 | 1994 | 1995 | 1996 | 1997 | 1998 | 1999 |
|---|---|---|---|---|---|---|---|---|
| All people employed, | 72.1 | 70.9 | 68.5 | 66.4 | 66.0 | 64.7 | 63.7 | 64.0 |
| Including: | | | | | | | | |
| In public and municipal undertakings | 49.7 | 37.6 | 30.6 | 28.0 | 27.7 | 25.9 | 24.4 | 24.4 |
| In private sector | 13.2 | 19.9 | 22.6 | 22.8 | 23.5 | 25.8 | 26.6 | 28.3 |
| In public organizations | 0.6 | 0.6 | 0.5 | 0.5 | 0.4 | 0.4 | 0.4 | 0.5 |
| In joint undertakings | 0.2 | 0.3 | 0.3 | 0.4 | 0.6 | 0.7 | 0.8 | 1.2 |
| In organizations of mixed ownership | 8.4 | 12.5 | 14.5 | 14.7 | 13.8 | 11.8 | 11.5 | 9.6 |

*Sources: Rossija v tsifrax . Kratkij stat. Sbornik. Goskomstat Rossii. 1999*
*Rossijskij statisticheskij ezhegodnik. RF State Statistics Committee. 2000*

**Table F4.** Distribution of citizens employed in economy, by industry (%)

| | 1992 | 1993 | 1994 | 1995 | 1996 | 1997 | 1998 | 1999 |
|---|---|---|---|---|---|---|---|---|
| All people employed, including: | 100 | 100 | 100 | 100 | 100 | 100 | 100 | 100 |
| Manufacturing | 29.6 | 29.4 | 27.1 | 25.9 | 24.8 | 23.0 | 22.2 | 22.4 |
| Construction | 11.0 | 10.1 | 9.9 | 9.3 | 8.9 | 8.7 | 8.5 | 7.9 |
| Agriculture and forestry | 14.3 | 14.6 | 15.4 | 15.1 | 14.4 | 13.4 | 13.0 | 13.7 |
| Transport and telecommunications | 7.8 | 7.6 | 7.8 | 7.9 | 7.9 | 7.9 | 7.9 | 7.6 |
| Retail and public catering | 7.9 | 9.0 | 9.5 | 10.1 | 10.3 | 13.5 | 14.0 | 14.6 |
| Housing and public utilities and Non-production domestic services | 4.1 | 4.2 | 4.4 | 4.5 | 4.9 | 5.2 | 5.8 | 5.3 |
| Health care, physical culture and social Provision | 5.9 | 6.0 | 6.4 | 6.7 | 6.9 | 6.8 | 7.1 | 7.0 |
| Education, culture and art | 10.4 | 10.2 | 10.8 | 11.0 | 11.1 | 11.1 | 11.3 | 11.1 |
| Science and research services | 3.2 | 3.2 | 2.7 | 2.5 | 2.3 | 2.2 | 2.2 | 1.9 |
| Finance, lending and insurance | 0.7 | 0.8 | 1.1 | 1.2 | 1.2 | 1.2 | 1.2 | 1.2 |
| Local government | 1.9 | 2.1 | 2.2 | 2.8 | 4.0 | 4.0 | 4.0 | 4.5 |
| Other | 3.2 | 2.8 | 2.7 | 3.0 | 3.3 | 2.7 | 2.8 | 2.8 |

*Sources: Rossija v tsifrax . Kratkij stat. sbornik/ Goskomstat Rossii, 1999*
*Rossijskij statisticheskij ezhegodnik. RF State Statistics Committee. 2000*

**Table F5.** Official unemployment in some regions , 1999

| | % |
|---|---|
| Russian Federation | 1.8 |
| Krasnodarsky kraj | 0.7 |
| St. Petersburg | 0.9 |
| Novosibirsky oblast | 0.9 |
| Moscow | 1.0 |
| Nizherodsky oblast | 1.0 |
| Permsky oblast | 1.0 |
| Saratovsky oblast | 1.1 |
| Tchelabinsky oblast | 1.1 |
| Kursky oblast | 1.4 |
| Uljanovsky oblast | 1.5 |
| Irkutsky oblast | 2.1 |
| Tumensky oblast | 2.3 |
| Vologodsky oblast | 2.3 |

*Sources: Goskomstat Rossii, Mintryd RF.*
*Rossijskij statisticheskij ezhegodnik. RF State Statistics Committee. 2000*

**Table F6.** Employment and Unemployment, 1992–1999

| | 1992 | 1993 | 1994 | 1995 | 1996 | 1997 | 1998 | 1999 |
|---|---|---|---|---|---|---|---|---|
| Number of people employed, million people | 72.1 | 70.9 | 68.5 | 66.5 | 65.9 | 64.7 | 63.7 | 64.0 |
| Number of unemployed people looking for job (the unemployed by ILO definition): | | | | | | | | |
| million people | 3.9 | 4.3 | 5.7 | 6.5 | 7.3 | 8.1 | 8.9 | 9.1 |
| percent of EAP | 5.2 | 6.0 | 7.7 | 9.0 | 9.9 | 11.2 | 12.3 | 12.9 |
| Number of people officially registered as unemployed: | | | | | | | | |
| million people | 0.58 | 0.84 | 1.64 | 2.33 | 2.51 | 1.99 | 1.93 | 1.27 |
| percent of EAP | 0.8 | 1.1 | 2.2 | 3.1 | 3.4 | 2.8 | 2.7 | 1.8 |

*Sources: Rossija v tsifrax . Kratkij stat. sbornik/ Goskomstat Rossii, 1999*
*Rossijskij statisticheskij ezhegodnik. RF State Statistics Committee. 2000*

**Table F7.** Length of unemployment in 1992–1998 .

| | 1992 | 1993 | 1994 | 1995 | 1996 | 1997 | *1 part* 1998 |
|---|---|---|---|---|---|---|---|
| Up to 1 month | 34,6 | 18,9 | 13,0 | 10,6 | 9,9 | 9,7 | 8,1 |
| 1–4 months | 44,9 | 39,9 | 35,4 | 32,8 | 28,7 | 27,8 | 26,3 |
| 4–8 months | 16,6 | 26,5 | 26,2 | 24,6 | 23,0 | 21,3 | 25,9 |
| 8–12 months | 3,7 | 12,2 | 16,5 | 18,0 | 20,2 | 18,2 | 17,2 |
| More than 12 months | 0,3 | 2,5 | 9,0 | 14,0 | 18,2 | 23,0 | 22,5 |

*Sources: Goskomstat Rossii, Mintryd RF.*

**Table F8.** Underemployment in 1993–1998

| | 1993 | 1994 | 1995 | 1996 | 1997 | 1998 | 1999 |
|---|---|---|---|---|---|---|---|
| Number of employees sent on administrative leave: | | | | | | | |
| percent of EAP | 6,9 | 10,3 | 8,4 | 10,4 | 7,3 | 7,1 | 4,7 |
| Percent of the employed | 6,9 | 11,4 | 9,2 | 11,4 | 8,0 | 8,2 | 7,4 |
| Underemployment: | | | | | | | |
| percent of EAP | 2,2 | 6,7 | 2,8 | 4,7 | 3,0 | 6,4 | 3,9 |
| Percent of the employed | 2,2 | 7,5 | 3,1 | 5,2 | 4,0 | 7,4 | 4,5 |

*Source: Goskomstat RF*

# G. Principles of Market-Oriented Labor Market Policies

John T. Addison

## 1 Introduction

Gradually in the western industrialized nations we have seen a movement toward active labor market policies and away from measures that simply support the individual's job search while offering a modicum of relocation assistance. The new emphasis is on training, job subsidies, and job search policies. To be sure, there has also occurred a reduction in the generosity of income maintenance – either in unemployment benefit replacement rates and/or entitlement periods – imparted by periodic deregulatory thrusts, but such developments have been distinctly secondary in importance to the development of proactive labor market policies.

The immediate backdrop to active labor market policies offering skills acquisition and reemployment assistance is of course the deteriorating position of less skilled workers as a result of (biased) technological change and heightened international trade. Such forces have led to falling relative (even absolute) wages of unskilled workers and, in those circumstances where wage flexibility is constrained, to rising levels of unemployment and greater unemployment persistence. The United States is typically cast as an example of the former case and continental Europe as illustrative of the latter. More generally, active labor market policies have been advocated as a means of addressing actual and prospective threats to competitiveness.

As a practical matter, however, despite the widespread popularity of manpower policy – as it used to be called – our understanding of the efficacy of such measures is still rather rudimentary. Much of what has been learned stems from the U.S. experience, because of that nation's long tradition of subjecting policy to appraisal and moving forward on the basis of demonstration projects. That said, account has also to be taken of regime differences between the United States and Europe and, within Europe, between advanced western nations and the transition economies. Fortunately, the sheer diversity of U.S. policy initiatives serves to cover many of the bases while the evaluations have general relevance.

## 2 The Case for Active Manpower Policy

Arguments in favor of active labor market policies have a basis in market failures and distortions. Among the more obvious distortions are unions, so-called 'efficiency wages,' and statutory or de facto wage minima. Minimum wages may prevent employers from employing low skill workers – or at least training them – while unions and efficiency wages may similarly elevate wage rates above market clearing levels. The (second-best) solution takes the form of skills training or subsidized employment.

In the same vein, capital market imperfections can be used to justify training programs (for relevant skills) because liquidity constraints can lead to underinvestment in human capital. In addition, it has been argued that excessive turnover and uncertainty lead firms to underinvest in both the general and firm-specific capital of their workers (the maintained hypothesis being that training is neither exclusively general nor specific)(see the essays contained in Booth and Snower, 1996). However, these underinvestment arguments are by no means uncontroversial in advanced market economies because of the lack of strong empirical support for credit constaints (see Cameron and Heckman, 1992) coupled with evidence that job shopping is a productive activity (Topel and Ward, 1992; Neumark, 1998).

Less controversial are the externalities associated with the public goods nature of labor market information. In principle, these externalities offer support for a state agency that collects and disseminates labor market information. The efficiency of the public job broking function is of course another matter (see the pessimistic evaluation in Addison and Portugal, 2000, and the empirical studies referred to therein). Externalities of a social nature also provide the basis for programs geared toward unskilled youth. Raising the income of such workers can mitigate crime and teenage pregnancy, and justify programs that do not pass a conventional benefit-cost test.

Relatedly, Heckman et al. (1998) have recently stressed the important role of dysfunctional families in the United States. The argument here is that some families do not provide adequate learning environments, thereby justifying policies aimed at disadvantaged children. The policies aim to improve the home environment of children, impart parenting skills, or provide alternative places for learning. This is by way of a long-term solution to tackling the skill deficit problem and is crucially linked to the empirical finding of a strong positive association between formal schooling and postschool training investments – the notion of universal complementarity (*vulgo*: skill begets skill). At issue is the point in the life cycle at which skill remediation fails.

Another justification for intervention arises from negative duration dependence, namely, the tendency for escape rates out of unemployment to decline with the spell length of joblessness. Abstracting from other imperfections, the tendency for unemployment duration to be time dependent does not by itself provide a basis for policy intervention since it may simply reflect a sorting phenomenon, whereby the least employable come to make up an ever larger share of the unemployment pooled. However, true duration dependence resulting from labor market "scarring" may give rise to inefficiencies. When unemployed individuals come to be ranked by employers on the basis of their spell length of unemployment, the better (among those workers separated for economic reasons) will not be able to signal their higher productivity and will be screened out in favor of employed job seekers and the shorter-term unemployed (see Blanchard and Diamond, 1994). Here a case can be made for direct job creation to break the cycle. True duration dependence can also arise from skill depreciation but the policy implications are here altogether less transparent – in terms of both compensation and training – outside of situations where major regime shifts have occurred; the most obvious case in point being the change from a centrally-planned economy to a market economy.

In the above we have commented on the broad efficiency case for an active labor market policy. Equity considerations may be no less important – both goals are formally recognized in the U.S. Job Training Partnership Act (see section 3). An important issue in the analysis of manpower policy is the extent to which the two are in conflict. If so, they should be reflected in the design of policy; for example, it may be inefficient to train older workers but appropriate to subsidize their employment if not their human capital.

To varying degree, all the above considerations are relevant to the transformation economies – particularly the social externalities of poverty and unemployment and credit market imperfections – and are underwrittten by the requirement for different skills than those previously acquired. But as usual the devil is in the detail.

## 3 Active Labor Market Policy in the United States

U.S. active labor market policy can be traced back to the 1962 Manpower Development and Training Act (MDTA). The intention of the Act was to offer training to technologically dislocated workers, but the emphasis was to shift in favor of disadvantaged workers as a result of the Economic Opportunity Act of 1964. Thereafter, the MDTA targeted welfare recipients and low income youth via classroom training, referrals to vocational schools, and on-the-job training. A key component of the MDTA was the Job Corps – established in 1964 and ongoing – which offered training for disadvantaged youth. The distinguishing characteristic of the Job Corps was, and remains, the provision of an extensive range of program services in a residential setting.

MDTA was replaced by the Comprehensive Employment and Training Act (CETA) in 1973. CETA gave states and local authorities the authority to operate training and other programs, and provided them with federal grants. The legislation also introduced public service job creation in response to the economic downturn 1970–71. Through time the latter program was to expand and account for a little under one half of all manpower outlays.

The stance of public policy again shifted in 1982 with the passage of the Job Training Partnership Act (JTPA). The legislation retained and strengthened the decentralized apparatus of CETA, giving primary responsibility for its implementation to the states, local authorities, and the business community. It also eliminated the public service employment component and generally reduced real outlays on the reemployment services offered the disadvantaged under Title IIA of the program. But the JTPA did include – under Title III – special assistance for dislocated workers, thereby supplementing the provisions of separate legislation on trade adjustment assistance.[1]

The Economic Dislocation and Worker Adjustment Assistance (EDWAA) Act of 1988 amended Title III of the JTPA. Under EDWAA, states were required to develop 'dislocated worker units' with the ability to react to major layoffs and plant closings, and help workers find and qualify for new jobs. Dislocated workers could receive retraining services (classroom, occupational skills, and/or on-the-job training), readjustment assistance (testing and counseling, job search and placement, supportive services to include child care and transportation allowances, and relocation assistance and pre-layoff assistance), as well as needs-related payments in the event of unemployment benefit exhaustion. As we shall see, the JTPA is in the process of being replaced by the Clinton administration's Workplace Investment Act.

The most important services offered disadvantaged workers under JTPA-Title IIA were classroom training in occupational skills plus basic education where this was adjudged deficient (44% of JTPA enrollees): job search assistance, covering instruction on how to locate jobs, prepare for interview, and write resumes (15% of enrollees); subsidized on-the-job training and work experience in private sector firms (15% of enrollees), providing up to 50% of the wage over 6 months; and short-term work experience in the public sector and not-for-profit organizations (6% of enrollees). But, as noted by LaLonde (1995, p. 154), training services varied markedly by demographic group. Thus, adults participating in classroom training were more likely to be females receiving vocational instruction, while youths were are more likely to be receiving remedial education. On-the-job training participants were disproportionately job-ready men, unlike those in work experience programs who were mainly adult females and youths without recent labor market experience.

Before addressing recent changes to mainstream manpower policy, it is important to note that welfare recipients, covered by the Aid to Families with Dependent Children (AFDC) program, have long been *mandated* to participate in separate employment and training programs. Under the 1967 Work Incentive

[1] Trade adjustment assistance (TAA) was first authorized under the Trade Expansion Act of 1962. It offered supplemental unemployment benefits to workers who lost their jobs because of trade liberalization. The program was expanded in 1974 under the Trade Act, as a result of which workers had only to show that import competition had 'contributed importantly' to their job loss. Amendments to the enabling legislation in 1981 sought in the first instance to reduce the cost of the program - by restricting supplementary benefits to the unemployment compensation levels obtaining in the relevant state - and, second, by placing more emphasis on training. Under the 1988 Omnibus Trade and Competitiveness Act, job training was made a specific requirement for eligibility under the program. Finally, as a result of the North American Free Trade Agreement, TAA was augmented by a so-called 'transitional adjustment assistance program' (NAFTA-TAAP). This offers the same benefits and services as TAA proper for those workers displaced by trade with Canada or Mexico, or whose jobs were relocated to either country. The claimant has again to be enrolled in an approved job training scheme in order to receive program benefits and services.

program (WIN), such welfare recipients were provided with job search assistance. Subsequently, a work experience (i.e. workfare) component was added. WIN was superseded by the Job Opportunities and Basic Skills Program (JOBS) in 1988. This more comprehensive legislation was designed to extend the type of assistance offered AFDC recipients via classroom and job training; in practice, however, funding limitations meant that the degree of supplementation was modest.

The 1996 Personal Responsibility and Work Opportunity Reconciliation Act (PRWORA) replaced the JOBs program (and AFDC) with the Temporary Assistance for Needy Families (TANF) block grant. The TANF grants give states the flexibility to design their own welfare programs in circumstances where they require recipients to engage in work or work-related activities for their welfare checks (now limited to 5 years in total). Post PRWORA initiatives include the Welfare-to-Work Grants Program and a Welfare-to-Work Tax Credit. Both seek to create job opportunities for the hardest-to-employ TANF recipients. Under the former initiative, resources can be used for job creation, on-the-job training, job placement and post-employment services, and job retention and supportive services. For its part, the tax credit for each eligible worker hired is equal to 35% of qualified wages for the first year of employment and 50% for the second year. Qualified wages are capped at $10,000 per year.

The most recent variant of mainstream manpower policy is the 1998 Workforce Investment Act (WIA) (see Manpower Report of the President, 1999, pp.127–129; Manpower Report of the President, 2000, pp. 162–164). The legislation seeks to integrate/consolidate a variety of programs/services at the street level in so-called 'one-stop centers,' designed to make the delivery system more accessible to individuals and businesses. WIA also sets up self-directed 'individual training accounts.' These are supposed to allow workers more choice over their training and retraining. To facilitate this process, the legislation requires training providers to give information on their performance along the dimensions of job placement, earnings, and job retention.

The one-stop centers offer universal access to core employment services, including unemployment insurance.[2] About 1,000 such centers, funded by the federal government in partnership with the states, have already have been set up. Their performance is to be carefully monitored. That is, states and local authorities will have to meet performance standards, and are subject to sanctions for failure to meet job placement, earnings, and worker retention goals. Training providers for their part have to be certificated and a condition for their continued eligibility is their meeting performance standards issued by the local Workforce Investment Board (dominated by members of the business community) - information on which is then transmitted to the one-stop centers. Youth councils are also established under each WIB. The goal is to improve coordination among the various

---

[2] A group of internet tools have been established under a so-called 'career kit.' This includes web sites listing job vacancies (http://www.ajb.dni.us/), resumes (http://www.atb.org), and information on occupational employment trends and job training requirements (http://www.acinet.org/acinet/).

agencies serving youth and to provide 12-month follow up services in respect of each program.[3]

## 4 Evaluation of U.S. Employment and Training Programs

A distinguishing characteristic of the U.S. evaluations, apart from their sheer number, is that they have often been conducted on an experimental basis. That is, assessment proceeds on the basis of random assignment of individuals either to a treatment group, which is allowed access to the program or to a nontreatment group, which is excluded from it. In principle, random assignment ensures that the two groups do not differ systematically in any way other than in their access to the program, so that outcome differences between the treatment group and the controls can with more assurance be attributed to the program. Classical experiments of this nature get around the difficult problem of controlling directly for characteristics that affect program outcomes but cannot be observed. (In practice, as we shall see in the next section, the process of randomization is never complete, neither is it a panacea.)

The emphasis on experimental methods in the United States reflects that nation's preoccupation with reducing welfare rolls/dependence. As noted by Heckman et al. (1999, fn. 96), experiments proliferated in the 1980s after the federal government authorized states to operate as demonstration projects workfare programs (i.e. community work experience programs) for their welfare populations.

Following the literature (and, in particular, the surveys by LaLonde, 1995; Heckman et al., 1999), we shall first distinguish between experimental and nonexperimental studies of programs designed for these disavantaged workers before turning to examine the effects of policies geared to the nondisadvantaged dislocated worker population. We conclude with findings from experimental unemployment insurance (UI) initiatives and some 'early intervention' policies. Additional interpretation and caveats are remitted to section 5.

### *Disadvantaged Workers – Nonexperimental Studies*

We begin by summarizing the results of nonexperimental studies of the early manpower programs – MDTA and CETA – that usually involve the construction of some control group having characterics similar to those of program participants (on which, see section 5).

[3] Another element of current policy is lifetime learning. This has two main components: a lifetime learning tax credit and a Learning Anytime Anywhere Partnership program. The former applies to the first $5,000 of a family's qualified educational expenses ($10,000 after 2002). The latter supports partnerships between the educational sector, businesses, and community organizations to address challenges in lifelong learning and postsecondary education.

Studies of MDTA and CETA indicate that, where successful, the programs raised subsequent earnings by between $1,000 and $2,000 per year (see LaLonde, 1995, Table 1, for 13 such studies). Given the modest cost of the programs – other than the Job Corps – earnings gains of this magnitude would, if sustained, imply a high rate of return on the investment. But most such studies usually follow program participants for only several years after the training event, so that much hinges on extrapolation.

No less important, gains of this order of magnitude are by no means observed across the board. Indeed, variability in impact is the hallmark of the nonexperimental literature, and not simply across cohorts but also within program cohorts and by the particular training service provided. Nonetheless, certain patterns are discernible in the studies. First, earnings improvement is consistently largest for disadvantaged adult females. For example, Ashenfelter's (1978) famous study of programs funded under MDTA reports earnings gains for white (nonwhites) adult females of $1,740 ($1,540) in the 12 months following the training event (1990 dollars). Second, although adult females always record earnings improvement, the same in not always true of adult males (see for example Kiefer, 1979; Dickinson et al., 1986). Where positive, earnings gains for adult disadvantaged males are always smaller than for their female program counterparts. Third, when one considers the results for disdavantaged youth it is typically found that exposure to program services typically *lowers* subsequent earnings. These findings are prima facie consistent with stigma effects attaching to program participation and/or opportunity costs in the form of sacrificed labor market experience. The principal exception is a study by Mallar et al. (1982) of the Job Corps, which points to large earnings gains (particularly for male youth) that persist for at least four years after the training event. Although substantial, these gains fall far short of covering the costs of the intensive Job Corps program, support for which thus hinges on a wider benefit-cost calculation emphasizing social savings from reduced criminal activity, the value of reduced use of other transfer and training programs, the value of output produced by participants during training, as well as earnings projections beyond the initial four-year follow-up interval. Not surprisingly, controversy attaches to each component magnitude (see LaLonde, 1995, p.164; Heckman et al., 1999, p. 2068).

### Disadvantaged Workers – Experimental Studies

The experimental literature was in no small part generated by the substantial variance in outcome indicators reported in the nonexperimental studies. Detailed summary findings from the now substantial literature on the WIN/JOBS and JTPA programs, and separate initiatives such as the National Supported Work demonstration, are provided by Heckman et al. (1999, Table 22), who identify social cost and employment/earnings outcomes by program service and demographic group. Overall, the experimental studies yield smaller earnings gains than their nonexperimental counterparts but nonetheless suggest that access to program services can benefit both the individual and society.

As before, the strongest results are observed for adult females. Although annual earnings gains are typically modest, they tend to persist over the survey interval and to accrue over a variety of (incremental) program services, such as job search assistance, work experience, and classroom training/on-the-job-training. Furthermore, they are often internally efficient. (The issue of deadweight losses and other external costs are discussed in section 5.) Some of the strongest evidence that access to training can improve the position of disadvantaged adult females comes from the National Supported Work (NSW) demonstration (see Hollister et al., 1984). The NSW operated from 1975–1979 and was designed to provide subsidized employment opportunities of 9 to 18 months' duration to trainees. It was targeted on long-term AFDC recipients (as well as ex-drug addicts, ex-criminal offenders, and disadvantaged youth). Adult females in the program experienced higher earnings than the controls for at least seven years after the training event ended (Crouch, 1992, Table 1). Earnings gains of similar magnitude are recorded for adult females under the more recent National JTPA study, with persistence over a 30–month post-training interval (see Bloom et al, 1992; Bloom et al.,1997).

The evidence from a smaller number of experimental studies pertaining to adult males is less conclusive, with some studies showing earnings gains vis-a-vis the controls and others pointing to zero or even negative impacts. Here the results are sensitive to the type of treatment offered. Thus, there is the suggestion that work experience does not lead to significantly higher earnings (e.g. the NSW demonstration). Rather, positive earnings effects appear to hinge on the provision of more intensive services such as job search assistance combined with on-the-job training if not classroom training (the National JTPA study).

Finally, there is no evidence from any U.S. experimental study that disadvantaged youth benefits from access to employment programs. Thus, the NSW demonstration indicates that none of the estimates of the treatments' relative earnings effects was statistically significant in the seven years following their exposure to lengthy work experience. Similarly, analysis of the JOBSTART demonstration that offering participants a wide range of program services (broadly replicating Job Corps services, but without the residential setting) fails to indicate earnings gains vis-à-vis the controls over a four-year follow up period (Cave and Doolittle, 1991). Similarly, the National JTPA provides no evidence that youths gained from any service strategy (classroom training, on-the-job training and/or job search assistance, or other services), this time over a 30–month follow-up period (Bloom et al., 1997).

### Evaluations of Dislocated Workers

Reflecting the preoccupation of U.S. manpower instruments with disadvantaged workers, there is comparatively little information on the effects of training and other programs for dislocated workers. Most of the evidence comes from some early demonstration projects. This evidence, while pointing to clear gains to dislocated workers from their exposure to job search assistance, fails to detect any incremental earnings advantage from the provision of additional services in the form of classroom training or even on-the-job training (see the survey by Leigh, 1990). More recent work suggests that the effects of some services, most notably classroom training, may have been more positive than first thought. Thus, for example, the New Jersey UI demonstration points to positive incremental effects of classroom training on participant earnings over a 10–quarter follow- up interval (Anderson et al., 1991).[4] Moreover, a study by Jacobson et al. (1994) reports that dislocated workers derive long-term earnings gains from completing rigorous vocational and academic community college level courses. As far as on-the-job training is concerned, however, there has been no real clarification of the disappointing results reported in the earlier literature.

### Other Evaluations

We conclude this section with some results from U.S. unemployment insurance (UI) experiments and a very different literature on the effects of early intervention policies for the disadvantaged.[5] For their part, the UI experiments have taken two main forms: cash bonus and job search programs. Both have been carefully surveyed by Meyer (1995).

The first UI bonus program was operated in Illinois in 1984. It offered all claimants – irrespective of their previous earnings or level of benefits – a $500 bonus (about four times the then average weekly UI benefit).[6] To receive the bonus, participants had to start a job within 11 weeks of filing (the qualification period) and retain the job for over 4 months (the re-employment period). The apparent success of the Illinois program directly led to three other bonus experiments in Pennsylvania, Washington, and New Jersey, which were more varied. For example, the two former experiments used different combinations of benefit amount and qualification period, while New Jersey experiment combined the provision of the bonus with job search assistance (see above).

The Illinois experiment produced very favorable results. Specifically, mean weeks of benefits fell by 1.15 weeks for those offered the bonus, while their earnings were modestly higher in the third quarter after filing the UI claim and significantly higher over a 12-month period (consistent with more weeks being worked). The reduction in benefits was achieved without having to pay a large number of bonuses and thus produced savings to the UI system. Because earnings also increased, the benefit-cost calculation was also favorable to the government and society. However, the results of the other experiments were less compelling. All yielded a reduction in benefits for those assigned to the claimant treatment, but this amounted on average to just one-half a week (average compensated jobless spells of the controls ranged between 15 and 20 weeks). As a result, there were mostly negative effects on the UI system. In addition, earnings gains among the

[4] See also the study by Corson et al. (1993) of classroom training under the trade adjustment assistance program.

[5] On UI self-employment demonstrations, see Benus et al. (1994).

[6] We do not dwell on that component of the Illinois experiment offering the $500 bonus to the employer (rather than the individual), other than to note that there were no statistically significant differences in duration of UI payments and subsequent earnings as between the treatment and control groups in this case - although it has been alleged that the voucher mechanism may have stigmatized participants by identifying them as less skilled or less motivated (Burtless, 1985).

treatment group were found in just one of the experiments, so that the costs to government and society were also broadly negative.

One reason for the dissonance in results between Illinois and the three follow-up experiments reflects the fact that its reemployment bonus effect combines a very large estimated effect for workers eligible for extended benefits (under the federal program) with a much smaller effect among workers eligible for the regular state funded benefits (Davidson and Woodbury, 1991). The former group appears to have disproportionately increased its search activity in response to the bonus payments. But any inference that such bonus payments might be of especial interest to continental European countries has to be qualified by the likelihood of 'displacement' effects, discussed in the next section.

Results of the UI job search experiments on the other hand are rather more favorable. There have been five such experiments – in addition to the hybrid New Jersey demonstration – each of which sought to intervene relatively early in the unemployment spell and, in varying degree, to provide enhanced job search assistance and more frequent checks of claimant eligibility. As noted, the effects of the experiments on weeks of benefits and earnings are reviewed in Meyer (1995). In all cases, the combination of job search assistance with enhanced enforcement of the job search requirement led to fewer weeks of unemployment benefits for the treatments. (Interestingly, in the case of the Washington experiment, one of the treatments eliminated all checks on work search, as compared with the traditional UI programs which required three employer contacts per week to justify continued receipt of benefits. For this treatment it was found that found that the duration of benefit receipt *increased* by 3.34 weeks.) At the same time as benefit duration decreased among the treatments – the magnitude being similar to that observed in the more costly bonus experiments – earnings actually increased for the more intensive approaches. While cautioning that the earnings effects are estimated with imprecision, Meyer concludes that program benefits exceeded costs from the perspectives of the UI system, the government, and society.

At issue, of course, is the relative contribution of job search assistance on the one hand and tighter enforcement of the work requirement on the other. To the extent that most treatments were a combination of both, it is impossible to determine the component magnitudes – a similar problem arises in evaluating the mainstream manpower policies reviewed earlier. It is important to make this determination for a number of reasons. For example, if better job matches dominate then it is less likely that we will observe displacement – namely, a reshuffling of the unemployed – and also more likely that employers will make greater use of the public employment service.

Another bright spot in the employment and training literature, now very broadly defined, is the apparent success of high quality early childhood interventions in yielding subsequent labor market benefits to the disadvantaged participant Heckman et al. (1998, Table 6) review ten of these programs. One such (experimental) study is the Perry Pre-school program in which disadvantaged subnormal children were randomly assigned to a treatment group (offered intensive high quality pre-school services for up to two years coupled with weekly home visits with parents) and a control group denied these benefits (see Schweinhart et al., 1993). Over the 22-year follow up period, the treatments not only achieved better test scores throughout but also higher high-school graduation rates (21%), lower grade retention (21%), reduced criminal activity (e.g. 2.3 lifetime arrests by age 27 as compared with 4.6 arrests for the controls), and considerably improved monthly earnings ($453 at age 27). Not surprisingly, the benefit-cost appraisal is highly favorable.

Here as elsewhere there is an issue of external validity since controversy attaches to the efficacy of the broad-based federal program Head Start (see, for example, Haskins, 1989). Nevertheless, the findings summarized in Heckman et al. do suggest that early intervention has considerable promise as a long-term solution to the labor market problems confronted by the disadvantaged.

## 5 Interpretation of the U.S. Evidence

Interpretation of the U.S. evidence has proceeded at the policy and technical levels. Dealing with policy first, one interpretation of the evidence would be that the benefits of employment policy have been modest at best and incapable of addressing the earnings and unemployment problems of low skilled workers. Opponents of manpower policy would focus on the low returns to conventional programs compared with private-sector training and argue that private sector training is broadly optimal to begin with or perhaps seek to encourage it through tax incentives and subsidies rather than through inefficient manpower programs. On this view, the only solution to skill deficits resides in early intervention – ensuring that students have a proper educational foundation – reflecting the complementarity between schooling investments and subsequent labor market investments, underwritten by the long period over which returns may be realized. A market solution would be no less relevant here, with a focus on school vouchers and charter schools rather than further infusions of monies into the public school system.

An alternative view would be that manpower policy has not yielded greater payoffs largely because public spending on low-income individuals has been modest, at least in respect of the scale of the skill deficits that policy-makers are seeking to address. Note that this view does not imply immediate across-the-board increases in subventions but, rather, increased expenditures that are targeted toward programs with the greatest payoffs on the basis of what has been learned from the experimental and nonexperimental studies. Its proponents would therefore emphasize the gains made by disadvantaged adult females across a variety of treatments; gains that have persisted through time and often yielded societal benefits. But implicit in this view is the argument that large gains do require more expensive services, even if the content has yet to be determined on the basis of additional demonstrations (e.g. the jury being still out on the efficiency of the Job Corps). Presumably, this view would also see scope for wage subsidies to facilitate the employment of residual groups.

An intermediate view would see the U.S. experience as illustrating that helping the existing disadvantaged must always be an incremental process, and one that is buttressed by favorable economic conditions. Sustained economic growth in the United States has already produced a modest reversal of rising skill differentials and begun to redress in part the large deficits in earnings that manpower policy is supposed to address. Tight labor markets have also encouraged employers to revise their stereotypes and offer employment and training to those previously statistically screened out. Unfortunately, the appropriate use of active manpower policy in favorable states of nature has received inadequate attention from researchers.

In all of this there is little disagreement on the need for policies that tackle skill deficits prior to labor market entry. Although the methods to improve schooling are at issue, there is much interest in early intervention programs based on the findings of the suggestive experimental studies. There are also signs that the thrust of manpower policy is also changing to reflect lifelong learning considerations through support for continuing human capital investments, though it is palbably the case that this shift has not been informed by as much evidence as has been assembled in the debate over more conventional manpower instruments.

It is sometimes claimed that the extant U.S. experience is of marginal relevance to Europe because of the focus of its policy on the disadvantaged. Thus, for example, might not less disadvantaged European youth gain more from their exposure to training programs than their U.S. counterparts? We have therefore also to consider European studies. In an important sense, however, this charge misses the important point that perhaps the main relevance of the U.S. experience resides in the framework used to inform discussion in the United States. We refer of course to the experimental and nonexperimental evaluation exercises that have helped shape public-sponsored programs since the mid-1970s.

A number of problems attach to both types of evaluation. Nonexperimental studies have sought to identify the (mean direct) effect of programs on those who receive program services (i.e. the effect of the treatment on the treated). The unobserved counterfactual is what program participants would have earned had they not received program services. The counterfactual is estimated using data on nonparticipants. Program participants are paired with an externally selected comparison group and adjustments made for inherent differences beween the two groups using a variety of estimators. There are a number of difficulties in using nonparticipant outcomes as the counterfactual. In particular, when individuals choose (or are chosen for) a treatment group, the participation decision will reflect unobservables that are likely linked to earnings. For example, if participants select to participate because of the poor alternatives otherwise available to them, there will be negative selection bias – that is, nonparticipants will have higher earnings than participants would have had if they had not participated. Accordingly, mean program effects will be understated. Conversely, if participants have unobservables that make them more likely to have higher earnings in the absence of a program, there will be positive selection bias and hence an overstatement of program effects. (Note, however, that it may still be more efficient to provide training to these individuals.)

An influential paper by LaLonde (1986) provided evidence that nonexperimental strategies involving the construction of comparison groups from alternative data sets and the application of available econometric techniques – most notably for dealing with selection bias – failed to replicate the experimentally generated results. That is, LaLonde compared actual results from the National Supported Work (NSW) demonstration with nonexperimental estimates that would have been obtained if no information had been available from the NSW's control group. The nonexperimental results were based on a variety of samples from general population surveys and various approaches for dealing with selection bias. As noted, none of the nonexperimental estimators passed muster – either in replicating the experimental estimates or passing conventional specification tests. Not surprisingly, LaLonde's study stimulated the use of experimental methods. Even if subsequent work was to call into question the generalizability of LaLonde's findings (see below), it is not in doubt that the comparisons used in the evaluations of the MDTA and CETA programs were inappropriate (Heckman et al., 1999).

In principle, random assignment gets round the problem of selection bias arising from missing data on common factors that affect participation decision and outcomes. (Strictly speaking it does not remove selection bias but, rather, balances the bias between the participant and nonparticipant samples.) However, as Heckman and Smith (1995) and Heckman et al. (1999) demonstrate, there are some important limitations of the experimental approach, quite apart from its cost and the ethical issues associated with denial of treatment. In particular, the actual implementation of experiments actually creates new forms of selection that require the application of nonexperimental procedures for making statistical adjustments. First, there is the problem of treatment group dropout and control group substitution important for all manpower programs other than the NSW).[7] The dropout problem means that the majority of experimental studies measure the mean-difference effects of an offer to treat rather than the effect of a treatment on the treated. Substitution bias refers to a situation in which members of the control group have access to substitutes for the experimental treatment, so that control-group outcomes may no longer correspond to the untreated state. Although this problem is common to both experimental and nonexperimental studies, the effect is that an important advantage of an experimental study is lost, so that auxiliary nonexperimental analysis may again have to be performed. Second, a problem unique to experimental studies is randomization bias, which arises when "random assignment causes the type of persons participating in a program to differ from those who would participate in the program as it normally operates," or "from changes in participant behavior due to the threat of service denial" (Heckman and Smith, 1995, p. 99). Third, there is the problem of calculating the effects of individual components of program services that are offered in sequence. This requires that randomization be conducted at each stage in the sequence. In practice, this has not been achieved under extant experimental evaluations of programs offering tiered services. Fourth, it is impossible to use an experimental design to obtain estimates of the impact on training on post-program wages or the duration of subsequent jobless spells – as opposed to the effects on earnings and employment rates. Consider wages for example. If the treatment affects employment, as any well-designed program should, then the sample of employed treatments will have diff-

---

[7] Note that dropping out is different from sample attrition since treatment dropouts will remain in the sample. The problem is that since attrition rates are nonrandom (being higher for those with poorer labor market characteristics) and larger for the control sample, experimental estimates of program impact will be biased. This selection bias must again be tackled using nonexperimental techniques

erent characteristics than the employed controls. If, as is likely, individuals recording zero wages are less skilled, then the experimental impact estimate will compound wage effects with its selection into employment effects. Here again a complementary nonexperimental analysis would be required to recoup the wage effects.

These and other criticisms,[8] do not vitiate experiments – indeed, since some of them not a by-product of random assignment, they contain suggestions for improved experimental design – but they do make the sensible point that experiments are not a panacea. Experimental data need on occasion to be supplemented with nonexperimental analysis. For the future, there are promising developments in the theory and practicė of nonexperimental methods that may offer unique solutions to many of the problems with experimental studies, given appropriate control group data. These theoretical insights and nonparametric estimators are set out in Heckman et al. (1999). The fact remains that evaluative research using extant datasets in nonexperimental analysis have provided less reliable conclusions of program impact than their experimental counterparts.

A final issue that cannot really be addressed through the application of experimental methods – even if the results of such exercises can inform as to the scope of the problem – is the need to consider indirect as well as direct effects. This consideration is especially relevant to Europe. Analyses of the programs considered here have examined the effect of treatment on the treated or the offer of treatment. In each case, it is typically assumed that the no-treatment outcomes in a given regime mirror those would obtain in a no-program regime. If the programs cause a substitution of program graduates for the non-treatments, however, program effects will be incorrectly estimated. In low-skill labor markets with overly high wage minima, the introduction of wage subsidies can produce sizeable displacement effects among previously employed low-skill workers even if unemployment and output is unaffected. Heckman et al. (1999, p. 2035) show that in these circumstances all commonly used estimators will produce misleading estimates of program impact since they focus only on the program effects on subsidized workers (i.e. direct effects).

The ideal way to evaluate programs in these circumstances is via a general equilibrium approach. One such approach has been applied in the context of the Illinois UI bonus experiment, considered earlier. Davidson and Woodbury (1993) offer an equilibrium model of the labor market, that allows them to determine the direct effect of the Illinois program through its effect on the search behavior of those offered the bonus as well as its indirect effect via the impact on equilibrium employment and the search behavior of those who do not receive bonus offers. Data from the Illinois experiment is used to infer values for the unobservable parameters of their search model, which is then solved to derive estimates of the displacement effect. The model distinguishes between eligibles who search more

[8] There are additional limitations of experimental studies. These include issues such as the determinants of program applications (which can generally not be addressed through experiments), and the general inability of experimental data to yield useful information about the overall distribution of program effects (i.e. the experiments yield only mean-difference estimates of a program's effects).

and ineligibles who have at once less incentive to search because of the competition from eligibles and more incentive because a job gained today offers a second bite of the cherry, namely, the prospect of a bonus payment in the future. Although the two effects are a wash, the rate of job acquisition falls, while for those ineligibles who will never qualify for the bonus (permanent ineligibles), only the reduced search effect obtains – unambiguously raising their unemployment. Unemployment falls on net, and even though the magnitude of the displacement effect nowhere exceeds 1.9 workers per thousand, this is sufficient to generate a displacement effect that is 30 to 60% of the gross employment effect of the bonus program.

## 6 European Evidence

It should come as no surprise to learn that micro studies of the effects of active labor market policies in Europe produce very mixed results. The vast majority of studies are nonexperimental and thus involve all the usual problems in constructing a relevant comparison group and selection issues. That said, many of the studies do contain more detailed information on trainee/control characteristics than their U.S. counterparts using administrative data, and have the added advantage of being able to exploit wage (rather than overall earnings) data.

Heckman et al. (1999, Table 25) summarize the results of 39 studies of employment and training programs in 9 European countries. Just three of the studies are experimental. Two of the three experimental studies look at UI job search-type programs in Sweden and the United Kingdom (see, respectively, the summary in Bjorklund and Regner, 1996; White and Lakey, 1992). Consistent with the U.S. evidence, both studies find that job search assistance plus 'prodding' serve to significantly raise employment rates of the treatments – for up to five years in the British (Restart) experiment.

Most of the studies point to reductions in unemployment rates/higher unemployment hazards or increased employment rates/lower employment hazards across a variety of programs. There is, however, no discernible hierarchy of effects with respect to the measures (classroom training, on-the-job training, and work experience, and so on). That said, some studies report statistically insignificant and even negative effects of employment and training policies.

Of the 39 studies reviewed by Heckman et al. (1999), significantly positive wage effects (if not earnings) are much less commonly encountered and a number of these are anyway rather implausible given the limited training exposure of the treatments. Again, some studies yield negative effects on wages. A case in point is Dolton et al. (1994), whose analysis of the British Youth Training Scheme (YTS) using data from the third cohort of the Youth Cohort Study indicates that YTS is associated with either lower earnings (for females) or insignificantly higher earnings (males). However, subsequent British research has suggested that there may be 'good' and 'bad' types of YTS training: bad where it is the only form of training provided, and good when it is accompanied by other types of private-sector training (Makepeace and Johnson, 1995). (But even the good YTS is not necessarily justified, since it may have been provided by employers in the absence of government subsidies.)

If European programs have had little positive impact on wages but an often (if not universally) positive impact on employment, the suggestion may well be that displacement of nonparticipants has occurred. Heckman et al. (1999, p. 2080) argue that the very scale of the European programs, taken in conjunction with their tendency to focus on on-the-job training, implies that "cost-benefit analyses based on the [observed] impact effects ... probably overstate the net social benefit derived from active labor market policies in Europe."

Necessarily, Heckman et al. (1999) can only go so far in summarizing the European evidence. Most notably, they rather neglect German research and nowhere consider the transition economies. The recent German evidence is evaluated in Fitzenberger and Speckesser (2000). (On the wider training issue, see also Pfeiffer, 2000.) Fitzenberger and Speckesser survey evidence on two important components of German active labor market policy, namely, continuing training and retraining on the one hand, and subsidized employment and wage subsidies on the other. They provide evidence from 20 training studies (12 for the former DDR and 8 for western Germany) and 4 subsidized employment studies (all for eastern Germany).[9] As far as the results of training programs in eastern Germany are concerned, only one study reports distinctly positive effects; the majority of the studies obtain no significant effects on either unemployment/employment or wages. The results for training in western Germany are mixed, arguably because of the linkage between public- and private-sector training. Yet three studies report significantly negative effects on such outcomes as labor market search, employment stability, employment, and wages. For its part, subsidized employment yields consistently positive outcomes for unemployment in only one study, the three other evaluations finding negative effects on unemployment hazards.

These are rather disappointing results, especially for eastern Germany. Abstracting from the very real problems of interpretation stemming from selection bias in nonexperimental studies – and the fact the positive effects, where observed, are modest – it remains the case that the research deals with only two aspects of active labor market policy in Germany while at the same time neglecting their acknowledged heterogeneity.

Although the labor market problems (and constraints facing) the transition economies have been well documented, together with certain institutional innovations to the employment problem – see, in particular, the comparative evidence assembled on ten transitional economies by Nesperova (1999) – very little is known about the impact of their employment policies. One of the more interesting evaluations is Burda and Lubyova's (1995) comparative analysis of active labor market policy in the Czech and Slovak republics, 1991–94. The authors use a 'matching function' – not to be confused with the matching method used in cross-section

[9] Also examined are five macroeconomic evaluations, dealing with short-and long-term unemployment, and labor market mismatch. The results are generally more favorable for subsidized employment than before in suggesting some diminution in structural unemployment, while training is associated with some reduction in long-term unemployment (but see below).

evaluations of employment and training measures – that links, at the district level, monthly flows of exits from unemployment to lagged stocks of unemployment and vacancies (see also Boeri, 1997). Additional determinants of the outflows from unemployment are individual district and fixed-time effects and of course various active labor market policies pursued (in the Czech case, proxied by either the number of participants in publicly-provided jobs and job creation schemes, or spending on those measures; in the Slovak case, captured by administrative staffing levels or expenditures).

For their preferred specification and most comparable results, it is reported that the expenditure measure is associated with significantly higher outflows from unemployment, the coefficient estimates being broadly similar for the two countries. In addition to providing estimates of the efficiency of policy in the two countries (in terms of bang per Koruna), since the Slovak republic slashed its manpower subventions by 71% in 1993, the authors attempt to estimate how much higher the outflows would have been – and, inferentially, how much lower steady state unemployment – without this cutback. They report that outflows from unemployment would have been 30% higher and the steady state unemployment rate 9.7% lower. Actual unemployment in the Slovak republic was 14.4% in 1993.

The actual magnitudes reported by Burda and Lubyova have to be taken with more than a pinch of salt; most generally because of the parsimonious nature of the matching model, and more specifically as regards the above projections because of omitted general equilibrium considerations and the implied regime change. Nevertheless, the consistency of the expenditure effects of employment policies in the two countries is of interest.

As was alluded to earlier, indirect effects are likely to be of especial concern in (western) Europe because of the prevalence of wage subsidies. Although there is some cross-country evidence that active labor market measures do serve to reduce aggregate unemployment, the estimates are often small and sometimes insignificant. Even if some of the smaller (absolute) point estimates reflect the presence of outliers, the overall conclusion would seem to be one of material displacement effects even where, say, the derivative of the unemployment rate with respect to the participation rate in manpower programs exceeds unity (see Scarpetta, 1996, p. 63).

The negative effects of employment and training measures have been addressed by Calmfors (1994). In addition to some effects that would hopefully be captured in microevaluations (such as reduced search activity and stigmatization effects), he also identifies deadweight effects (jobs that would have been created in irrespective of hiring subsidies), tax effects (changes in output in sectors taxed to pay for training and employment subventions), substitution effects (the change in relative wage costs causes the substitution of some categories of worker for others), and displacement effects (jobs generated by a program are at the expense of other jobs). Calmfors provides evidence from the Swedish experience that the deadweight and substitution in particular can tip the balance and outweigh the benefits. (It is interesting that Sweden is the principal outlier referred to above.) More formally, we have argued that there is no real substitute for general equilibrium techniques for measuring the indirect effects of training and employment practices. The European literature has instead used reduced form approaches (see

Heckman et al., 1999, p. 2036), although general equilibrium models have been used in Denmark to quantify the consequences of other measures to include the potential effects of EU enlargement.

In such reduced form analyses it is now conventional to account for the endogeneity of policy, that is, to formally recognize that policy initiatives may be undertaken in response to anticipated adverse labor market conditions in the future. For this reason, it is sometimes argued that the point estimates from microevaluations might provide a lower bound of the true effects. But there are other sources of policy endogeneity. Labor market policies are not solely to be viewed as a technocratic response. They can also be analyzed in public choice theoretic terms. Crudely put, active labor market policies might provide a cover for politicians who wish to appear to be doing something about unemployment, perhaps unemployment resulting from other policies (thus, the 'social chapter' inserted into the Treaty of Amsterdam might be construed as a means of mopping up unemployment resulting from the imposition of pan-European labor standards introduced under the social charter and social chapter initiatives).[10] This is doubtless overstating the case, but the political nature of employment and training policy has to be reckoned with. One important issue here is that these policies may massage the unemployment problem in the same manner as have early retirement measures and disability programs. Participants in most of the programs considered here will not be counted as unemployed, and the phenomenon of cycling between training or subsidized unemploynent and traditional UI benefits may create the illusion that the key problem of long-term unemployment has been lessened (see also Boeri, 1997). It follows that analysts should be particularly wary of using 'narrow' measures of unemployment in aggregative studies. More generally, assessment of policy should be informed by the demand for (e.g. on the part of employed 'insiders') and supply of (by politicians) of active labor market policy measures. It is of course a moot point whether interest groups that help determine the shape of policy are less entrenched in the transition economies

## 7 Concluding Remarks

Given four decades of experience, the lessons from market-oriented labor market policies – and for reasons of tractability I have restricted my attention to active labor market policies rather than the gamut of employment protection mandates (for an evaluation of which, see Addison and Hirsch, 1999) – might appear thin. One view of active labor market policy in western nations would be that it is all too easy to design and implement ineffective training programs, an assertion underscored by public choice considerations. But we have argued that some programs have been successful, even if we have yet properly to account for program heterogeneity, and much has been learned about how to measure program impact.

[10] This is not to deny certain positive features of the employment chapter, most notably its emphasis on benchmarking to best-practice standards which might improve the evaluation exercise.

The main lessons may nonetheless have more to do with what does not work than what does.

As for the transition nations, wherein rising unemployment may indeed be indicative of the progress made in the reforming their economies, and where the generosity of UI systems (replacement rates and/or duration of benefits) has already been cut, there is no alternative to the use of active labor market policies on a fairly wide scale. Policies should focus in the first instance on a very much improved job broking function (to include mobility incentives), start-up loans coupled with technical support, subsidized employment measures for youth to create new jobs, and some targeted wage subsidies for the disadvantaged. The training function would at all times benefit from close employer involvement which would also seem to imply the extension of training to employed workers. But programs have to reflect the real risk of long-term unemployment, and attempts to reduce this exposure will inevitably involve some cycling between program participation and unemployment benefits and limit the intensity of service provision.

Policy must be responsive to experience and labor market conditions, and must increasingly be guided by evaluation exercises and foreign experience in this regard. Thus far we have some idea about placement rates of various programs (see Nesperova, 1999, p. 59) but this falls far short of what is needed, namely, an assessment of the internal effectiveness of programs and calculation of indirect effects. Extant assessments on the basis of labor market matching functions do show evidence of increased turnover of the unemployment pool. This is useful in terms of the immediate need to limit exposure to long-term unemployment, but it says nothing about net program impact. Pilot projects are now under way under the aegis of World Bank and EU financing that should shed light on how program participants have fared relative to nonparticipants. Here as elsewhere, however, attention will then have to turn to evaluate the effects of policies on nonparticipants.

## References

Addison JT, Hirsch BT (1997) The Economic Effects of Employment Regulation: What Are the Limits? In: *Government Regulation of the Employment Relationship*, Industrial Relations Research Association, Madison, Wisc., pp 125–178

Addison JT, Portugal P (2000) Job Search Methods and Outcomes. Unpublished Paper, Department of Economics, University of South Carolina (Forthcoming in *Oxford Economic Papers*)

Anderson P, Corson W Decker P (1991) The New Jersey Unemployment Insurance Reemployment Demonstration Project Follow-Up Report. Unemployment Insurance Occasional Paper 91-1, U.S. Department of Labor, Washington DC

Ashenfelter O (1978) Estimating the Effect of Training Programs on Earnings. *Review of Economics and Statistics* 60: 47–57

Benus JM, Wood M, Grover N (1994) A Comparative Analysis of the Washington and Massachusetts UI Self-Employment Demonstrations. Abt Associates, Bethesda, Maryland

Bjorklund A, Regner R (1996) Experimental Evaluation of European Labor Market Policy. In: Schmid G, O'Reilly J, Schomann K (eds) *International Handbook of Labor Market Policy and Evaluation.* Edward Elgar, Aldershot, pp 89–114

Blanchard O, Diamond P Ranking, Unemployment Duration, and Wages. *Review of Economic Studies* 61: 417–434

Bloom HS, Orr LL, Bell SH, Cave G, Doolittle F, Lin W, Bos JM (1997) The Benefits and Costs of JTPA Title II-A Programs. *Journal of Human Resources* 32: 549–576

Boeri T (1997) Learning from Transition Economies: Assessing Labor Market Policies across Central and Eastern Europe. *Journal of Comparative Economics* 25: 366–384

Booth A, Snower D (eds) (1996) *Acquiring Skills – Market Forces, Their Symptoms and Policy Responses.* Cambridge University Press, Cambridge

Burda M, Lubyova M (1995) The Impact of Active Labor Market Policies: A Closer Look at the Czech and Slovak Republics. Discussion Paper No. 1102, Center for Economic Policy Research, London

Burtless G Are Targeted Wage Subsidies Harmful? Evidence from a Wage Voucher Experiment. *Industrial and Labor Relations Review* 39: 105–114

Calmfors L (1994) Active Labor Market Policy and Unemployment – A Framework for the Analysis of Crucial Design Features. *OECD Economic Studies* 22: 7–47

Cameron S, Heckman JJ (1992) Dynamics of School Attainment for Blacks, Whites, and Hispanics. Unpublished Paper, University of Chicago

Cave G, Bos H, Doolittle F, Toussaint C (1993) JOBSTART: Final Report on a Program for School Dropouts. Manpower Demonstration Research Corporation, New York NY

Corson W, Decker P, Gleason P, Nicholson W (1993) International Trade and Worker Dislocation: Evaluation of the Trade Adjustment Assistance Program. Mathematica Policy Research, Princeton NJ

Couch KA (1992) New Evidence on the Long-Term Effects of Employment Training Programs. *Journal of Labor Economics* 10: 380–388

Davidson C, Woodbury SA (1991) Effects of a Reemployment Bonus under Differing Benefit Entitlements, or, Why the Illinois Experiment Worked. Unpublished Paper, Department of Economics, Michigan State University

Davidson C, Woodbury SA (1993) The Displacement Effect of Reemployment Bonus Programs. *Journal of Labor Economics* 11: 575–605

Dickinson K, Johnson T, West R (1986) An Analysis of the Impact of CETA on on Participants' Earnings. *Journal of Human Resources* 21: 64–91

Dolton PJ, Makepeace GH, Treble JG (1994) "Public- and Private-Sector Training of Young People in Britain." In: Lynch LM (ed) *Training and the Private Sector. International Comparisons.* University of Chicago Press, Chicago, Ill., pp 233–281

Economic Report of the President (1999) United States Government Printing Office, Washington DC

Economic Report of the President (2000) United States Government Printing Office, Washington DC

Fitzenberger B, Speckesser S (2000) Zur wissenschaftlichen Evaluation der Aktiven Arbeitsmarktpolitik in Deutschland: Ein Uberblick. Discussion Paper No. 00–06, Center for European Economic Research/ZEW, Mannheim

Haskins R (1989) Beyond Metaphor: The Efficacy of Early Childhood Education. *American Pychologist* 44: 274–282

Heckman JJ, LaLonde RJ, Smith JA (1999) The Economics and Econometrics of Active Labor Market Programs. In: Ashenfelter O, Card D (eds) *Handbook of Labor Economics.* Vol. 3A, Elsevier, Amsterdam, pp 1865–2097

Heckman JJ, Lochner L, Taber C (1998) The Effects of Government Policies on Human Capital Investment, Unemployment and Earnings Inequality. In: *Third Public GAAC Symposium: Labor Markets in the U.S.A. and Germany*, Center for European Economic Research/ZEW, Mannheim, pp 305–336

Heckman JJ, Smith JA (1995) Assessing the Case for Social Experiments. *Journal of Economic Perspectives* 9: 85–110

Hollister R, Kemper P, Maynard R (1984) The National Supported Work Demonstration. University of Wisconsin Press, Madison, Wisc.

Jacobson L, LaLonde RJ, Sullivan D (1994) The Returns to Classroom Training for Displaced Workers. Unpublished Paper, Federal Reserve Bank of Chicago

Kiefer N (1979) *The Economic Benefits of Four Employment and Training Programs.* Garland Publishing, New York NY

LaLonde RJ (1986) Evaluating the Econometric Evaluations of Training Programs with Experimental Data. *American Economic Review* 76: 604–620

LaLonde R (1995) The Promise of Public-Sector-Sponsored Training Programs. *Journal of Economic Perspectives* 9: 149–168

Leigh D (1990) *Does Training Work for Displaced Workers?* A Survey of Existing Evidence. W.E. Upjohn Institute for Employment Research, Kalamazoo, Mich.

Makepeace GH, Johnson DH (1995) Does Vocational Training Pay? Lifetime Earnings, YTS and Vocational Training. Unpublished Paper, Department of Economics, University of Hull

Mallar CS, Kerachsky S, Thornton C, Long D (1982) Evaluation of the Economic Impact of the Job Corps Program: Third Follow-Up Report. Mathematica Policy Inc., Princeton NJ

Meyer BD (1995) Lessons from the U.S. Unemployment Insurance Experiments. *Journal of Economic Literature* 33: 91–131

Nesporova A (1999) *Employment and Labor Market Policies in Transition Economies.* Organisation for Economic Co-operation and Development, Paris

Neumark D (1998) Youth Labor Markets in the U.S.: Shopping Around Vs. Staying Put. Working Paper 6581, National Bureau of Economic Research

Pfeiffer F (2000)Training and Individual Performance in Europe: Evidence from Microeconometric Studies. Discussion Paper No. 00–28, Center for European Economic Research/ZEW, Mannheim

Scarpetta S (1996) Assessing the Role of Labor Market Policies and Institutional Settings on Unemployment: A Cross-Country Study. *OECD Economic Studies* 26: 53–113

Topel R, Ward M (1992) Job Mobility and the Careers of Young Men. *Quarterly Journal of Economics* 107: 439–480

White M, Lakey J (1992) The Restart Effect: Does Active Labour Market Policy Reduce Unemployment? Policy Studies Institute, London

# H. Rent-Seeking and Rent-Setting: Government Versus Competition (The Case of St. Petersburg)

Andrei Zaostrovtsev

## 1 Introduction

The proliferation of rent-seeking practices in Russia's post-communist economy has been explained in different ways. Most theories focus on the behavioral peculiarities of former state-owned companies, their incapacity, for a variety of reasons, to compete in a free market and provide quality that meets consumer needs (Alfandari, Fan and Freinkman, 1997; Earle, Estrin and Leschenko, 1997; Braguinsky, 1997; Kuznetsov, 1997). One other explanation links the dominance of rent-seeking practices in the Russian economy to missing markets (Polishchuk, 1997).

This paper mainly investigates the behavior of the government. The point is that the demand for artificially created rents does not originate solely from the business community, individual companies or interest groups. To a greater extent, this demand originates from the rent creator itself - the government, its politicians and bureaucrats. Models of rent-seeking behavior usually feature corrupt bureaucrats who lay claims to a part of the rent in the form of bribes by fashioning an environment that encourages rent-seeking (Appelbaum and Katz, 1987; Hillman and Katz, 1987). In this case, the government acts as the rent-setter.

The validity of this assumption was further corroborated by economists studying corruption practices. For instance, V. Tanzi (1998, p. 582) argued that "rigidities and rules are not exogenous and unmovable features of a society; a society is not born with these rigidities. They are created and, in fact, they may be intentionally created by public officials to extract bribes. When rules can be used to extract bribes more rules will be created." Maximizing their own utility, politicians and bureaucrats create an environment compelling the private sector to seek rent and thus to bring obvious benefits to the former. The more conducive the environment is to rent-seeking, the less suitable it is for competition. The consumer suffers, as competition is always to his advantage.

A competition analysis for Russian economy reveals a multiplicity of diverse administrative barriers that combine to form a nourishing medium for rent-seeking practices. For evidence, we can refer to a paper on the subject published by the Bureau of Economic Analysis (BEA, 1999a; 1999b). Moreover, rent-seeking environments have been increasingly acquiring regional traits.

In this paper, we will attempt to show how the authorities, by means of regional decision-making and regulations, knowingly and purposefully foster the institutions of a rent-seeking society in St. Petersburg - Russia's second largest city. We chose St. Petersburg for a reason. In the early 1990s, the city was, not undeservedly, considered a "showcase" of Russia's market reforms. The emergence, in the following years, of an environment that discourages fair competition in St. Petersburg may serve as a good indicator of competition problems in Russia overall, showing how the omnipotent bureaucracy employs administrative tools to suppress competition.

## 2 Industrial Policy and Rent-Seeking

For St. Petersburg authorities, industrial policy is one of the ways to encourage rent-seeking. City Hall's industrial policy is initiated and implemented mainly by the Committee for Economics and Industrial Policy (CEIP). The very existence of such a committee in a market economy is highly questionable. With its help the authorities effectively interfere with company management, manipulate taxes and arbitrarily grant or deny companies access to capital resources and land. In other words, the authorities invest taxpayers' money in business as they see fit in the light of their immediate priorities. Furthermore, there are no reliable guarantees of any returns on such investment.

### *Government Encouragement of Investment as an Incentive for Rent-Seekers*

In recent years, attempts have been made to legally institutionalize the city's industrial policy. In 1998, the Legislative Assembly of St. Petersburg passed a package of laws that, according their official interpretation, purported to encourage investment in the city. In reality, these laws created rent-seeking incentives for businesses by compelling them to fight for various institutionalized privileges.

In this sense, St. Petersburg law "*On Government Incentives for Investment in St. Petersburg*" dated July 30, 1998, is of particular note. Article 4 of that law provides for the following types of government incentives for investment:

- City Hall guarantees for any loans taken out by investors seeking to invest in the city;
- tax breaks for investors;
- profit tax rebates for banks and other credit institutions providing loans to investors;
- attractive lease terms on property leased by investors in St. Petersburg with a view towards investing in that property;
- deferral of payments due on real estate for up to 5 years;
- financial assistance to investors out of St. Petersburg budget.

The procedure of guarantee issuance set forth in Art. 9 of the above-mentioned law envisages certain restrictions that have to be observed by parties seeking to obtain a City Hall guarantee. For example, the amount of a guarantee may not exceed a certain limit specified within St. Petersburg's *Budget* Law adopted in the relevant fiscal year.

Meanwhile, the same Article 9 grants huge powers and discretion to bureaucrats. St. Petersburg city administration is given the power to make guarantee decisions at its sole discretion or, in effect, to select guarantee recipients provided that they meet certain requirements mentioned in the law. One of such requirements is that the payback period of investment made with loan money taken out under government guarantees may not exceed 6 years from the date of first investment. It is also required that the applicant have no tax and social security debts and show no signs of impending bankruptcy as defined by federal law.

However, none of the requirements and restrictions set out in the said law have been consistently enforced. By January 1, 2000, the city had run up guarantees worth 22% of St. Petersburg's entire debt (Komitet Finansov..., p. 16). Not infrequently, City Hall does not require payback details from the applicant before issuing a guarantee. For example, the guarantees issued for the liabilities of *Dvorets Sporta* (Sports Palace) open joint stock company were never formally substantiated as far as payback is concerned. Likewise, it is not known how much the Ice Palace really cost to build. That notwithstanding, by January 1, 2000, the city had guaranteed the Ice Palace's liabilities to the tune of US $18.3 million and Rbl 106.4 thousand. Moreover, these liabilities are maturing in 2000 (Komitet Finansov..., p. 31).

## Economic Development Zones

There are special areas – miniature tax havens – in St. Petersburg, called "Economic Development Zones." The concept of EDZ was developed and put into effect by St. Petersburg government in its Executive Order of January 28, 1999, entitled "*Re: The Concept of Economic Development Zones*." The concept envisages EDZs to be set up along the lines of urban development, manufacturing and transportation.

As transpires from the experience of economic development zone operation in the city prior to the Concept, EDZs of a manufacturing nature have a tendency to turn into a form of granting special benefits to certain companies to the detriment of market competition. For example, the operating zone Northern Shipyard encompasses the territory of an eponymous shipbuilding company. Northern Shipyard has been exempted from all municipal tax for three years.

Another EDZ - Pushkinskaya - belongs to the Electromechanical Factory. Pushkinskaya has been exempted from 40% of all municipal taxes and charges for five years.

In the above cases, tax benefits are granted to specific companies and serve no urban development purpose whatsoever. This is a typical element of the city's industrial policy compelling other potential beneficiaries to engage in rent-seeking practices. As an example, we can cite the St. Petersburg Shipyards EDZ project now being lobbied in the government. If pushed ahead, this project may bring numerous benefits to the shipbuilding companies based on the chosen project site.

Curiously, the economic development zone concept initially met with vehement opposition on the part of the St. Petersburg Agency of the Russian Anti-Monopoly Policy Ministry ("TU MAP"). Later on, the benefits that went with the EDZ concept were incorporated into St. Petersburg Law "*On Tax Benefits*" which deprived TU MAP of legal grounds to resist this practice effectively.

According to a generally accepted practice, in the event of a local law coming into conflict with the Russian Federal Law "*On Competition and Restriction of Monopoly Practices in Commodity Markets*" ("The Russian Competition Law"), all a local anti-monopoly agency can do is appeal to the prosecutor's office who will process the appeal and issue its determination to the local law-making institution who may, in turn, appeal against it in court. Meanwhile, the Russian Competition Law contains no clear definition of "unjustified benefits." It may be very hard to prove in court that a benefit was granted "without due justification." As a result, local anti-monopoly agencies and prosecutor's offices know better than to become entangled in court litigation with local law-makers when Art. 7 of the Russian Competition Law is violated. As the matters stand, Art. 7 of the Law is targeted to combat artificial benefits and thus suppress rent-seeking.

## 3 Rent-Seeking Through Social Merit

Under St. Petersburg Law "*On Assessment of Rent on Non-Residential Premises Let by the City of St. Petersburg*" dated July 22, 1998, rent due on non-residential space is set at a market rate multiplied by the premises' social merit coefficient.

Social merit coefficient values are determined annually, as are lists of entities eligible for special benefits. As a result, lobbying campaigns rage every year to have those coefficients revised (reduced), and companies fight to have their business put on a list of "meritorious" categories of business. This state of things plays into the hands of St. Petersburg Legislative Assembly representatives who have the power to amend local laws. The initial draft of the Law, debated in 1997, listed 10 categories of socially important business. Now there are 32.

There is plenty in it for the bureaucrats, as well. There is a number of categories of business that never qualify as "socially meritorious" unless the "socially meritorious" turnover of the company's goods or services constitutes at least 70% of the its total turnover. Other types of business are subject to a different rule: in order to enjoy a rebate, the tenant has to use at least 70% of leased building or space for socially important activities. According to the Law, compliance with these requirements is monitored annually by "a competent sectoral agency of St. Petersburg city administration."

It goes without saying that these criteria are just about vague enough to give a free hand to bureaucracy and create formidable opportunities for corruption. Consider, for instance, the socially meritorious business (coefficient 0.5, i.e. the tenant pays half of the market rate) of selling "independently produced" dairy, meat and vegetable produce and derivative products.

First of all, it is not an easy task to determine how the products were made (usually the term "independently produced" refers to someone's vegetable patch or farm in which no hired labor is used). Anyhow, the question of whether or not a product qualifies as "independently produced" may easily become the subject of bargaining between the parties concerned.

Second of all, it is equally complicated in this case (as well as, for that matter, in all other cases mentioned in the Law) to determine the actual percentage of sales meeting this qualifying criterion. It is easy to play with this percentage during the year, adjusting it as necessary from time to time, and by all means before an annual audit. Once again, there's plenty of bargaining room for businesses and bureaucrats.

The list of examples can be continued. Organizations and solo entrepreneurs dealing in used merchandize with at least 25% wear have been granted social merit coefficient 0.1. It is clearly impossible to control the actual percentage of wear.

It is also notable that many types of business entitling their owners to lower rent can hardly qualify as "socially meritorious." Very often social merit coefficients merely reflect the lobbying clout of the rent-seekers involved. For instance, bar associations renting premises for their management offices and legal consulting business are entitled to social merit coefficient 0.2 (i.e. they pay 20% of the market price). Independently practicing notaries public are entitled to coefficient 0.4; law firms enjoy coefficient 0.3.

Essentially, this law violates the fundamentals of fair competition. Under its provisions, coefficient 0.3 is granted to retailers of fruit, vegetables, dairy and baked products, provided that the share of these products in their total turnover is at least 70%. What happens if the share of these product categories is 69% with one business, and 71% with another? The former will have a hard time trying to compete, as the latter business would be enjoying very sizeable perks.

In certain instances, the Law provides for a particularly favorable environment for public sector businesses. Thus state-owned unitary companies whose main business is in above-ground passenger carriage services pay only 0.05 of applicable market rent on any premises they lease directly for their main business activity. This effectively means they use their premises at no cost. Needless to say, no other companies, with the exception of the aforesaid state-owned unitary entities, are entitled to this privilege.

It is no wonder the municipal authorities are not even close to considering the idea to allow privatization of commercial space in the city. So far, only 3% of St. Petersburg's non-residential space is privately owned (Sinochkin, p. 4). Combined with a set of arbitrary and constantly changing rent policies, lease of municipally owned commercial space creates an ideal environment for rent-seeking and corruption.

## 4 The Vesting of Monopoly Power

Not infrequently, St. Petersburg's executive authorities simply allot a set of exclusive rights to a selected company thus leaving all or most of its competitors far behind. This is usually the case with socially important services funded by the city.

On March 14, 1997, the governor of St. Petersburg issued a directive appointing, practically without competition, an authorized commercial bank (BaltUNEX-

IMBank) to handle municipal budget accounts that had earlier been held with several city banks. Later on, under pressure from the banking community and TU MAP, the governor rectified the situation somewhat by adopting a new directive (St. Petersburg Governor's Directive of March 23, 1997).

It should be noted that even if all the necessary laws and regulations are in place, the authorities are still at liberty to vest monopoly power in selective business entities. This is evidenced, *inter alia*, by how the principle of competitive bidding has been consistently ignored in affording municipal contracts. A number of crucial commodity groups have been supplied to the city in violation of the Russian President's Decree of April 8, 1997, "*On Priorities in Deterring Corruption and Reducing Budget Spending on Commodity Purchases for State Needs.*" One example are fuel supplies to municipally-funded companies and organizations (Passazhiravtotrans, emergency trouble-shooting services, Spetstrans, Khlebtrans, the police, health institutions and ambulance services). Technically, fuel supplies to these companies are to be procured through a municipal ordering system on a competitive basis. In fact, fuel supplies are arranged by direct bargaining with public or - more frequently - private suppliers who don't usually have direct contracts in place with fuel producers; instead, they outsource fuel from different wholesalers.

Despite the requirements of the above-referenced presidential Decree and St. Petersburg Governor's directive of December 16, 1996, ordering organizations authorized by the city to award contracts to building and installation contractors have, so far, adhered to their practice of awarding municipal contracts on a target basis to a limited number of contractors with whom they are connected. According to TU MAP data, of all building contracts awarded by City Hall's Construction Committee (mainly housing and social utility properties), only 10% were awarded in a competitive tender in the first 6 months of 1998, and about 15% were awarded in a tender in the first 6 months of 1999 (TU MAP, 1999).

The process of municipal ordering of pharmaceuticals for community groups entitled to rebates created the opportunity for a council of experts headed by a senior vice-governor to select suppliers arbitrarily at their full discretion during the preliminary screening process. Between 1996 and 1998, the said council consistently awarded orders of varying supplies to the same group of suppliers. According to TU MAP, the number of companies so selected did not exceed 11 compared to 500 operating in the marketplace (TU MAP, 1999).

On July 23, 1998, the Governor of St. Petersburg issued a directive introducing a "*Process of Statutory Monitoring of Legal Compliance of Alcoholic Beverage Circulation and its Conformity to Standards Applicable in St. Petersburg*" which designated, on a competitive basis, 15 authorized wholesale warehouses (out of about 130 similar entities duly licensed to sell alcohol). These authorized warehouses would have tax police posts stationed on their premises. All other suppliers were obligated to take their products to the authorized warehouses for mandatory inspection, so the authorized warehouses were essentially free to grant or deny clearance to their competitors.

Pursuant to St. Petersburg Governor's directive of December 29, 1998, entitled "*Re: Toll Parking Areas in St. Petersburg*," the state-owned unitary company Municipal Parking and Garage Center was given a go-ahead to charge parking toll in key downtown streets and squares. In other words, the entire toll business was thus delegated to a commercial entity. Moreover, it became that company's main source of earnings. It was a municipally sanctioned monopoly, a one-company market sector.

The Municipal Parking and Garage Center did not limit its business to collecting toll from individual drivers. Soon its toll parking area was expanded to cover, for instance, Badayev Warehouses where they introduced a paid entry system (10 rubles for automobiles; 20 for trucks). In addition to a flagrant infringement on the property rights of the warehouse owners and their customers, this system interfered with competition in the warehousing services market. The owners of Badayev Warehouses found themselves in a situation where they were no longer able to fairly compete with other warehousing service providers in the city. A city court has recently granted St. Petersburg Prosecutor's Office appeal to invalidate the gubernatorial directive on toll parking.

City Hall's outdoor advertising rules compel advertising agencies (customers for advertising space) to sign contracts with the Municipal Center for Advertisement Placement, another state-owned unitary company authorized by the city, vested with supervisory functions and, on top of that, allowed by its Charter to engage in gainful activity of its own in advertising. That company has a discount policy it applies selectively to grant very considerable advantages to a few major advertising agencies out of the 45 to 50 similar agencies operating in the city.

## 5 Licensing as Rent-Seeking

In Russia, official licensing is increasingly becoming a wide-spread practice. Licensing is administered under the Russian Federal Law "*On Licensing of Certain Types of Business*" dated September 25, 1998 ("The Russian Licensing Law") which more than doubled the list of activities requiring official licenses compared to an earlier governmental executive order on licensing. As of 1999, licensing of the absolute majority of business activities in St. Petersburg is the responsibility of the Licensing Office (LO).

### *Licensing Office: Power Usurped*

LO is an office with pronounced expansionist leanings. Irrespective of the type of business a license is sought for, the practice of licensing necessarily involves a pre-licensing background check of the applicant in order to verify compliance with license requirements and conditions.

At the same time, the Russian Licensing Law provides for an independent background check involving a third organization contracted for a fee in only one case: when the license applicant appeals to court against the licensing authority's decision to deny license. Only the applicant himself may decide to seek an independent background check. Any other background check for a fee by an extraneous corporate entity or individual would be against the law.

There is plenty of evidence that LO has been routinely abusing its usurped powers. Pre-licensing checks are conducted both by LO surveyors, and by expert centers accredited with LO. An audit conducted by TU MAP has revealed that, between July 1, 1999 and November 19, 1999, those expert centers administered 1424 background checks, while LO experts performed only 586 (TU MAP, 1999). An audit of assignment letters issued by LO to the expert centers instructing them to perform pre-licensing checks, further revealed that the scope of issues constituting the object of such a background check consists exclusively of verifying whether the applicant's information and submissions to LO were full and correct.

LO has been consistently stretching its powers outside licensing proper, occasionally organizing tenders to award local government contracts. This has been made possible by the Economics and Industrial Policy Committee who recommends LO as a tender consultant to heads of St. Petersburg City Hall's local area and sectoral arms. In 1999, LO organized 11 tenders for the supply of the following product and service categories:

- car fuel, oil and lubricants;
- design of energy consumption meters;
- refurbishment of outdoor lighting systems;
- rebuilding of tram tracks and trolley bus lines.

Conduct of competitive tenders is not mentioned among the functions of a licensing body as defined by Art. 5 of the Russian Licensing Law.

The powers usurped by LO in this area imply the option of awarding contracts to those business entities to whom LO is also inclined to delegate some of its licensing functions.

### *Licensing Office as Rent-Setter*

The functions of LO make it the public institution playing a crucial role in nurturing a rent-seeking environment.

An audit of LO, conducted by TU MAP, has revealed that some of the "independent" expert organizations accredited with LO to conduct background checks were, in fact, commercial entities and competition to some of the applicants. For instance, such accredited "expert" organizations as Nefto Kombi Servis ZAO (a filling station chain operator), St. Petersburg Center - the Civil Engineering Section of the Russian Engineering Academy (design of buildings and installations), Preventative Disinfection Station (disinfecting services), and others may conceivably emerge as competitors to some of the license applicants.

An agreement signed between LO and PTC-Terminal Limited Liability Company (petrochemicals dealer and filling station operator) provides that, in the event the licensing authority sees fit to carry out an audit of a license holder's production facilities, the licensing body agrees to contract PTC-Terminal LLC to perform the same. The agreement further stipulates that, if so instructed by the licensing authority, PTC-Terminal would conduct laboratory tests of petrochemicals and assure their quality. As we see, in this case the power of a public institution to monitor license compliance has been delegated to a commercial organization. On top of it, that organization is a competitor to those whose compliance it is required to monitor.

The oil and petrochemicals market is not the only sector where a commercial entity may combine the functions of competitor and supervisor vis-a-vis the entities it supervises. The retail market of alcoholic beverages is another example. According to a cooperation agreement signed between LO and the state-owned unitary company Peterburgalcoholcontrol in November 1999, the latter is authorized to help supervise alcohol retailers. However, according to its Charter, Peterburgalcoholcontrol is a company established to generate profit, and one of its intended objects of business is to engage in activities requiring prior official licensing.

A determination issued by Peterburgalcoholcontrol as to whether the license applicant complies with the terms and conditions of the license it is seeking constitutes grounds for decision-making on granting or denying a license to retail alcoholic beverages.

Under the Russian Federal Law "*On Government Regulation of the Production and Circulation of Ethyl Alcohol, Alcoholic Beverages and other Products Containing Alcohol*" (Edition of January 7, 1999), any documents submitted by an applicant seeking a license to deal in alcoholic beverages must be processed exclusively by the licensing institution. The law precludes the involvement of business entities in the process of government oversight of the alcohol market.

LO has thus effectively introduced a mechanism for additional license compliance supervision of alcohol retail license applicants. Such additional supervision is administered by Peterburgalcoholcontrol with violations of federal law, including the anti-monopoly provisions of Art. 7 of the Russian Competition Law.

LO's activities undermine competition in the very market of expert survey services. According to an established practice, a license applicant is not allowed to choose its expert from among those accredited with LO. Upon submission of his license application, the applicant is referred by LO to one of its accredited experts at LO's discretion. At the same time, there is an element of coercion in this system whereby applicants are forced to pay a commercial organization contrary to the freedom-of-contracting principle prescribed by Russian civil law.

An agreement between LO and Nevsky Institute of Independent Survey ZAO binds the licensing institution (LO) to heed the findings in the Institute's pre-license processing in its decisions to issue or deny licenses in the housing and utilities sector.

A cooperation agreement between LO and Legal Consultancy #6 requires that the licensing institution refer its corporate and individual applicants engaging or proposing to engage in a licensed activity, to the said law offices. This creates a competitive advantage for the above-mentioned law firm in the market of legal consulting services.

In a memorandum of intent between LO and LUKOIL Insurance Company ZAO, the licensing institution undertakes, *inter alia*, to grant the said insurance company, free of charge, access to LO's databases on hazardous insurable industrial properties, thus creating a competitive advantage for a private company in the relevant sector of insurance services.

Under the Russian Licensing Law, the licensing institution is solely empowered to make decisions as to whether or not a license applicant fulfills the terms and conditions of its desired license. Under Art. 7 of the Russian Competition Law, delegation to third-party experts of the licensing institution's function of verifying the fullness and correctness of applicants' submissions constitutes unlawful vesting of the functions and discretion of a public executive authority in a business entity.

In the course of their surveys, commercial organizations administering the functions of "independent expert surveyors" are entitled to obtain access to the applicant's documentation, production facilities, payroll and other essentials of the applicant's business.

First of all, this practice gives said organizations a number of unfair advantages in their pursuit of the licensed business activity to which their survey pertains. Second of all, it creates opportunities for the exercise by those organizations of unfair competition methods. Finally, it violates the license applicant's right to protect its trade information.

## 6 Protectionism

Article 74 of the Russian Constitution proscribes any local authority in the Russian Federation to create customs borders, duties, charges or any other barriers for free circulation of goods, services or finance streams. Art. 1 of the Civil Code of the Russian Federation also provides for unrestricted circulation of goods, services and finance throughout the Russian Federation. Restrictions on goods circulation may be imposed solely in the interests of security, the safety of human life and health, environmental protection or protection of cultural heritage.

Failure to observe the aforesaid provisions, or any of the corresponding provisions of the Russian Competition Law, is interpreted as an offense against anti-monopoly law. The provision of Art. 7 of the Russian Competition Law precluding local authorities from creating barriers for goods circulation has no exceptions: any such barriers limiting competition or infringing upon the lawful rights of businesses or individuals are to be suppressed by anti-monopoly agencies.

Nevertheless, administrative regions of the Russian Federation frequently employ protectionist measures against each other, especially in the alcohol market. According to a survey conducted by the Russian Anti-Monopoly Committee in 1997, more than 40 regional authorities of the Russian Federation had executive orders out restricting the inflow of alcoholic beverages from other Russian regions (BEA 1999b, p. 225).

Until recently, St. Petersburg wasn't one of those regions. The city's authorities made their first protectionist policy moves in the alcohol market in the summer of 1998 (cf. the above-mentioned "authorized wholesale warehouses"). As of that time, any alcoholic beverages brought in from other regions have had to be presented for "registration" at those warehouses. No registration was required for local distillers. According to Kommersant newspaper, this system alone boosted St. Petersburg distillers' sales 50% (Kommersant, 1999, p. 11).

In a further policy move, a gubernatorial directive was issued introducing a regional "control stamp" in St. Petersburg (the sole rationale behind setting up the state unitary company Peterburgalcoholcontrol). Those stamps are affixed to both local and other regions' alcoholic beverages. St. Petersburg City Hall touted the move as a major consumer protection initiative. In actual fact, as an addition to the existing federal excise stamp with its 12 levels of protection, the "control stamp" appears to serve no purpose whatsoever except for increasing the product's price.

St. Petersburg administration officials have often reiterated that, unlike many other Russian regions, the price of that stamp is the same in St. Petersburg for local and "guest" distillers (out-of-the-region suppliers). They have maintained that the introduction of the "control stamp" is in no way a violation of fair competition. However, as far as outside suppliers are concerned, the very mechanism of procuring local "control stamps" implies higher costs for them compared to local distillers. The problem is that the only way to affix local "control stamps" to bottles brought in from other regions is to manually unpack the crates, affix stamps to each bottle, then to repack the crates. These operations add to production cost as they require extra labor and rent of warehouse space for a few extra days.

St. Petersburg City Hall's protectionist policy also manifests itself in discrimination against outside suppliers through the municipal ordering system. Art. 7 of St. Petersburg's *Municipal Ordering* Law dated May 20, 1999, provides for only three cases when a municipal contractor is allowed to outsource products in another region: when the outside supplier, in return, promises to purchase products made in St. Petersburg on a reciprocal basis (in this case, the value of products sourced outside St. Petersburg must be equal to the value of products purchased in St. Petersburg by the outside supplier); when the desired product cannot be manufactured in St. Petersburg; and when the prices of products sourced outside St. Petersburg are at least 15% lower than the prices offered by St. Petersburg-based suppliers (in this case, the company proposing to outsource has to furnish an expert report stating that it is not feasible to purchase a similar product manufactured in St. Petersburg).

Under Art. 8 of the above-mentioned law, St. Petersburg suppliers are entitled to certain preferences and quotas during their bid processing, the scope and extent of which is fixed annually by the Legislative Assembly as proposed by the Governor of St. Petersburg.

Finally, it is relevant to note that, in its protectionist effort, the local authorities tend to infringe upon the purview of federal authorities by introducing supplementary international trade barriers. In his Directive No. 881-p of September 3, 1999, the Governor of St. Petersburg binds local and sectoral arms of City Hall to use exclusively domestically manufactured products and equipment when designing, building, renovating or rebuilding properties funded out of St. Petersburg budget. In those cases when a product is not available domestically, the customer proposing to import the same is required to obtain a prior permission from City Hall's Committee for Economics and Industrial Policy.

## 7 Conclusion

In the late 1990s, an environment conducive to rent-seeking evolved much faster in St. Petersburg compared to the previous years. Indeed, steps were taken to institutionalize rent-seeking by making appropriate laws and regulations. As a result, more room was created for discretionary decision-making by certain government institutions, such as the Licensing Office of St. Petersburg. Not infrequently, the aforesaid laws and regulations contradict Russian federal anti-monopoly law. Nevertheless, most of them continue in full force and effect.

This state of things fits in perfectly with the concept of «seeking rent by setting rent.» Some of the most vivid manifestations are the city's industrial policy, business licensing policy, and management of municipally-owned commercial property. All these policies have enabled St. Petersburg authorities to legalize and perpetuate rent-seeking, and even to make it law. Notably, regulations and selective benefit schemes encouraging rent-seeking were, for the most part, initiated by the authorities, particularly the executive branch, rather than the business community. Whenever the rules of the game stop being the same for all players, and selective preferences emerge, the powers of bureaucracy are expanded; bureaucracy turns into a benefactor meting out favors at its discretion and enriching itself in the process.

## References

Alfandari G, Fan Q, Freinkman L (1997) Government Financial Transfers to Industrial Enterprises and Restructuring. In.: Commander S, Fan Q, Schaffer M (eds) Enterprise Restructuring and Economic Policy in Russia. EDI and World Bank, Washington DC, pp 166–203

Appelbaum E, Katz E (1987) Seeking Rents by Setting Rents: The Political Economy of Rent Seeking. The Economic Journal 97: 685–699

Braguinsky S (1997) Producer's Behavior in a Transitional Economy – Theoretical and Empirical Analysis with an Application to the Russian Economy. Economic Systems 21: 265–295

Earle J, Estrin S, and Leschenko L (1997) Ownership Structures, Patterns of Control, and Enterprise Behavior in Russia. In: Commander S, Fan Q, Schaffer M (eds) Enterprise Restructuring and Economic Policy in Russia. EDI and World Bank, Washington DC, pp 205–252

Hillman A, Katz E (1987) Hierarchical Structures and the Social Costs of Bribes and Transfers. Journal of Public Economics 34: 129–142

Komitet Finansov Administratsii Sankt-Peterburga (2000) Itogi upravleniya gosudarstvennym dolgom. 1999 god. SPb.

Kommersant (1999) 2 fevralya.

Kuznetsov Ye (1997) Learning in Networks: Enterprise Behavior in the Former Soviet Union and Contemporary Russia. In: Nelson JM et al (eds) Transforming Post-Communist Political Economies. National Academic Press, Washington, pp 156–174

BEA (1999 a) Ogranichenie konkurentsii na reginalnykh tovarnykh rynkakh tovarov i uslug mestnymi organami vlasti i upravleniya. Moskva

BEA (1999 b) Obzor ekonomicheskoi politiki v Rossii za 1998 god. ROSSPAN, Moskva, pp 217–232

Polishchuk L (1997) Missed Markets: Implications for Economic Behavior and Institutional Change. In: Nelson JM et al (eds) Transforming Post-Communist Political Economies. National Academic Press, Washington, pp 80–101

Sinochkin D (2000) Rynochnyi makiyazh gossobstvennosti. Ekspert Severo-Zapad No. 4 (1999). Spravka po resultatam proverki Litsenzionnoi Palaty Administratsii Sankt-Peterburga. SPb: Sankt-Peterburgskoe TU MAP (mimeo)

Tanzi V (1998) Corruption Around the World. IMF Staff Papers 45

# I. Powerful Groups and Corruption

Frank Bohn

## 1 Introduction

The model-theoretic literature on corruption typically focuses on its consequences, e.g. on output as in Ehrlich and Lui (1999), or on government policy as in Acemoglu and Verdier (2000). By contrast, this paper offers a new approach by incorporating the political power structure in the analysis.

Ehrlich and Lui (1999) develop an endogenous growth model with optimizing rent-seeking individuals. Agents can choose between growth enhancing human capital investment and socially unproductive investment in political capital. Multiple steady state equilibria obtain a stable growth path, an unstable development equilibrium, and a stable, but stagnant poverty trap. It is shown, for instance, that a rise of the level of government intervention may hurt poor countries (who are already in the poverty trap) and prevent countries at a critical take-off level from reaching the path of economic growth. Interdependencies between government intervention, in this case public investment and growth are also captured in Tanzi and Daroodi (1997).

Inefficiencies caused by rent-seeking agents are also modeled in Dabla-Norris (2000). Multiple equilibria may again exist in this game-theoretic framework. It is also shown that some corruption may be optimal in a two-tier government setting. In contrast, Thiele (1999) asserts that optimal corruption is determined by moral hazard. Acemoglu and Verdier (2000) include self-interested bureaucrats in a standard model of government intervention. They derive the optimal level of regulation, but again leave room for optimal corruption.

In this paper, corruption depends on the political power structure. The government is only interested in securing support from various groups in society. Corruption is determined in a game with corrupt capitalists who can secure a larger share of national production and raise their profits by paying bribes to bureaucrats. Corruption and output depend on the relative power of various groups in society and/or the costliness of corruption. Based on this positive analysis, normative interpretations are possible: which parameters should be changed and how should this be brought about?

## 2 The Power Index Model

### *Agents and Their Income*

The model is based on the assumption that there is a link between the well being of various groups in society and their support for government. Abstracting from non-pecuniary aspects each group's well-being can be expressed by its total income (I) accrued (instead of a utility function). Total government support is, therefore, a function of these income levels, in its simplest form modeled as a general Cobb-Douglas function. A rational government's objective will be to maximize this weighted product of income levels subject to the government budget constraint (to be specified further down):

$$\max \quad I_A^{\alpha} * I_C^{\gamma} * I_E^{\varepsilon} \quad , \tag{1}$$

where A, C, and E represent various groups in society (as described further down). $I_{\circ}^{\circ}$ refers to the aggregate income of each group, not to income per person in different groups. Parameters α, γ, and ε are weights attributed to groups' incomes. They can be interpreted as exogenous power indices (not in the game theoretic sense) where an increase means growing power of the respective group in society. In other words, a rising value for a particular power index reflects the government's acknowledgement that the support of that group has become more important. Hence the government will devote more attention to increasing the income level of that group.

In a parsimonious framework, it suffices to capture three groups:

- Bureaucrats or administrators (A) are the potential recipients of bribes. Their aggregate income is a straight sum of their salaries (S) and the bribes (B) received:

$$I_A = S + B \quad . \tag{2}$$

- Corrupt capitalists (C), for instance so-called oligarchs in Russia, are only interested in raising their profits. By paying bribes to bureaucrats they can secure a larger share of national production. Hence bribes are a positive argument in their production function. For simplicity, their production function is assumed to correspond to their profit function $Y_C(B)$. The costs of bribery are b*B, where $b \geq 1$ and exogenous. Furthermore, tax rate $t_C$ is applied to profits $\tau(B)$. Given that bribery-induced additional profits may be partly evaded from tax payments, it is save to assume that $\tau(B) \leq Y_C(B) \quad \forall B$. Corrupt capitalist's aggregate income equals:

$$I_C = Y_C(B) - b*B - t_C*\tau(B) \quad . \qquad (3)$$

- Honest entrepreneurs (E) are the only group in society which experiences a negative effect of bribery. Their profit share is modeled as the difference between total profits ($Y(B)$) and those absorbed by corrupt capitalists ($Y_C(B)$). Tax rate $t_E$ applies and net-of-tax aggregate income of entrepreneurs is, therefore:

$$I_E = (1-t_E) * (Y(B) - Y_C(B)) \quad . \qquad (4)$$

From the modelization it is already clear that bureaucrats and entrepreneurs are passive agents, i.e. they do not have any policy variables at their disposal. (One possible extension would be to model bureaucrats' willingness to accept bribes.) By contrast, corrupt capitalists may use bribery as a policy variable to maximize their income. At the same time, the government is maximizing support by setting three income distribution variables: taxes for entrepreneurs ($t_E$) and corrupt capitalists ($t_C$), as well as salaries (S) for bureaucrats. The model captures interdependencies between political support sought by the government and corruption induced by private agents.

### Bribery and Profits

It has already been mentioned in the previous that bribery has an effect on GDP and profits for each group and for society as a whole. Functional assumptions are based on first principles. In a stationary economy, total profits in the non-corruption case are a sum of profits accrued by both groups in society, $\overline{Y_C}$ by potentially corrupt capitalists and $\overline{Y_E}$ by entrepreneurs. Assuming that corruption leads to less efficiency, the effect of corruption on total profits is captured by a downward sloping convex function in B:

$$Y = Y(B) = \overline{Y_C} + \overline{Y_E} + f(B) \qquad (5)$$

*with* $\quad f(B) < 0$

$\quad f'(B) < 0$

$\quad f''(B) > 0 \quad .$

Decreasing marginal costs are assumed. Moving from an (almost) non-corrupt environment to some corruption typically bears considerable distortions. By contrast, if there are already larger distortions further payments of bribes are probably not quite so harmful.

The share of profits secured by corrupt capitalists can be increased using bribes. This is captured by an upward sloping function with decreasing marginal returns:

$$Y_C = Y_C(B) = \overline{Y_C} + g(B) \qquad (6)$$

*with*
$$\overline{Y_E} + f(B) > g(B) > 0$$
$$g'(B) > 0$$
$$g''(B) < 0 \quad .$$

Entrepreneurs suffer from both effects. Their profits are reduced because total GDP and profits are reduced and because corrupt capitalists secure a larger share:

$$\begin{aligned} Y_E = Y_E(B) &= Y(B) - Y_C(B) \\ &= \overline{Y_E} + f(B) - g(B) \end{aligned} \qquad (7)$$

*with*
$$f(B) - g(B) > 0$$
$$f'(B) - g'(B) < 0$$
$$f''(B) - g''(B) > 0 \quad .$$

It is a stylized fact that the tax base of corrupt capitalists is smaller than their profits. The simplifying assumption here is that entrepreneurs and capitalists pay taxes for their entire non-corruption profits $\overline{Y_C}$ and $\overline{Y_E}$, respectively. The additional income of capitalists due to corruption is only partly taxed. The capitalists' tax base is, therefore:

$$\tau = \tau(B) = \overline{Y_C} + k(B) \qquad (8)$$

*with*
$$g(B) \geq k(B) \geq 0$$
$$g'(B) \geq k'(B) > 0$$
$$g''(B) \leq k''(B) < 0 \quad .$$

These assumptions are represented graphically in figure I1. The $Y_C(B)$ curve is always above the $\tau(B)$ curve. The curves $Y(B)$ and $Y_C(B)$ do not intersect. The curve $Y_E(B)$ corresponds to the vertical distance between $Y(B)$ and $Y_C(B)$. Either $\overline{Y_C}$ or $\overline{Y_E}$ may be larger with no effect on the results.

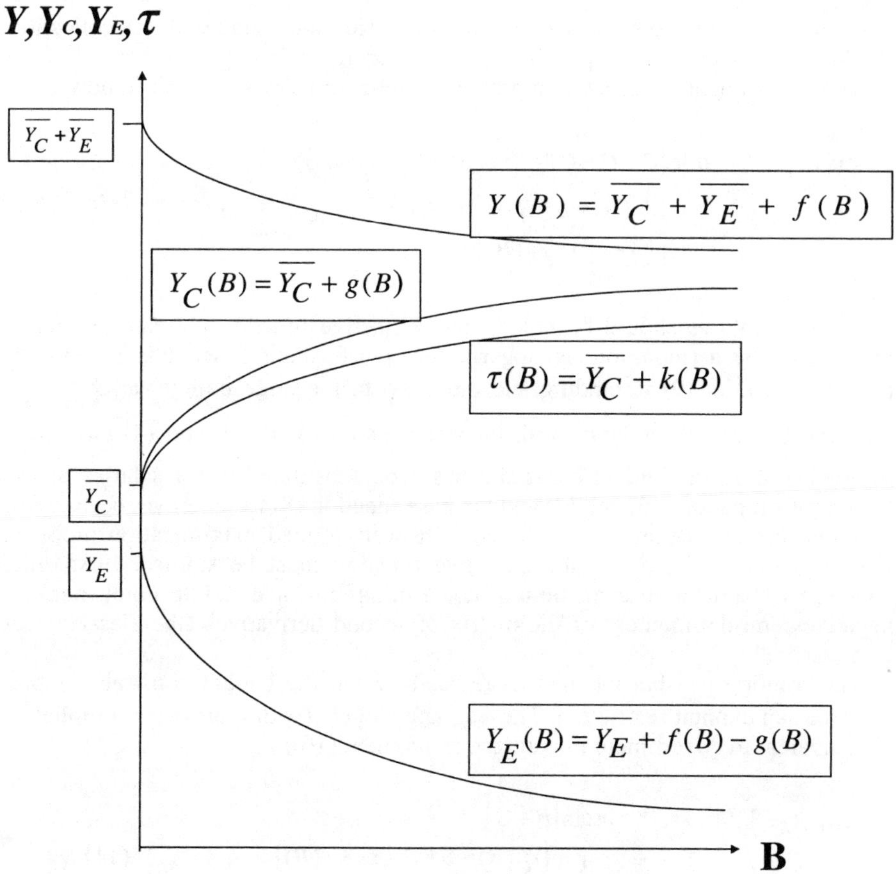


**Fig. I1.** Bribery and Profits

### *Government and Its Maximization Problem*

The government budget constraint is given by:

$$S \leq (1-\theta) \left[t_C * \tau(B) + t_E * Y_E(B)\right] \quad . \tag{9}$$

Taxes are the only source of revenue in the absence of seigniorage income and international loans. Tax rate $t_C$ applies for the tax base $\tau(B)$ of corrupt capitalists (which is only part of their profits $Y_C(B)$ ). In contrast, $t_E$ is the tax rate for entrepreneurs, whose entire profits $Y_E(B)$ are taxed. A standard assumption is that a fraction θ of taxes is lost due to inefficiencies associated with tax collection. As there is no public goods provision, salaries are the only expenditures.

The government maximization problem can be formally summarized now:

$$\begin{aligned} \max_{t_C, t_E} \quad & \alpha \ln\left[B + (1-\theta)\left(t_C * \tau(B) + t_E * Y_E(B)\right)\right] \\ + \quad & \gamma \ln\left[Y_C(B) - b * B - t_C * \tau(B)\right] \\ + \quad & \varepsilon \ln\left[(1-t_E) * Y_E(B)\right] \end{aligned} \quad . \tag{10}$$

Several features should be noted: first, objective function (1) can be equally represented by a (monotonous) logarithmic transformation; second, government budget constraint (9) is binding and only two to the three policy variables $t_E$, $t_C$, and S are independent; third, income equations (2), (3), and (4) have been inserted; fourth, the budget constraint has been substituted in for salaries S; and fifth, profit functions (6) and (7) and tax base function (8) have not yet been used.

To ensure that equation (10) describes a well-defined maximization problem, the concavity properties of the objective function must be studied. First order conditions characterize a maximum, not a minimum or a saddle point, because negative semi-definiteness of the matrix of second derivatives (the Hessian) has been verified.

The solution can be obtained more easily when the budget constraint is preserved as an explicit restriction. The Lagrangian (11) (with Lagrange multiplier λ) is equivalent to government maximization problem (10):

$$\begin{aligned} L(t_C, t_E, S, \lambda) = \quad & \alpha \ln\left[B + S\right] \\ + \quad & \gamma \ln\left[Y_C(B) - b * B - t_C * \tau(B)\right] \\ + \quad & \varepsilon \ln\left[(1-t_E) * Y_E(B)\right] \\ + \quad & \lambda * \left[S - (1-\theta)\left(t_C * \tau(B) + t_E * Y_E(B)\right)\right] \end{aligned} \quad . \tag{11}$$

The maximum is attained for the following first order conditions:

$$S = \frac{-\alpha}{\Sigma} * Z - B \tag{12}$$

$$t_C = \frac{\gamma}{\Sigma} * \frac{Z}{(1-\theta) * \tau(B)} + \frac{Y_C(B) - dB}{\tau(B)} \tag{13}$$

$$t_E = \frac{\varepsilon}{\Sigma} * \frac{Z}{(1-\theta) * Y_E(B)} + 1 \tag{14}$$

*with* $Z = dB - B - Y(B) < 0$

$\Sigma = \alpha + \gamma + \varepsilon$ .

The government's optimal choice of salaries and tax rates largely depends on the power structure. Given that Z is negative, an increase in the relative weight attributed to bureaucrats, i.e. a rise in the ratio of power index $\alpha$ to the sum of all power indexes, causes the government to raise salaries for state employees. Similarly, increasing the relative weight of entrepreneurs (or corrupt capitalists) leads to a reduction of the respective tax rate and taxes collected from this group. However, this result is only valid for unchanged levels of corruption. The interaction with corrupt capitalists and their optimal choice of bribery is considered in the next section.

### Equilibrium and Perturbation Results

In this paper, it is assumed that corrupt capitalists and the government play a (non-cooperative) Nash game. Obviously, corrupt capitalists cannot make reliable commitments, but this assumption makes also sense for the government if the model is applied to a situation with bribery in a country with considerable political instability (e.g. Russia). The government cannot credibly precommit to particular policy decisions (here on tax rates and bureaucrats' salaries) because majorities and/or governments may change. Neither corrupt capitalists nor the government can, therefore, be a leader (and force the other into a Stackelberg game). A prime example is Russia in the 1990s. It would, however, be an extension to compare the results obtained in a Nash game to the Stackelberg outcome. By doing so, the model could be applied to a more general set of situations and the impact of stabilizing the political system could be inferred.

In the Nash game, the government maximizes its objective function (to secure political support) for a given value of B (as already done in the previous section). At the same time, corrupt capitalists maximize their profits by choosing the desired level of corruption for given government decisions, in particular for given tax rate $t_C$:

$$\max \quad Y_C(B) - dB - t_C * \tau(B) \quad . \tag{15}$$

From the assumptions in equation (8) and from figure I1 it can be seen that equation 15 is concave in B. The first order condition is:

$$Y_C'(B) \;=\; b \;+\; t_C * \tau'(B) \tag{16}$$

In economic terms, this means that corrupt capitalists achieve their optimum when the marginal gain in gross-of-tax profits equals the marginal costs of bribery (b) plus marginal taxes, i.e. additional taxes caused by the marginal unit of bribes.

The Nash outcome for B, S, $t_E$, and $t_C$ can be calculated from equations (12), (13), (14), and (16). However, the focus here is on perturbation results, i.e. on the impact on bribery for changes in exogenous variables. Based on (13) and (16) implicit function I is defined so that changes in indexes α, γ, and ε (reflecting the power structure) can be analyzed:

$$I(\alpha,\gamma,\varepsilon;B) = 0 = \frac{\gamma}{\Sigma} * \frac{dB - B - Y(B)}{(1-\theta)*\tau(B)} + \frac{Y_C(B) - dB}{\tau(B)} - \frac{Y_C'(B) - b}{\tau'(B)}. \tag{17}$$

The Implicit Function Theorem is applied for each of the parameters $\circ = \alpha,\gamma,\varepsilon$ and its corresponding function $B = \varphi_\circ(\circ)$:

$$\frac{dB}{d\circ} = \varphi_\circ'(\circ) = -\frac{\frac{\partial I}{\partial \circ}}{\frac{\partial I}{\partial B}} \tag{18}$$

Results for $\circ = \alpha,\gamma,\varepsilon$ are identical except for an expression containing the power indexes:

$$\frac{dB}{d\circ} = -\frac{\frac{\partial I}{\partial \circ}}{\frac{\partial I}{\partial B}} = -\frac{\Omega(\alpha,\gamma,\varepsilon)*\frac{dB - B - Y(B)}{\Sigma^2(1-\theta)*\tau(B)}}{\frac{\partial I}{\partial B}} \tag{19}$$

$\Omega(\alpha,\gamma,\varepsilon)$ is positive for $\circ = \alpha,\varepsilon$ and negative for $\circ = \gamma$. The expression $\frac{dB - B - Y(B)}{\Sigma^2(1-\theta)*\tau(B)}$ is positive, and $\frac{\partial I}{\partial B}$ is also unambiguously positive for nicely behaved functions $\tau(B)$ and $Y_C(B)$[1]. The overall effect on B can be read from column two of table I1. The value of $\Omega(\alpha,\gamma,\varepsilon)$ is given in each case. These are the "unconstrained" perturbation results: the marginal change of one of the power indexes in not offset by an opposite change of another, i.e. the value of Σ changes.

[1] Formally, the condition is that $\frac{k(B)}{k'(B)} \geq \frac{g(B)}{g'(B)}$ and $\frac{k'(B)}{k''(B)} \leq \frac{g'(B)}{g''(B)}$. These conditions are fulfilled with equality for simple increasing and concave functions when g(B) and k(B) have identical functional formats and only differ in parameters. Examples are pairs of the square root function ($g(B) = a * B^{1/2}$ and $k(B) = c * B^{1/2}$) or of the log function ($g(B) = a * \ln(B+1)$ and $k(B) = c * \ln(B+1)$).

The next four columns refer to unchanged values of Σ. Formally, columns 3, 4, and 5 give the results for $\frac{dB}{d\circ} - \frac{dB}{d\bullet}$, where $\circ,\bullet = \alpha,\gamma,\varepsilon$ and $\circ \neq \bullet$. For instance, raising γ at the expense of α (column 3) results in a stronger increase in bribery ($\Omega = \alpha + \gamma + \varepsilon$) than raising γ without constraint (column 2). Column 6 refers to unchanged values of Σ when the change in one of the power indexes is offset by both others. The last column presents the effect on output Y. This result is straightforward because equation (5) contains the assumption that bribery B has a negative effect on output.

Perturbation results (for changes of power indexes) can also be obtained for government choice variables, salaries S and tax rates $t_E$, and $t_C$, but are not contained in table I1. If bureaucrats become more powerful (α↑), salaries go up, but the income obtained from bribes goes down. If corrupt capitalists get more power (γ↑), the government is more reluctant to tax them (under specific conditions). Similarly, if entrepreneurs turn more powerful (ε↑), their tax burden will be lowered (under certain conditions). All effects of a group's power index on policy variables affecting another group are less clear-cut. The perturbation effect of exogenous bribery costs b (born by corrupt capitalists) on bribes is also not included in table I1. As expected corruption decreases, if b goes up.

**Table I1.** Response of Corruption and Output

| Raise: | Uncon-strained: | At the expense of: | | | | What happens to output? |
|---|---|---|---|---|---|---|
| | | α | γ | ε | both others | |
| α<br>(Ω=) | B↓<br>(γ) | ——— | B↓<br>(α+γ+ε) | 0 | B↓<br>½(α+γ+ε) | Y↑ |
| γ<br>(Ω=) | B↑<br>(α+ε) | B↑<br>(α+γ+ε) | ——— | B↑<br>(α+γ+ε) | B↑<br>(α+γ+ε) | Y↓ |
| ε<br>(Ω=) | B↓<br>(γ) | 0 | B↓<br>(α+γ+ε) | ——— | B↓<br>½(α+γ+ε) | Y↑ |

# 3 Conclusion

The idea of this model is to capture the effects on corruption of changes in the power structure of society, i.e. shifts in the relative values of power indices (as defined in the previous chapter). Based on this positive analysis, normative interpretations are possible: which parameters should be changed and how should this be brought about?

Results in table I1 suggest that corruption can be reduced by either increasing the power of bureaucrats and honest entrepreneurs or by reducing the power of corrupt capitalists. Even though bureaucrats and entrepreneurs are modeled differently, making them more powerful has exactly the same quantitative effect. In fact, it only matters how powerful the only group actively soliciting corruption is ($\gamma$) relative to all other groups ($\alpha+\varepsilon$). Bureaucrats are one of these "other" groups, even though they are the recipients of bribes.

Given that the government is a player in the game how can these exogenous power indexes be affected, how can the underlying power situation be changed? In principle, there are three options: first, part of the government may not be involved in the short run effort to secure political support, e.g. the president; second, a popular initiative may be based on media support and/or the public conscience; and third, foreign governments or institutions may be able to exert pressure.

Various policies are conceivable to achieve a reduction of bribery. The obvious measure is a public campaign against corruption. A media campaign in democratic countries and an official campaign in less democratic countries may have similar effects. Consider anti-corruption efforts by Putin in Russia or by the communist party in China. Once the top government level has initiated the campaign, all levels of government may be affected. The entire government would be forced to distance itself from support obtained from corrupt groups. In terms of the model, the power index of the corrupt group would be reduced.

Privatization initiatives had an enormous impact on the power structure of transformation countries. In Russia, for instance, powerful financial tycoons and capitalists emerged from the privatization of Gazprom and other monopolies (valuable shares were given to the nomenclatura at low prices) and from the "loans for shares" scheme (banks became shareholders by extending loans to firms). Many of these new capitalists (so-called oligarchs) turned out to be corrupt. A privatization campaign to create new small and medium-sized firms and to establish a class of entrepreneurs might increase the power of a less corrupt group in society (even though some of the entrepreneurs will, of course, be corrupt as well). Thus different types of privatization may have exactly opposite effect with respect to their impact on corruption.

The institutional framework may also be decisive for the power structure of society. The legal system and the rule of law is crucial for reducing the power of corrupt groups. Such reforms may be supported publicly and requested by foreign countries and institutions. Nonetheless, it can only be initiated if some part of the government, which itself is a player in the game, does actually manage to break out of the vicious circle of seeking support from powerful corrupt groups.

Overall, the power index model presented in this paper illustrates the link between the power structure of society and corruption. The model shows that the change of power of various groups in society generates responses by private agents and by the government and, thereby, affects corruption.

The power index model is still in its early stages. The virtue of this new approach is, however, that it offers a general framework for a number of extensions: costs of corruption could be endogenized, reputation could be included in the government objective function, and extensions for workers, the military, or social welfare are straightforward.

## References

Acemoglu D, Verdier T (2000) The Choice Between Market Failures and Corruption. American Economic Review 90: 194–211

Dabla-Norris E (2000) A Game-Theoretic Analysis of Corruption in Bureaucracies., IMF Working Paper WP/00/106

Ehrlich I, Lui FT (1999) Bureaucratic Corruption and Endogenous Economic Growth. Journal of Political Economy 107: 270–293

Tanzi V, Daroodi H (1997) Corruption, Public Investment, and Growth. IMF Working Paper WP/97/139

Thiele H, Eskeland GS (1999) Optimal Corruption and Moral Hazard. Presentation at the Econometric Society European Meeting 1999

# J. Regional Dimension of the Market Transformation in Russia

Ruslan Grinberg and Leonid Vardomsky

## 1 Introduction

In the 1990s economic liberalization in Russia has not ensured any positive dynamics in the development of national economy, has not impelled a structural economic shift in favor of branches with the high added value and provided no growth in real income for the majority of the population.

This may be explained by subjective factors (ineffective economic measures, excessive political influence on economic life, incompetence, lack of political will necessary to implement the approved projects, contradictory interests of political and economic elites, criminalization of economy etc.), combined with objective factors (severe global competition, volatile conjuncture on global markets, inevitable backlog of measures of the currency, customs and tax control from accepted liberalization plans, the inert present economic structure etc.). At the same time regional factors have played an important role in the failure of Russian reform. As the experience in the 1990s has shown, inadequate perception or underestimation of regional factors has resulted in social pathologies, economic losses and a threat to the country's integrity. In our opinion, the key aspects to estimating the regional constituent of the Russian reforms are:

1. characteristics of the Russian economic space at the moment when the transformation began;
2. the power decentralization carried out in 1992–1998, which has essentially changed the central/regional authorities ratio in Russia;
3. a specific character of the economic policy, pursued by regional authorities;
4. results of the regional development in the 1990s.

## 2 Nonmarket Characteristics of the Russian Economic Space

For decades Russia has been isolated from the external world. Military-strategic priorities have had a strong effect on its economic structure. That conditioned the extensive development of the Russian economy, financial and human resources being deficient. As a result, Russia did not manage to develop a solid, geographically monolithic economic nucleus, like in the countries of Western and Central Europe and neighboring China and Turkey. The territorial structure of the Russian economy has historically developed as an aggregate of industrial bases formed in the process of economic advance to the east. The majority of them is situated in the heart of the continent far apart from each other.

The country has inherited vast sparsely populated areas. So, in 32 territories of the Russian Federation the density of population does not exceed 10 inhabitants per sq. km, while the country's average index is 8.5 inhabitants per sq. km. Sparsely populated regions, occupying the most part of Siberia, the whole Far East and European North, account for almost 4/5 of the country's territory.

**Table J1.** Some structural characteristics of the Russia's territory (1995)

| Territories of the Russian Federation with the density of population (inhabitants per sq.km): | Number of regions | Share in the area, % | Share in the population, % | Share in GDP, % |
|---|---|---|---|---|
| 1. Less than 10 | 32 | 79.6 | 16.9 | 25.8 |
| 2. 10 - 24.9 | 16 | 10.3 | 21.1 | 19.1 |
| 3. 25 - 39.9 | 14 | 4.0 | 15.5 | 13.0 |
| 4. 40 - 55 | 10 | 3.2 | 16.8 | 12.7 |
| 5. More than 55 | 17 | 2.9 | 29.7 | 29.4 |
| Total | 89 | 100.0 | 100.0 | 100.0 |

*Estimated on the basis of a statistical report "Russian Regions", M., Goskomstat, 1997; a forecast of the socio-economic development of the Russian Federation up to 2000, developed by the Ministry of Economy of the Russian Federation.*

At the same time, 17 of the most densely populated territories of the Russian Federation account for less than 3% of the country's territory and for almost 30% of its population. The Moscow region (the capital and its region, Vladimir, Ivanovo and Tula regions), Povolzhye region (Tatarstan, Chuvashiya and Samara region), Baltic region (St. Petersburg with the Leningrad region and Kaliningrad region) and Northern Caucasus are the most densely populated.

A low density of the population in the majority of the territories of the Russian Federation is associated to that in Russia as a whole. The greatest clot is concentrated in the Moscow region - 10.4% of the Russian population (5.9% in Moscow and 4.5% in the region). In two regions (Petersburg and Krasnodar Territory) the population amounts to 5–7 million. In 10 regions it varies within the limits of 3–5 million, in 11 regions – 2–3 million and in 31 – 1–2 million. In the remaining 42 territories of the Russian Federation the population is less than 1 million, including 18 regions with less than 0.5 million inhabitants.

The small total population conditions low consumer capacity of the majority of regional markets and a high degree of its dispersion owing to a low density of the population. Market capacity is a particularly important factor for the stable development of regional economy, as within the territories of the Russian Federation there are usually vast blank spots between the regions with a high degree of the economic concentration.

The smaller the population and the lower its density, the more specialized regional economy is. The degree of specialization grows the further east one looks. Infrastructural conditions for economic activity deteriorate as well. In this sense Russia's European regions have more advantages than the Asian ones. For example, the radius of 1 thousand km around Saratov embraces about 40% of the Russia's population and 45% of regional gross products, whereas the same radius from Irkutsk – about 5% of the population and almost the same share of gross regional product.[1]

A fundamental feature of Russia's territory is also an inland location of key export industries. More than 60% of the export potential is situated at a distance of 3–4 thousand km from European and Far East frontiers. The country's main export bases are located in sparsely populated regions (Khanty-Mansiysk and Yamalo-Nenetsk autonomous districts, Krasnoyarsk Territory, Vologda, Irkutsk and Murmansk regions).

Thereupon it is necessary to emphasize that in case of the inland location of export-oriented raw materials and fuel production its yield is steady, provided that the current exchange rate of the ruble is 150% more than the purchasing power parity. In 1992 this excess averaged 940%, in 1993 – 400%, in 1994 – 240%, in 1995 – 175%, in 1996 – 142%, in 1997 – 135%, in 1998 – 181%.[2]

In 1995 the regions with a low population density (Table J1) produced more than a quarter of total GDP. The share of other regions in total GDP was less than their share in the country's population. Only in the group of the most densely populated regions were these two indices almost equal.

The lack of correlation between the region's share in the population and in GDP reflects one more important feature of Russia's territory — striking inter-regional contrasts at the level of socio-economic development. The highest figures of per capita GDP are characteristic of the sparsely populated regions, disposing of large oil and gas resources, and the lowest – for the densely populated republics of Northern Caucasus with their underdeveloped economy. In 1995 per capita GDP in Yamalo-Nenetsky autonomous district (Rub 67 million) was almost 1200% more than that in the Dagestan Republic (Rub 0.56 million). In the Russian Federation this index averaged Rub 9 million.[3]

In view of the above-stated, the important characteristic of Russia is a vast periphery and a small number of central regions. In the center-periphery relations the economic initiative comes from centers. They are the focal points of financial

---

[1] Estimated on the basis of a statistical report "Russian Regions", M., Goskomstat, 1997.

[2] L. Vardomsky, A. Treyvish. Problemy ustoychivosti ekonomicheskovo prostranstva Rossii v kontekste vneshneekonomicheskoy liberalizacii [Stability problems of Russia as an economic area in the context of external liberalization]. In: Vneshneekonomicheskiye svyazi i regionalnoye razvitiye v Rossii [Foreign economic relations and regional development in Russia], Moscow Epikon, 1999. p. 210

[3] Estimated on the basis of a forecast of the socio-economic development of the Russian Federation up to 2000, developed by the Ministry of Economy of the Russian Federation.

flows and technological innovations, the places where commercial and administrative decisions, influencing the periphery's economic life, are taken.

Provincial regions are characterized by economic, educational and infrastructural gaps, prevailing in one or two kinds of traditional economic activities, poor receptivity of innovations, limited potential for self-development and economic dependence on central regions. On the whole the province is more conservative. Main impulses for its development come from a center, influencing it.

Russia has inherited an asymmetrical center-periphery territorial structure, by which one central region (the Moscow metropolitan) manifestly prevails. The following tier is formed by several subcentral regions with their centers in the largest Russian cities: Leningrad, Sverdlovsk, Kazan, Ufa, Samara, Rostov, Novosibirsk, Krasnoyarsk, Nizhniy Novgorod. These cities influence more than just the corresponding republics, territories and regions.

There is no doubt that the inherited properties of Russia's territory, such as an inland, sparse, dispersed location of population and industry, a great number of provincial territories and the contrasts between regions, are objective impediments for the market transformation.

In a closed command economy enterprises were being allocated according to criteria of the economic optimality, based on home prices. Price liberalization made the inherited patterns of the raw materials and fuel supply, as well as of products sales mostly unprofitable. Infrastructural underdevelopment in combination with a low density of the population and enterprises, geographical "gap" between the production of objects of labor and consumer goods and the seasonal nature of many Russian industries objectively raise turnover costs and call forth increased requirements of the economy for circulating assets. Furthermore, allocation of the most basic enterprises in the regions with the extreme or hard geoclimatic conditions increases production costs and makes it harder for a single producer to sell goods and services. Credits being expensive, circulating assets are formed mainly on the account of profit, so the enterprises' tendency to increase the latter by means of a rise in prices is easy to understand. Taken together, all these factors result in inflation, on the one hand, and high risks in investment activity, on the other.

The inherited structural asymmetry of the Russian territory has a rather strong effect on macroeconomic dynamics. However, wide power decentralization within the framework of new federalization at the beginning of reforms also starts to influence economic processes in the country.

## 3 Political and Economic Factors of Decentralization

The first steps towards decentralization were made during Gorbachev's "perestroika". In 1989–1990 the regional sovereignty was used as a small change in the struggle for power between Boris Yeltsin and Mikhail Gorbatchev. The declaration of Russia's independence (June, 1990) has given a powerful stimulus to the spontaneous decentralization. In the heat of political fight B.Yeltsin offered subordinated regions "to take as much sovereignty, as they can swallow". At the same time "a parade of sovereignties" became a prerogative of national autonomies. Prospects of devolution for regions and territories were associate then to getting the status of special economic zones (SEZ). In 1990-91 twelve SEZ were declared. Though that project has remained on paper, it provoked "a zonal fever": more than 100 administrative-territorial units of different levels came out with the same initiative – to create a free zone in their territory.

The spontaneous decentralization was put into legal framework, when on March 31, 1992 the Federative Treaty was signed (however, Chechnya and Tatarstan have not joined the Treaty). It has secured sovereignty for 21 republics and has given the status of a subject of federation to territories, regions, Moscow and St.-Petersburg. Accepted at the end of 1993, the Constitution of the Russian Federation has given equal rights to all subjects of federation, having the priority of republics kept.

Afterwards "a parade of sovereignties" was replaced by "a parade of treaties". In February, 1994 Tatarstan was the first to sign the treaty concerning the division of the terms of reference and powers between the government of the Russian Federation and that of a subject of the Russian Federation. This republic did not participate in referendum on the Constitution of the Russian Federation and in elections to the State Duma.

The Treaty gave Tatarstan a special status and thus was contrary to the newly accepted Constitution. The republic had special relations with the federal budget and a noticeably wider frame of reference for natural resources and property management and international activity, than other regions did. That was supposed to be an exception. But soon after, similar agreements were signed with Bashkortostan, the Sakha Republic, Northern Ossetiya, Udmurtiya etc.

The greatest number of agreements were signed in 1996. In the year of the presidential election, the federal center has decided to balance the situation and started signing agreements with the territories and regions, claiming for equal rights. These later agreements were supposed to be a kind of compensation for the regional authorities' loyalty. But the federal authorities did not bother with their implementation. In 1997–1998 the number of the signed agreements was reduced. By 1999, when this practice was given up, 47 treaties were signed.

In Vladimir Lysenko's opinion, by means of those agreements the Center pursued the policy of an individual asymmetry, which added to a group asymmetry already confirmed by the Constitution, giving extra rights to certain subjects of federation, foremost to republics. Lysenko explains a great enthusiasm for such treaties because of the traditional mentality of the Russian authorities, having gotten used to tackling regional problems on the basis of personal relations between chiefs, not of laws[4].

The country's financial and economic situation significantly influenced the progress of decentralization. The restrictive financial policy and inefficient privatiza-

[4] V. Lysenko, Perspektivy razvitiya federalizma v Rossii: simmetrichnaya ili asimmetrichnaya federaciya [Perspectives for the development of federalism in Russia: symmetric or asymmetric federation], in: Vtoraya mezhdunarodnaya konferenciya po federalizmu [Second international conference on federalism], Moscow, December 16-17, 1997. Moscow Editorial URSS 1999, p. 54-56.

tion resulted in a protracted economic recession. The government financial resources decreased sharply. The total capital flight over that period is estimated at USD150-200 billion. By the beginning of 1999 foreign debt stock of the state and private sector increased from USD103 billion (inherited from the Soviet period) up to USD186 billion[5], while direct foreign investment, accumulated during the years of reforms, made up USD12–14 billion.

The currency and customs policy of the federal center before the August crisis of 1998 did not favor an increase in financial resources. Strengthening the ruble by means of overrating made export of many goods losers and at the same time stimulated imports, suppressing the domestic producer.

The consolidated budget revenue decreased from 30.6% of GDP in 1993 to 24.5% in 1998, having halved in dollar terms in 1992–1998[6]. In the process of disorderly economic liberalization the Federal center has been losing control over decreasing private incomes and enterprises' revenues.

Tax collection fell to 65% in 1996. The federal budget entailed deficit until 1999. Both revenues and expenditures did not correspond to budget laws. In these circumstances the federal center was trying to transmit more and more responsibilities for social expenditures to the regional level. At the same time it delayed leveling-off transfers from the federal budget, payments to federal organizations and to the military-industrial establishment; the approved federal programs were not financed.

Under such conditions regions of the Russian Federation had to assume more and more responsibility for their social and economic situation. The federal center had to meet regions' claims to increase their share in the country's budget. Over the course of 1992–1998 the share of regions of federation in expenditures of the consolidated budget of the Russian Federation has increased from 38.6% up to 58.1%[7].

'In 1998 the federal authorities made an attempt to change their relations with regions. The struggle with regional privileges began. The treaties of the division of terms of reference were not signed any more. A number of bills, regulating the separation of powers between the government of the Russian Federation and those of subjects of the Russian Federation, was introduced in the parliament. But this process was interrupted by the August crisis of 1998 – a result of failures in economic and financial policy pursued by the federal center.

Given the above-mentioned disproportions characteristic of Russia's territory, the transfer of administrative functions to subjects of federation has caused a number of serious contradictions. First, subjects of federation have different material resources for exercising their powers. In 1998 per capita gross regional product in the Yamalo-Nenetsky autonomous district was almost 4000% more than that in the Aguinsky Buryatsky district (Rub 47.5 and 1.2 thousand correspond-

[5] Dolgi tayut na glazakh [Depts are melting at sight], in: Ekspert, № 20, 29.05. 2000, p. 7.

[6] Rossiyskiy statisticheskiy yezhegodnik [Russian statistical yearbook] 1999, Moscow Goskomstat, 1999.

[7] A. Arinin, G. Marchenko, Uroki i problemy stanovleniya rossiyskovo federalizma [Lessons and problems from the creation of Russian federalism]. Moscow 1999, TOO Inteltekh, p. 172.

ingly)[8]. Regions also differ very much in regards to the tax collection and budget provision of the population. In 1998 per capita budget revenue in the Yamalo-Nenetsky autonomous district (Rub 26012) was 8900% more than that in Dagestan (Rub 292). Inter-budget relations are supposed to smooth this disparity over, but they are far from perfection. The disparity of per capita budget expenditures in 1998 reached 2400%[9]. Up until 1999 the federal budget did not meet its commitments to regions, at the same time demanding them to pay taxes promptly. The second contradiction is conditioned by the legal asymmetry of subjects of the Russian Federation. Depending on their status they transfer different shares of collected taxes to the federal budget. So, the shares of taxes actually transferred to the federal budget by Tatarstan and Bashkortostan (in percentage to the total sum of collected taxes) were much less, than those transferred by other subjects of federation[10].

**Table J2.** Shares of Taxes Transferred to the Federal Budget

| Year | Tatarstan | Bashkortostan | The Russian Federation on the average |
|---|---|---|---|
| 1992 | 0.1 | 0.1 | 51.7 |
| 1993 | 0.0 | 0.0 | 37.1 |
| 1994 | 16.6 | 12.5 | 30.2 |
| 1995 | 22.7 | 26.2 | 40.9 |
| 1996 | 19.0 | 27.0 | 43.7 |
| 1997 | 24.6 | 27.0 | 43.7 |
| 1998 | 11.1 | 17.8 | 37.1 |

Asymmetrical decentralization of budget resources in 1992–1997 was combined with concentration of the country's financial resources in Moscow. The share of the metropolitan region in the assets of the Russian banking system has increased from 65% in the beginning of 1993 up to 85% in the beginning of 1998. The majority of the 200 first-rate banks (about three fourths) and almost all backbone banks were located in the capital. Up until the August crisis of 1998, first-rate exercised financial drainage of the province and used the accumulated funds

[8] Ekonomika i zhizn', Moscow May 19, 2000, p. 31.

[9] V. Seliverstov, I. Podporina, O. Boracheva, Formirovaniye byudzhetnykh i drugikh finansovykh resursov regionalnoy politiki dlya vyravnivaniya regionalnoy asimmetrii. Regionalnaya politika, napravlennaya na sokrashcheniya socialno-ekonomicheskoy i pravovoy asimmetrii [Allocation of budgetary and other financial ressources of regional politics for balancing regional asymmetry. Regional politics focused on reducing the socio-economic and legal asymmetry], № 2, Novosibirsk 2000, Sibirskoye soglasheniye [Sibirian agreement], p. 143.

[10] A. Lavrov, Komu platit federalny centr [The federal center is paying whom]? Moscow 1999. Moskovskiy centr instituta Vostok-Zapad [Muscovite Center of the East-West Institute], p. 58.

for investment in GKO, foreign securities and for purchase of export-oriented enterprises. So, the third contradiction of the Russian decentralization is connected with the fact that devolution was accompanied by a constant reduction in financial resources in most regions. It is even more apparent at a local government level.

## 4 Characteristics of the Economic Policy Pursued by Subjects of the Russian Federation

The extension of economic powers of subjects of the Russian Federation in the context of new federalism encouraged local initiatives concerning possible ways of stable regional economic development. These initiatives resulted in working out and enactment of regional constitutions, regulations and development programs, attracting investment, support of businesses etc. It is necessary to emphasize that the regions finding themselves in a relatively favorable budget situation, and therefore attractive for foreign investment and credits, were the most active ask for development of their own socio-economic policy.

The majority of regions are not able to pursue a more or less steady policy due to the lack of resources required for development.

We would like to stress the fact, that in view of federalization and liberalization of foreign economic relations, the latter essentially defines the financial situation in every subject of the Russian Federation. The difference between regions regarding the foreign economic activity conditions is the disparity of financial resources they have at their disposal for consumption and savings. On the average, regions-extraverts, reporting high absolute and relative indices as for the development of foreign economic relations, find themselves in a better financial position (budget self-sufficiency, enterprises' revenue and incomes of the population) than regions-introverts. In 1999 seventeen of the Russian first-rate regions-exporters (with exports more than USD 1 billion) have provided two-thirds of total tax receipts of the country's budget.

A survey carried out by the Institute for Economics of the Russian Academy of Sciences have shown that an increase in industrial output in Russia over the period of October 1998 – January 2000 is for the most part (86.6%) determined by export[11]. It means that regions, possessing a large export base, have a greater potential for the economic development than those without such a base.

The policy, pursued by regional authorities, reflects the way regional elites interpret the socio-economic and political situation and the means of solving problems of their region. In this interpretation, history of the regional development, structural economic characteristics, as well as mental patterns of the population and educational level of the regional government get their refraction.

The motivation of the regional authorities' policy is practically the same all over the country. It is determined by efforts to ensure in-payments to the regional budgets, social stability and economic growth. But these goals are being achieved

[11] N. Rayskaya, Mify ekonomicheskovo rosta [Myths of economic growth]. Vedomosti, April 04, 2000.

by different means, according to regional specifics. The regional authorities' policy gets more and more individual.

Application of decentralization to structural, national and cultural characteristics of Russia's territory prompted few types of regional economic regimes. In particular, a national-clannish economic model has developed in national republics, a state-bureaucratic model – in regions of the "red belt", bureaucratic-criminal – in Primorye Territory and Kaliningrad region, bureaucratic-capitalist – in Moscow, Moscow region and St.-Petersburg, bureaucratic-oligarchic – in Yamalo-Nenetsky and Khanty-Mansiysky autonomous districts and the Omsk region.

The common feature of all these different models is regional protectionism, which is somehow presented in the economic policy of all subjects of the Russian Federation.

Regional protectionism contradicts Article 8 of the Constitution of the Russian Federation, declaring the unity of economic space, free movement of goods, services and capital, freedom of competitiveness and of economic activities. This phenomenon is due to the imperfection of this Constitution, having legalized a wide range of subjects of joint government, weakness of federal center and development of regional (ethnic, cultural, geographical) identity. Besides, it is a result of an active support of the seven first-rate Russian banks by the federal center.

Regional authorities try to resist capital outflow, to restrict a potential competitiveness of non-residents on their regional market, to control production and sales of the goods most important for their region. Extreme manifestations of such a regulatory policy are the export prohibition for foodstuffs and agricultural raw materials for reasons of market protection (Krasnodar Territory, Voronezh region, Tatarstan etc.) and the creation of the closed regional alcohol markets.

As a result of protectionism the risks of regional enterprises become lower at the expense of their growth in business of non-residents. A study carried out by the McKinsey Global Institute has shown that significant potential for risks in Russia is conditioned by the federal and regional authorities' support of a number of chosen enterprises. These enterprises are usually not very effective because of tax and customs privileges, state orders, low energy prices, mutual reckoning and barter.

On the whole, regional protectionism is a kind of regional authorities' response to a sharp increase in transborder capital mobility (due to globalization), combined with weakening the federal center and a continuous production recession.

Another important element of economic policy pursued by subjects of the Russian Federation is a struggle for receiving one or another relative advantage (privilege, power, federal transfers and programmes, investment). The national product gets redistributed for the benefit of successful regions.

For example, until 2000 the economic activity in offshore zones (Ingoushetia, Kalmykia, Altai and other regions and closed administrative-territorial formations) was stimulated by an introduction of a preferential tax regime for companies-non-residents. These were mainly engaged in importing and selling imported goods across Russia, other regions suffering double damage: collecting less taxes at the place of offshore companies' operations and the advance of imported goods onto regional markets, bringing about difficulties for producer-residents.

Now regions are also competing for investment. They adopt appropriate regulations, providing tax privileges and credit guarantees to investors. It looks like a competition between investment laws of different subjects of the Russian Federation. By the beginning of 1999 such laws were enacted in 54 subjects. The most liberal laws are in the Leningrad, Novgorod and Yaroslavl regions, Tatarstan and St.-Petersburg. Tax privileges granted to foreign investors influence regional budgets considerably. Regional authorities stop budget gaps by credits, thus allowing their debts to grow and financial position to deteriorate.

In some cases the competitiveness of equal partners may, for a long time, paralyze making decisions important for the federation. A vivid example is a struggle between St.-Petersburg and the Leningrad region for the new port capacities, which are undoubtedly essential for Russia. St. Petersburg is trying to attract investment to reconstruct its port, and the region – to construct new ports in the Finnish gulf. The story began just after the USSR disintegration, but no progress for solving of the problem was found until 1999. On Russian and international markets many regions act as competitors. While on a home market Russian consumers benefit by this competition, on foreign markets foreign consumers do, and Russian producers lose. The budget loses as well.

In Tatarstan, the Saratov, Samara and Moscow regions the regional land codes are enacted, so we can speak about formation of regional land markets and about land pledging for security of attracted financial resources.

Enactment of liberal regional laws by regions gives certain advantages for attracting financial resources to them and thereby intensifies structural economic transformation. Gaps of 2–3 years, required for the familiarization of legislative innovations, result in an advantage for a vanguard group, materialized in investment attracted.

## 5 Some Results of Decentralization

During the years of reforms Russia's territory became more asymmetrical, and this mainly concerns a system of center-periphery relations. Metropolitan regions increasingly overtake the rest of Russia. The share of Moscow and its region in total GDP has increased from 13.6% in 1995 up to 20.3% in 1998, the share of the Leningrad region – from 4.2% up to 4.6%. Due to metropolitan regions, the total share of subjects of the Russian Federation with the highest density of population in GDP has increased from 29.4% in 1995 up to 35.3% in 1998[12].

The largest cities have adjusted to the new economic situation. As a result of system changes the former ties between centers and periphery were broken, and the new contacts have not been established yet. Most of the country's leading centers find themselves in an initial stage of economic re-structuring, carried out

[12] Estimated on the basis of: Russian Regions: Economic Conjuncture (Socio-Economic Information), Moscow: Center for Economic Conjuncture by the Government of the RF, 2000. Vol. 2. p. 401-402.

mainly at the expense of the province. At the same time the centers' weak economic position does not allow livening up the economy of corresponding regions.

The Moscow central region and most subcentral regions are main recipients of foreign direct investment, which plays an important role in their market adaptation.

In 1993–1999 only 21 subjects of the Russian Federation accumulated more than USD100 million of FDI each. These subjects accounted for more than 90% of all FDI, attracted to the country over that period. The first-rate FDI recipients are capitals and metropolitan regions (the Moscow and Leningrad regions), gas- and oil-producing regions (the Tyumen and Sakhalin regions, the Republic of Komi) and the largest industrial regions (Sverdlovsk, Chelyabinsk, Volgograd regions, republic of Tatarstan – this may be considered among oil-producing regions as well). Half of these regions are frontier (coastal), and in more than a half of them the main city's population is more than one million.

Economic liberalization in Russia promotes (directly and indirectly) the European orientation in regional contacts and economic structure. The historical tendency of economic expansion eastwards has stopped. In previous decades the government has made sufficient efforts to develop the country's North and East. As the financial support is cut back, this process has stopped. The fact that the people have migrated back to the European part of Russia and foreign investment has concentrated there as well is evidence of a new stage in Russia's regional development, decentralization being unable to prevent it.

**Table J3.** Ten first-rate regions as for foreign investment in 1995 and 1999 (in percentage to total investment in the Russian Federation)

| 1995 | | 1999 | |
|---|---|---|---|
| Region | % | Region | % |
| Moscow | 46.9 | Moscow | 27.8 |
| Moscow region | 7.4 | Sakhalin region | 10.7 |
| Tatarstan | 5.8 | Omsk region | 9.3 |
| St.-Petersburg | 5.6 | St.-Petersburg | 7.3 |
| Tyumen region | 3.7 | Krasnodar Territory | 5.3 |
| Samara region | 2.5 | Moscow region | 4.6 |
| Tver region | 2.4 | Nenetsky autonomous district | 3.6 |
| Nizhniy Novgorod region | 2.2 | Leningrad region | 3.0 |
| Novosibirsk region | 2.1 | Krasnoyarsk Territory | 2.1 |
| Sakhalin region | 1.8 | Sverdlovsk region | 1.8 |
| Share of ten regions | 80.4 | Share of ten regions | 75.5 |

*Sources: Finansoviye izvestiya, 13.04.96; The socio-economic performance in the Russian Federation in January—February 1999. M.: Goskomstat of the Russian Federation.*

So, despite new federalization, the 1990s are marked by economic centralization and weakening of the province. In particular it is proved by decreased shares of subjects of the Russian Federation with the low density of the population in GDP. In regions with up to 10 inhabitants per sq. km this index has fallen from 25.8% in 1995 to 23.5% in 1998, in regions with 10-25 inhabitants per sq. km – from 19.1% to 16.9%[13].

The growing of inter- and intra-regional disproportion is closely connected with an increase in the centers/periphery polarization in 1990s. In 1998 the maximum level of per capita GDP was observed in the Yamalo-Nenetsky autonomous district – Rub 47.5 thousand, which was almost 4000 % more than the minimum level (in the Aguinsky Buryatsky autonomous district) – Rub 1.2 thousand, the average level in Russia being Rub 16.9 thousand[14]. The growth of disproportion can be interpreted as the shrinkage of the territory favorable for running business. This shrinkage occurs at the expense of remote and provincial regions.

**Table J4.** Accumulated FDI (1993—1999)

| Region | FDI, USD million | Share in total FDI in the RF, % |
|---|---|---|
| Moscow | 6921 | 37.7 |
| Moscow region | 1978 | 10.8 |
| Sakhalin region | 1367 | 7.5 |
| St.-Petersburg | 1339 | 7.3 |
| Krasnodar territory | 794 | 4.3 |
| Tyumen region | 745 | 4.1 |
| Leningrad region | 461 | 2.5 |
| Samara region | 436 | 2.4 |
| Novosibirsk region | 370 | 2.0 |
| Komi Republic | 267 | 1.5 |
| Sverdlovsk region | 267 | 1.5 |
| Chelyabinsk region | 218 | 1.2 |
| Khabarovsk territory | 216 | 1.2 |
| Primorye Territory | 215 | 1.2 |
| Magadan region | 207 | 1.1 |
| Volgograd region | 170 | 0.9 |
| Kaluga region | 166 | 0.9 |
| Tatarstan | 145 | 0.8 |

[13] Ibid.

[14] Ekonomika i zhizn', • 19, May 2000, p. 31.

| | | |
|---|---|---|
| Irkutsk region | 135 | 0.7 |
| Nizhniy Novgorod region | 118 | 0.6 |
| Oryol region | 101 | 0.5 |

*Estimated on the basis of the statistics, published by Goskomstat and Ministry of Economy of the RF.*

Inter-regional disproportion is specific for the regional development in a market economy, as some regions have relative advantages. However, in the developed countries discrepancies of 200-300% between regions are considered a serious social pathology. Regional disproportion in Russia by thousands per cent exceed the limits admissible for EU countries.

One more result of the regional development in the 1990s is the country's increased disintegration. Regional protectionism and formation of specific economic models in subjects of the Russian Federation contribute to the creation of separate territorial formations. In other words, the case in point is the Russia's fragmentation, decentralization being its catalyst.

Decentralization has enhanced the effect of regional isolation based on long distances and high prices for freight services. Fragmentation is manifested in formation of regional markets, differing as for the level of prices for consumer goods, energy carriers, labor, real estate etc. The regional authorities and businesses try to substitute long (from the point of view of the transport costs and effectiveness/safety) technological cycles with shorter ones and to increase a share of finished goods, that is, the value added produced in a region. Thereby it is possible to improve or at least stabilize the enterprises' and regions' financial situation during economic recession. It is a kind of regional economy's structural adjustment to the high risks of inter-regional economic relations.

V.I.Ishayev and P.A.Minakir estimate that by the beginning of reforms in the Far Eastern region the inter-regional contacts accounted for 75% of all economic relations, foreign trade – for 5% and intra-regional contacts – for 20%. Today the latter prevail in this region's structure of contacts (70%). Foreign trade accounts for 15%, inter-regional contacts – for 10% of all economic relations.[15] This process is observed at the level of both large economic zones and individual subjects of the Russian Federation.

For subjects of the Russian Federation, the potential of fragmentation is limited by their market capacity. At the same time, widening territorial bounds of fragmentation encounters the neighbors' policy of regional protectionism. Inter-regional barriers turn into a serious obstacle for the development of regional economies and for the Russian economy as a whole.

Given deficiency of financial resources, the power decentralization, which was supposed to stimulate regional development, has turned into a source of conflicts and contradictions both in "vertical" relations – between the federal center and

[15] V. Ishaev, P. Minakir, Dal'ny Vostok Rossii: real'nosti i vozmozhnosti ekonomicheskovo razvitiya [The Far East of Russia: realities and possibilities of economic development]. Khabarovsk 1998, p. 92.

subjects of the RF, between the latter and the local authorities, – and in "horizontal" relations – between subjects of Federation and local governments. The contradictions arise mainly in the budget and tax spheres. But the conflicts over regulations concerning the use of natural resources are also frequent. For example, the Buryatiya and Irkutsk regions clash over the volume of Baikal waters required for maintaining stable work of the "Irkutenergo" joint-stock company, the Far Eastern regions – over fishing quotas etc.

## 6 A Change in the Federal Center's Position and Imperatives of the Regional Policy

The country's current regional problems, along with some other vital issues, like paying debts, make the federal center reestablish the vertical power and to reinforce the elements of power centralization.

The federal authorities intend to increase the power centralization, pursuing a liberal course in economy. The main purpose of strengthening the vertical power is to centralize the country's budget resources and to reduce regional protectionism and fragmentation of the Russia's territory. In 1999 a share of the federal budget in the country's consolidated budget increased up to 50%. According to the federal budget law, in 2000 this share will rise up to 52%, and it is supposed to grow up to 65–70% as a result of the tax and budget reforms, which are now being carried out.

The problems of protectionism and fragmentation are planned to be solved by toughening control over regional authorities and reducing their political influence. For this purpose, the procedure of forming of the Council of Federation is being changed, and a mechanism of federal intervention in case the regional authority break a federal law is being created. In seven federal regions the representatives of the President of the Russian Federation have already began their work. At the same time, the law on increasing dependence of local governments on the federal and regional authorities is being passed.

This parallels with specifying federal, regional and local fields of competence, which are supposed to release regional and local authorities from some federal functions and to centralize a considerable part of the country's budget resources. Thus, it might be possible to pass on to the civilized forms of decentralization, preserving the strong federal center.

Deregulation of the power system for the benefit of the center in combination with the liberal priorities in economy will actually lead to speeding up the change in regional structure of the Russian economy and to its faster adaptation to an open economy. As a matter of fact, such a policy answers the interests of large Russian and foreign companies now facing problems for having numerous differences with the local authorities.

In this context the institute of President's representatives in federal regions, who is expected to see to the observance of federal laws and stop manifestations of regional protectionism, will rather promote inter-regional differences, than hamper them. The removal of regional barriers will facilitate the movement of production resources within Russia, as they will move to the regions where good use can be made of them.

The fragmentation of Russia's territory will go on, but the integration of small fragments around the largest economic centers will begin. The "integration of fragmentation" will also be promoted by forming federal regions.

Such a policy being pursued, the concentration of economy in the European part of Russia is very likely to increase, and a key role in the coming territorial structure will be played by the economic axis Moscow - St.-Petersburg and the belt Minsk - Moscow - Nizhni Novgorod - Kazan - Ekaterinburg. The same tendency will be manifested in a "drift" of the Russian economy towards the Baltic and Black Seas and the country's western borders.

At the same time, the heightened business risks in southern Russia will direct the main vector of economic development to the north. The current investment placing and the change in the regional production and income structure are the evidence of such a scenario. This allows us to assume that the gap in the socio-economic development and market transformation between Russia's European north and south will increase.

This growing polarization will inevitably provoke separative tendencies, reducing the country's integrity and strategic stability. Therefore, leveling of the federal center's regional policy and federal investment in education and infrastructure of underdeveloped regions should be the focus of the power reform.

The federal center can influence financial flows either through the budget redistribution, or by means of the special fiscal policy in respect of the regions with heightened business risks. Today the object is set to centralize budget resources and to strengthen control over the private capital. This policy can bring about positive change only if the strategy of the country's regional development is elaborated. It should include the general issues of adaptation of the Russian regional economic structure to the globalization. In particular, one of the main directions of adaptation is the gradual, but steady transformation of the inherited "inverse pattern" of allocating the export-oriented enterprises. It will allow to make the country's participation in the economic globalization more effective and to begin transition from an inland to continental-coastal allocation of enterprises.

The reconstruction of the Russian economy's territorial structure will allow for smoothing over a problem of polarization, to accelerate inter-regional integration on a market basis and to introduce elements of partnership and cooperation to the relations between centers and periphery. However, this reconstruction evidently requires large-scale and long-term investment. At first sight the tendency of the federal authorities to centralize public finances also looks evident. However, the situation is not so simple.

## 7 Political Imperatives of Harmonizing Economic Relations between the Center and Regions

Despite the appreciable economic recovery, the crisis of the Russian state system is still acute. As a matter of fact, there are two possible scenarios: either the federal center, supported by regions, overcomes the crisis and proposes to the society an effective strategy of the socio-economic development, or the further regional differentiation as for the development and incomes level, combined with the disintegration of economic space, actually threatens the integration of Russia as a federate state.

The problems of federalism have turned strongly towards the focus of discussions on the future of the Russian state system. This fact is due to the following circumstances.

First, we have to admit that in the course of liberal transformation in Russia a real multi-party system was not formed for a variety of reasons. In our view, the main reason is that parties as such remained "unclaimed" by the constitution. Therefore, the society could not be structured by a party criterion. Furthermore, the structural vacuum, natural for a transitory period, appeared in the society: the former social relations were destroyed, and the new connections were not yet established. It is clear, that in these circumstances regions or, to be exact, subjects of federation became a backbone of the state. Hence, there is a direct dependence between the country's integrity and the "quality" of its federate structure.

Secondly, it is necessary to take into account the fact that the federate structure was formed for purely political reasons, not in the process of evolution. At that time Russian authorities tried to get rid of the supposedly predatory center. As a result a federation of 89 subjects, divided according to resources, was formed. The constitution declares the principle of equal rights for subjects of federation, at the same time allowing a serious imbalance between them because of their real status and economic potential. Of course, this has caused many problems in conditions of a long and profound recession. Some regions believe that they give away too much, others – that they receive too little, and everyone is dissatisfied with the federal center.

Thirdly, it is important to emphasize that there is practically no system of financial relations between the center, regions and local authorities. Due to lack of precisely formulated criteria, the distribution of public resources has become, so to say, feudal-arbitrary. The privileges and subsidies are usually granted to regions without sufficient economic substantiation, let alone calculation of expected results. A sensible idea of differentiated approaches and regulations, based on the existent regional differentiation, is being realized in the form of individual privileges, given in consideration of taste. Moreover, the lion's share of financial transfers is destined for consumption, not investing. As a result, the regional polarization still increases.

And finally, it is necessary to point out the legal uncertainty in the center/subjects relations. In particular, there are no clear regulations for realizing joint authorities, which constantly provokes conflicts. Besides, there are rather serious discrepancies in the federal and regional legislation, and this is true for the majority of subjects of federation.

How are these problems and contradictions to be solved? Is it possible to achieve the consent of the federal and regional political elite concerning prospects of the Russian state system? Expert opinions are diametrically opposed.

Some experts believe that the fundamental change of the present federative structure is required to overcome the centrifugal tendencies in the country and to prevent its disintegration. An extreme variant of this point of view is an idea of liquidating national formations and passing over to the unitary state. Some arguments count in favor of such an approach, which seem sensible enough. For example, it is noted, that "the "canonical" federation is established by means of the voluntary integration treaty, concluded by sovereign states... A similar process took place when forming the USSR, as distinct from the present Russian "Federation". This is the only thing which prejudices the legitimacy of the Russian federalism and the propriety of granting the status of "a subject of federation" to territories, areas, cities, let alone autonomous districts and republics... Hence, autonomism, not federation, should be considered a principle of the administrative system appropriate to the realities and history of Russia. Autonomism... is able to provide regional self-dependence, on the one hand, and on the other – to limit this self-dependence in the interests of the state as a whole."[16]

Professor V.P.Fyodorov holds a similar opinion. He notes, in particular, that the federal center should place emphasis on "the absolute legal equality of all subjects of federation irregardless of what they are called",[17] in order to stop separative tendencies in republics of the Russian Federation. Furthermore, he considers that only local authorities should be elected. "At the higher levels of elective authorities there should only be a representative branch; heads of executive authorities should be nominated; heads of subjects of federation and mayors of these subjects' capitals should be nominated by the country's president, elected in the course of nation-wide voting".[18] Those supporting such an approach see the possibility of recovering the executive vertical in eliminating the asymmetry of the Russian Federation, on the one hand, and limiting regional rights considerably, on the other.

No wonder representatives of the political elite of the first-rate regions (first of all republics) keep to the opposite opinion. They believe that all the problems arising in the process of public transformation are due to insufficient decentralization of the country's economic policy and poor exercising of existing regional powers. So, the councilor of the President of Tatarstan points out the necessity of keeping "as far as possible" from the federal center: "It seems that references to the common economic space of Russia have played a wicked trick [with the republic]... Being guided by the federal policy, Tatarstan is threatened not only with economic lag, but also with losing sovereignty and becoming an average region... Nowadays the responsibility for developing the national policy should be born by regions. They should develop their own "policy of survival", while at the same time uniting with other regions for the purpose of setting the country's policy"[19]. Another high official from Tatarstan writes: "Such a model is evidently closer to confederation or a milder form of federation".[20]

---

[16] L.B.Reznikov. Plus autonomization of the whole country, in: «Vremya-MN », № 175, Oct.18, 2000

[17] V.P.Fyodorov, "Sovremennaya Evropa", No.3, 2000, p. 16

[18] V.P.Fyodorov, "Sovremennaya Evropa", No.3, 2000, p. 17

[19] P. Khakimov. The Tatarstan's future – the challenge of the moment, in: "Economy of Kazakhstan after August 18", Kazan, 1999, p.77

[20] p.74

We think that under present circumstances both approaches, however sensible some of their arguments may be, are counter-productive.

In a case of liquidating national-state formations on the territory of Russia, it is highly probable that results will be opposite to those expected. The point is not that a real threat for realizing the subsidiarity principle will arise, especially as the process of optimizing the distribution of authority between levels of administration is at the initial stage. Passing over from the federation to the unitary state by administrative means alone is similar to opening Pandora's box, for it is fraught with conflicts, being potentially acute and very hard to settle.

In our view, recovering the unitary state under conditions of globalizing the country's economy will result in an increase in the socio-economic polarization of Russia. 25-30 % of GDP of financial resources potentially controllable by the center as a result of possible reunitarization, are insufficient for stopping undesirable centrifugal processes. The total control over the country's financial resources is necessary for this purpose. This kind of control is only made feasible by giving up market reforms and returning to the state monopoly on external economic activities. The unacceptability of such measures seems indisputable.

Besides, the unitary state structure reduces possibilities for taking into consideration a diversity of Russian regions in a concrete socio-economic policy. For all criticism, leveled at the Russian regional policy of the 1990s, we have to admit that the decentralization, carried out in its framework, has created preconditions necessary for adaptation of unified federative regulations to concrete regional conditions. It is mainly regional leaders, facing needs and asperity of the population due to a rapid change of the former way of life, who has so far prevented the country from social explosions.

It is clear that the movement of the Russian state system towards confederation is not acceptable. Both from economic and political points of view, priority should be given to the imperative of the country's unity and integrity. We are convinced, that the federative foundations of the state should remain stable, and the only question to be discussed is the means of perfecting these foundations. In any case, the decisions in this field should be imposed neither by the center, nor by the regions. These decisions must be a product of civil agreement, a result of conscious and voluntary manifestation of the citizens' will.

So, for today's Russia it is essential to find the most effective ratio of federal, regional and local authorities, being in line with the subsidiarity principle, within the framework of the federative structure. For us it is absolutely clear that a correct balance will accelerate the country's economic development, and incorrect one will impede it. In this context it makes sense to dwell on one important circumstance.

The fact is that in modern Russia, apparently owing to an orthodox-liberal way of thinking, dominating in the Establishment, the efficiency of the state's participation in smoothing regional disproportion in the process of system transformation is being more and more frequently prejudiced. It is claimed, in particular, that the stable economic growth in itself will solve the problem of balancing-out the local disproportions, though not straight away. "Every region has its own disproportions and weak points, and at an initial stage of growth they manifest themselves more vividly. But later on the regional diversity starts working for the benefit of the whole nation, as the variety of regional complexes, complementing each other, becomes an important additional factor of growth".[21] We believe that such an approach obviously exaggerates the possibilities of self-regulation in smoothing regional disproportion. The international experience is clear evidence of the fact that however stable and long economic growth might be, there is an absolute need for a systematic regional policy as an instrument of correcting market failures/adjusting market mechanism. In modern Russia, where subjects of federation differ as for per capita incomes level by more than 1000% (in EU – by 450%), such a policy should be an unconditional imperative of the state interventionism.

We have come to the following conclusions:

1. In Russia the regional economic structure is now adjusting to conditions of an open market economy. This process has just begun, and weakening regional authorities for the benefit of the center when liberalizing economy will accelerate it, aggravating social and political pressures. More smooth and controllable "re-planning" of the territorial economic structure is in the interests of Russia and its federal center.
2. In the process of globalization Russia has gotten into a system of global center-periphery relations, which makes the task of leveling regional development and living standards almost impracticable in the foreseeable future. But the acuteness of this problem can be alleviated by a steady policy, pursued by the federal center in cooperation with regional authorities and investors.
3. From our perspective, the proposed power restriction for regional administrations only makes sense if their powers correspond with their responsibilities. The powers of regional authorities should be balanced with their functions by means of material resources.
4. Regional laws must correspond with the federal legislation, especially in regard to ensuring equal competitiveness for businesses and maintaining the common economic space. In this connection it is necessary to encourage large-scale economic projects with participation of two or more subjects of federation. The trans-territorial economic activity naturally narrows a scope for separative tendencies. For the same reason it is necessary to counteract the partition of natural monopolies now integrating the country's economic space.
5. From our point of view, it is necessary to struggle resolutely for separation of authorities from businesses, first of all at a regional level. In this connection it is necessary to encourage privatization in subjects of the Russian Federation in every possible way. Limiting regional elites' possibilities to manipulate the public property in their own political interests and forming the private capital objectively promote the country's integrity.
6. Within the framework of reconstructing the regional economic structure two interconnected objectives should be set in the middle- and long-term policy of the federal center: economic growth in the regions, possessing a potential for that, and emigration of the population from the territories, having no chances for economic recovery in the near future. As a matter of fact, it suggests crea-

[21] G.A.Granberg. Transformation of the Russia's economic space: threats and prospects, in: "Rossiyskaya ekonomika na novykh putyakh", 2000, № 8, p. 25

tion of mechanisms regulating and coordinating capital and population flows. The achievement of these goals will eventually demand some change in the administrative division, that is, depriving the "bankrupt" subjects of federation of their status. In our view, the idea of changing the administrative territorial division, including integrating existent subjects of federation or breaking them up into smaller units, is now untimely.

7. From our point of view, certain amendments to the Russian constitution are necessary for successful economic reforms and effective control over the complicated situation in the provinces. First, the country requires a government possessing real authorities. It should not be a kind of economic-administrative department of the presidential administration any more. Secondly, the country needs a parliament, being able to exercise effective control over the government. And thirdly, the institution of presidency should be essentially democratized. All of this presupposes that the presidential republic should be transformed into the parliamentary republic with all ensuing consequences, including: first of all, rising public demand for political parties and energizing the party construction on a national scale as a factor of strengthening federalism in the country.

# K. Foreign Trade Policies in Transformational Russian and Ukrainian Economies

Olga Nosova

## 1 Introduction

The majority of world countries succeeded in the restoration of their financial systems after the destructive financial crisis in 1998. Countries in transition restored their economies, but they continue to encounter serious problems that are considered the consequences of crisis. Eastern European countries are at starting positions for integrating into the global economy. For transition countries, the interaction of domestic distortions in the tradables sector and in the overall economy combined with adverse external shocks naturally make sustained economic opening up difficult. The process of economic liberalization is expected to bring about real income gains through the realization of comparative advantages – associated with structural changes –, access to a richer variety of goods and the positive impact of import competition. Rising import competition will bring about pressure on domestic firms to become more efficient; to the extent that firms are really responsive in behavior, technological choice and product assortment, as well as the phasing in of import competition is expected to bring about economic benefits. However, a high responsiveness of firms can hardly be expected if firms have not yet been privatized. Moreover, adjustment is partly in parallel with gross investment so that stable conditions for investment financing are important for east European transition countries.

However, a slow pace of market reform, high budget deficits, current account deficits and capital flight plus high foreign debt reflect the urgent problems of many transition countries. This is all the more crucial since one cannot rule out that shocks in global financial markets or regional economic shocks undermine progress in domestic and fiscal stabilization. As is well known, countries with large current account deficits largely financed through long-term foreign direct investment face fewer problems than countries that mainly rely on portfolio capital inflows. This does not imply that one should overlook the possibility that in transition countries with a short history of FDI inflows, cumulated FDI stock could indeed contribute to a rising current account deficit since foreign subsidiaries often have a preference for imported capital goods. Moreover, if FDI inflows mainly occur in the non-tradables sector there are few reasons to expect that FDI will stimulate net exports of goods and services in the medium term. However, FDI inflows into the tradables sector can be expected to contribute with some delay to net exports, provided that government conducts a trade enhancing policy and that there will be no strong real appreciation of the currency. Such appreciation can occur both through high sustained portfolio capital inflows and through overshooting effects in the context of a Dornbusch model.

There are different approaches regarding trade and FDI interconnection. FDI can be a substitute for trade, others consider FDI a complement of trade, while still some think FDI and trade are fully interdependent of each other. FDI plays an important role in accelerating the transformational process. Foreign affiliates contribute to the growth of value added and account for a significant share of world exports. To the extent that FDI inflows raise per capita income, the opportunities for intra-industry trade will improve.

Unstable exchange rate movements can impair expansion of the tradables sector. In the case of free capital movements a real appreciation of the currency will result in import growth, and it might eliminate long-term export growth. Devaluation of national currency makes imports more expensive, and exports cheaper while stimulating the rise in import demand. Foreign trade policy instruments that are used for stimulation are competitive protection of domestic production, the rise of export income and a source of budget revenues.

## 2 Global Capital Movements and Capital Flows

The processes of globalization and internationalization of world economies suggest an enlargement and deepening of interdependencies; globalization in the form of rapidly rising FDI clearly reinforces the role of multinational companies and in the context of vertical FDI – eg the parent company relying in intermediate imports from a foreign subsidiary – creates stronger economic ties among countries. Hence the very asymmetric FDI inflows into eastern Europe and Russia indirectly create a structural asymmetry among transition countries.

Globalization provides access to new resources and more affective distribution, stimulates free exchange of information, knowledge, development of competition, and new forms of management. The global movement of capitals and commodities is usually explained by basic trade theories: comparative advantages theory, production costs theory, the international product life cycle theory, and the "preference similarity" theory, etc. Modern trade theories are considered foreign trade from supply or demand side economy. In comparison with the neoclassical trade theory, one should mention that without institutional arrangements it is impossible to get advantages from the free movement of capital. When the factor proportions vary widely among countries, pressures exist for the most abundant factors to move to countries with greater scarcity, where they can command a better return. Similarly, capital will tend to move away from countries in which it is abundant to those in which it is scarce. Capital movement stipulates the development of international markets, increases trade and foreign investment. The development of international trade benefits in the creation of international markets of products, makes lower production costs, contributes to competition between domestic and foreign goods, and provides the satisfaction of consumer choice.

Rapid integration of national economies worldwide through trade, financial flows, technology spillovers and information networks contribute to deepening social divisions of labor. The process of global integration spreads to capital goods from the level of commodities and services. Globalization of capital markets is accompanied by a huge capital movement among countries. CEE and CIS absorbed 15 percent of total capital flows to developing and transition countries in the period 1990-1995. Net resource inflows were much lower taking into account debt service and capital flight. Private capital flows to developing countries increased dramatically during the 1990s, with the surge of FDI and portfolio equity investment (From Plan to Market, 1996, 136). In accordance with the view of IMF directors, the negative role of globalization is explained with the scope limit of countries to pursue policies incompatible with medium-term stability, increasing the costs of economic distortions and imbalances. (see IMF Annual Report, 1997, 24, p.35).

The substantial fluctuations in international financial markets affect global development. Developed countries with solid and competitive banking systems – and professional banking supervision – can withstand adverse global shocks. They are not so vulnerable to the financial shocks because of the protection of world financial regulation systems. The process of market adjustments to world events after financial crisis is quick in such countries. The liberalization of transition countries makes them more open to external shocks, and causes fluctuations of capital flows. Decentralization is accompanied by the satisfaction of internal needs, bringing macroeconomic instability in the country. In spite of the considerable improvement of the global economic situation, the threat of feasible deterioration of the economic situation in transition countries exists. The present fall of oil prices can evoke the reduction of demand on the main group of resource commodities.

The process of globalization affects the liberalization of foreign trade, which in turn creates incentives for liberalizing FDI policies. The relative importance of trade within the eastern European region shrank to 14 % in the first half of 1998 on the export side, and remained a stable 10 % for imports. The position of the Russian Federation and other CIS countries as export markets were stable, and equaled 8 %. The CIS share of total eastern European imports declined from 10 % in the first half of 1997 to 8 % in the same period of 1998. The CIS region's overall trade surplus decreased by almost 60 % to $6 billion due to a decline in the Russian surplus and deterioration in other CIS countries (Economic Survey of Europe, 1998, p.77, 94). The main indicators of economic integration among countries have traditionally been measured by the relative importance of international trade, and also FDI flows and stocks. For the world as a whole, the ratio of FDI stock (inward plus outward) to GDP increased steadily from its point in 1980, with rates of increase higher for developing countries (Figure K1).

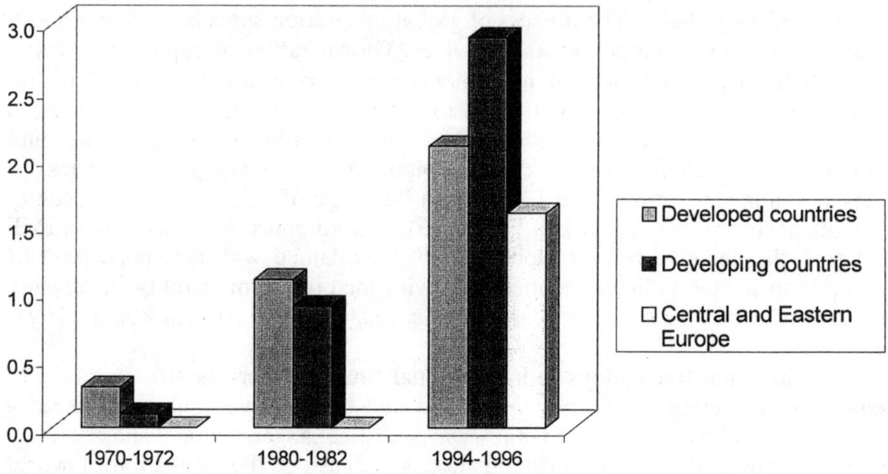


**Fig. K1.** FDI Inflows Plus Outflows (Percentage of GDP)
*Source: World Investment Report: Trends and Determinants, 1998, p.8.*

The ratio of world FDI flows (inflows plus outflows) to GDP has also risen, with developed countries in the lead (Figure K2).

The ratio of world trade (imports plus exports) had an overall change to world GDP in all countries in total during the same period (Figure K3).

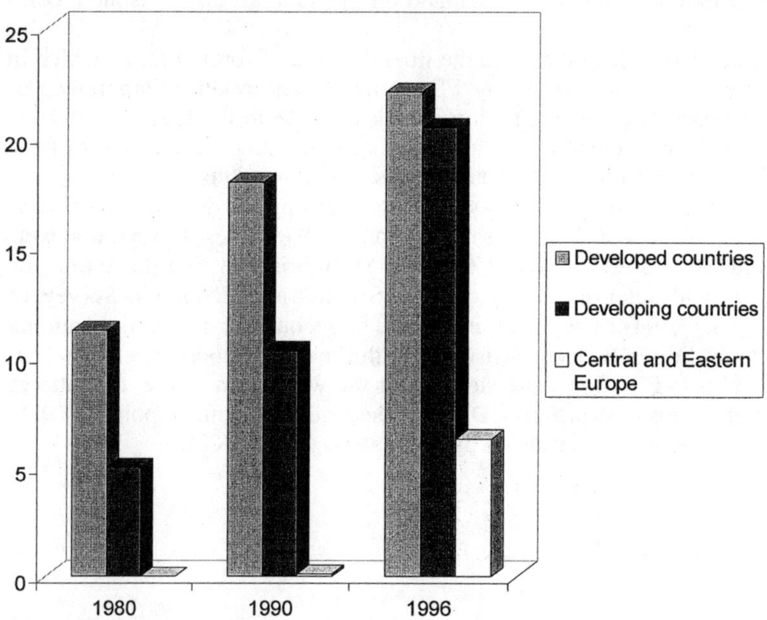


**Fig. K2.** FDI Inward Stock Plus Outward Stock (Percentage of GDP)
*Source: World Investment Report: Trends and Determinants, 1998, p.8.*

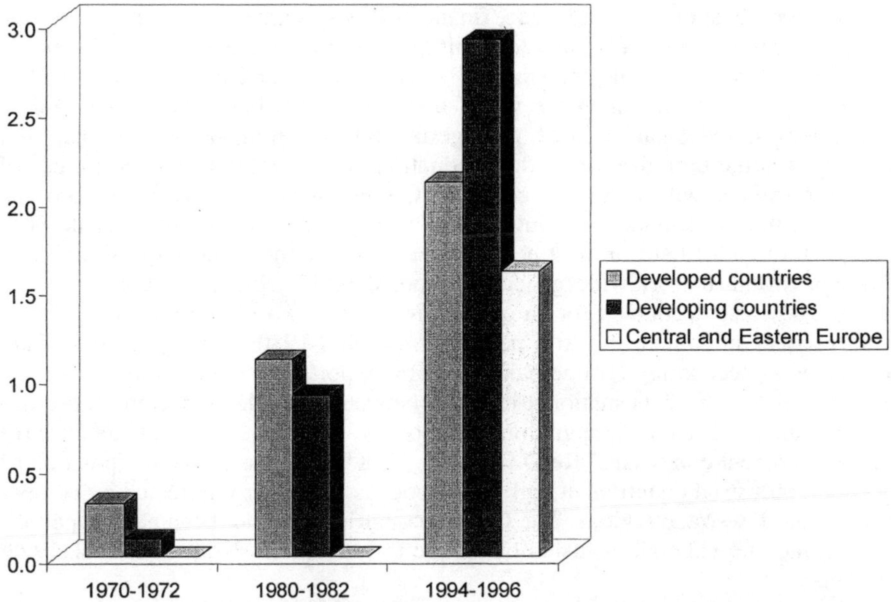


**Fig. K3.** Exports Plus Imports (Percentage of GDP)
*Source: World Investment Report: Trends and Determinants, 1998, p.8.*

In comparison to export plus imports, the rising FDI indicators suggest that the global integration has proceeded more rapidly through FDI than through trade (World Investment Report, 1998, p.7). Kojima and Ozawa emphasize the significant effect that FDI has to economic development through an increase in trade, which occurs as a result of improved comparative advantage leading to an increase in the share of goods requiring a higher level of skilled labor and advanced technology (Wysokinska Z., 1998, p.69).

The economic liberalization of trade and capital has a negative effect on the balance of payments. In the short run, after import liberalization, balance of payments can be deteriorated. This is explained in the discrepancy between the immediate increase of imports and the lag in exports, as companies have to reorganize production in accordance with global requirements. In the case of simultaneous liberalization of trade and capital inflow, this effect can be bigger. The results of liberalization in Hungary were different. Foreign trade had been liberalized parallel to capital inflow in Hungary; the jump of imports emerged only later in 1991, while the exports grew at a faster rate. The main reason was a long-lasting and strong depression in overall home demand. Hamar points out the role of joint ventures in foreign trade, which have been much more dynamic in exports and imports than in domestically-owned companies. In 1992, almost the whole deficit was produced by joint ventures (Hamar J., 1994, p.186). Intra-trade, which determines diversified manufactured products, is very intensive among developed countries, and it is weakly developed in transition countries.

The liberalization of world trade, financial flows, market deregulation, and the development of principally new technological informational systems with broad functions of receiving and transmitting information extend the sphere of TNC's influence and penetration in the world markets. TNC's bring additional capital, technologies, and organizational, managerial and marketing skills. The main aim of TNC's is the optimization of the production process on the basis of the use of scarce resources with minimum costs. TNC's provide diversification of production, and the dissemination of investment management on the world scale. The role of foreign affiliates in host countries has become more and more significant. Foreign affiliates worldwide generated more than $2 trillion in value added in 1997. They also accounted for an increasing share in world GDP, close to 7 percent in 1997 in comparison to 5 percent in the mid-1980s. Foreign affiliates are estimated as accounting for one–third of world exports in 1995 (World Investment Report, 1998, p.6). Transnational linkages between firms have become more important in acquiring and upgrading technology because foreign affiliates have access to parent companies' R&D facilities. H. Klodt suggests that the position of Western industrial countries in high-tech goods is no longer unaffected by competition from low-wage regions. The CMEA-countries have not been able to participate in the international diffusion of mobile technical knowledge (Klodt H.,1992, p.119).

The consequences of the Asian crisis is reflected in the fall of net long-term financial flows to developing countries from $338 billion in 1997 to $275 billion in 1998, including both private and official finance. Net long-term flows from bonds, banks, lending, and equity fell from $136 billion in 1997 to $72 billion in 1998. The rate of world trade growth is projected to decline from 4.8 % in 1998 to 4.2 % in 1999. Import volume growth is expected to slow in Europe and Central Asia, as a result of transitional problems in Russia and the Ukraine (Figure K4).

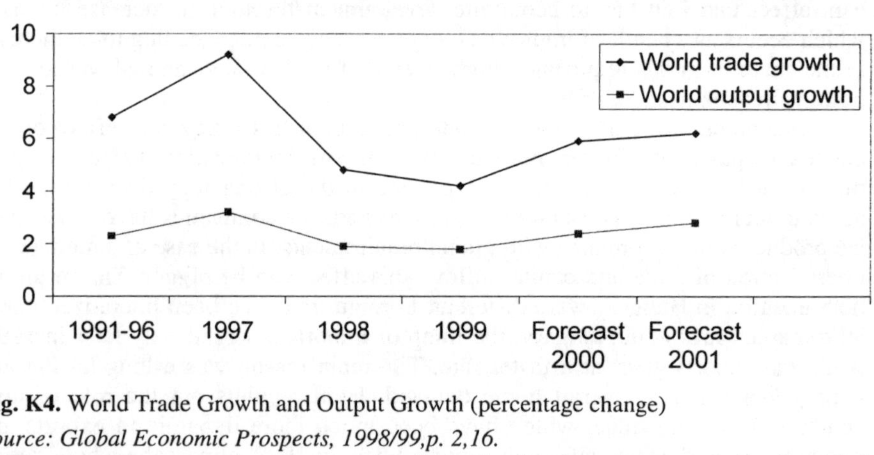


**Fig. K4.** World Trade Growth and Output Growth (percentage change)
*Source: Global Economic Prospects, 1998/99,p. 2,16.*

Low saving and accumulation rates impede the functioning of the financial sector. FDI in developing countries is slowing down in response to slow growth in global output and in world trade, which negatively affects corporate earnings in some countries and restricts access to finance. Aid flows to developing countries have been shortened. The ratio of FDI to private investment is less than 30 percent in major recipient countries, which illustrates that the rise in private investment exceeds the direct impact of an increase in FDI (table K1).

**Table K1.** Ratio of FDI to private investment in major recipient countries

| Country | 1994 | 1995 | 1996 | 1997[a] |
|---|---|---|---|---|
| China | 40.2 | 31.8 | 29.5 | 29.1 |
| Brazil | 3.6 | 4.1 | 9.4 | 14.3 |
| Mexico | 16.2 | 23.8 | 19.9 | 18.7 |
| Argentina | 6.3 | 11.0 | 10.7 | 11.4 |
| Poland | 15.4 | 23.5 | 22.6 | 20.1 |
| Chile | 27.2 | 27.6 | 35.1 | 29.9 |
| Malaysia | 22.0 | 15.5 | 17.5 | 16.5 |
| Thailand | 2.9 | 3.6 | 3.9 | 8.9 |
| Venezuela | 19.6 | 25.5 | 66.1 | 79.7 |
| Russian Federation | 1.2 | 3.9 | 3.6 | 8.6 |

[a] - Preliminary.

*Source: Global Economic prospects 1998/99, World Bank, p.53.*

In the majority of transition countries, the share of foreign debt to GDP increases, GDP per capita reduces, and the income gap between the basic groups of population grows. These processes mark the economic and social consequences of globalization for Eastern European countries. V. Choros emphasizes two directions of IMF recommendations toward export - import liberalization in the improvement of host country's balance of payments (Choros V., 1999, p.117). The first deals with import liberalization, which strengthens competition in the domestic market and positively affects the balance of payments. The second relates to the export of natural resources, import of obsolete technologies, and production of articles that negatively influence a country's economic position.

Major benefits for Eastern European economies from openness and the switch to relatively free trade can be had only on the basis of trade liberalization and institutional transformation. An open and liberal system of capital movements fostered economic growth and prosperity by contributing to an efficient allocation of world savings and investment. The capital account liberalization should be a permanent process, fostering a realization of macroeconomic policies and setting up strong financial systems. Removal of trade restrictions should be accompanied by structural reforms.

FDI can help boost host country exports. MNCs are likely to face lower costs in exporting than local firms due to knowledge of international market conditions and access to marketing and distribution networks (Aitken B., Hanson G., and Harrison A., 1997, p.103). FDI in developing and transition countries made up $155 billion in 1998, 16 times more than in 1990. The result of global production nets, world trade makes up one-third of total volume (Usuf Sh., 1999, p.2). The elimination of trade barriers and the development of trade liberalization allow access to FDI; challenge the appearance of new company's ties; provide the expansion of production nets; and stimulate production specialization, development management, and marketing skills. However, there are considerable differences across transition countries that differ in size, per capita income and policy orientation, as well as with respect to the role of foreign indebtedness. While EU accession countries in eastern Europe enjoy the advantage of having an institutional anchor in all policy fields through prospects for EU membership, the situation in Russia and the Ukraine is much different and indeed more difficult. This does not rule out the possibility that these and other transition countries could draw lessons either on the basis of theoretical analysis or from the numerous experiences in transformation policies and in the economic liberalization of Newly Industrialized Countries.

## 3 Foreign Trade Policies in Russia and Ukraine in Transition

Developing countries and the CIS are becoming increasingly linked to the global economy. This process affects development of market integration, interdependence among countries, and provides opportunities to exploit country's comparative advantages. The main aims of transition – trade liberalization, effective privatization and macro stabilization – have not been fully achieved in the CIS. M. Porter contends that most developing countries are at the first stage of development and are building comparative advantages in labor-intensive and natural resource-intensive goods (Wysokinska Z., 1998, p.65). Further progress in providing reforms can be ensured via the restructuring and privatizing of key enterprises, through reorganization of the banking sector, and investment in capital-intensive branches. The openness of the country is closely connected with the development of well-functioning market-based institutions, an efficient state management of public business, the guarantee of property rights, and adherence to the rule of law.

State regulation policy toward foreign trade is directed toward the stimulation of domestic products in the foreign markets through exports, the increase in the supply of competitive products, and improved access of these goods to convertible-currency markets. The protection of the economy from undesirable imports and the lowering competitiveness of imported goods positively influence the foreign trade policy of the country. There are basic methods of state regulation, import-promotion, and export-promotion. Government policy of economic openness, the dismantling of import and export barriers, foreign trade and FDI liberalization promote adjustment of domestic prices to world market prices. It results in decreasing prices on some domestic goods in case of saturation of their internal market, while simultaneously increasing the competitiveness of goods. The market determines necessity and profitability of production goods. The competition policy is the basis for creation and preservation of industrial structure in the economy of the future. Searches for new kinds of competitive products, new markets, and production of new commodities force competition among producers, affect the reduction of production costs, and raise export revenues.

Foreign trade policy is divided in its policies based on export substitution or import substitution. The export substitution policy is based on the expansion production of exported goods of a country, which leads to the aggravation of trade conditions in favor of trade partners. The import substitution policy results in the broadening of the production of a country's imported goods, thereby leading to the improvement of trade conditions in the country towards its trade partners. As a result, the better the trade conditions that appear in a country, the worse they become for trading partners. Such investment stimulation into import substitution policy promotes domestic production, decreases relative import prices, and raises relative export prices. Studies support the export-enhancing policy but emphasize difficulties in its implementation.

This liberal-institutional industrial policy marks new strategies in transition countries. It involves government's promotion of economic development, entrepreneurial activities, and competition, thereby promoting orientation. The protection of infant industries is suggested in the initial stages of development. After a period of protection, industries become competitive and assistance is no longer needed. In most countries, protective tariffs or quantitative bans or restrictions regarding specific industries were set up. These measures correspond to the need to develop a policy of sustaining competitive advantage (Gorynia M., 1998, 18). The protection of the domestic market via import duties and the development of more efficient domestic production seek to strengthen the country's trade position.

Import substitution is a rather doubtful strategy, as experiences from Latin America in the 1970s and 1980s have shown. A strategy of reorientation toward import substitution policy could be based on the development of high technological productions in the country; this, however, only makes sense if there is a relatively strict domestic competition policy combined with adequate innovation policies. It is unclear whether political systems in transition countries can develop such policies. Given a high endowment of human capital in Russia and the Ukraine, there are arguments for considering policy options aimed at enhancing the growth of manufacturing industries that produce skill-intensive – and sometimes capital-intensive – products. Investments in the production of capital-intensive and skill-intensive products will stimulate economic growth in the production sector of the economy. The structure of export in transition countries changed from one dominated by raw materials and low-cost labor-intensive products to one in favor of capital-intensive and skill-intensive products. In countries, that were less successful in acquiring FDI in early stages of transition, relying rather on Western Europe's outward processing trade, a large proportion of exports were provided by unskilled labor-intensive products. According to UN data, Russia's specific share in world foreign trade decreased from 2.5 % at the beginning of $90^{Th}$ to 1.3 % in 1998.

The barter negatively affects relative prices and development in financial and banking sectors. In 1997, Russia's barter trade was about 6% of exports and 8% of imports, where CIS countries account for the majority of Russian barter deals (Economic Survey of Europe, 1998, p.92, 103). The Ukraine has continued to rely on international barter because of its significant share of arrears to Gazprom, Russia's natural gas monopoly. The barter operations share in Ukrainian export decreased to 4.3% in nine months during 1999 in comparison with 7.8% in 1998, making up 6.3% of imports in 1999 compared with 3.4% in 1998 (Informational Bulletin, 1999, p. 61, 62, 72). The reduction of barter shares in export and import in the Ukraine during 1999 is explained due to the government policy substantially limiting barter operations.

**Table K2.** Russia, Ukraine: Selected Economic Indicators, 1990 – 1996

| Russia | 1990 | 1993 | 1994 | 1995 | 1996 |
|---|---|---|---|---|---|
| GDP, RUR bn, nominal | 644 | 171510 | 610592 | 16305956 | 2256000 |
| Real gross rate, % | - 3.0 | - 8.7 | - 12.7 | - 4.2 | - 6.0 |
| Gross investment, RUR bn, nominal | 249.1 | 27124.5 | 108810.0 | 266974.0 | 370000.0 |
| Real gross rate, % | 0.1 | - 11.5 | - 24.0 | - 10.0 | - 18.0 |
| Retail trade, RUR bn | 280 | 58762 | 213430 | 553466 | 753287 |
| Real gross rate, % | 12.0 | 1.9 | 0.1 | - 7.0 | - 4.0 |
| Ukraine | 1990 | 1993 | 1994 | 1995 | 1996 |
| GDP,UAH mn, nominal | 1.671 | 1483.0 | 12037.7 | 52933.1 | 80510.0 |
| Real gross rate, % | - 2.6 | - 14.2 | - 23.0 | - 11.8 | - 10.0 |
| Gross investment, UAH mn, nominal | 0.311 | 283.8 | 2280.0 | 9378.2 | 12557.0 |
| Real gross rate, % | 1.9 | - 10.3 | - 22.5 | - 20.0 | - 22.0 |
| Retail trade, UAH mn | 0.783 | 438.2 | 3369.7 | 11964.0 | 15700.0 |
| Real gross rate, % | 12.0 | - 35.0 | - 13.6 | - 13.9 | - 11.0 |

*Source: Countries in Transition 1997. p 89, 95.*

The main economic indices of GDP, gross investment, and retail trade have been aggravated in Russia and Ukraine since 1990 (table K2). Currently, the economic situation in both countries is beginning to improve slightly.

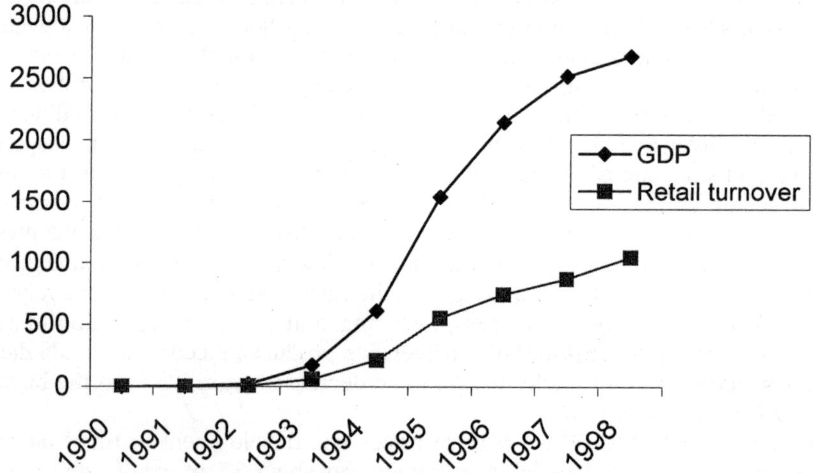


**Fig. K5.** GDP and Retail Trade in Russia (Bill. Roubles)

*Source: Constructed on the data Review of Economic Policy in Russia in 1998, p.584, 605.*

The bigger rate of GDP increase in comparison with retail trade in Russia does not reflect the improvement of living standards for the common people; the CPI made up 100 % in 1995 and reached 249,3 % in 1998. According to state statistical data, foreign trade turnover decreased to 17.6% in Russia during 1998, compared with the same period in 1997, as is illustrated in table K3.

**Table K3.** Foreign Trade in Russia in 1990 – 1998 (Bill. dollars US)

| | Export (fob) | Including oil, oil products | Including gas | Import (sif) | Machinery products | Foreign trade balance |
|---|---|---|---|---|---|---|
| 1990 | 71.1 | - | - | 81.8 | 36.3 | -10.7 |
| 1991 | 50.9 | - | - | 44.5 | 15.8 | 6.4 |
| 1992 | 53.6 | - | - | 43.0 | 13.9 | 10.6 |
| 1993 | 59.6 | - | - | 44.3 | 9.1 | 15.3 |
| 1994 | 68.1 | - | - | 50.5 | 13.6 | 17.6 |
| 1995 | 81.3 | 17.3 | 10.8 | 60.9 | 15.7 | 20.4 |
| 1996 | 88.4 | 23.1 | 15.8 | 61.5 | 14.6 | 26.9 |
| 1997 | 88.4 | 21.9 | 16.4 | 73.6 | 18.5 | 14.8 |
| 1998 | 73.9 | 14.5 | 13.3 | 59.5 | 15.6 | 14.4 |
| 9 months 1999 | 50.82 | - | - | 29.31 | - | 21.51 |

*Source: Goskomstat of Russian Federation.*

The share of Russian foreign trade with non-CIS countries made up 78.5% of total turnover in 1998. The foreign trade turnover with distant countries reduced to 16.7% in 1998 compared with the same data from 1997.

Russia accounts for 50 percent of exports and 40 percent of imports in total regional trade among the CIS. Russia's CIS-destined exports consisted of 54% of its natural gas, crude oil and oil products. The second most important export commodities were base metals and chemicals, which made up a 16% share (Economic Survey of Europe, 1998, p.100). The price rise compared with import prices from distant countries and the low quality of products resulted in the increased use of state trading and bartering operations. Import reduction from CIS made up 16%, whereas the rest-of-world countries (ROW) equaled 32%. The Russian export value is highly sensitive to changes in world commodity prices. The share of machinery, equipment and vehicles decreased in total export volume, depicting a problem in foreign trade, namely a reduction of the above-mentioned items. There were changes in the commodity structure of Russian exports to non-CIS countries. Russian exports of mineral products and metal – making up two-thirds of its total non-CIS products – fell in the first half 1998. The export of precious metals and stones doubled. Exports of chemical products decreased, as can be seen in table K7. After the financial crisis in 1998, the export of oil products rose to 20%, natural gas and coal increased to 17%, timber to 44%; vodka increased to 65% in the second quarter of 1999 compared to the same period the previous year in Europe. European analysts contend that East European trade growth may be set to slow, at least in short to medium run, as exports are likely to suffer more deeply than imports. (Economic Survey of Europe, 1998, p.85).

The falling prices of fuels and raw materials, the devaluation of the ruble, and a discrepancy involving overestimated exchange rates of ruble to US dollar caused the reduction of Russian exports in the second quarter of 1998. The appreciation of the Russian ruble reinforced increased import demand. Russian export discrimination in foreign markets impedes the development of foreign trade. European Union countries and the USA use the protection regime for their domestic goods. The export of technically-complicated manufactured articles to the European Union is limited. Discrepancies exist concerning the main economic characteristics of devices and equipment. The main distinguishing feature of Russian export is resource specialization, which can be explained by the low competitiveness of domestic goods, inefficient policy of export stimulating and a decreasing share of finished articles in total export volume. From the point of political and strategic interests, the USA and countries of the European Union block the export of technically-advanced (military) products.

The commodity structure of imports from countries abroad is characterized by a significant decrease in deliveries of machinery and equipment to 60%, transport equipment and medicine to 40%, clothes and footwear to 44%, and a rise in frozen meat to 30% in second quarter of 1999 in comparison to the same period in 1998. The same tendencies can be observed among the countries of the CIS. The foreign trade turnover of Russia with the CIS decreased to 20.8%, and made up $28.6 billion. The export share of the Ukraine was 40% in total volume of exports, Belarus 34%, and Kazakhstan 14%. Germany exported 10.9% of total imports to Russia, USA 8.6%, and Italy 5.6% (Figure K6).

In order to lower the competitiveness of Eastern European and Baltic exports, Russian authorities introduced a 3 percent import surcharge (abolished in October 1998), which considerably increased import duties on raw sugar and eliminated tax concessions in tolling arrangements. Foreign investment is considered an important source for attracting foreign capital in the economy.

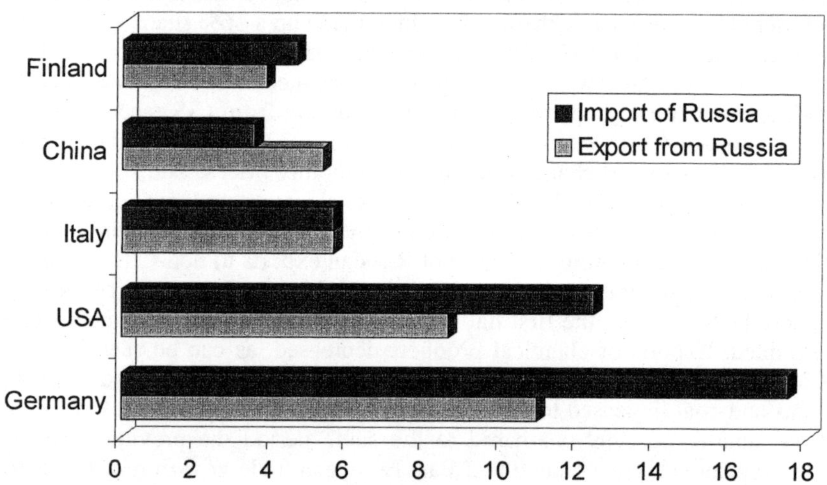


**Fig. K6.** The Importers and Exporters of Russian Production in 1998 (Percent)
*Source: Goskomstat of Russia.*

The total volume of foreign investment equaled $11.77 billion US in 1998, making up 95.8% of foreign investment in 1997, and capital outflow from Russia has continued (table K4).

**Table K4.** Structure of Foreign Investment in Russian Economy (Mn. US Dollars)

| | 1995 | | 1996 | | 1997 | | 1998 | |
|---|---|---|---|---|---|---|---|---|
| Total | 2983 | 100 | 6970 | 100 | 12295 | 100 | 11773 | 100 |
| Including: | | | | | | | | |
| Direct | 2020 | 67.72 | 2440 | 35.00 | 5333 | 43.38 | 3361 | 28.55 |
| Portfolio | 39 | 1.30 | 128 | 1.84 | 681 | 5.53 | 191 | 1.62 |
| Other | 924 | 30.98 | 4402 | 63.16 | 6281 | 51.09 | 8221 | 69.83 |

*Source: Goskomstat of Russia.*

The FDI branch distribution of working foreign capital in Russia can be seen in table K5. The calculated efficiency, based on the total volume of production per worker in enterprises with foreign capital, exceeds the average level of the same indicator in Russian enterprises twofold. The distinguishing feature of foreign investment policy is the rise of intensity of FDI import activity, especially in trade, food catering and industry. The enterprise's export with respect to foreign capital is resource-oriented. It includes oil, chemical commodities, timber, fish products, non-ferrous metals, and waste materials. Reduction in the growth rate of FDI exports is explained by the decrease in foreign investor activity in the extractive industry and the redistribution effect among specific sectors of economy. The rise of FDI foreign trade operations is based on deepening FDI inflow within industry, as well as the expansion of equipment imports and details for domestic production. Enterprises with FDI produce about 5% of Russia's GDP.

**Table K5.** The Branch Structure of FDI in Russia in 1998

| Branch | % |
|---|---|
| Trade and food catering | 35.2 |
| Industry | 26.4 |
| Transport and communication | 8.5 |
| Building | 6.8 |
| Commercial activity | 6 |

*Source: Goskomstat of Russia.*

The experiences of Central European and Baltic countries reveal the significant role of FDI in covering current account deficits and boosting export growth. For example, FDI is financing a large share of current account deficits in Hungary and the Baltic States. The existence of fiscal problems and the devaluation of national currencies are affecting the exchange rate of national currencies in Russia and the Ukraine. Current account deficits are not excessive in these countries. The shares of current account deficits covered by FDI inflows can be seen in table K6.

**Table K6.** Shares of current account deficits covered by FDI inflows, (%)

| | 1996 | 1997 | January – June 1998 |
|---|---|---|---|
| Russian Federation | -20 | -214 | 44[a] |
| Ukraine | 44 | 47 | 48 |

[a] - January - March

*Source: UN/ECE secretariat, estimates based on national statistics.*

The impact of lower prices for key commodities and weak demand caused a reduction in the value of exports in the first half 1998 in the Ukraine, a country intensely reliant on exports of ferrous metals. The consequences of the Asian financial crisis resulted in a reduction of demand for cheap Ukrainian steel from some Asian countries, which subsequently reduced their steel imports. The Ukrainian government raised import tariffs on over 600 primarily consumer goods, eliminated tax exemptions in 1998, and increased its control over trade. The total volume of foreign merchandise trade by commodities made up $16.684 billion US during nine months in 1999 within the Ukraine and decreased to 19.9% when compared with the same period in 1998, including exports in the amount of $8.251 billion US and imports valued at $8.433 billion US (Figure K7, K8).

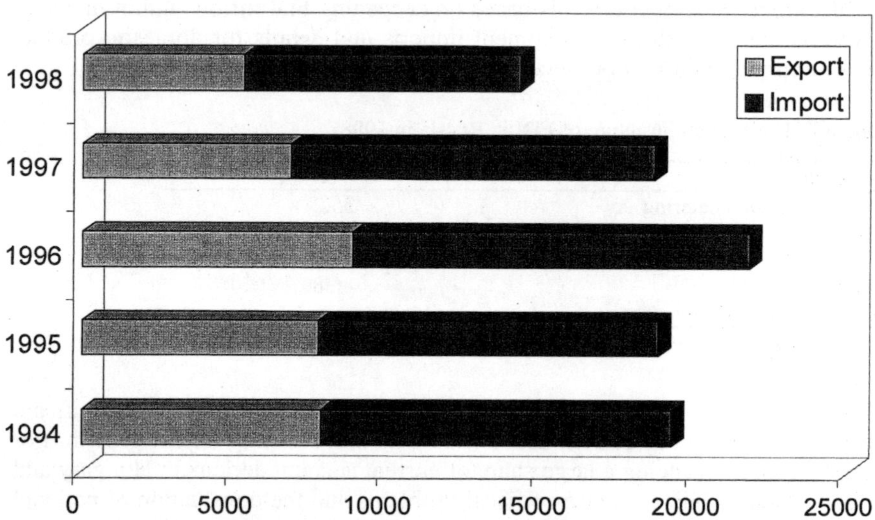


**Fig. K7.** Ukrainian foreign trade in goods with FSU (mn US dollars)
*Source: Informational Bulletin of State Statistics, 1998, p.61.*

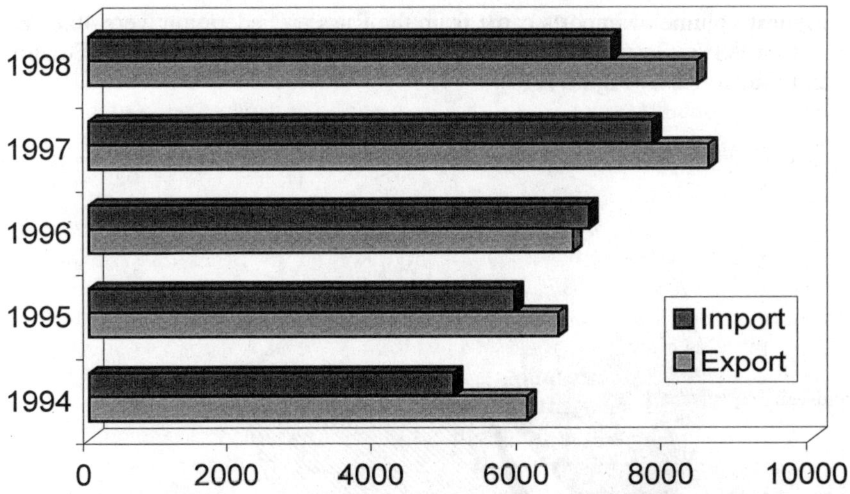


**Fig. K8.** Ukrainian trade in goods with the rest of the world (mn US dollars)
*Source: Informational Bulletin of State Statistics, 1998, p.61.*

The Ukraine carried out foreign trade operations with 179 countries throughout the world. The biggest volume of commodities exports were sent to Russia, making up 20.2% of the total export volume, followed by China 7.1%, Turkey 6%, Germany 5.1%, Italy 4%, USA 3.6%, Belarus 3%, and Bulgaria 2.6% (Figure K9).

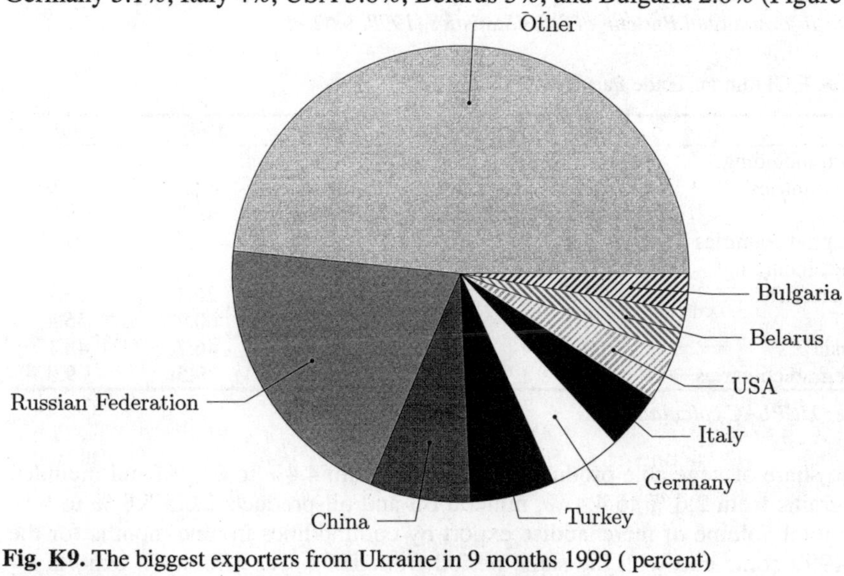


**Fig. K9.** The biggest exporters from Ukraine in 9 months 1999 ( percent)
*Source: Informational Bulletin of State Statistics, 1998, p.62.*

The biggest volume of imports came from the Russian Federation were 46.8 %, Turkmenistan 8.3%, Germany 7.5%, USA 3%, Belarus 2.9%, Italy 2.3%, Poland 2.2 %, and France 1.8% (Figure K10).

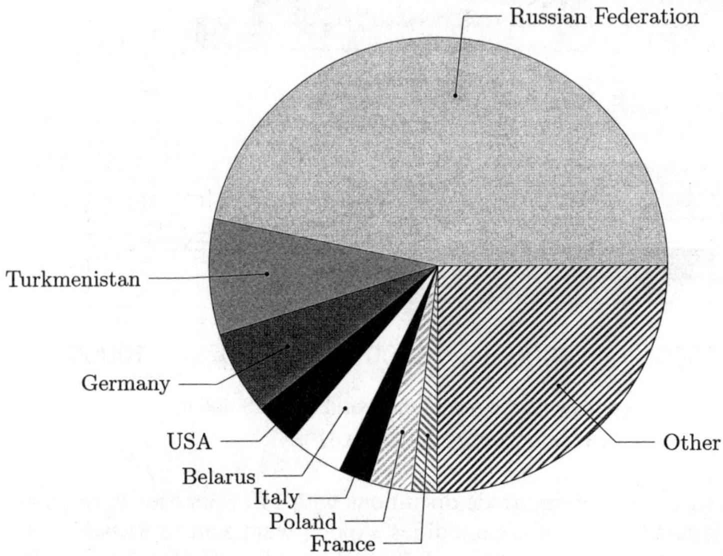


**Fig. K10.** The biggest importers from Ukraine in 9 months 1999 (percent)
*Source: Informational Bulletin of State Statistics, 1998, p.62.*

**Table K7.** Ukrainian Trade Partners (%)

| | 1994 | 1995 | 1996 | 1997 | 1998 |
|---|---|---|---|---|---|
| Export, including: | | | | | |
| EU countries | 9.0 | 11.7 | 10.9 | 12.1 | 16.9 |
| FSU | 57.8 | 54.3 | 54.1 | 40.8 | 35.1 |
| Visegrad countries | 5.5 | 6.9 | 7.4 | 9.4 | 9.4 |
| Import, including: | | | | | |
| EU countries | 13.3 | 19.1 | 14.1 | 20.4 | 22.7 |
| FSU | 76.3 | 67.3 | 67.8 | 60.4 | 56.4 |
| Russia | 60.6 | 52.9 | 48.0 | 46.7 | 48.1 |
| Visegrad countries | 4.4 | 8.3 | 6.0 | 9.5 | 9.9 |

*Source: UEPLAC calculations.*

The share of vegetable production increased from 4.4% to 6.2 %, and included food grains from 2.6 % to 4.4 %, mineral oil and oil-products from 3.8 % to 6 % in the total volume of merchandise export by commodities in nine months for the year 1999 compared with the same period from 1998. The Ukraine's exports remain vulnerable to unfavorable changes in trade regimes, as indicated by severe problems for metal exporters caused by the quantitative restrictions of trading partners. Exports on ferrous metal products decreased from 5.3% to 3.6%, mechanical machinery and equipment from 6.3% to 5.2%, ferrous metals from 34.9%

to 33.5%. The reduction of the share of metal products in the total export volume indicates the necessity for modernization of the export structure. The negative balance is formed primarily because of the mineral fuel, oil and oil-processing products, rubber, and machinery products. The share of mineral oil and oil products increased from 38.3% to 46.1% and the share of mechanical machinery and equipment – including all vehicles except railway transport – decreased from 5.7% to 3.6% in the total volume of merchandise import. The export of services from the CIS decreased to 5.4%. The import of services from the CIS decreased to 39.6%, including that within Russia to 37.3%. The share of import reduction of services from Great Britain decreased to 29.5%, Germany 20.8%, and USA 7%. The barter negatively affects relative prices and development of the banking sector. Ukraine continually relies upon international barter because of a significant share of arrears to Gazprom, Russia's natural gas monopoly. The barter operations share in Ukrainian export decreased to 4.3% in nine months during 1999 in comparison with 7.8% in 1998; imports made up 6.3% in 1999 compared to 3.4% in 1998 (Informational Bulletin, 1999, p. 61,62, 72). The reduction of barter share in export and import in 1999 is explained by the Ukrainian policy toward substantial limitation of barter operations.

According to State Statistics, the cumulative volume of FDI to the Ukraine on October 1, 1999 made up $3.122 billion US. The USA invested 18.3% in the Ukraine, the Netherlands 9.5%, the Russian Federation 9.2%, Germany 7.7%, the United Kingdom 7.6%, and Cyprus 5.5%. The branch structure of FDI includes machinery and metal processing 11%, oil processing 6%, food catering 20%, foreign trade 17%, finance and credit 6%, building 4%, and other 36%. The absence of effective export specialization reveals a low share of finished articles in the total volume of exports. Reorientation of the export mechanism from natural resources to finished articles will stimulate the accumulation of export revenues. The capital account of the host country's balance of payments can benefit from the establishment of multinational company (MNC) subsidiaries used as an export supply source.

## 4 Foreign Trade Policy Instruments

A prime task of foreign trade policy in several CIS countries is membership in the WTO, which would help to avoid unfair anti-dumping procedures in OECD markets. At the beginning of the 21st century, Russia has yet to become a member. While China's accession to the WTO certainly provides encouragement for Russia to become a member, the structure of the Russian economy implies particular problems, e.g. the large role of oil and gas exports that face markets with volatile price movement. Moreover, Russia could be a major agricultural exporter but is likely to face sudden and strong protection in EU countries and elsewhere.

Another important task of foreign trade policy in transition countries is to get access to the CIS markets, provide growth of export products, increase the share of competitive products in total volume of export, and stimulate the increase of export revenues. The government can use different instruments of state regulation on trade policy: tariffs, quotas, subsidies, and duties. The negative role of import tariffs is shown through the drop of world trade, the increase of tax burden for consumers, the blast of the country's export, and the reduction of the overall level of employment. The positive side of tariffs deals with the protection of infant industry, the stimulation of domestic production and the source of budget incomes. The income from custom duties makes up 3.4% of the Russian GDP. The Russian structure of state income through custom duties distinguishes it from the majority of other countries. Three-fourths of state income is comprised of the export tariff and one-fourth through import duties. (Kireev A., 1999, p. 226). The producer's subsidies are considered a more favorable method of import restriction in comparison with tariffs and quotas, because they bring smaller losses for the national economy.

P. Welfens points out two arguments in favor of uniform tariffs. Tariff revenues could generate considerable government revenues in the medium term although it seems appropriate to reduce tariff rates in the long-run. Temporary tariff protection will give manufacturing industry more breathing space to prepare for full competition (Welfens P., 1999, 102). V. Novikov and T. Golayshova suggest setting up stepped custom duties that would reflect the difference in world and domestic prices. The absence of import duties results in budgetary and custom losses (Novikov V., Golaysheva T., 1999, 83). P. Sutela emphasizes a crucial question of the central authorities to tax some revenue received by the exporters to use for infrastructure maintenance and redistribution that should be shared across regions (Sutela P., 1999, p. 21). The economic strategy of foreign trade policy aims at protecting the domestic market, providing for the development of competitive products, and stimulating structural changes.

Russia and the Ukraine signed the "Treaty on Economic Co-operation for 1998 –2007" on February 27, 1998, directed at unifying tariff and tax policies and expanding trade relations. The Russian government reduced the maximum tariff rate from 30 to 20 percent on some consumer goods in 1998, but nevertheless considerable differences still exist between Russia and WTO members.

The Russian foreign trade turnover with European Union countries makes up 34% of total turnover, 40% of investment flows, and 40% of joint ventures (Petrov G., Perska V., 1999, 15).

A. Vodaynov, V. Lapenin, and G. Isakov analyze average autonomous rates of import tariffs, average conventional rates of import tariffs, and average nominal and average weighted ad valor rates of import tariffs. The main conclusion of their research deals with the fact that the Russian foreign trade regime is more liberal on foreign goods inside its domestic market than compared with WTO countries (Vodaynov A., Lapenin V., Isakov G., 1999, 49). The equal economic opportunities for domestic and foreign investors are the prerequisite for the effective development of the real economy sector. V. Perska considers the creation of the independent group (commission), which would be responsible for the world organizational cooperation, and will provide an assessment of the international organization's role in transformational economies (Petrov G., Perskay V., 1999, p.18). The main direction of Russian membership to the WTO is real foreign trade liberalization, free access to the European markets of high technologies, improvement tax, custom legislation, and infrastructure development.

The different level of asymmetry of a liberalizing economy is the primary problem of Ukrainian trade relations with countries of the European Union. There are quantity restrictions of Ukrainian exports to the European Union. The share of foreign trade relations in the Ukraine with countries of the European Union made up 19% in 1998, exceeding 1997 levels. The Ukrainian foreign trade balance of commodities and services with countries of the European Union was positive in the first half 1999 when compared to the same period in 1998 (Sotnikov O., 1999, p.6). The main condition for Ukrainian accession to the WTO is the reduction of the import tariffs on agricultural production, state subsidies to agriculture, and the use of varied control instruments of trade volumes. The WTO members apply rigid tariff restrictions for protecting their domestic markets; this can be observed, for example, with respect to the progressive increase of import tariffs adequate to the degree of processing of imported products. Economic restructuring is the basis for future progressive development, and a condition for Russia and the Ukraine becoming members of the WTO.

Russian and Ukrainian membership in the WTO will favorably benefit the trade regime for these countries and provide an access to the world mechanism for concluding international transactions. The basic obstacles for foreign trade development in Russia and the Ukraine are exchange rate regulations, which are directed at the necessity of getting licenses on imported capital. Customs regulations in both countries are not stable and not attractive for foreign investors. Foreign trade tax systems do not affect producers in an effective way, nor do they stimulate tax collection. The procedure of getting products certified is complicated. There is no internal mechanism of protection on the market against low quality of products.

The main efforts of foreign trade policy should be directed towards the liberalization of trade, reorientation toward export substitution policies in highly technological branches, export orientation activity of enterprises with FDI, and the use of different import duties as the source for receiving import revenues. The experience of Central European countries shows that firms with foreign participation are more trade-intensive on average than domestic companies. Some sectors have become more export or trade-oriented as a result of the activity of enterprises with foreign capital. The attraction of foreign capital in technology-intensive areas is the condition of fostering a rise in the export propensities of companies with foreign participation to export. The direction of change in trade composition toward capital-intensive and technology-intensive exports leads to Russia's and the Ukraine's increased participation in the international division of labor.

The most urgent problems in the sphere of foreign trade should be solved:

- to simplify the custom regulation for imported goods;
- to improve the regulated procedure of getting licenses;
- to develop export strategy from capital-intensive and labor-intensive to technology-intensive;
- to raise price competitiveness of exports on the basis of the development of domestic production with high processing share;
- to stimulate export growth on the basis of state guarantees of export credits and export insurance;
- to use the world system of imposing zero export tax;

- and to provide entrance to the WTO.

One should not overlook that there are vested interests in both transition countries as well as in many OECD countries. Moreover, rapid and broad capital market liberalization in transition countries that often have weak banking sectors – and inadequate prudential supervision – could undermine efforts to achieve sustained growth of trade.

# Appendix

**Table K8.** Non-CIS trade of the Russian Federation by selected commodities, 1994–1998 (Shares in %)

| | Exports | | | Imports | | |
|---|---|---|---|---|---|---|
| | 1994 | 1997[a] | 1998[a] | 1994 | 1997[a] | 1998[a] |
| Agricultural products (I – III) | 1.2 | 0.7 | 1.0 | 13.4 | 15.5 | 14.7 |
| Food, beverages and tobacco (IV) | 0.6 | 0.5 | 0.2 | 17.0 | 11.7 | 15.2 |
| Mineral products (V) | 41.5 | 51.5 | 44.2 | 2.9 | 2.9 | 2.6 |
| Chemical and allied products (VI) | 7.3 | 6.7 | 6.6 | 8.8 | 12.8 | 12.8 |
| Textiles and textile articles (XI) | 1.8 | 0.9 | 1.0 | 5.3 | 2.5 | 2.3 |
| Precious metals and stones (XIV) | 12.7 | 1.7 | 4.2 | 0.1 | 0.4 | - |
| Base metals and articles (XV) | 20.8 | 23.6 | 25.8 | 3.9 | 4.4 | 4.3 |
| Machinery and equipment (XVI) | 2.9 | 2.7 | 3.6 | 27.6 | 24.8 | 23.1 |
| Vehicles, transport equipment (XVII) | 3.3 | 3.9 | 5.0 | 4.7 | 8.9 | 8.6 |
| Precision and optical equipment (XVIII) | 0.2 | 0.3 | 0.7 | 5.4 | 3.8 | 4.4 |
| Arms and ammunition (XIX) | 0.9 | 0.4 | 0.2 | - | - | - |
| Total above | 93.4 | 92.9 | 92.5 | 89.2 | 87.8 | 88.1 |
| Total | 100.0 | 100.0 | 100.0 | 100.0 | 100.0 | 100.0 |

[a] - January – June

*Source: Economic Survey of Europe, 1998, p.97.*

**Table K9.** Branch structure of export in Ukraine in 1993–1997 (%)

| Branch | 1993 | 1994 | 1995 | 1996 | 1997 |
|---|---|---|---|---|---|
| Fuel and Energy: | 2.2 | 2.2 | 3.4 | 3.3 | 3.2 |
| Oil and gas | 0.3 | 0.0 | 0.3 | 0.0 | 0.9 |
| Coal | 1.2 | 0.3 | 0.7 | 0.7 | 0.7 |
| Electrical Energy | 0.7 | 1.2 | 0.7 | 0.6 | 0.6 |
| Chemical and oil-chemical | 8.5 | 12.3 | 13.2 | 13.8 | 12.4 |
| Metallurgy | 34.1 | 39.6 | 36.4 | 36.1 | 44.9 |
| Forestry, wood-working industry | 0.8 | 1.1 | 1.2 | 1.4 | 1.7 |
| Building materials | 1.0 | 2.5 | 1.6 | 1.8 | 1.4 |
| Agricultural | 16.2 | 16.2 | 22.6 | 22.8 | 13.4 |
| Light industry | 7.8 | 4.3 | 3.2 | 2.9 | 3.6 |
| Machinery and metal-working industry | 22.3 | 20.3 | 17.6 | 15.9 | 14.9 |
| Medicine and microbiology | 0.1 | 0.5 | 0.3 | 0.5 | 0.7 |

*Source: Derzhgomstat of Ukraine.*

**Table K10.** Ukraine's merchandise exports by commodity groups and regions (balance of payments data in mn US dollars)

| | 1996 | 1997 | 1998 | 1999 Q1 | 1999 Q2 |
|---|---|---|---|---|---|
| Total of which | 15547 | 15418 | 13699 | 2785 | 3110 |
| to FSU | | 6841 | 5273 | 880 | 964 |
| to ROW | | 8577 | 8426 | 1905 | 2146 |
| Food, beverages and agricultural prod. | 3045 | 1802 | 1379 | 393 | 316 |
| to FSU | | 1185 | 652 | 158 | 171 |
| to ROW | | 617 | 727 | 235 | 145 |
| Fuel and energy, incl. Ores | 1156 | 1142 | 1023 | 213 | 285 |
| to FSU | | 215 | 177 | 31 | 28 |
| to ROW | | 927 | 846 | 182 | 257 |
| Chemical and related products | 2207 | 2015 | 1735 | 292 | 344 |
| to FSU | | 959 | 818 | 124 | 139 |
| to ROW | | 1056 | 917 | 168 | 205 |
| Wood and articles of wood | 193 | 209 | 238 | 68 | 82 |
| to FSU | | 117 | 116 | 29 | 2 |
| to ROW | | 92 | 122 | 39 | 80 |
| Textiles; footwear, stone, ceramic and glass products | 620 | 643 | 672 | 145 | 137 |
| to FSU | | 184 | 143 | 20 | 25 |
| to ROW | | 469 | 529 | 125 | 112 |
| Non-precious metals | 4628 | 5904 | 5336 | 1032 | 1200 |
| to FSU | | 1715 | 1324 | 175 | 192 |
| to ROW | | 4189 | 4012 | 857 | 1008 |
| Machinery and equipment, incl. Vehicles | 2081 | 1970 | 1721 | 324 | 336 |
| to FSU | | 1370 | 1102 | 164 | 197 |
| to ROW | | 600 | 619 | 160 | 139 |
| Other | 1617 | 1733 | 1595 | 318 | 410 |
| to FSU | | 1096 | 941 | 179 | 210 |
| to ROW | | 637 | 654 | 139 | 200 |

*Source: Ukrainian Economic Trends (1999), December, p. 81.*

**Table K11.** Ukraine's merchandise imports by commodity groups and regions (balance of payments data in mn US dollars)

| | 1996 | 1997 | 1998 | 1999 Q1 | 1999 Q2 |
|---|---|---|---|---|---|
| Total of which | 19843 | 19624 | 16283 | 3371 | 2801 |
| to FSU | | 11820 | 9040 | 2242 | 1503 |
| to ROW | | 7804 | 7243 | 1129 | 1298 |
| Food, beverages and agricultural products | 1447 | 898 | 1052 | 187 | 198 |
| to FSU | | 137 | 225 | 39 | 37 |
| to ROW | | 761 | 827 | 148 | 161 |
| Fuel and energy, incl. Ores | 8868 | 8280 | 6170 | 1175 | 883 |
| to FSU | | 7714 | 5801 | 1708 | 855 |
| to ROW | | 586 | 369 | 67 | 28 |
| Chemical and related products | 1954 | 2151 | 1821 | 284 | 408 |
| to FSU | | 653 | 529 | 87 | 125 |
| to ROW | | 1498 | 1292 | 197 | 283 |
| Wood and articles of wood | 529 | 500 | 473 | 94 | 95 |
| to FSU | | 188 | 175 | 42 | 39 |
| to ROW | | 312 | 298 | 52 | 56 |
| Textiles; footwear, stone, ceramic and glass products | 734 | 745 | 743 | 132 | 172 |
| to FSU | | 199 | 187 | 28 | 35 |
| to ROW | | 546 | 556 | 104 | 137 |
| Non-precious metals | 760 | 666 | 629 | 87 | 103 |
| to FSU | | 361 | 318 | 42 | 55 |
| to ROW | | 305 | 311 | 55 | 48 |
| Machinery and equipment, incl. Vehicles | 2990 | 3687 | 3172 | 456 | 562 |
| to FSU | | 1266 | 957 | 164 | 228 |
| to ROW | | 2421 | 2215 | 292 | 334 |
| Other | 2561 | 2697 | 2223 | 356 | 380 |
| to FSU | | 1302 | 848 | 132 | 129 |
| to ROW | | 1385 | 1375 | 224 | 251 |

*Source: Source: Ukrainian Economic Trends (1999), December, p. 81.*

## References

Aitken B, Hanson GH, Harrison AE (1997) Spillovers, Foreign Investment, and Export Behavior. Journal of International Economics 43: 103–132

Choros V (1999) Globalization and Periphery Countries. World Economy and World Relations 12: 111–119

Dohrn R (1996) EU Enlargement and Transformation in Eastern Europe, Consequences for Foreign Direct Investment in Europe, Konjunkturpolitik 42

Economic Survey of Europe (1998), United Nations, New York and Geneva, • 3.

Gorynia M (1998) The Polish Economy's International Competitiveness and Economic Policy. Russian and East European Finance and Trade 34, No. 4 (July-August): 7–25

Hamar J (1994) Foreign Direct Investment and Privatization in Hungary. Acta Oeconomica 46: 183–198

Helpman E, Krugman PR (1985) Market Structure and Foreign Trade. MIT Press, Cambridge

Hirsh S (1976) An International Trade and Investment Theory of the Firm. Oxford Economic Papers 28: 258–270

IMF (1997) Annual Report of the Executive Board for the Financial Year Ended. April 30, International Monetary Fund, Washington DC

Kireev A (1998) World Economy. Mezhdunarodnaye otnosheniya Vol.1, 2

Klodt H, Welfens PJJ (eds) (1992) Multinationals in the New Europe and Global Trade. Springer, Berlin

Novikov V, Golayshova T (1999) Custom Duties and Prices. Economist. 7: 78–84

Petrov G, Perska V et al (1999), Prospects of Integration of the countries of Central and Eastern Europe in the European Union. Economic Annals 10: 14–20

Sotnikov O et al (1999) Economy of Central and East European Countries in the Reorganization Period. Economic Annals 10:, 4–10

State Committee of Ukrainian Statistics, Informational Bulletin of State Committee of Ukrainian Statistics No. 10–12 (62–64), October-December, IBA, Uzhgorod

Sutela P (1999) Russia: Rise of Dual Economy. Transition 10 (5): 20–21

Usuf Sh (1999) Globalization and Localization, Changes of Development Forms. Transition 4: 1–2

Vodaynov A, Lapenin V, Isakov G (1999) Russian Foreign Trade Policy in Case of the Entrance to WTO. No.7, pp 44–57

Welfens PJJ (1999) EU Enlargement and the Russian Transformation Crisis. Springer, Berlin

WIIW (1998) Countries in Transition 1997. WIIW Handbook of Statistics, WIIW

World Bank (1996) From Plan to Market. World Development Report 1996, Oxford University Press

World Bank (1998) Global Economic prospects 1998/99. World Bank, Washington DC

Wunner N (1998) Trade Liberalization and Political support in Transition Economies. Economics of Transition 6 (2): 409–425

Wysokinska Z (1998) Impact of Foreign Direct Investment on Export Competitiveness. Russian and East European Finance and Trade 34 (4) July-August: 64–87

Zagashvili V (1999) Russian Integration into World Economy: Structural Problems. World Economy and World Relations 7: 22–30

# L. The Role of Foreign Direct Investment in Transformation

Roland Doehrn and Natalja v. Westernhagen

## 1 Theoretical Background

In the theoretical literature, various channels are discussed through which FDI may contribute to growth in transforming economies:

- *FDI contributes to national capital stock and increases employment.* FDI contributes both to the stock of human and physical capital increasing and modernizing physical capital and creating new working places with the rise of production (Bellak, 1998). Investments in physical capital and an increase in employment in turn create positive real income effect which raises demand for the products of domestic firms.
- *FDI is a channel of technology transfer.* The most important contribution of FDI to the economic growth consists in the characteristic of FDI as an important vehicle for knowledge and technology transfer (Borenstein et al. 1995; Blomstroem and Sjoeholm, 1999).
- *FDI raises the productivity of the Foreign Investment Enterprises (FIEs).* Combination of advanced managerial skills and technology with domestic labor and inputs result in higher productive efficiency of FIEs and allows them to derive products at lower costs than domestic firms. Thus FIEs are more productive than domestic firms and hence contribute to the growth more than domestic investment. But FIEs can only then be more productive in comparison to domestic firms when the countries possess over the minimum threshold stock of human capital (Bellak, 1998; Borenstein et al., 1995).
- *Intra-firm spillover efficiency:* In order to avoid leakages, Multi-National Companies (MNCs) are eager to transfer modern and complex technologies only on an intra-firm basis and less willing to accept any other arrangements. That is why transfer of technologies on an intra-firm basis is the most quickly and qualitatively better way (Blomstroem, 1991).
- *Restructuring effect.* Integration into the MNCs' networks is an important impulse for the restructuring of the enterprises which enforces the competitiveness of the enterprises at the world markets and makes them stronger against domestic firms (Bellak, 1998). The restructuring effect also plays a role when FDI means just a change of ownership and is not connected with the transfer of capital. The importance of *the restructuring effect* for transformation economies is especially meaningful in the context of privatization since state enterprises in the former Soviet times were oversized and characterized by the insufficient structures with weak control possibilities (Welfens, 1999).

- *Economies of scale.* FIEs are normally larger than domestic firms and have higher R&D intensity that allows them to exhibit the economies of scale at the host markets (Bellak, 1998).
- *FDI intensifies competition towards to local firms.* Introduction of new management, increased specialization and restructuring as well as new knowledge and technologies give FIEs competitive advantages against local firms (Borenstein et al., 1995; Blomstroem, 1991).
- *FDI increases the productivity of local firms.* FDI does not "crowd out" domestic investment but through complementary effects in production and through spillover-effects and externalities from knowledge and technology transfer makes domestic firms more productive[1] (Borenstein et al., 1995). The most important spillover-effects which bring productivity gains to local firms are: the increased competition between FIEs and local firms; spillovers from labor and management training; "supplier" spillover effect which forces domestic suppliers to improve local facilities and has a positive effect on the whole economy (Blomstroem, 1991).
- *MNCs speed up technological upgrading of domestic firms.* New technologies and new products introduced by MNCs would hasten domestic firms to become accessible to a particular technologies and to imitate knowledge inferred in new products which would speed up technological upgrading of domestic firms (Blomestroem 1991).
- *FDI changes the specialization pattern.* With the further development the share of intra-industry FDI as well as intra-industry trade would increase like it is in highly developed countries which represent competitors of similar differentiated products. The network channels of MNCs and the intra-firm trade are likely to provide these changes. The domestic firms in opposite occur technologically and financially week to initiate structural changes (Bellak, 1998).
- *FDI increases trade.* FDI creates secondary flows in the form of exports of machinery and other capital goods, generates also demand for manufactured production imports as well as for imports of services (expertise, finance, accounting and so on). FDI provides a positive effect on the balance of payments in the long run: each dollar of outward FDI is associated with $2 of additional exports and with a bilateral trade surplus of $1.7 dollars. Since FDI are associated with industrialization and change of the specialization pattern it hastens the expansion of the "increasingly technologically-sophisticated manufactured exports" (OECD, 1998).

Figure L1 tries to give a systematic overview over these diverse effects. They can be summarized in the two main channels. First, by adding to the stock of physical capital and increasing employment in the host country, having positive effects on real income, raising the demand for products of domestic firms and promoting, thus, their expansion. Second, by the productivity gains attained from the technology transfer and "spillovers" that spread to the entire economy. Knowledge and technology transfer, higher managerial skills, restructuring effect as well as in-

[1] Borensztein, E. (1995) : "One dollar increase in the net inflow of FDI is associated with an increase in total investment in the host economy of more than one dollar".

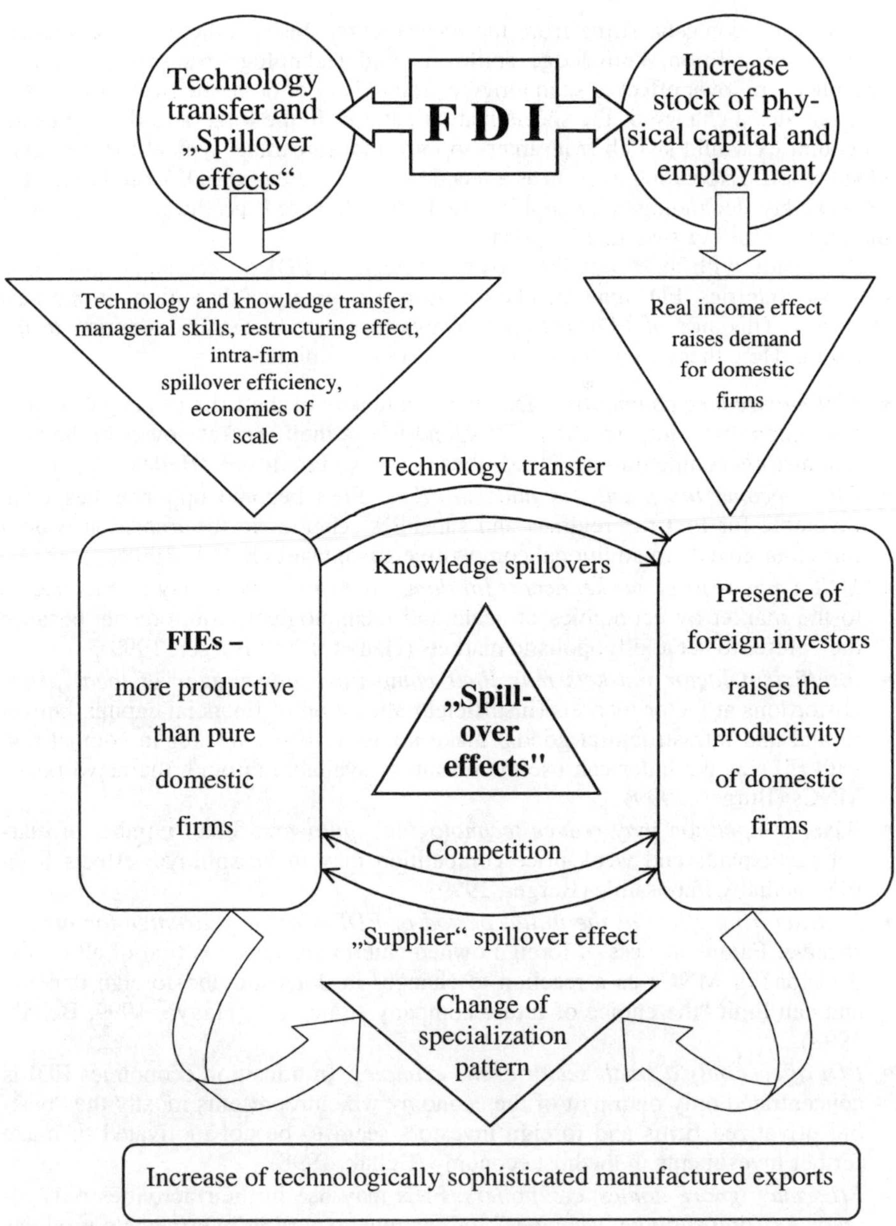


**Fig. L1.** The Positive Effect of FDI on Economic Growth

tra-firm spillover efficiency make FIEs more productive in comparison to domestic firms. Higher productivity and economies of scale give FIEs additional competitive advantages at the host market. But there is an evidence that FIEs don’t "crowd out" domestic firms from the local market. Such spillover effects as increased competition, knowledge spillovers and technology transfer as well as "supplier" spillover effect raise in turn the productivity of domestic firms. Likewise, FDI initiates a change of the specialization pattern. In the long period the transition countries would switch from inter- to intra-industry trade, typical for the developed world. Expending exports as a reaction to the increased FDI would represent increasingly technologically-sophisticated manufactured products - a positive indicator of further sustainable growth.

Alongside with these possible positive effects of FDI on economic growth in the host countries, FDI may also be a reason for numerous distortions in the host countries. This side of FDI does not always receive a necessary attention in the literature. Here there are some critic or "courteous" points:

- *FDI may reduce competition.* Due to the intensity of the FIEs to get gains from the oligopolistic imperfections FIEs tend to use their market power in the way that distorts competition and leads thus to the welfare losses (Bellak, 1998).
- *FIEs become tax privileges and subsidies.* FIEs become opportunities from favorable for FDI tax regimes and subsidies schemes in the transition economies that give them additional competitive advantages (Bellak, 1998).
- *MNCs may restrict market access for domestic firms.* MNCs may restrict access to the market by economies of scale and technological requirements because they prefer to act at oligopolistic markets (Hanya, 1999; Burger, 1999).
- *Insufficient factor markets may limit competitive advantages of local firms.* Distortions at factor markets (insufficient allocation of financial capital, human capital and infrastructural goods) make domestic firms weaker in competition with FIEs as the latter can use the resources available through the networks of MNCs (Burger, 1999).
- *Weak competition may reduce technological spillovers.* Small number of market participants and weak price competition may make spillover-effects from FDI factually impossible (Burger, 1999).
- *Restructuring effect at the initial period of FDI is not a guarantee for further success.* Future success of foreign owned enterprises depends first of all on the decisions of MNCs as a reaction to changes in domestic and foreign demand and can limit "the choice of future company strategies" (Hanya, 1999; Bellak, 1998).
- *FDI affects only a small sector of the economy.* In transition economies FDI is concentrated only on a part of the economy which represents mostly the "best-of" privatized firms and foreign investors seem to be not motivated to make further investments in the host economy (Bellak, 1998).
- *FIEs may ignore domestic suppliers.* FIEs may use in their activities only already existing supplier "schemes" for example exporting intermediate products from neighboring and more advanced transition economies and does not involve domestic suppliers in their activities. Although it could have technological advantages for MNCs, from the other side, it restricts "supplier" effect on the economy with it's price and quality effects on the intermediate products in the host country and may kill domestic supplier (Bellak, 1998).

- *FDI reinforces polarization between high and low-income regions.* As FDI is directed to the regions with abanderous factor endowments, human capital and technologies, spillover effects in these regions strengthen their economic growth. From the other side, the limited diffusion of knowledge and unwillingness of MNCs to invest into regions with poor factor endowments will lead to further lagging behind of poor regions (Hanya, 1999).
- *FIEs may limit local R&D activity.* FIEs limit local R&D activity as the highly skilled human resources reallocated towards MNCs and competition for high-standard products within MNCs is much stronger relative to domestic firms (Hanya, 1999).
- *Local companies may not be able to adsorb and imitate technologies.* Local companies that doesn't invest in learning are not able to get opportunities from externalities and spillover effects. In this case MNCs should not be afraid of technological leaks and "borrow" more than "give" to the host markets (Burger, 1999).
- *The conflict of interests between MNCs and domestic firms.* MNCs try to prevent positive technology spillovers and externalities to domestic firms (Bellak, 1998).

So far, expectations in FDI should not be too far-reaching, bearing in mind that high inflows can be followed by set-backs owing to the factors mentioned.

## 2 Statistical Background

Measuring FDI is a rather difficult task, something that especially holds for transition countries, whose statistical systems are undergoing a transformation too. The term FDI is defined for balance of payment purposes. All capital inflows that create "a lasting interest of an entity resident in one economy (direct investor) in an entity resident in another economy (direct investment enterprise)" (IMF, 1993, p. 41) are defined as FDI. The share of the investor in the foreign enterprises' equities should exceed 10% to ensure that he has a voice in the decisions of the company. It is important to stress at this point that (a) the definition is linked to capital inflows only and (b) it is essential that the investor takes control over the foreign investment enterprise. How the capital is used in the direct investment enterprise – to form fixed or financial assets – is not part of the definition. In other words, FDI statistics only cover a potential source of financing fixed capital formation abroad but not the amount of fixed capital (Graham, 1995).

Furthermore, measuring FDI is also difficult in a more technical sense. Even in a country with a well developed statistical system actual FDI may be significantly misreported in the official figures. In the case of Germany, e.g., estimates suggest that incoming FDI is underreported by a factor 4 to 6 whereas outflows seem to be overestimated at least to some extent (Jost, 1997). In a transforming economy, technical problems to measure FDI can be expected to be even larger, if there are not even strong reasons to overstate incoming FDI, as it is widely understood as a measure of the success of transformation.

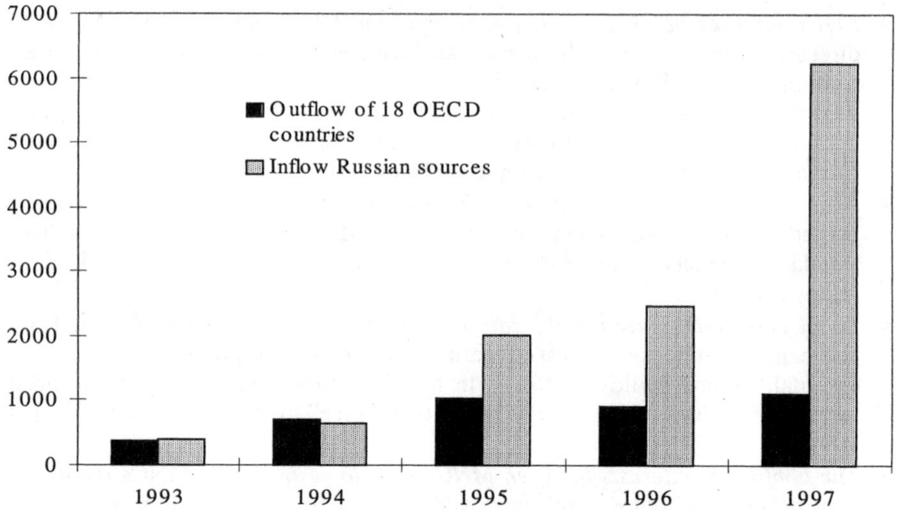


**Fig. L2.** Measuring FDI in Russia: National and International Sources, 1993–1997; mill. US$
*Source: IMF, OECD.*

A commonly used approach to judge the potential measurement error is to compare inward investment in the receiving country with data on outward investment in the investors' countries (JOST, 1997; Doerhn and Heilemann, 1999). In the case of Russia, information on inward FDI can be taken from IMF sources that refer to data compiled by the Russian central bank. Figures on outflows to Russia are available for 18 OECD countries. The discrepancy between the two sources is astonishingly large (Figure L2): Whereas Russia reports inflows of more than $6 bn. in 1997, outflows of the 18 OECD members only add up to approximately $1 bn.. Even when considering that also some FDI has been made in Russia from Non-OECD countries, the differences are extremely pronounced suggesting that Russia is severely overreporting FDI inflows.

Some factors might help to explain these differences: The figures on inflows might also contain some Russian money that is recycled in the form of FDI; furthermore, tax laws might make it favorable for Russian investors to involve a foreign partner, even if the latter transfers no money in the end; finally, the inflows shown in Russian statistics might in part refer to planned (notified) FDI, that is not covered by statistics of most OECD countries and of the stocks statistics as well.

Another method to shed some light on the quality of FDI data is a comparison of FDI stocks and inflows. Especially in the case of Russia, where little FDI has been made before 1990, cumulated inflows should come close to stocks after the inflows having been corrected for exchange rate movement (s. Appendix). However, the difference between the two is striking: In 1997, cumulated inflows have been more than ten times as large as stocks, although both figures are published by Russian authorities (Figure L3).

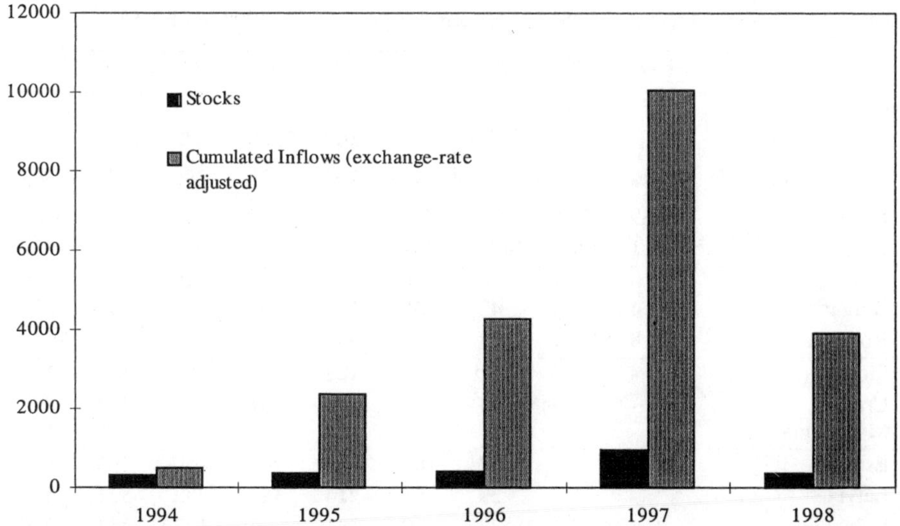


**Fig. L3.** Comparison of Stocks of FDI in Russia and Cumulated Inflows, 1994–1998, mill. US$

*Source: IMF.*

The above calculation highlights another problem, too, that becomes especially relevant for countries which experienced large exchange-rate movements in the past. The marked devaluation of the ruble in Russia in 1998, e.g., resulted in a drop of FDI-stocks measured in US dollar to almost one third of the 1997 value, without substantial outflows of FDI having taken place. Hence, a good deal of changes in stocks in the end reflects exchange rate movements rather than changes in foreign hold equities (Doehrn, 1996a).

As it is already partly discussed above there are several problems in measuring FDI. It is worth pointing out one more problem connected with different definitions of FDI used in different countries that lead to variation in FDI statistics. The problem is that not all transition economies capture in the balance of payments statistics on FDI reinvested earnings and capital loans. Most transition economies record only the equity capital component of FDI. Some countries in the region began to alter the FDI statistics. For example Poland (since 1990) recorded reinvested earnings and inter-company debt. Calculating the data we followed the definition of IMF so that the data for Poland might shine to be overestimated in comparison with others which in tern represent lower bound estimates[2].

[2] Direct investment comprises not only the initial transaction establishing the relationship between the investor and the enterprise but also all subsequent transactions between them and among affiliated enterprises, both incorporated and unincorporated (IMF, 1993) Further according to the IMF definition, there are three main components to FDI: (i) equity capital - the purchase of shares of the investor in a foreign country; (ii) reinvested earnings; and (iii) capital loans - the borrowing and lending of funds between direct investors and affiliates (EBRD Transition Report 1998).

**Table L1.** Foreign Direct Investment in Eastern Europe, 1990 – 1998, mill. US$

| | 1990 | 1991 | 1992 | 1993 | 1994 | 1995 | 1996 | 1997 | 1998 |
|---|---|---|---|---|---|---|---|---|---|
| CSFR | 173 | 583 | 1073 | - | - | - | - | - | - |
| Czech Republic [1] | - | - | 988 [a] | 568 | 862 | 2568 | 1435 | 1286 | 2554 |
| Slovak Republic [1] | - | - | 85 [a] | 199 | 203 | 183 | 280 | 174 | 562 |
| Poland | 89 | 291 | 678 | 1715 | 1875 | 3659 | 4498 | 4908 | 6365 |
| Hungary | 311 | 1462 | 1479 | 2339 | 1145 | 4519 | 1982 | 2079 | 1936 |
| Albania | 0 | 0 | 20 | 58 | 53 | 70 | 90 | 48 | 45 |
| Bulgaria | 4 | 56 | 42 | 55 | 105 | 90 | 109 | 505 | 537 |
| Romania | -18 | 40 | 77 | 94 | 340 | 419 | 263 | 1215 | 2031 |
| Slovenia | - | - | 111 | 113 | 128 | 176 | 185 | 321 | 165 |
| Croatia | - | - | - | - | 98 | 101 | 533 | 487 | 873 |
| Macedonia | - | - | - | - | 24 | 9 | 11 | 16 | 118 |
| Estonia | - | - | 82 | 162 | 214 | 201 | 150 | 266 | 581 |
| Latvia | - | - | 29 | 45 | 214 | 180 | 382 | 521 | 357 |
| Lithuania | - | - | 27 | 30 | 31 | 73 | 152 | 355 | 926 |
| Russian Federation | -400 | -100 | 700 | 400 | 637 | 2017 | 2479 | 6243 | 2764 |
| Ukraine | - | - | 170 | 200 | 159 | 257 | 521 | 623 | 743 |
| Belarus | | | | | 11 | 15 | 73 | 200 | 144 |
| Kazakhstan | - | - | - | 473 | 635 | 964 | 1137 | 1321 | 1158 |
| other CIS Countries [a] | - | 50 | 35 | 223 | 320 | 607 | 823 | 1434 | 1485 |
| Total | 159 | 2382 | 4523 | 6675 | 7055 | 16108 | 15105 | 22002 | 23343 |

*Source: IMF, EBRD. National Sources. - [1]Without FDI-relations between the Czech and the Slovak Republic. - [a] estimate.*

Table L1 gives an overview of total FDI inflows of all transition economies in Eastern Europe since 1990. As can be seen, total FDI climbed from less than $200 mill. in 1990 to more than $23 bn. in 1998. The distribution of FDI to CIS and other Eastern European countries did not occur equally. Before 1997 Poland and Hungary have been the preferred destinations of FDI, only in 1997 they have been surpassed by Russia, although these figures are questioned above. To do justice to Russia's position among the transitions countries, the current account position must be taken into account: Russia is the only case among the economies considered having a current account surplus which necessarily is reflected in the capital account balance, too. However, compared to inflows into industrialized countries – the OECD members attracted $260 bn. in 1997 – total FDI in Eastern Europe is still small with respect to the size of its population. Among Eastern European countries in per capita terms Hungary still holds leading position. FDI in Russia in per capita terms absolutely does not correspond the size and demand of the Russian market. Ukraine and especially Belarus are far behind in per capita terms. If one would compare Ukraine with Poland and Belarus with Hungary in terms of population than Ukraine accounts only for ca. 7,7% of Polish FDI per capita and Belarus only 2,6% of Hungarian.

**Table L2.** FDI-Stocks in Selected Eastern European Countries, 1997

| | FDI Stocks US-$ mill | Population Mill. | FDI p.c. US$ |
|---|---|---|---|
| Russian Federation | 970 | 148,0 | 7 |
| Romania | 3617 | 22,6 | 160 |
| Lithuania | 1041 | 3,7 | 281 |
| Slovak Republic | 1804 | 5,4 | 334 |
| Poland | 14587 | 38,6 | 378 |
| Latvia | 1272 | 2,5 | 509 |
| Czech Republic | 6763 | 10,3 | 657 |
| Estonia | 1148 | 1,5 | 765 |
| Slovenia | 2120 | 2,0 | 1060 |
| Hungary | 15869 | 10,0 | 1587 |

*Source: IMF.*

This view is strongly supported by the stock data (table L2): In 1997, FDI per capita in Eastern Europe ranges between $1500 on the top (in Hungary) and only $7 in Russia. Even when using cumulated inflows for the calculation, the situation in Russia does not look much brighter, as FDI per capita will reach only $80. In comparison: In Spain FDI-stocks per capita come close to $3000, in Belgium even $14000.

To sum up, FDI in Eastern Europe and even more in the CIS countries is relatively small up to now. But the quality of the data is uncertain. There is some indication, at least according to the experience in OECD countries, that as a rule data on outflows is more accurate than data on inflows, and that stock data is more reliable than cumulative inflow data. Therefore, the calculations in the next section are based on information that is taken from stock statistics on outward investment of OECD countries.

# 3 Determinants of FDI and Projections for Selected CIS and other Eastern European Countries

## 3.1. Determinants of FDI

As a next step in our analysis it is helpful to draw a picture where flows and stocks of FDI can be considered „normal" in Russia's case, Ukraine and Belarus. The estimates presented below are based on a more general modeling of FDI relations between different countries, using a gravity-model type approach. Generally speaking, $FDI_{ij}$ from country i in country j is seen in this type of models as a result of the interaction between several push factors $Y_i$, determining the size if investment flowing out of country i, with pull factors $Y_j$ determining the attractiveness of country j, and, finally, certain factors $D_{ij}$ hampering or promoting flows from i to j such as geographical or cultural distances. Following Newton's gravity law the relation between these factors can be written as

$$FDI_{ij} = Y_i^{\alpha_1} \cdot Y_j^{\alpha_2} \cdot D_{ij}^{\alpha_3},$$
$$\text{with: } \alpha_{1,2} > 0, \alpha_3 < 0.$$

Earlier work on gravity models made evident that size measured by GDP as well as research intensity of the investor's country are main push factor, whereas size of the market in the host country is a main pull factor, underpinning that FDI as a rule is used as an instrument to develop and serve foreign markets (Doehrn, 1996b). The role of wages in this context is subject to some controversy. All in all, a survey of literature suggests that regressions testing the impact of wages on FDI may lead to quite different results depending very much on the selection of countries included in the analysis and on the definition of wages used (RAINES et al., 1999, p. 3). Especially, the explanatory power of wage-variables in such models often appears to be inferior to other determinants, especially to cultural factors (Doehrn, 1996b; Morsink and Molle, 1991). On the other hand, most analyses support the role of geographic distances as an obstacle to FDI. Concerning the model employed here, we follow this specification proposed by earlier analyses without scrutiny.

The appropriate estimation technique to parameterize gravity models is an aspect that is often neglected, although it will have considerable impact on the elasticities estimated. A first problem in these estimations is linked to the specification of the error term of the gravity model. A procedure often employed is to make the model linear by transforming all variable to their logarithms. An OLS estimate of this transformed equation in the end minimizes the logarithms of a multiplicative error-term, which is the same as minimizing a percentage error. However, data on FDI are characterized by extremely large differences in their dimensions. The smallest figure found in our sample is US-$1 mill. only, the largest is nearly $200 000 mill. in the case of Japanese investment in the U.S. Given these differences, minimizing a percentage error means that small figures have an enormous impact on the coefficients estimated as they are associated by large percentage errors as a rule (Doehrn and Milton, 1992). An alternative procedure is, to put an additive error term to the gravity equation which requires a non-linear estimation technique.

The second problem is caused by the fact that the matrix used to estimate the gravity model contains many cases where no information is available. These cases reflect that statistics of many countries only report on FDI that exceeds a certain threshold. Hence, the data omitted as a rule represent cases with particularly low FDI causing a selection bias in our sample. Technically speaking, the data are censored, requiring an estimation technique for censored data such as a Tobit-estimator. However, software available can process linearized models only and thus employ a multiplicative error term.

In table L3, both estimates are presented. The data used refer to FDI-stocks abroad in 1995 and are taken from OECD sources[3]. They cover investment of 15 OECD countries in 25 industrialized and emerging economies. FDI relations that were not reported where substituted by minimum values derived from the statistics of the individual reporting countries to conduct the Tobit estimates.

**Table L3.** Estimates of a Gravity Model of FDI Stocks, 1995

| | Estimation 1: Non-linear | estimation 2: Tobit |
|---|---|---|
| Constant | 0,025 | -4,850 |
| | (2,1) | (3,6) |
| GDP of Investors' country ($ bn) | 0,833 | 1,064 |
| | (18,4) | (12,5) |
| GDP of Host country ($ bn) | 0,868 | 1,302 |
| | (25,4) | (14,6) |
| Distance (km) | -0,178 | -1,353 |
| | (6,3) | (14,6) |
| Expenses on Research and Development, investors country (% of GDP) | 1,492 | 1,336 |
| | (5,8) | (4,1) |
| Wages investors' country ($ 1000 per worker) | - | 1,504 |
| | | (4,9) |
| Wages host country ($ 1000 per worker) | - | 0,078 |
| | | (0,6) |
| Common language (Dummy-variable) | 0,979 | 1,164 |
| | (12,2) | (3,6) |
| Official language English in host country (Dummy-variable) | 1,007 | 2,161 |
| | (12,0) | (8,7) |
| $R^2$ adj. | 0,830 | 0,696 |
| number of observations | 395 | 464 |

*Source: Author' calculation. In brackets: t-values*

The two estimates show many common features, but they also exhibit some differences. The most obvious contrasts are related to the impact of wages and distances: Wages have no significant influence – and therefore are excluded in equation (1) – and the parameter of the distance variable is smaller by far in the non-linear estimate. Furthermore, elasticity with respect to market size in the host country is less than unity in equ. 1 but above in equ. 2. It is worth of noting that the latter seems to be caused by the estimation method used rather than by the larger sample, including a large number of cases of very small FDI in the Tobit estimate; when the non-linear method is applied to the Tobit data set similar coefficients are gained. According to this regression, labor costs in the host country have no measurable impact on FDI, although specifying the wage variable is diffi-

[3] The regressions are based on data provided by 16 OECD-Countries(Australia, Germany, Finland, France, Italy, Japan, Canada, Netherlands, Norway, Austria, Poland, Sweden, Switzerland, South Korea, United Kingdom, United States) in 31 Countries (the 16 already mentioned plus Belgium, Brazil, Denmark, Greece, Hong Kong, Ireland, Mexico, New Zealand, Portugal, Singapore, Spain, Taiwan, Czech Republic, Turkey, Hungary)

cult. This is relevant insofar, as it is often argued that cheap labor is one of the main motivations for investing in Eastern Europe (Dmochowski, 1995, p. 305).

It might be argued that being unable to detect an influence of wage costs might be a consequence of measurement problems or a selections bias. International comparisons of levels of labor costs are difficult and as a rule one has to use estimates and proxy variables. Indeed, other analyses, e.g. Lansbury et al. (1996, p. 111), found an influence of labor costs on the distribution of FDI among Eastern European countries, although they only examine three countries. Anyhow, FDI is only one way to make use of differences in labor costs. Many companies highly sensitive to labor costs refrain from making long term investments abroad and instead decide on subcontracting or imports to make use of cost differentials.

This is not the place to discuss these estimates in detail and the implications of the different methods. There is neither priori information nor any empirical evidence which estimator leads to better results. Therefore, both are used subsequent to calculate „normal“ FDI relations between Russia and the OECD countries alternatively.

### 3.2. Projections for Investigated CIS Countries and Eastern European Countries

The gravity model results for the five countries examined are represented in table L4. In the upper half of the table, projections of FDI-stocks under different growth scenarios are given, in the lower half annual inflows are derived that are needed to reach this level starting from actual 1995 stocks. A first scenario – the *no change scenario* – starts from the actual 1995 figures of GDP and calculates FDI stocks assuming the transformation countries would have followed the „normal“ sample characteristic for developed market economies in that year. It also represents two more scenarios where it is assumed that these countries would exhibit light catching up process during following ten years with the GDP growth in the *scenario 2005 I* of 2%- points above OECD growth equal to 2,5%-points and in the *scenario 2005 II* of 4%-points above the OECD level. Considering recent GDP growth, the catching up scenarios seem to be too optimistic for most countries examined. Only Poland experienced rates that were in the reach of scenario 2005 II; in Hungary expansion came close to the assumptions of scenario 2005 II. In Russia and the Ukraine real GDP shrank in the second half of the 90s, Belarus experienced high growth in some rates, but development is unsteady. However, we choose the same catching up scenario for all five countries to provide a better basis for comparison. As no stock figures for the Ukraine and Belarus are available, and the stock data on Russia is inconsistent with the inflows, adjusted cumulated inflows are the starting point of our projections.

The results for Hungary proclaim an interesting picture which is not surprising if we take into account unequal distribution of FDI among the Central and Eastern European countries and CIS as mentioned above. The gravity model results shows that FDI already cumulated is far above its potential level. One could guess that ample FDI is primarily connected with the transformation process, in particular with the role of foreign companies in the privatization of Hungarian enterprises. In the long run FDI can be expected to come down to its „normal" level. In other words, the FDI inflows during the initial stage of catching up obviously tend to be much larger in comparison to the steady-state. Therefore, the gravity model which shows „normal long run FDI" pattern among developed market economies underestimates inflows into successful transformation economies at their initial stage. It can be expected that FDI into Hungarian economy has already reached its peak and will come down to its normal pattern in the years to come. Anyhow, the negative FDI inflows, given in the lower half of table L4, should not be taken at their face value.

Poland tends to come close to the Hungarian case, but the stocks estimated still hint at a considerable unused potential. In this context it should be noted that Poland represents a substantially larger market than Hungary and, consequently, is more attractive for foreign investors. In order to reach this potential Poland should accumulate between $87 mill. to $981 mill. per year according to estimate 1 and between $1082 mill. to $1584 mill. corresponding with estimate 2.

**Table L4.** Projections of FDI 1995–2005, mill. US$

| Country | Estimate | observed 1995[1] | Scenario[2] | | |
|---|---|---|---|---|---|
| | | Cum. inflows | no change | 2005 I | 2005 II |
| Hungary | Estimate 1 | 8324 | 2756 | 4962 | 5850 |
| | Estimate 2 | 8324 | 933 | 3120 | 3994 |
| Poland | Estimate 1 | 7108 | 7973 | 14354 | 16922 |
| | Estimate 2 | 7108 | 5360 | 17926 | 22946 |
| Russia | Estimate 1 | 2368 | 19475 | 35059 | 41332 |
| | Estimate 2 | 2368 | 7330 | 24514 | 31378 |
| Ukraine | Estimate 1 | 312 | 2799 | 5039 | 5941 |
| | Estimate 2 | 312 | 457 | 1530 | 1958 |
| Belarus | Estimate 1 | 23 | 992 | 1785 | 2105 |
| | Estimate 2 | 23 | 165 | 552 | 706 |
| | | Average annual inflows required to reach | | | |
| Hungary | Estimate 1 | | -557 | -336 | -247 |
| | Estimate 2 | | -739 | -520 | -433 |
| Poland | Estimate 1 | | 87 | 725 | 981 |
| | Estimate 2 | | -175 | 1082 | 1584 |
| Russia | Estimate 1 | | 1711 | 3269 | 3896 |
| | Estimate 2 | | 496 | 2215 | 2901 |
| Ukraine | Estimate 1 | | 249 | 473 | 563 |
| | Estimate 2 | | 15 | 122 | 165 |
| Belarus | Estimate 1 | | 97 | 176 | 208 |
| | Estimate 2 | | 14 | 53 | 68 |

*2005 I: Yearly growth in country 2%-points above OECD growth*
*2005 II: Yearly growth in country 4%-points above OECD growth.*
*Source: Author's calculations.-[1]C.f. Table L9.-[2]No change: income of 1995*

In the three CIS countries, on the other hand, actual FDI in 1995 was far below its potential:

- In Russia, actual values accounted for only 12% resp. 32% of FDI predicted in the *no change scenario,* depending on the estimate used. According to estimate 1, an annual inflow of $1.7 bn. would be necessary to achieve the 'normal' level within 10 years, even if GDP did not grow. In this case, the Russian GDP will rise considerably, the annual inflow required would go up to $3.9 bn. in the *2005 II scenario*. Estimate 2 will lead to lower figures in general, but also require substantial investment.
- In the Ukraine, cumulated inflows accounted for 11% resp. 68% from the potential pattern in the *no change scenario*. To bridge this gap, the Ukraine should accumulate between $249 mill. and $563 mill. per year due to the first estimate, but only $15 mill. to $165 mill. according to the second estimate.
- Belarus shows the largest gap. The 1995 accumulated FDI was only 2,5% resp.14% of the expected value in the *no change scenario*. The FDI necessary to reach „ natural" FDI stock vary from $97 mill. to $208 mill. according to the first estimate and from $14 mill. to $68 mill. according to the second estimate.

At a first glance, the FDI inflows needed for CIS countries to compensate the backlog do not sound too high, given the fact that actual FDI inflows in 1997 were more than $6 bn. in Russia, more than $600 mill. in Ukraine and $200 mill. in Belarus. However, one should keep in mind that the data on inflows into these countries might be over-optimistic since they are not mirrored in the outflows from the OECD that are much lower. Furthermore, all calculations are based on constant prices and exchange rates from 1995. Inflation, however, will lead to a higher need of inflows to achieve the stocks shown, and the same would follow from a depreciation of the currency in these countries.

## 4 FDI, Capital Formation, and Structural Change

Assessing the impact of FDI on capital formation and thus on the restructuring of the economies in the investigated countries has to take several aspects into account. Firstly, the size of gross fixed capital formation necessary to bring investigated countries forward in transformation must be discussed. Secondly, the contribution of FDI to gross fixed capital formation has to be examined, as well as against the background of the projections of FDI made above, as well as in the light of other emerging economies. Thirdly, sectoral aspects should be taken into consideration.

### 4.1. The Size of Gross Fixed Capital Formation

There is no reliable information on the size and structure of capital stocks in investigated economies. Therefore, capital formation cannot, as preferable, be derived from considerations about discrepancies between existing and necessary capital stocks. Another approach that is applied here is to take investment rations from other emerging economies as reference. Table L5 shows the share of gross fixed capital formation (GFCF) in GDP in several Asian emerging economies and in some European transition countries. There is a significant difference between the two regions: In the Asian case, GFCF is between 35% and 42% of GDP, and even in 1998, the year of the Asian crisis, the quotas were above Eastern European values. In Eastern Europe, the same relation ranged between about 15% and slightly more than 30% over the last six years. In the European transition economies, however, figures are on the rise, whereas Russia and the Ukraine experienced a relative fall in investment from nearly 24% in 1992 to less than 18% in 1998.

One might ask whether investment ratios as they are found in the Asian emerging economies are necessary especially against the background of some „over-investment“ in these countries that was unveiled by the Asian crises. But it is equally clear that more investment than observed in the last years is needed to modernize the transition economies successfully within a reasonable time. For simplicity it is assumed in the calculations to follow, that all investigated countries need a ratio of investment to GDP of 30%, which admittedly is arbitrary, and from today's point of view quite unrealistic in the case of the CIS countries, but it may be necessary to bring forward restructuring of their economies.

**Table L5.** Share of Gross Fixed Capital Formation in GDP in Selected Emerging Economies, 1992–1998, %

| | 1992 | 1993 | 1994 | 1995 | 1996 | 1997 | 1998 |
|---|---|---|---|---|---|---|---|
| South Korea | 37,0 | 36,2 | 36,0 | 36,7 | 36,8 | 35,1 | 29,4 |
| Malaysia | 36,6 | 38,9 | 40,2 | 43,6 | 42,5 | 43,1 | 26,8 |
| Thailand | 39,3 | 39,4 | 39,9 | 41,8 | 40,8 | 32,3 | 26,7 |
| Czech Republic | - | 28,0 | 28,7 | 32,8 | 33,0 | 30,7 | 28,1 |
| Estonia | 20,9 | 24,4 | 27,0 | 26,0 | 26,7 | 27,9 | 29,1 |
| Hungary | 19,9 | 18,9 | 20,1 | 19,1 | 21,6 | 22,3 | 23,4 |
| Poland | 16,8 | 15,9 | 16,2 | 16,9 | 19,0 | 21,2 | 22,1 |
| Belarus | 25,4 | 33,9 | 33,2 | 25,0 | 21,8 | 26,0 | 27,0 |
| Russia | 23,9 | 20,4 | 21,8 | 21,3 | 21,2 | 19,6 | 17,7 |
| Ukraine | 27,4 | 24,5 | 23,7 | 23,4 | 20,9 | 18,4 | - |

*Source: Author's calculations based on IMF data.*

## 4.2. The Contribution of FDI to Capital Formation

At this point, we should recall that FDI does not necessarily mean the formation of fixed capital. If a foreign investor, e.g., acquires a company, least in the short run no capital formation will be made by this acquisition; only the ownership of the company changes, although modernization and reorganization might have a considerable impact on production capacities in the medium term. On the other hand, fixed investment can also be made by foreign companies without making use of FDI, e.g. by financing a project using bank credits. Therefore, the most appropriate view of FDI is that of being one source among the other of financing capital formation abroad (Doehrn, 1996b; Graham, 1995). Ratios of FDI to GFCF should be interpreted accordingly.

Subsequently, data for the three CIS countries will be given only, as in Hungary and Poland, when FDI has already reached a level that does not allow for interpreting the FDI inflows derived in Table L4 in an appropriate manner. All figures in table L6 are expressed in US-Dollars, as it is the easiest way to correct the calculations for the large exchange rate movements some of the CIS countries experienced. Then, taking together the assumptions on GDP underlying the scenarios presented above, the FDI inflows from these scenarios and the investment ratio discussed in the previous chapter, it is possible to derive the contributions of FDI to GFCF.

Our estimates suggest that FDI inflows will contribute between 0.5% and 2.6% to GFCF in Russia. For the Ukraine, the figures range between 0.1% and 3.5% and for Belarus between 0.5% and 4.8%. At first glance, these figures do not seem to be too high, but they must be put into a historical as well as a cross-section context.

**Table L6.** Contribution of FDI to Gross Fixed Capital Formation 1995 to 2005 averages, %

| | | | Scenario | |
|---|---|---|---|---|
| Country | Estimate | no change | 2005 I | 2005 II |
| Russia | 1 | 1.6 | 2.4 | 2.6 |
| | 2 | 0.5 | 1.7 | 1.9 |
| Ukraine | 1 | 2.2 | 3.3 | 3,5 |
| | 2 | 0.1 | 0.9 | 1,0 |
| Belarus | 1 | 3.2 | 4.6 | 4.8 |
| | 2 | 0.5 | 1.4 | 1.6 |

*Source: Author's computations based on Table L4.*

How do these figures compare to other countries? In developing countries, that include the emerging markets in the terminology of UNCTAD, the ratio of FDI inflows to GFCF was 8.4% in 1996 and even 10.3% in 1997. Reducing this comparison to countries with an income per capita that comes close to those in Eastern Europe and to the period, our calculations were made for, the weighted average in the reference group listed in the table L7 accounts for 10.6% over the period 1994–1996.

These figures, however, must be taken with a grain of salt. They are very high in small, low income economies, coming close to 100% in some extreme cases. This is partly caused by poor GFCF in these countries, partly because it is also due to misreporting FDI; investment in financial services that leads to a low formation of fixed capital seems to have some influence, too. Restricting the comparison to larger medium income economies, experience is mixed. In the case of India, e.g., the 1996 ratio was 2.9% and thus of the same dimension as the projections for Russia. In Brazil, the ratio was 7.5% in 1996, although in the years before it also came close to the figure projected for Russia. In China, on the other hand, the ratio exceeded 17% in each year since 1994, and approximately the same is true for Mexico.

In an historical context, it is worth noting that the role of FDI in the process of catching up was limited in many cases. In emerging Asian countries like South Korea, Taiwan or Thailand, ratio of FDI to GFCF never exceeded 3% before the mid 1980s, and the same is true for economies in Europe that caught up such as Spain and Portugal. Exceptions to that rule, again, are rather small countries such as Hong Kong, Singapore, or Ireland. Going back further into the past, Bellak (1998, p. 11) states that FDI also played a minor role in Austria's catch up after World War II. When taking this into consideration, the figures seem to draw a reasonable picture of the role FDI can play.

Two methodological aspect should be kept in mind: First, the projections with the gravity model are annual averages with no respect either to the profile of inflows over time nor to any policies to promote FDI. When discussing the model results for Hungary and Poland, it has already been stressed that especially in the first years of a transformation process, when industries are privatized, inflows may be very high, especially in countries that benefit from first mover advantages. Second, the projections are based on cross section data for one year only and thus do not reflect any dynamics of the FDI/GDP ratio over time. Between 1995 and 1998, the share of FDI in World-GDP (in $) nearly doubled from 1.2 to 2.2%, even if this change may have be influenced by the Asian crisis and the sharp drop of GDP in that region when measured in Dollars on the one hand, and the sharp increase of the number of mergers of companies in industrialized countries[4].

[4] According to UNCTAD estimates, the two largest cross-border mergers in 1998 accounted for 15 % of FDI flows world wide.

**Table L7.** Selected Indicators of the Importance of Inward FDI, 1996

| Country | FDI inward stock as a share of GDP 1996, % (Per cent) | FDI inward stock per capita, 1996, in $ | FDI inflows over gross fixed capital formation, 1994–1996, % |
|---|---|---|---|
| Central and Eastern Europe[1] | 4,8 | 147,9 | 6,5 |
| Hungary | 34 | 1490 | 30 |
| Estonia | 19 | 551 | 23 |
| Latvia | 17 | 335 | |
| Albania | 11 | 84 | |
| Czech Republic | 11 | 537 | 11 |
| Poland | 11 | 339 | 18 |
| Moldova, Republic of | 9 | 34 | 36 |
| Slovakia | 5 | 161 | 4 |
| Bulgaria | 4 | 51 | 5 |
| Lithuania | 4 | 80 | |
| Romania | 4 | 55 | 6 |
| Croatia | 4 | 185 | |
| Slovenia | 4 | 366 | 5 |
| Ukraine | 3 | 26 | 4 |
| Russian Federation | 1 | 45 | 2 |
| TFYR Macedonia | 1 | 20 | |
| Belarus | - | 6 | 1 |
| Reference group[1] | 16,5 | 559,3 | 10,6 |
| Trinidad and Tobago | 77 | 2996 | 46 |
| Grenada | 71 | 2016 | 22 |
| Malaysia | 49 | 2014 | 12 |
| Fiji | 39 | 925 | 21 |
| Costa Rica | 36 | 915 | 22 |
| Botswana | 33 | 942 | 31 |
| Chile | 27 | 1356 | 17 |
| Mexico | 22 | 783 | 15 |
| Panama | 22 | 646 | 13 |
| Tunisia | 22 | 470 | 7 |
| Belize | 15 | 762 | 15 |
| Peru | 15 | 374 | 23 |
| Thailand | 12 | 328 | 3 |
| Colombia | 11 | 261 | 16 |
| Mauritius | 7 | 252 | 2 |
| Turkey | 3 | 92 | 2 |
| Syrian Arab Republic | 2 | 74 | 1 |
| Lebanon | 2 | 61 | 2 |

*Source: UNCTAD, FDI/TNC database. – [1]Weighted averages, using population as weights*

## 4.3. Sectoral Aspects

The impact of FDI on transformation depends a lot upon which sectors it is directed at, i.e. whether inflows are allocated to the "right" sectors. It is a difficult task to find reliable and comparable data on sectoral reallocation of FDI in investigated countries. As a reference one could take UNCTAD source although the definitions of FDI used differ from IMF approach in some cases, in which portfolio investment and bank credits are also covered to some extent. Table L10 represents sectoral and industrial distribution of inward FDI stock in five transformation countries. The data for Belarus is a special case since it refers to the distribution of the number of foreign investing firms.

What "right" sector is concerned, the interpretation of "right" is changing alongside the transformation process (Bellak, 1988), since FDI tends to play different roles at different stages of transformation. In the early stage, it may contribute to the stabilization of the economy by supporting existing firms and modernizing their capital stock. Thus, the early stage is characterized by investment in sectors that either are traditionally strong in the host country or in which foreign investors want to get market access. At that time, foreign investors provide little input to the restructuring of the economy in the form of moving from resource and labor intensive industries to R&D and capital intensive industries. In a second stage, investment will focus on restructuring and will be directed predominately towards new growing industries, compensating existing production gap.

The more advanced transformation economies such as Hungary and Poland have already overcame the first stage and moved up to the next "restructuring" ladder, as the data on sectoral FDI confirm. The food industry and the textiles sector, which have been preferred investment sectors in the first stage, have already been replaced by investment in machinery and equipment industry, chemical industry which are the most skill- and technology- intensive, and are the major contributors to economic growth in transition economies. The investment in these sectors was simultaneously followed by investment in services: wholesale and distributive trade, finance (banking and insurance), transport and telecommunications which can be supposed to support restructuring process.

The tendencies for three CIS countries look less optimistic and show that FDI is still primarily directed into traditional sectors. In other words, the countries are still in the first stage mentioned. For Russia, the picture given in table L8 may even be too optimistic concerning the importance of the service sector, as the figures do not relate to FDI in the sense used in this study, but to foreign capital including bank credits. Much FDI in finance sector is owed to this statistical concept. Nevertheless, even given these limitations, 16% of FDI in Russia was made in the fuel industry, which is a considerably high figure in comparison to the other transition economies. Anecdotal evidence supports the predominance of the fuel industry as well as it makes evident the problems of measuring FDI: One of the largest transactions a Western company made in Russia was the acquisition of 2.5% share of the gas producer Gazprom by the Germany based Ruhrgas which was worth US-$660 mill.. However, this deal should not be counted as FDI at all, because the share of the foreign owner is below 10%. FDI in machinery and equipment still remains very low which is a serious obstacle on the way towards restructuring and sustainable growth. FDI as a whole as well as distributive trade are also considerable. Some large projects were started in the transport and communications sector coinciding with the interest of investors in improving the infrastructure.

In the Ukraine, FDI is dominated by the industrial sector, giving some sign that restructuring has started. 9% of FDI was made in the machinery and equipment industries and 7% was made in the chemical industry. But on the other side, the food industry is still the major recipient of FDI in Ukraine. In the service sector considerable FDI was directed to the whole and distributive trade followed by banking, transport and telecommunications sectors.

In Belarus, figures given relate – as already mentioned – to the number of firms and are insofar not comparable to the other data. Here, industry obviously accounts for only a small part of FDI, with the food industry, textiles, wood industry dominating. Investment is in the machinery and equipment sector and the chemical industry is still small, although they are typical for the Belorussian industry. The largest number of investors are active in the wholesale trade and distributive trade sector. A remarkably high number of investments was made in the transport and telecommunications as well as in business services sector (including engineering and information services), they are important for successful transition.

To sum up. FDI made up to now in the investigated CIS was predominately directed to traditional sectors that were developed very well before and are also further called to play an important role in the economy. A shift towards new industries and above all towards manufacturing is not observed at the present (except for Ukraine to some extent). There is a slight tendency towards improvement in the service sector in Ukraine and Belarus (the banking sector in the Ukraine; in transport and telecommunications sector in both the Ukraine and Belarus). High foreign capital inflows into the banking sector in Russia were not supported by FDI in manufacturing, chemicals and other services necessary for a balanced development. Oppositely, Hungary and Poland exhibit the first steps in restructuring by increasing investment in machinery and equipment, chemicals and at the same time in service sectors.

**Table L8.** Sectoral Distribution of Inward FDI Stocks in Selected Central and Eastern European Countries, 1997, %

| Sector/Industry | Hungary | Poland[1] | Russia | Ukraine | Belarus[2] |
|---|---|---|---|---|---|
| Primary sector | 2 | 2 | 16 | 2 | 2 |
| Agriculture, hunting, forestry & fishing | 1 | 0 | .. | 2 | 2 |
| Mining, quarrying & petroleum | 1 | 2 | 16[a] | .. | 0 |
| Secondary sector | 39 | 61 | 23 | 50 | 34 |
| Food, beverages & tobacco | 9 | 21 | 9 | 20 | 7 |
| Textiles, leather & clothing | 2 | 3[b] | .. | 2[d] | 4 |
| Wood, paper, publishing & printing | 3 | 5 | 4 | 3 | 11 |
| Chemicals, chemical products, coke &, petroleum products | 8 | 5 | 3 | 7 | 3 |
| Non-metallic mineral products (cement & building materials) | 3 | 6 | .. | 7 | 1 |
| Basic metals & metal products | 2 | 1 | 3 | 3 | 2 |
| Machinery and equipment | 12[c] | 17[c] | 4[d] | 9 | 4 |
| Electrical machinery & apparatus | .. | .. | .. | .. | 2 |
| Automotive | .. | .. | .. | .. | 0 |
| Unspecified secondary | 0 | 3 | .. | .. | 0 |
| Tertiary sector | 59 | 38 | 51 | 40 | 65 |
| Electricity & water distribution | 14 | .. | .. | .. | 0 |
| Construction | 4 | 5 | .. | .. | 3 |
| Wholesale trade & distributive trade | 12 | 6 | 11 | 19 | 45 |
| Hotels &restructuring (tourism) | 2 | .. | 5 | .. | 1 |
| Transport, storage & telecommunica-tions | 8 | 5 | 2 | 5 | 6 |
| Finance (& banking & insurance) | 9 | 21 | 32 | 9 | 0 |
| Real estate, rental activities & business services | 8 | .. | .. | 2 | 6 |
| Public administration, health & social services | 2 | 0 | 1 | 5 | 3 |
| Unspecified | - | - | 10 | 8 | 0 |

*Source: UNCTAD, based on national reports and Helmstedt, 1998. These estimates are based on national statistical surveys and are not necessarily comparable with FDI data based on balance-of-payments figures; Belarus Economic Trends, April-June 1999 - [1]End 1996. – [2]Data are taken as % of total foreign investing firms. [a]Fuel industry. - [b]Includes other light industries - [c]Includes electrical machinery & automotive industries. – [d]Includes basic metals & metal products.*

# 5 Conclusions

Up to now, FDI in Russia was low in relation to the size of its economy and population, although official data even seem to overestimate FDI, as international comparisons suggest that FDI made actually might be much smaller. The Ukraine and Belarus also exhibit a large catch up demand in terms of FDI/GDP ratios as well as in per capita terms. Anyhow, there are many expectations linked to FDI and the role it may play in transition to the market economy, e.g. by transferring technology and tacit knowledge to economies of these countries.

Based on international evidence from other countries, this study makes an estimate on what FDI can be expected in selected CIS and Eastern European countries. Indeed, inflows will be significant, and they will be larger than observed over the 1990s on average. As foreign investors in general behave above all market seeking, growth in these countries is crucial to future volumes of FDI. Insofar, FDI on one hand is expected to contribute to growth, on the other hand growth is an important factor to attract FDI. However, relation between GDP and FDI is not a natural law, and thus it does not limit the possibilities of a country attracting foreign investors. Policy has the chance, to make a country attractive to foreign investors as well as it may deter them, e.g. by very restrictive privatization practices. Policy in the investigated countries up to now above all did the latter.

Nevertheless, even under optimistic assumptions concerning growth, FDI can only play a minor role in the process of capital formation, especially since countries have to increase their investment in fixed capital to bring forth transformation. In the long run, it is realistic to assume that FDI can contribute between 2 and 3% to the financing of capital formation, and there is again some room for higher shares given the static nature of the model employed here to derive these flows. But there is also room for lower shares, depending on policy as well as global trends in FDI. However, the lion's share of capital formation must be financed by domestic saving. Once more, policy is challenged to create conditions that increase income and allow higher savings. FDI will play an important role, but it will be complimentary only and cannot initiate a process of sustained growth.

As far as investment that has been made in CIS countries up to now, it seems to have been „backward looking“, concentrating on industries that were successful in the past. These investments are important to modernize these industries that will continue to be significant for the economy of these countries in the years to come. It will also be important to increase Russia's potential to export (the same is relevant for Ukraine and Belarus), although this may cause the problem of immiserization at the same time (Welfens, 1999, p. 146). On the other hand, there is little evidence that „forward looking“, restructuring investment in new industries is taking place in CIS countries to a significant extent.

## References

Bellak C (1998) Lessons from Austria's Post-war Pattern of Inward FDI for CEECs. WIIW-report 251, Vienna

Blomstroem M, Sjoholm F (1999) Technology transfer and spillovers: Does local participation with multinationals matter? European Economic Review 43: 915–923

Blomstroem M (1991) Host Country Benefits of Foreign Investment. In: McFetridge D (ed) Foreign Investment, Technology and Economic Growth. University of Galgary Press, Calgory, Mass.

Borenstein E et al (1995) How Does Foreign Direct Investment Affect Economic Growth? NBER Working Paper No. 5057, Cambridge

Brenton P, Mauro FD, Luecke M (1998) Economic Integration and FDI: An Empirical Analysis of Foreign Direct Investment in the EU and in Central and Eastern Europe. Kiel Working Paper No. 890, Kiel

Burger B (1999) Overcoming the Russian Transformation Crisis. Intereconomics 34: 115

Dmochowski A (1995) Foreign Direct Investment in Central Europe. Intereconomics 28(?): 305–312

Doehrn R (1996a) Direktinvestitionen und Sachkapitalbildung - Statistische Unterschiede und ihre ökonomischen Implikationen. RWI-Mitteilungen 47: 19–34

Doehrn R (1996b) EU-Enlargement and Transformation in Eastern Europe - Consequences for Foreign Direct Investment in Europe. Konjunkturpolitik 42: 113–132

Doehrn R, Heilemann U (1996) The Chenery Hypothesis and Structural Change in Eastern Europe. Economics of Transition 4: 411–425

Doehrn R, Heilemann U (1999) Zweifelhafte Grösse der Direktinvestitionen - Schwerwiegende Mängel der nationalen Statistiken. Neue Zürcher Zeitung 79, 7.4.1999: 25

Graham EM (1995) Foreign Direct Investment in the World Economy. Staff Studies for the World Economic Outlook Sep. 1995, Washington, D.C.: 120ff

Hunya G (1999) Central Europe Catching Up Through FDI? The Vienna Institute for International Economic Studies, Vienna

IMF (1993) International Monetary Fund, Balance of Payments Manual. 5th revision, Washington DC

Jost T (1997) Direktinvestitionen und Standort Deutschland. Diskussionspapier 2/97 der Volkswirtschaftlichen Forschungsgruppe der Deutschen Bundesbank, Frankfurt a.M.

Lansbury M, Pain N, Smidkova K (1996) Foreign Direct Investment in Central Europe Since 1990: An Econometric Study. National Institute Economic Review, May 1996: 104–114

Lorenz D (1990) West- und Osteuropa: Wirtschaftliche Probleme des Zusammenwachsens. Wirtschaftsdienst 70: 627–633

Meissner T (1999) Ausländische Direktinvestitionen in den mittel- und osteuropäischen Reformstaaten - eine Projektion. Wirtschaft im Wandel 1999 (5): 16–21

Meyer K, Pind C (1999) The slow growth of foreign direct investment in the Soviet Union successor states. Economics of Transition 7: 201–214

Morsink R, Molle W (1991) Direct Investment and Monetary Integration. In: Commission of the European Communities (ed.) The Economics of EMU. European Economy, Special edition No. 1, Brussels

OECD (ed) (1998) The Benefits of Trade and Investment Liberalization. OECD, Paris

Raines P, Doehrn R, Brown R, Scheuer M (1999) Labour Market Flexibility and Inward Investment in Germany and the UK. An Anglo German Foundation Report, London

UNCTAD (ed) (1998) World Investment Report. Trends and Determinants, New York and Geneva

Welfens PJJ (1999) Overcoming the Russian Transformation Crisis. Wirtschaftsdienst 79: 144–151

Welfens PJJ (1999) Institutions and Transition: On the Way to a Market Economy-Theory and Application to Russia. In: Welfens PJJ, Gavrilenkov E (eds) Proceedings of the Conference at the Higher School of Economics. Moscow

# Appendix

## On Calculating FDI Stocks from Inflow Data

For many countries, no data on FDI stocks provided by the statistical offices or central banks. In these cases, the missing data are often generated by using inflow data that are available for most countries. In this context, the influence of exchange-rates which differs between the two types of data often is neglected.

Data on *FDI inflows* are as a rule collected by national authorities and therefore expressed in national currencies. To convert them into a common currency, e.g. the US-$, the average exchange rate for the period is used. For many countries, among them the transition economies, data in US-$ are available only. Data on *FDI-stocks* mirror the share foreign investors hold in foreign direct investment enterprises at a given point of time, mainly at the end of a calendar year. As the balances of the enterprises are given in national currencies, they must be converted into a common currency as the $ by using the exchange rate at this point of time to obtain FDI stock in dollar. Therefore, data on FDI stocks do not reflect the flows only but also exchange rate movements.

To give an example: Assume, a foreign investor invested US-$ 100 mill. in Russia in 1997. This would translate, using the average rate for 1997, into an investment rbl. 578 mill., that also appears in the balance of the Russian subsidiary of the foreign investor. Ideally, the Russian subsidiary would report its balance to the Russian authority responsible for collecting FDI stocks at the end of 1998. Other things being equal, the share of the foreign investor would still be the same amount of roubles as in 1997. However, when this investment is converted in US-$ at the rate valid at 31st Dec. 1998, the investment would be US-$28 mill. only. In other words: FDI declined to one quarter of the original value due to the devaluation of the rouble.

This is not the place to discuss to what extent data on FDI stocks can be used to describe economic activities of foreign investors abroad. Having in mind the physical capital stocks behind the FDI inflows, adding up inflows even might be the more realistic estimate. However, to make figures gained by cumulating stocks comparable against information available in stocks, an exchange rate correction mechanism must be applied. In this paper the mechanism used is as follows:

$$FDI_T^a = \left( \sum_{t=0}^{T} fdi_t \cdot e_t^a \right) : e_T^e$$

with

$FDI_T^a$ Stocks of FDI in year T, adjusted,
$fdi_t$ Inflows of FDI in year t, in US-$,
$e_t^a$ exchange rate foreign currency per $ in the average of year t,
$e_T^e$ exchange rate foreign currency per $ at the end of year T.

**Table L9.** Cumulated Inflows and Stocks of FDI in Eastern European Countries, 1994–1998, in mill. US$

| | | 1994 | 1995 | 1996 | 1997 | 1998 |
|---|---|---|---|---|---|---|
| Hungary | cumulated inflows | 6931 | 11450 | 13432 | 15511 | 17447 |
| | cumulated inflows, adjusted | 5357 | 8324 | 8873 | 9099 | 10350 |
| | stocks | 7087 | 11919 | 14690 | 15869 | 18242 |
| Poland | cumulated inflows | 4659 | 8318 | 12816 | 17724 | 24089 |
| | cumulated inflows, adjusted | 3560 | 7108 | 10307 | 13005 | 19200 |
| | stocks | 3789 | 7843 | 11463 | 14587 | 22479 |
| Russia | cumulated inflows | 1037 | 3054 | 5533 | 11776 | 13959 |
| | cumulated inflows, adjusted | 505 | 2368 | 4259 | 10033 | 3922 |
| | stocks | 332 | 345 | 426 | 970 | 373 |
| Ukraine | cumulated inflows | 159 | 426 | 947 | 1570 | 2313 |
| | cumulated inflows, adjusted | 159 | 312 | 800 | 1407 | 1311 |
| | stocks | - | - | - | - | - |
| Belarus | cumulated inflows | 28 | 43 | 115 | 315 | 459 |
| | cumulated inflows, adjusted | 6 | 23 | 81 | 41 | 92 |
| | stocks | - | - | - | - | - |

*Source: Authors' calculations based on IMF and OECD figures.*

Table L9 represents the unadjusted and the adjusted cumulative inflows into the investigated countries and compares them to data on FDI-stocks, as far as they are available. As expected, the difference between unadjusted and adjusted cumulative inflows is considerable, given the large exchange rate movements in the countries considered. However, as pointed out above, the goal of the exercise is to gain internationally comparable estimates of FDI stocks and, therefore, adjusted cumulative inflows and stocks should be nearly the same. This seems to be true in the case of Poland, where official data on FDI-stocks are just in the middle between unadjusted and adjusted cumulative inflows. In the case of Hungary, stocks are even somewhat larger than cumulative flows, but the discrepancy is still within the usual inaccuracies, considering the experience from industrialized countries and the shortcomings of the reporting system. Another case is Russia, where stocks are far below unadjusted as well as adjusted cumulative inflows.

# M. Data Appendix

**Tabelle M1.** Macroeconomic Indicators of Russia, 1992–2002

| | Real GDP growth rate | Total investment expenditure | Exports of goods and services | Consumer price index inflation | Unemploy-ment rate |
|---|---|---|---|---|---|
| | % | % of GDP | % of GDP | % of GDP | % |
| 1992 | -18.60 | 23.94 | 67.13 | 1734.73 | 0 |
| 1993 | -13.01 | 20.39 | 35.83 | 878.79 | 5.29 |
| 1994 | -13.46 | 21.81 | 28.43 | 307.49 | 6.88 |
| 1995 | -4.16 | 21.29 | 28.21 | 198.02 | 8.14 |
| 1996 | -3.39 | 21.18 | 24.53 | 47.92 | 9.26 |
| 1997 | 0.86 | 19.76 | 24.50 | 14.66 | 10.81 |
| 1998 | -4.90 | 17.71 | 31.60 | 27.76 | 11.64 |
| 1999 | 5.40 | 15.83 | 44.61 | 85.72 | 12.63 |
| 2000 | 9.03 | 16.53 | 45.48 | 20.81 | 10.42 |
| 2001 | 5.05 | 19.09 | 37.68 | 20.70 | 8.69 |
| 2002 | 4.36 | 22.07 | 33.67 | 15.80 | 8.16 |

*Source: IMF World Economic Outlook Database.*

**Table M2.** Fiscal Indicators of Russia, 1992–2002

| | General government, total expenditure and net lending | General government, total revenue and grants | General government balance |
|---|---|---|---|
| | % of GDP | % of GDP | % of GDP |
| 1992 | 58.29 | 39.70 | -18.59 |
| 1993 | 43.55 | 36.19 | -7.36 |
| 1994 | 45.06 | 34.64 | -10.42 |
| 1995 | 39.54 | 33.47 | -6.07 |
| 1996 | 41.30 | 32.38 | -8.92 |
| 1997 | 44.71 | 37.11 | -7.60 |
| 1998 | 39.73 | 32.86 | -6.87 |
| 1999 | 34.22 | 34.03 | -0.19 |
| 2000 | 33.31 | 37.44 | 4.13 |
| 2001 | 34.23 | 37.07 | 2.84 |
| 2002 | 35.81 | 36.49 | 0.68 |

*Source: IMF World Economic Outlook Database.*

**Table M3.** Monetary Indicators of Russia, 1991–2002

| | Total debt outstanding at year end | Official debt outstanding at year end, creditor based | Nominal effective exchange rate, aop | Real effective exchange rate, aop |
|---|---|---|---|---|
| | % of GDP | % of GDP | Index | Index |
| 1992 | 123.14 | 79.43 | NA | NA |
| 1993 | 61.31 | 39.99 | 213.32 | 94.08 |
| 1994 | 47.23 | 28.63 | 162.95 | 91.12 |
| 1995 | 37.87 | 22.81 | 100.00 | 100.00 |
| 1996 | 32.48 | 18.47 | 97.06 | 122.10 |
| 1997 | 31.41 | 20.56 | 98.89 | 128.96 |
| 1998 | 56.01 | 31.87 | 80.31 | 114.23 |
| 1999 | 80.01 | 45.60 | 32.51 | 80.58 |
| 2000 | 54.18 | 32.61 | 34.46 | 90.27 |
| 2001 | 41.10 | 23.29 | 36.44 | 106.74 |
| 2002 | 35.24 | 19.33 | 34.83 | 111.20 |

*Source: IMF World Economic Outlook Database, International Financial Statistics.*

**Table M4.** Selected Trade Indicators of Russia 1991–2002

| | Balance on goods and services (resource balance) | Trade balance | Exports of goods | External current account balance |
|---|---|---|---|---|
| | % of GDP | % of GDP | % of GDP | % of GDP |
| 1992 | 1.50 | 6.90 | 61.29 | -1.40 |
| 1993 | 1.74 | 5.28 | 32.10 | 1.41 |
| 1994 | 4.74 | 7.14 | 25.11 | 3.04 |
| 1995 | 3.20 | 5.60 | 24.53 | 1.44 |
| 1996 | 2.71 | 4.24 | 21.61 | 0.91 |
| 1997 | -0.02 | 3.97 | 20.77 | -0.10 |
| 1998 | -0.43 | 5.97 | 26.51 | -0.57 |
| 1999 | 11.44 | 18.7 | 39.16 | 11.76 |
| 2000 | 17.44 | 23.38 | 40.66 | 17.47 |
| 2001 | 10.37 | 15.43 | 32.78 | 10.28 |
| 2002 | 7.06 | 12.23 | 29.31 | 6.98 |

*Source: IMF World Economic Outlook Database.*

# List of Figures

## K. Foreign Trade Policies in Transformational Russian and Ukrainian Economies



## L. The Role of Foreign Direct Investment in Transformation

## List of Tables

## List of Contributors

Prof. Dr. John T. Addison
Department of Economics
The Moore School of Business
University of South Carolina

Dr. Frank Bohn
Durham University
Department of Economics and Finance
Durham

Dr. Roland Doehrn
Rheinisch-Westfälisches Institut für Wirtschaftsforschung
Essen

Cathleen Faber
Potsdam University

Prof. Dr. Evgeny Gavrilenkov
Bureau of Economic Analysis and State University Higher School of Economics
Moscow

Prof. Dr. Ruslan Grinberg
Institue for International Economic and Political Studies
Russian Academy of Sciences
Moscow

Dr. Andre Jungmittag
European Institute of International Economic Relations (EIIW)
Potsdam University

Dr. Timothy Lane
International Monetary Fund
Washington

Dr. Leslie Lipschitz
International Monetary Fund
Washington

Dr. Alex Mourmouras
International Monetary Fund
Washington

Ass. Prof. Dr. Olga Nosova
Kharkov State Polytechnic University

Prof. Dr. Hans-Gerhard Strohe
Potsdam University

Dr. Leonid Vardomsky
Russian Academy of Sciences
Moscow

Prof. Dr. Paul J.J. Welfens
European Institute of International Economic Relations (EIIW)
Potsdam University

Ralf Wiegert
European Institute of International Economic Relations (EIIW)
Potsdam University

Dr. Natalja von Westernhagen
European Institute of International Economic Relations (EIIW)
Potsdam University

Prof. Dr. Andrei Zaostrovtsev
University of Economics and Finance
St. Petersburg

## Biographies

*John T. Addison* is Hugh C. Lane Professor of Economic Theory at the University of South Carolina. He is also professor-at-large at the Free University of Bolzano/Bozen (Italy), and is a research fellow at the Institute for the Study of Labor (IZA) and with the Center for Employment and Labor Law at New York University. Addison, a labor economist, was educated at the London School of Economics. He has published extensively in the major specialist and general economics journals, and is currently editing the International Handbook of Trade Unions, to be published by Edward Elgar in 2003.

*Frank Bohn* is a lecturer at the University of Essex. He holds a degree (B.A.) from Toulouse University. For his graduate diploma at Bonn University, he wrote a thesis on "The Transformation Process from a Centrally Planned to a Market Economy: Big Bang versus Gradual Change". He was awarded a 4-year scholarship by the German National Scholarship Foundation. After an internship at the Deutsche Bundesbank and an 18-month fellowship at Princeton University, he returned to Heidelberg University to complete his Ph.D.

His research is primarily in the fields of monetary economics and international macroeconomics, with two sessions at recent American Economic Association Meetings and a book publication on *Monetary Union and Fiscal Stability*. His most recent work has been in public choice theory (on political instability as well as on corruption). Frank mainly works with simulation and theoretical models.

*Dr. Roland Döhrn,* born in 1954, studied Economics at the University of Mainz and completed his Ph.D. at the University of Bochum. Since 1978, he has worked at the Rheinisch-Westfälische Institut für Wirtschaftsforschung (Rhenian-Westphalian Institute for Economic Research, RWI) in Essen and has headed the research group on International Economics since 1998. In addition, he is a lecturer at the University of Essen. His fields of interest are business cycle research, transformation in Eastern Europe, and Foreign Direct Investment.

*Cathleen Faber* is a research assistant at the Institute of Statistics and Econometrics at the University of Potsdam, where she is involved in a project to develop a web-based platform for teaching statistics interactively through the internet (e-stat). In addition, she is currently writing a doctoral thesis about "Problems in Measuring Consumer Price Indices in Transition Countries". On several occasions, Faber visited state statistical offices and met representatives not only in Russia, but also in the Ukraine and Georgia. She received her diploma of economics from the University of Potsdam in 1998.

*Andre Jungmittag* has been a senior researcher at the Department for Economic Policy/International Economic Relations and at the European Institute for International Economic Relations (EIIW) at the University of Potsdam since 1999. His research areas are applied econometrics; technological performance, competitiveness, structural change and economic growth; globalization of R&D and technology markets; and the analysis of national economic and innovation systems. From 1997 to 1999, he was a senior researcher and project manager at the Fraunhofer Institute for Systems and Innovation Research (ISI, Karlsruhe) in the "Technology Analysis and Innovation Strategies" Department, responsible for ISI's reporting on technological performance of Germany for the German Ministry for Education, Science, Research and Technology, as well as other subjects. Jungmittag was assistant of the Dean of the Faculty of Economics from 1990 to 1991 and was a research fellow at the Institute for Econometrics at the University of Münster from 1991 to 1997. He received his doctoral degree in 1995, having written his dissertation on "Long-term relations and short-term dynamics between foreign direct investment and exports".

*Timothy Lane* is Chief of Policy Review Division in the IMF's Policy Development and Review Department, where he is involved in work related to capital account crises, fiscal and external sustainability, the design of IMF-supported programs, and other issues. He previously served in the IMF's European I Department (where he worked on industrial countries including Italy and the United Kingdom) and.in the Capital Markets Division of the Research Department. During 1989-91, he participated in the IMF team working in support of Poland's stabilization and reform program; he subsequently wrote several papers on problems of transition economies. Prior to joining the IMF in 1988, he held positions as Assistant Professor of Economics at Michigan State University and at the University of Iowa. A Canadian citizen, he received his PhD from the University of Western Ontario.

*Nosova Olga* is Associate Professor at the Department of Economic Theory, where she is involved in delivering lectures, conducting seminars in International Economics, preparing reports, writing articles for conferences and journals. She investigates on foreign direct investment in the institutional transformation economy. She was a research scholar at the Kennan Institute for Advanced Russian Studies, Washington, DC in 1997. She took part in the Economic Programs in the Institute for Advanced Studies in Vienna, Hebrew University and Central European University. During 1998-2000 she participated in the joint Belgium-Ukrainian project in support new educational program in Ukraine. Currently she investigates the economic situation in transitional countries. A Ukrainian citizen, she received her PhD in Economics from Kharkov State University in 1992 and Habilitation in Economics from Kharkov State University in 2002.

*Nina Oding* is a Head of the Research Department in the International Centre for Socio-Economic Research "Leontief Centre", which was established in 1991 on the initiative of the Mayor of St. Petersburg and Wassily Leontief, a St. Petersburg-born economist and Nobel Price winner. As the Head of the Research dept., N.Oding has built up a vast experience in developing and managing research programs, in research of transition economy, regional development, land use policy, urban development, public sector reform, and in policy analysis and policy advise. She coordinates gathering data on local budget, employment and living level. Besides N.Oding is an editor in chief of the bi-monthly analytical review "The Socio-Economic Situation in St.Petersburg. A General Overview", publishing by the Leontief Centre.

N.Oding participated as a coordinator of large-scale research projects have been developed by the Leontief Centre under commission from the Russian Federal Government, City Administration. She is a team leader in the international projects of TACIS, projects in the framework of the World Bank loans (Historical Centre Rehabilitation, Housing Project, Review of Public Expenditure). N.Oding had fellowship in the research institutes in Sweden, Finland, Germany, and wrote several papers on regional economy and transition issues.

Since 1977 she worked in Leningrad Engineer- Economic Institute as a researcher. In 1990-1991 N.Oding was invited in the experts' team in the Committee for Economic Reform of Leningrad Executive Committee, which became a basis for the Leontief Centre.

*Hans Gerhard Strohe* is professor of statistics and head of the Chair of Statistics and Econometrics at the University of Potsdam, Germany. He is involved in the education of students of economics and business administration. He leads research projects on statistical analysis and econometric modelling of transition economics in East Europe and East Germany and on electronic teaching of statistics. He wrote several papers on this first topic. From 1991 to 1993, he was head of the Institute of Statistics at Humboldt University in Berlin, additionally serving as a professor of statistics there. In 1967 and 1978, he received his first (Ph.D. equivalent) and his second (German "habilitation") doctoral degree, respectively, from the Humboldt University in Berlin.

*Vardomskij, Leonid B.* Born in 1946, Vardomskij is Head of the Centre of Post-Soviet Economic Development and Cooperation, Institute of International Economic and Political Studies, Russian Academy of Sciences in Moscow. His main fields of Interests are regional processes and Policy in Transition Economy Countries, Russia's Integration into the World Economy and Cooperation among CIS countries.

*Paul J.J. Welfens* is the president of the *European Institute for International Economic Relations (EIIW)* at Potsdam University. He is the Jean Monnet Chair in European Economic Integration at Potsdam University, where he has taught Economic Policy and International Economic Relations since 1995. From 1990 to 1991, he was the McCloy Distinguished Research Fellow at AICGS/The Johns Hopkins University. From Spring 1991 to 1994, he was Chair of Eastern Europe and European Economic Integration at Münster University. Welfens has testified before Congress and the IMF on Eastern Europe/Russia. He has published articles and books on transition topics and on European integration issues as well as globalization and the New Economy (see www.euroeiiw.de). Welfens has conducted research for the European Commission and the European Parliament. He was also coordinator for the Russian project, financed by the Alfried Krupp von Bohlen and Halbach Foundation. A German citizen, he received his Ph.D. from Duisburg University.

*Natalja von Westernhagen* is employed with the Deutsche Bundesbank in the Department of Banking Supervision Research, where she deals with macroprudential analyses, analyses on stability of banking and financial systems, systemic risk, and impact of capital regulations on financial stability. Prior to joining the Deutsche Bundesbank in 2002, she completed her Ph.D. at the University of Potsdam.

*Ralf Wiegert* is a senior researcher at the European Institute for International Economic Relations (EIIW by its German acronym) and is in charge of heading the working group on Eastern Europe with specific emphasis on Russia and Systemic Transformation at the EIIW. Due to this function, he administrates an international research project on "Russia's Integration into the World Economy" at the EIIW. Working as a research assistant at the chair of Prof. Welfens for several years, he has gathered broad teaching experience in different fields of economics, namely economic policy. He received his Ph.D. in 2002 (thesis to be published in 2003) from Potsdam University, where he graduated as a Diplom-Volkswirt in 1997 as well. His main research interests include transition processes in Eastern Europe and Russia in particular; his special area of interest lies on the role of the financial sector in transition and economic development in general.

*Andrei Zaostrovtsev* is Associate Professor at the St. Petetrsburg State University of Economics and Finance, where he lectures on public economics. Since beginning of the 1990s, he has worked in the "Leontief Centre" (St.Petersburg), dealing with problems of urban economics under transition. He contributed to the development of World Bank programmes in St.Petersburg and World Bank Institute courses. He is a member of the editorial board for the journal "The Economic School" and of the ASPE (Association for Studies in Public Economics) Board. Zaostrovtsev was also honoured as a visiting scholar at the Stockholm School of Economics (1994, 1998) and Rochester Institute of Technology, College of Business (2001). He has published several papers on the problems of Russia's transitional economy. A Russian citizen, he received his degree from St. Petersburg State University.

## Further Publications by *Paul J. J. Welfens*

P. J. J. Welfens
**Market-oriented Systemic Transformations in Eastern Europe**
Problems, Theoretical Issues, and Policy Options
1992. XII, 261 Pages. 20 Figs., 29 Tab.,
Hardcover, ISBN 3-540-55793-8

M. W. Klein, P. J. J. Welfens (Eds.)
**Multinationals in the New Europe and Global Trade**
1992. XV, 281 Pages. 24 Figs., 75 Tab.,
Hardcover, ISBN 3-540-54634-0

P. J. J. Welfens (Ed.)
**Economic Aspects of German Unification**
Expectations, Transition Dynamics and International Perspectives
1992. XV, 527 Pages. 34 Figs., 110 Tab.,
Hardcover, ISBN 3-540-60261-5

R. Tilly, P. J. J. Welfens (Eds.)
**European Economic Integration as a Challenge to Industry and Government**
Contemporary and Historical Perspectives on International Economic Dynamics
1996. X, 558 Pages. 43 Figs.,
Hardcover, ISBN 3-540-60431-6

P. J. J. Welfens (Ed.)
**Economic Aspects of German Unification**
Expectations, Transition Dynamics and International Perspectives
2nd revised and enlarged edition
1996. XV, 527 Pages. 34 Figs., 110 Tab.,
Hardcover, ISBN 3-540-60261-5

P. J. J. Welfens
**European Monetary Integration**
EMS Developments and International Post-Maastricht Perspectives
3rd revised and enlarged edition
1996. XVIII, 384 Pages. 14 Figs., 26 Tab.,
Hardcover, ISBN 3-540-60260-7

P. J. J. Welfens (Ed.)
**European Monetary Union**
Transition, International Impact and Policy Options
1997. X, 467 Pages. 50 Figs., 31 Tab.,
Hardcover, ISBN 3-540-63305-7

P. J. J. Welfens, G. Yarrow (Eds.)
**Telecommunications and Energy in Systemic Transformation**
International Dynamics, Deregulation and Adjustment in Network Industries
1997. XII, 501 Pages. 39 Figs.,
Hardcover, ISBN 3-540-61586-5

P. J. J. Welfens, H. C. Wolf (Eds.)
**Banking, International Capital Flows and Growth in Europe**
Financial Markets, Savings and Monetary Integration in a World with Uncertain Convergence
1997. XIV, 458 Pages. 22 Figs., 63 Tab.,
Hardcover, ISBN 3-540-63192-5

P. J. J. Welfens, D. Audretsch, J. T. Addison, H. Grupp
**Technological Competition, Employment and Innovation Policies in OECD Countries**
1998. VI, 231 Pages. 16 Figs., 20 Tab.,
Hardcover, ISBN 3-540-63439-8

P. J. J. Welfens, G. Yarrow, R. Grinberg, C. Graack (Eds.)
**Towards Competition in Network Industries**
Telecommunications, Energy and Transportation in Europe and Russia
1999. XXII, 570 Pages, 63 Figs., 63 Tab.,
Hardcover, ISBN 3-540-65859-9

P. J. J. Welfens
**EU Eastern Enlargement and the Russian Transformation Crisis**
1999. X, 151 Pages. 12 Figs., 25 Tab.,
Hardcover, ISBN 3-540-65862-9

P. J. J. Welfens
**Globalization of the Economy, Unemployment and Innovation**
1999. VI, 255 Pages. 11 Figs., 31 Tab.,
Hardcover, ISBN 3-540-65250-7

P. J. J. Welfens, J. T. Addison, D. B. Audretsch, T. Gries, H. Grupp
**Globalization, Economic Growth and Innovation Dynamics**
1999. X, 160 Pages. 15 Figs., 15 Tab.,
Hardcover, ISBN 3-540-65858-0

R. Tilly, P. J. J. Welfens (Eds.)
**Economic Globalization, International Organizations and Crisis Management**
Contemporary and Historical Perspectives on Growth, Impact and Evolution of Major Organizations in an Interdependent World
2000. XII, 408 Pages. 11 Figs., 20 Tab., Hardcover, ISBN 3-540-65863-7

P. J. J. Welfens, E. Gavrilenkov (Eds.)
**Restructuring, Stabilizing and Modernizing the New Russia**
Economic and Institutional Issues
2000. XIV, 516 Pages. 82 Figs., 70 Tab., Hardcover, ISBN 3-540-67429-2

P. J. J. Welfens
**European Monetary Union and Exchange Rate Dynamics**
New Approaches and Applications to the Euro
2001. X, 159 Pages. 26 Figs., 12 Tab., Hardcover, ISBN 3-540-67914-6

P. J. J. Welfens
**Stabilizing and Integrating the Balkans**
Economic Analysis of the Stability Pact, EU Reforms and International Organizations
2001. XII, 171 Pages. 6 Figs., 18 Tab., Hardcover, ISBN 3-540-41775-3

P. J. J. Welfens, B. Meyer, W. Pfaffenberger, P. Jasinski, A. Jungmittag
**Energy Policies in the European Union Germany's Ecological Tax Reform**
2001. VII, 143 Pages. 21 Figs., 41 Tab., Hardcover, ISBN 3-540-41652-8

P. J. J. Welfens (Ed.)
**Internationalization of the Economy and Environmental Policy Options**
2001. XIV, 442 Pages. 57 Figs., 61 Tab., Hardcover, ISBN 3-540-42174-2

P. J. J. Welfens
**Interneteconomics.net**
Macroeconomics, Deregulation, and Innovation
2002. VIII, 215 Pages. 34 Figs., 30 Tab., Hardcover, ISBN 3-540-43337-6

D. B. Audretsch, P. J. J. Welfens (Eds.)
**The New Economy and Economic Growth in Europe and the USA**
2002. XII, 350 Pages. 28 Figs., 59 Tab., Hardcover, ISBN 3-540-43179-9

C. E. Barfield, G. Heiduk, P. J. J. Welfens (Eds.)
**Internet, Economic Growth and Globalization**
Perspectives on the Digital Economy in Europe, Japan and the U.S.
2003. XII, 388 Pages. 34 Figs., 67 Tab., Hardcover, ISBN 3-540-00286-3

J. T. Addison, P. J. J. Welfens (Eds.)
**Labor Markets and Social Security**
Issues and Policy Options in the U.S. and Europe, 2nd edn.
2003. X, 402 Pages. 56 Figs., 52 Tab., Hardcover, ISBN 3-540-44004-6

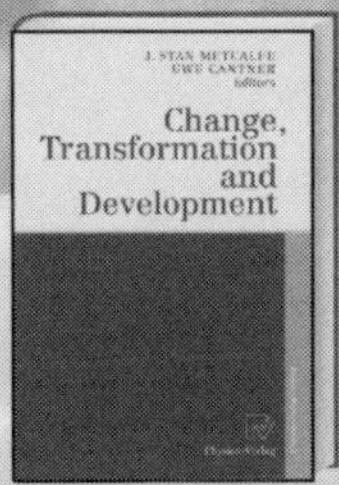

**J. S. Metcalfe,** University of Manchester, UK; **U. Cantner,** University of Jena, Germany (Eds.)

## Change, Transformation and Development

This volume contains a collection of papers all concerned with the exploration of economic and social dynamics in relation to the innovation process and its outcomes. There is a need for connecting principles to offset the dangers of intellectual fragmentation. Evolutionary economics and evolutionary analysis more generally, certainly provide some of these connecting principles.

2003. VIII, 450 p. 102 illus.
Hardcover
**€ 84.95**; sFr 141; £ 59.50
ISBN 3-7908-1545-4

**C. E. Barfield,** The American Enterprise Institute, Washington D.C., USA; **G. Heiduk,** University of Duisburg, Germany; **P. J.J. Welfens,** University of Potsdam, Germany (Eds.)

## Internet, Economic Growth and Globalization

### Perspectives on the New Economy in Europe, Japan and the US

Information and communication technology will affect productivity growth, production, the financial system and trade. Setting adequate rules for the digital economy is a key challenge for industrialized countries. Moreover, cultural and organizational challenges will also have to be met.

2003. XII, 388 p. 101 illus.
Hardcover
**€ 84.95**; sFr 141; £ 59.50
ISBN 3-540-00286-3

**E. Colombo,** University of Milan, Italy; **J. Driffill,** University of London, UK (Eds.)

## The Role of Financial Markets in the Transition Process

Financial Markets play an important role in economic development, channeling saving to investments and facilitating growth. The book offers a both theoretical and empirical analysis of financial markets in transitional economies. It investigates financial markets in Hungary, the Czech Republic, and Poland, and their role in the developments in the 1990s.

2003. VII, 225 p. 85 illus.
(Contributions to Economics)
Softcover
**€ 42.95**; £ 30; sFr 74
ISBN 3-7908-0004-X

**P. Cecchini,** Brussels, Belgium; **F. Heinemann,** Centre for European Economic Research (ZEW), Mannheim, Germany; **M. Jopp,** Institut für Europäische Politik, Berlin, Germany (Eds.)

## The Incomplete European Market for Financial Services

This analysis can be regarded as a modernised follow-up to the financial market part of the famous 1988 Cecchini Report "The cost of non Europe". Even in the Euro age, retail financial markets in the EU are heavily fragmented and the consumers pay a large price for this fragmentation. This weakens the growth perspective of EU and its international role.

2003. XII, 255 p. 106 illus.
(ZEW Economic Studies) Softcover
**€ 46.95**; sFr 80.50; £ 33
ISBN 3-7908-0013-9

**Please order from**
**Springer · Customer Service · Haberstr. 7 · 69126 Heidelberg, Germany**
**Tel.: +49 (0) 6221 - 345 - 0 ·Fax: +49 (0) 6221 - 345 - 4229**
**e-mail: orders@springer.de**
**or through your bookseller**

Springer

Druck: Strauss Offsetdruck, Mörlenbach
Verarbeitung: Schäffer, Grünstadt